THE HEROIC LEGEND OF
ARSLAN

STORY BY
YOSHIKI TANAKA

MANGA BY
HIROMU ARAKAWA

16

THE HEROIC LEGEND OF
ARSLAN

TABLE OF CONTENTS

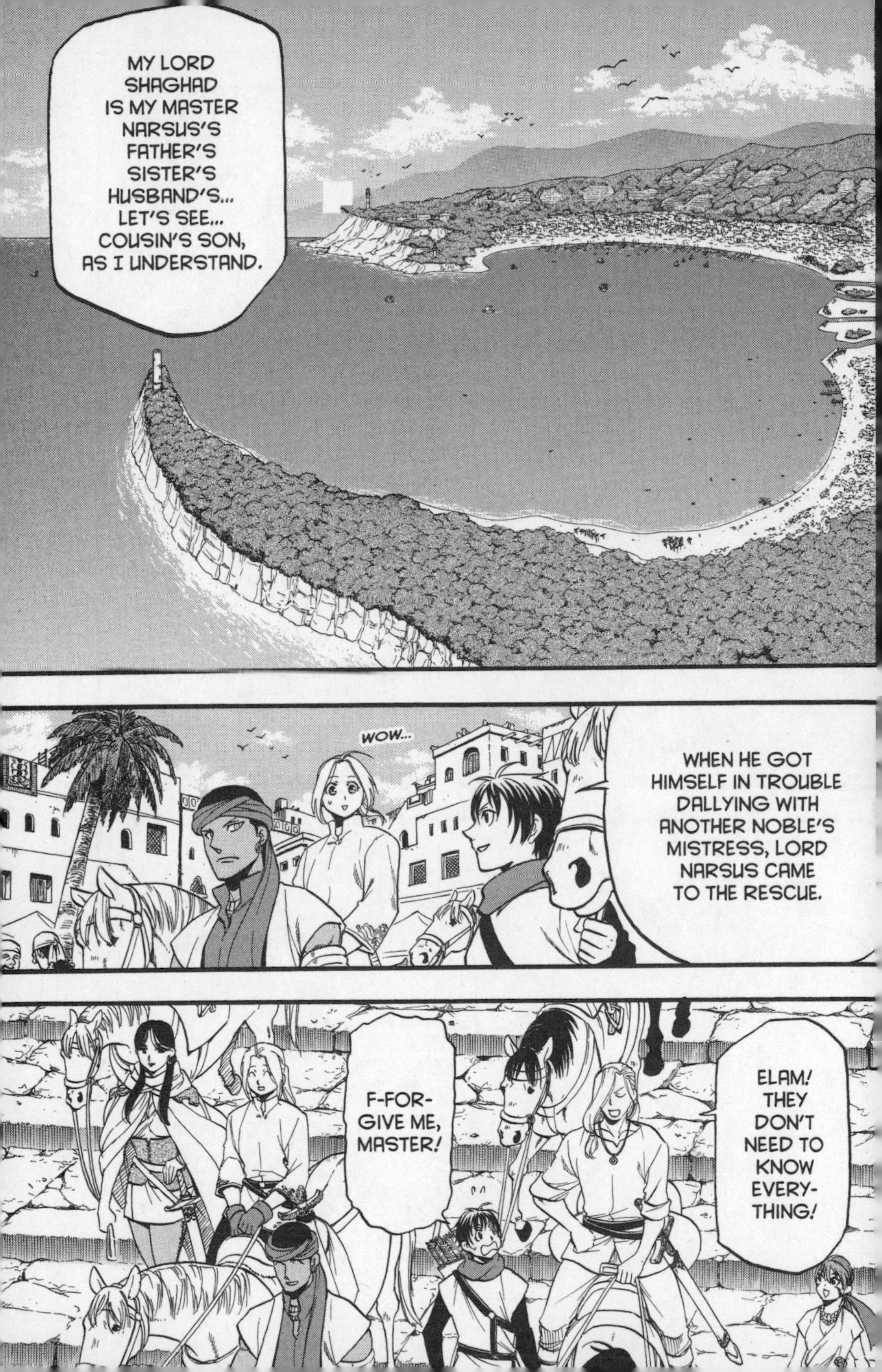
MY LORD SHAGHAD IS MY MASTER NARSUS'S FATHER'S SISTER'S HUSBAND'S... LET'S SEE... COUSIN'S SON, AS I UNDERSTAND.
WHEN HE GOT HIMSELF IN TROUBLE DALLYING WITH ANOTHER NOBLE'S MISTRESS, LORD NARSUS CAME TO THE RESCUE.
WOW...
ELAM! THEY DON'T NEED TO KNOW EVERY-THING!
F-FOR-GIVE ME, MASTER!

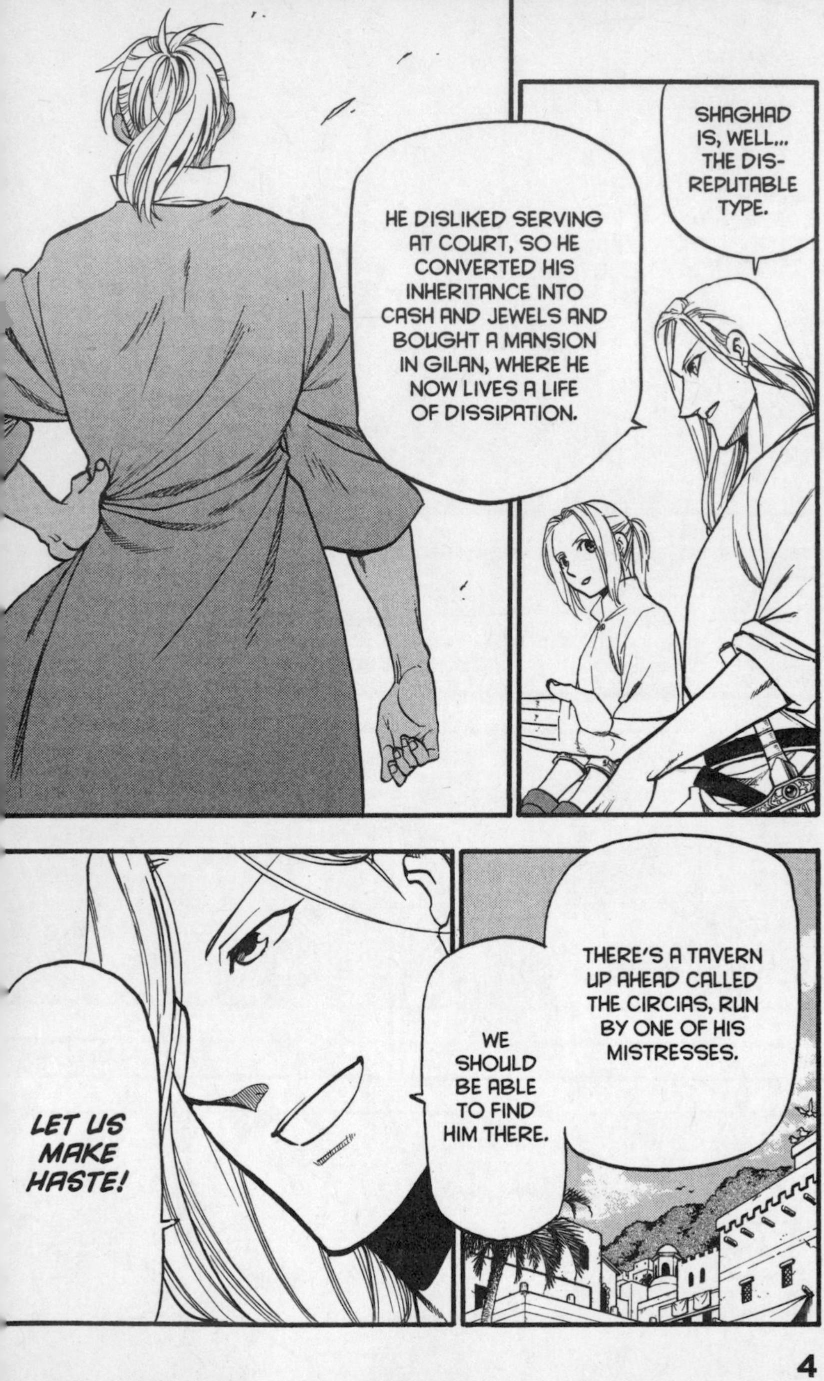
SHAGHAD IS, WELL... THE DIS-REPUTABLE TYPE.
HE DISLIKED SERVING AT COURT, SO HE CONVERTED HIS INHERITANCE INTO CASH AND JEWELS AND BOUGHT A MANSION IN GILAN, WHERE HE NOW LIVES A LIFE OF DISSIPATION.
THERE'S A TAVERN UP AHEAD CALLED THE CIRCIAS, RUN BY ONE OF HIS MISTRESSES.
WE SHOULD BE ABLE TO FIND HIM THERE.
LET US MAKE HASTE!

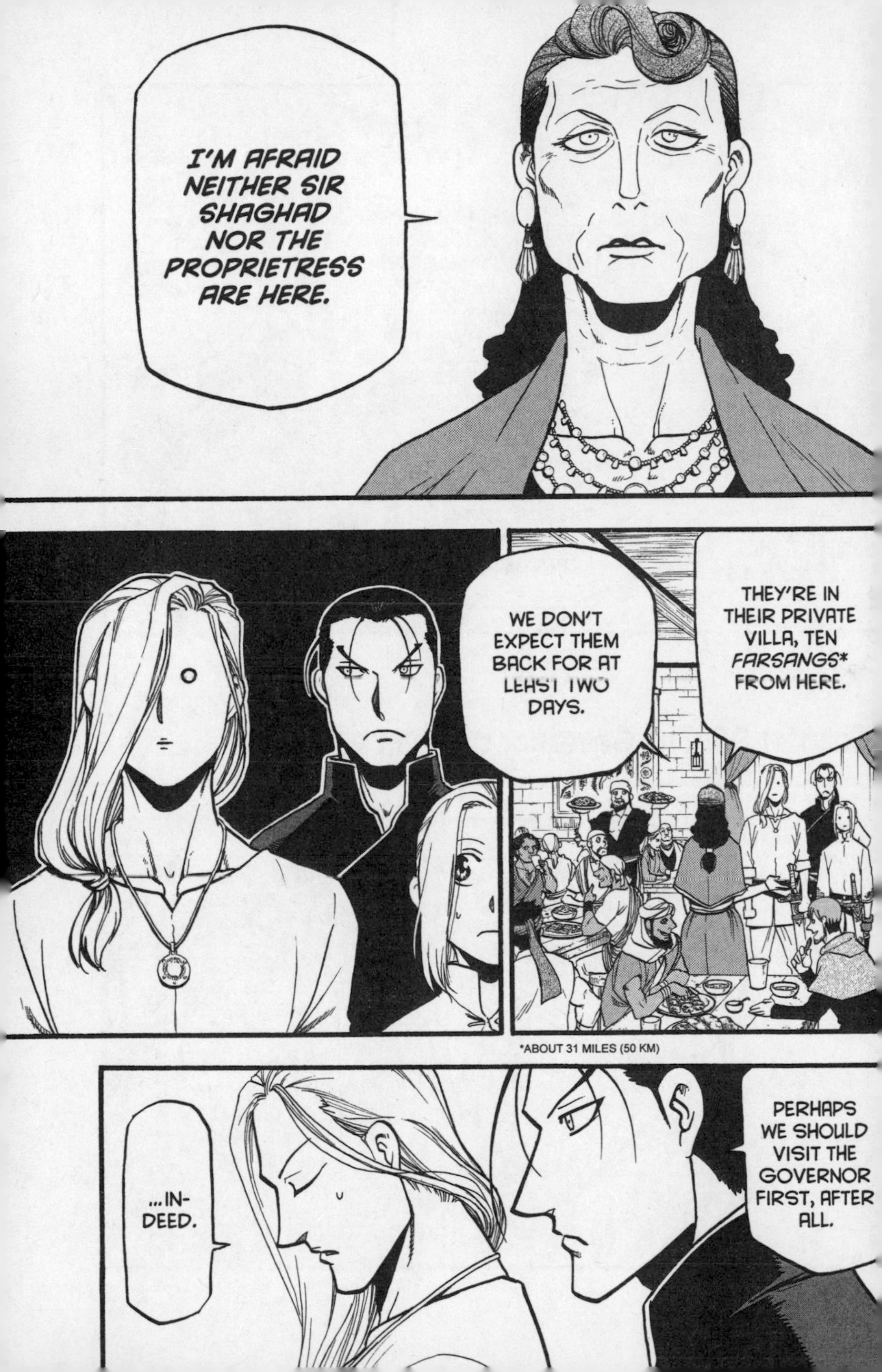
I'M AFRAID NEITHER SIR SHAGHAD NOR THE PROPRIETRESS ARE HERE.
THEY'RE IN THEIR PRIVATE VILLA, TEN *FARSANGS** FROM HERE.
WE DON'T EXPECT THEM BACK FOR AT LEAST TWO DAYS.
PERHAPS WE SHOULD VISIT THE GOVERNOR FIRST, AFTER ALL.
...IN-DEED.

*ABOUT 31 MILES (50 KM)

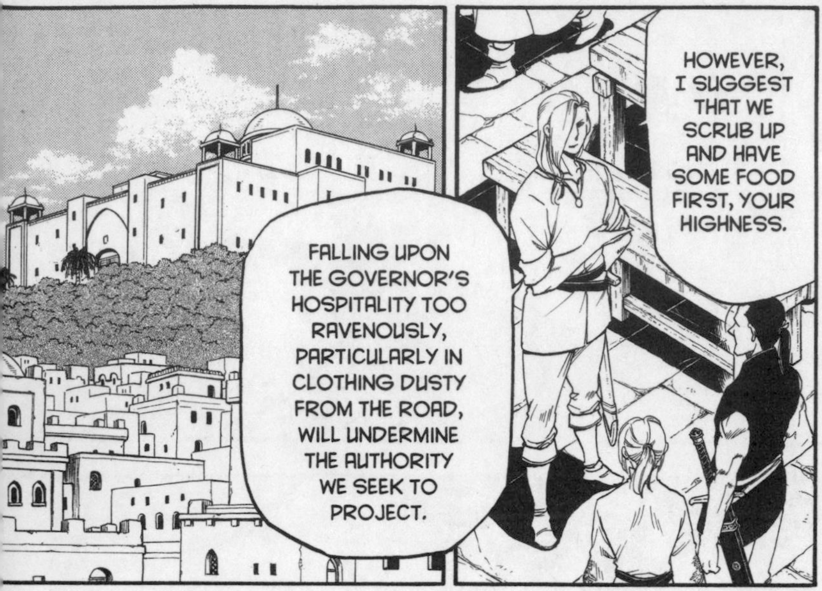
HOWEVER, I SUGGEST THAT WE SCRUB UP AND HAVE SOME FOOD FIRST, YOUR HIGHNESS.
FALLING UPON THE GOVERNOR'S HOSPITALITY TOO RAVENOUSLY, PARTICULARLY IN CLOTHING DUSTY FROM THE ROAD, WILL UNDERMINE THE AUTHORITY WE SEEK TO PROJECT.

Chapter 95: The Governor of Gilan's Disquiet

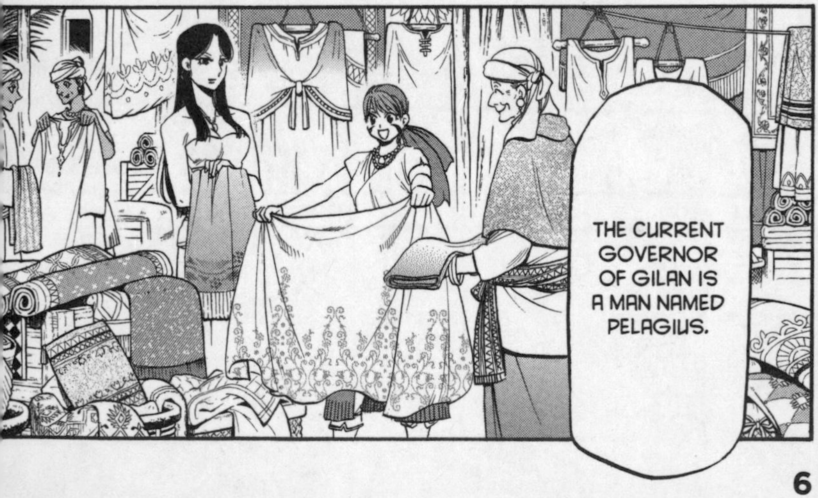
THE CURRENT GOVERNOR OF GILAN IS A MAN NAMED PELAGIUS.

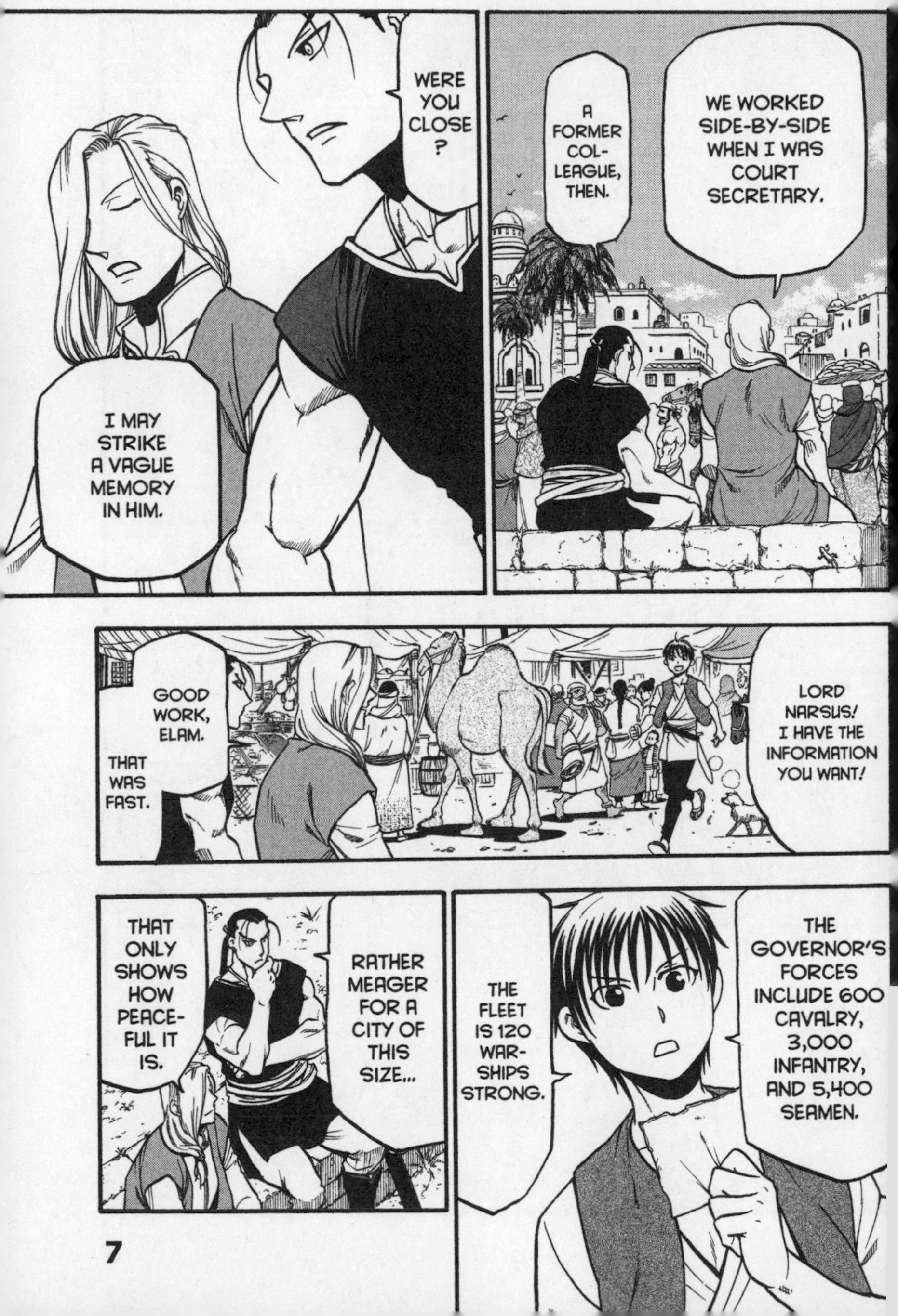
WE WORKED SIDE-BY-SIDE WHEN I WAS COURT SECRETARY.
A FORMER COL-LEAGUE, THEN.
WERE YOU CLOSE?
I MAY STRIKE A VAGUE MEMORY IN HIM.
LORD NARSUS! I HAVE THE INFORMATION YOU WANT!
GOOD WORK, ELAM.
THAT WAS FAST.
THE GOVERNOR'S FORCES INCLUDE 600 CAVALRY, 3,000 INFANTRY, AND 5,400 SEAMEN.
THE FLEET IS 120 WAR-SHIPS STRONG.
RATHER MEAGER FOR A CITY OF THIS SIZE...
THAT ONLY SHOWS HOW PEACE-FUL IT IS.

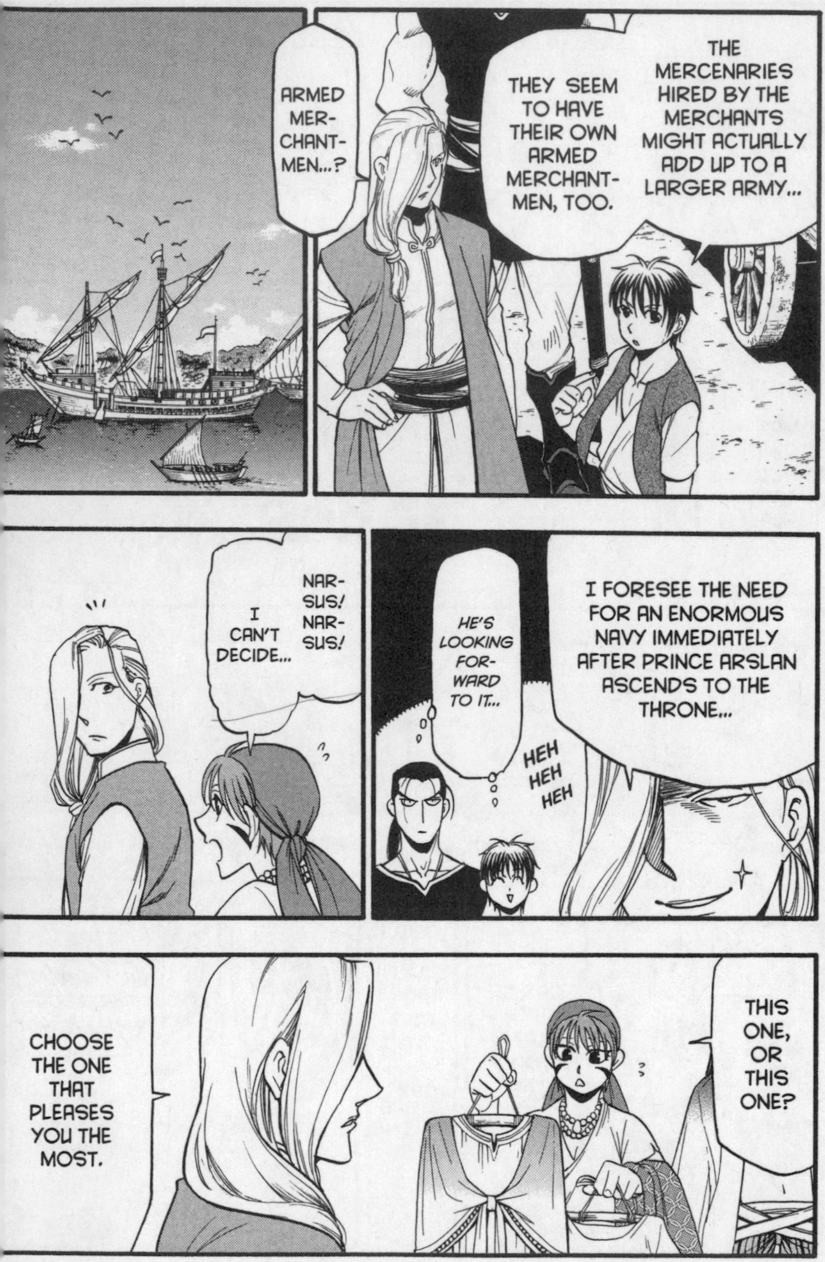
THE MERCENARIES HIRED BY THE MERCHANTS MIGHT ACTUALLY ADD UP TO A LARGER ARMY...
THEY SEEM TO HAVE THEIR OWN ARMED MERCHANT-MEN, TOO.
ARMED MER-CHANT-MEN...?
I FORESEE THE NEED FOR AN ENORMOUS NAVY IMMEDIATELY AFTER PRINCE ARSLAN ASCENDS TO THE THRONE...
HE'S LOOKING FOR-WARD TO IT...
HEH HEH HEH
NAR-SUS! NAR-SUS!
I CAN'T DECIDE...
THIS ONE, OR THIS ONE?
CHOOSE THE ONE THAT PLEASES YOU THE MOST.

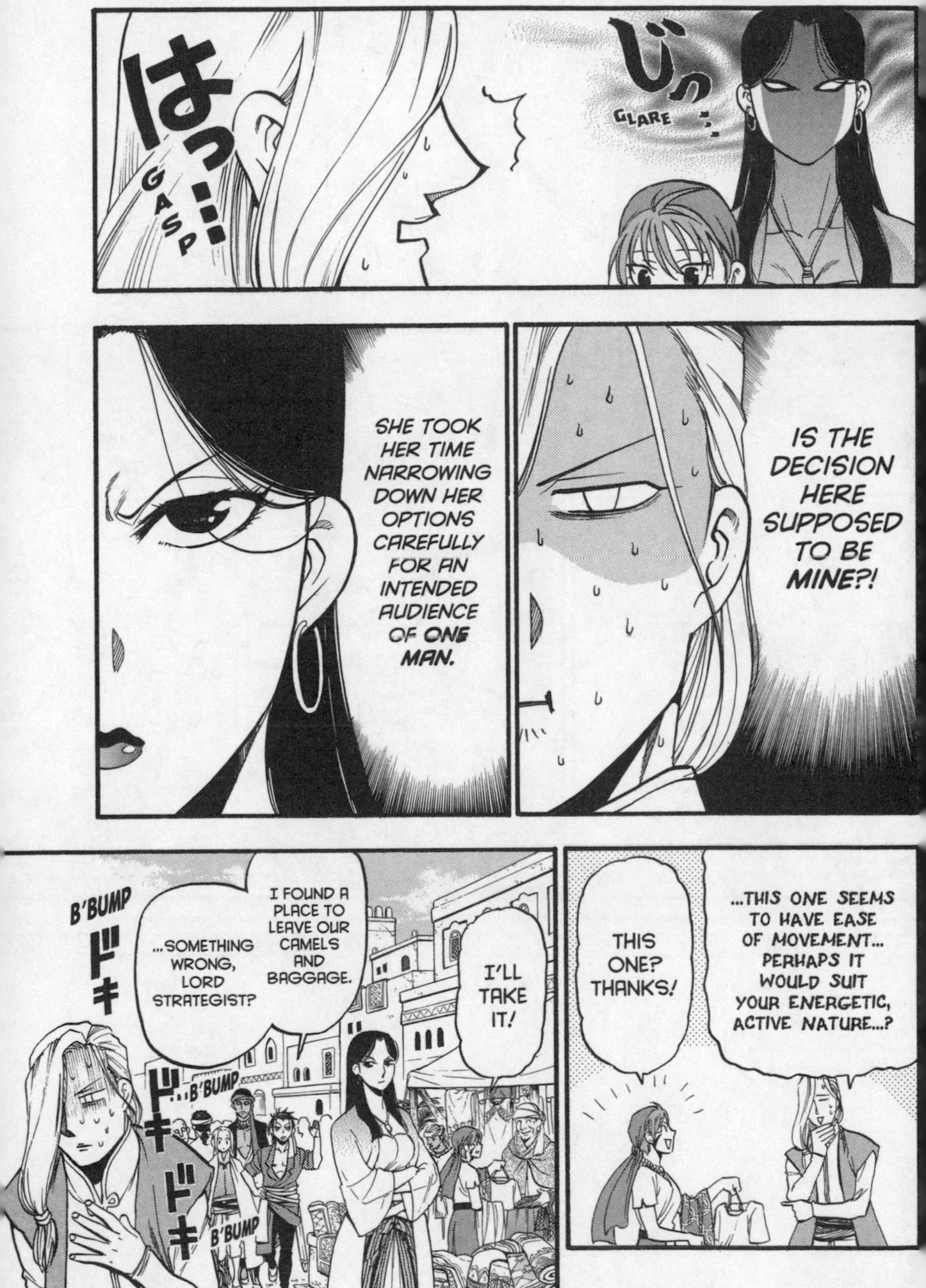
じっ
GLARE
はっ
GASP
IS THE DECISION HERE SUPPOSED TO BE MINE?!
SHE TOOK HER TIME NARROWING DOWN HER OPTIONS CAREFULLY FOR AN INTENDED AUDIENCE OF ONE MAN.
...THIS ONE SEEMS TO HAVE EASE OF MOVEMENT... PERHAPS IT WOULD SUIT YOUR ENERGETIC, ACTIVE NATURE...?
THIS ONE? THANKS!
I'LL TAKE IT!
I FOUND A PLACE TO LEAVE OUR CAMELS AND BAGGAGE.
...SOMETHING WRONG, LORD STRATEGIST?
B'BUMP
ドキ
ドキ
B'BUMP
ドキ
B'BUMP

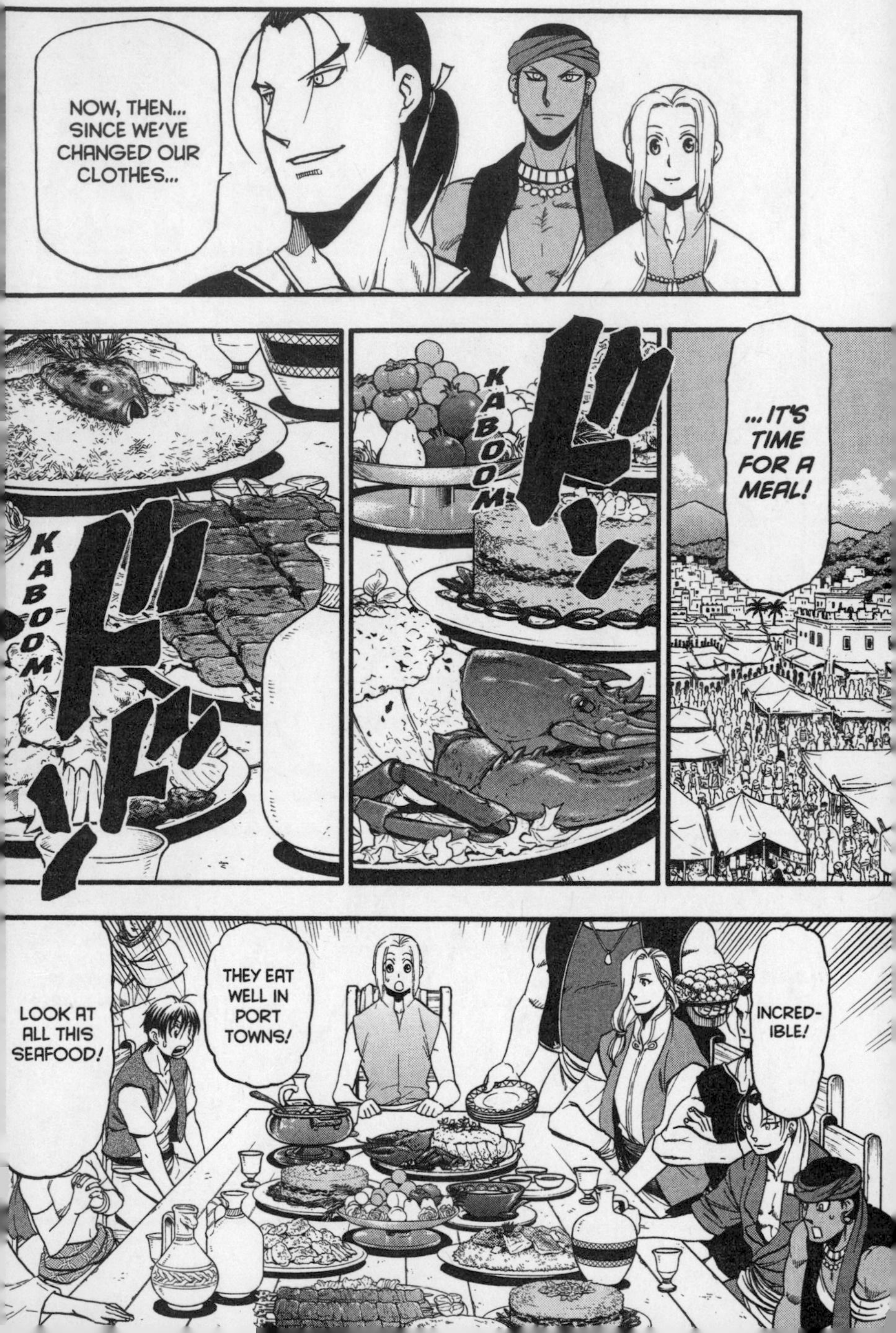
NOW, THEN... SINCE WE'VE CHANGED OUR CLOTHES...
...IT'S TIME FOR A MEAL!
KABOOM
KABOOM
INCRED-IBLE!
THEY EAT WELL IN PORT TOWNS!
LOOK AT ALL THIS SEAFOOD!

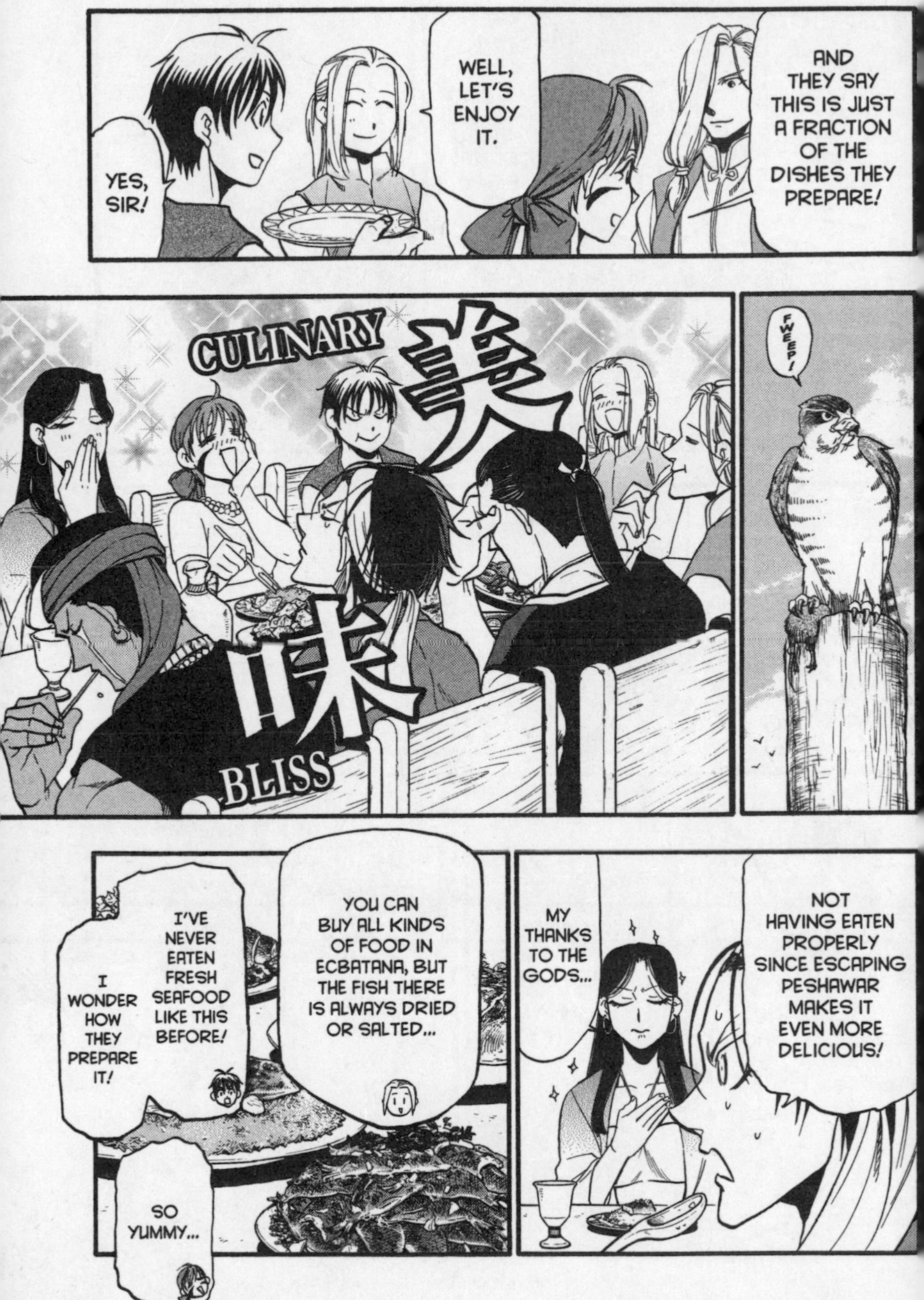
AND THEY SAY THIS IS JUST A FRACTION OF THE DISHES THEY PREPARE!
WELL, LET'S ENJOY IT.
YES, SIR!
FWEEP!
CULINARY
美
味
BLISS
NOT HAVING EATEN PROPERLY SINCE ESCAPING PESHAWAR MAKES IT EVEN MORE DELICIOUS!
MY THANKS TO THE GODS...
YOU CAN BUY ALL KINDS OF FOOD IN ECBATANA, BUT THE FISH THERE IS ALWAYS DRIED OR SALTED...
I'VE NEVER EATEN FRESH SEAFOOD LIKE THIS BEFORE!
I WONDER HOW THEY PREPARE IT!
SO YUMMY...

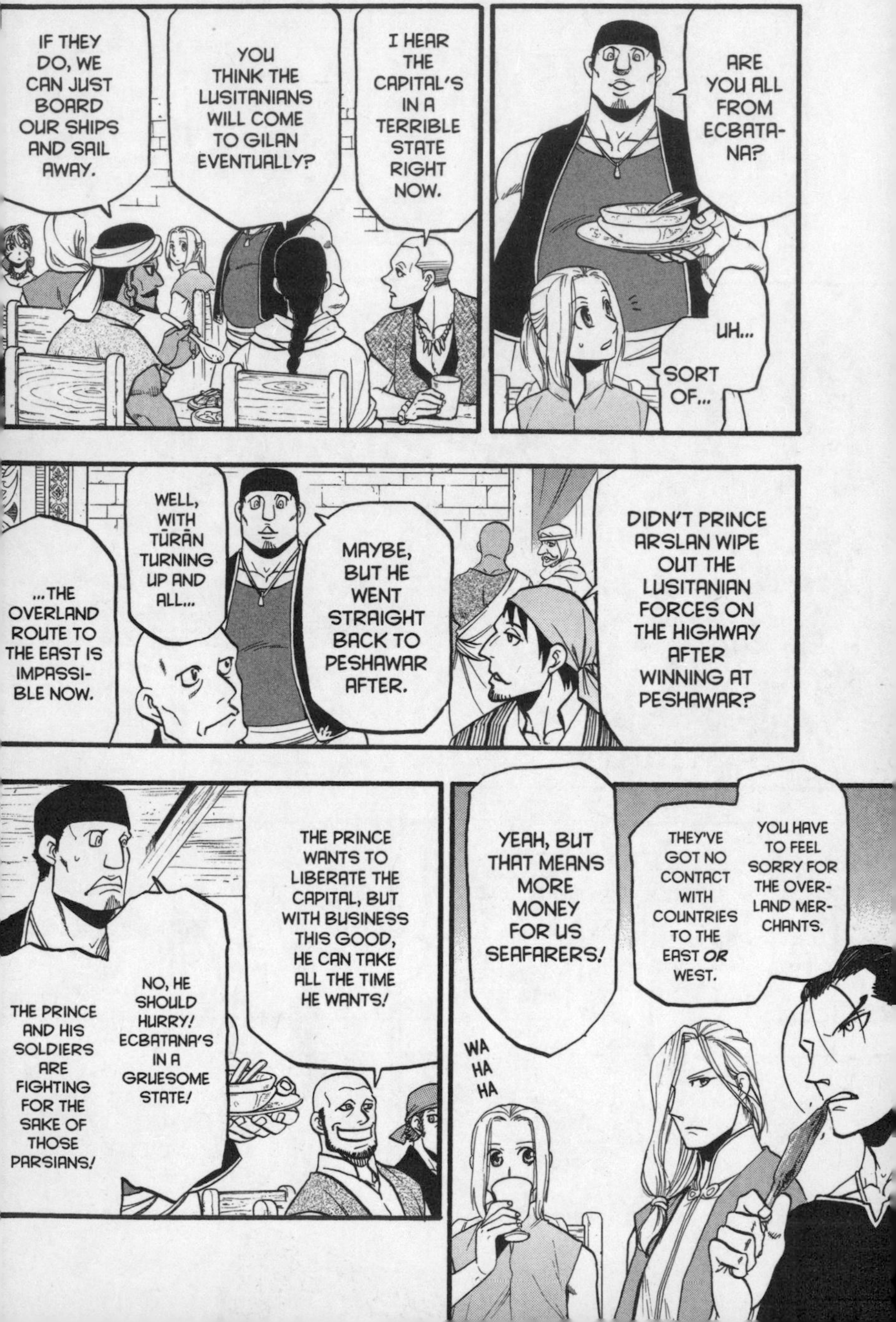
ARE YOU ALL FROM ECBATANA?
UH...
SORT OF...
I HEAR THE CAPITAL'S IN A TERRIBLE STATE RIGHT NOW.
YOU THINK THE LUSITANIANS WILL COME TO GILAN EVENTUALLY?
IF THEY DO, WE CAN JUST BOARD OUR SHIPS AND SAIL AWAY.
DIDN'T PRINCE ARSLAN WIPE OUT THE LUSITANIAN FORCES ON THE HIGHWAY AFTER WINNING AT PESHAWAR?
MAYBE, BUT HE WENT STRAIGHT BACK TO PESHAWAR AFTER.
WELL, WITH TŪRĀN TURNING UP AND ALL...
...THE OVERLAND ROUTE TO THE EAST IS IMPASSIBLE NOW.
YOU HAVE TO FEEL SORRY FOR THE OVERLAND MERCHANTS.
THEY'VE GOT NO CONTACT WITH COUNTRIES TO THE EAST OR WEST.
YEAH, BUT THAT MEANS MORE MONEY FOR US SEAFARERS!
WA HA HA
THE PRINCE WANTS TO LIBERATE THE CAPITAL, BUT WITH BUSINESS THIS GOOD, HE CAN TAKE ALL THE TIME HE WANTS!
NO, HE SHOULD HURRY! ECBATANA'S IN A GRUESOME STATE!
THE PRINCE AND HIS SOLDIERS ARE FIGHTING FOR THE SAKE OF THOSE PARSIANS!

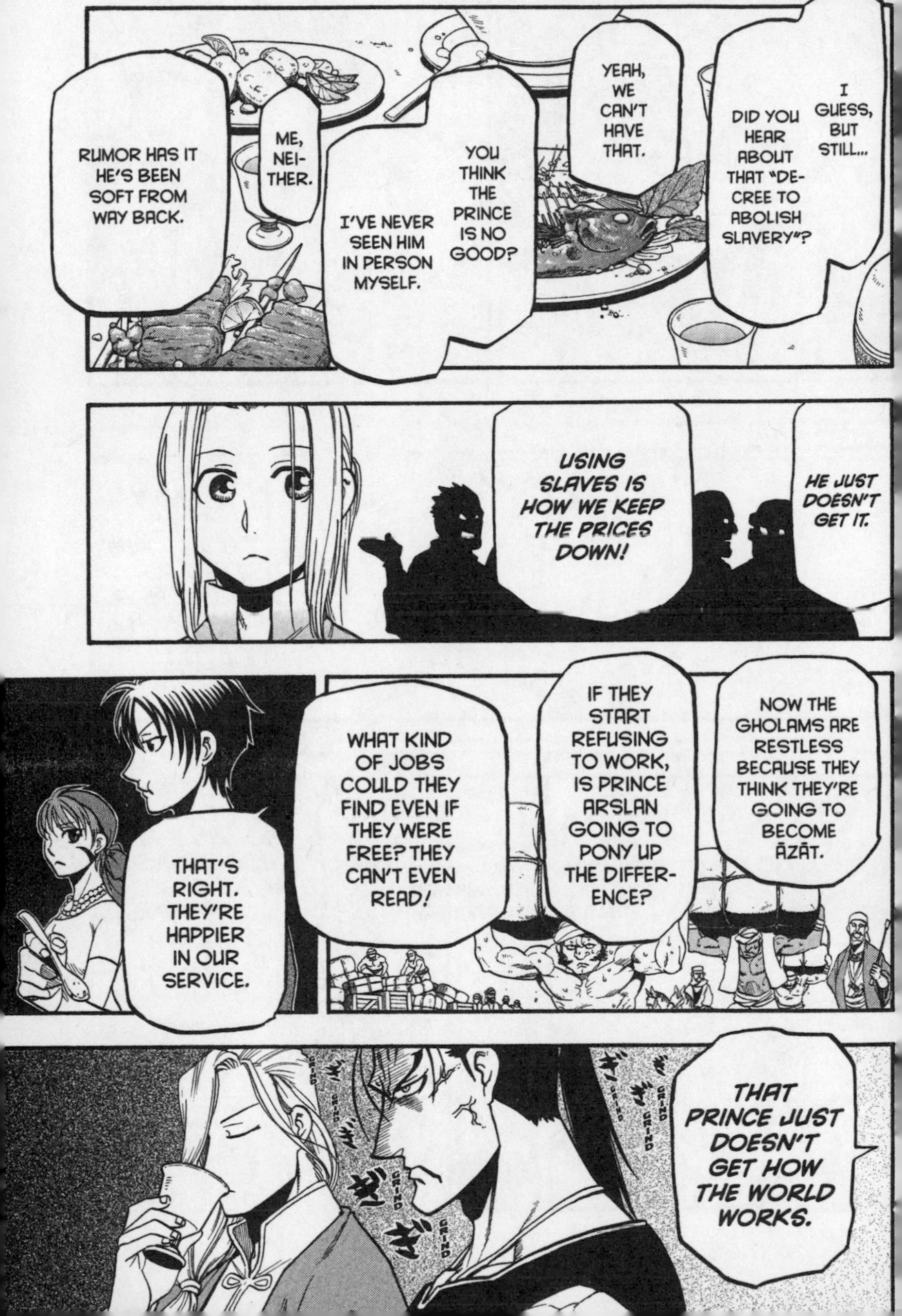
I GUESS, BUT STILL...
DID YOU HEAR ABOUT THAT "DE-CREE TO ABOLISH SLAVERY"?
YEAH, WE CAN'T HAVE THAT.
YOU THINK THE PRINCE IS NO GOOD?
I'VE NEVER SEEN HIM IN PERSON MYSELF.
ME, NEI-THER.
RUMOR HAS IT HE'S BEEN SOFT FROM WAY BACK.
HE JUST DOESN'T GET IT.
USING SLAVES IS HOW WE KEEP THE PRICES DOWN!
NOW THE GHOLAMS ARE RESTLESS BECAUSE THEY THINK THEY'RE GOING TO BECOME ĀZĀT.
IF THEY START REFUSING TO WORK, IS PRINCE ARSLAN GOING TO PONY UP THE DIFFER-ENCE?
WHAT KIND OF JOBS COULD THEY FIND EVEN IF THEY WERE FREE? THEY CAN'T EVEN READ!
THAT'S RIGHT. THEY'RE HAPPIER IN OUR SERVICE.
THAT PRINCE JUST DOESN'T GET HOW THE WORLD WORKS.
GRIND GRIND GRIND GRIND GRIND GRIND

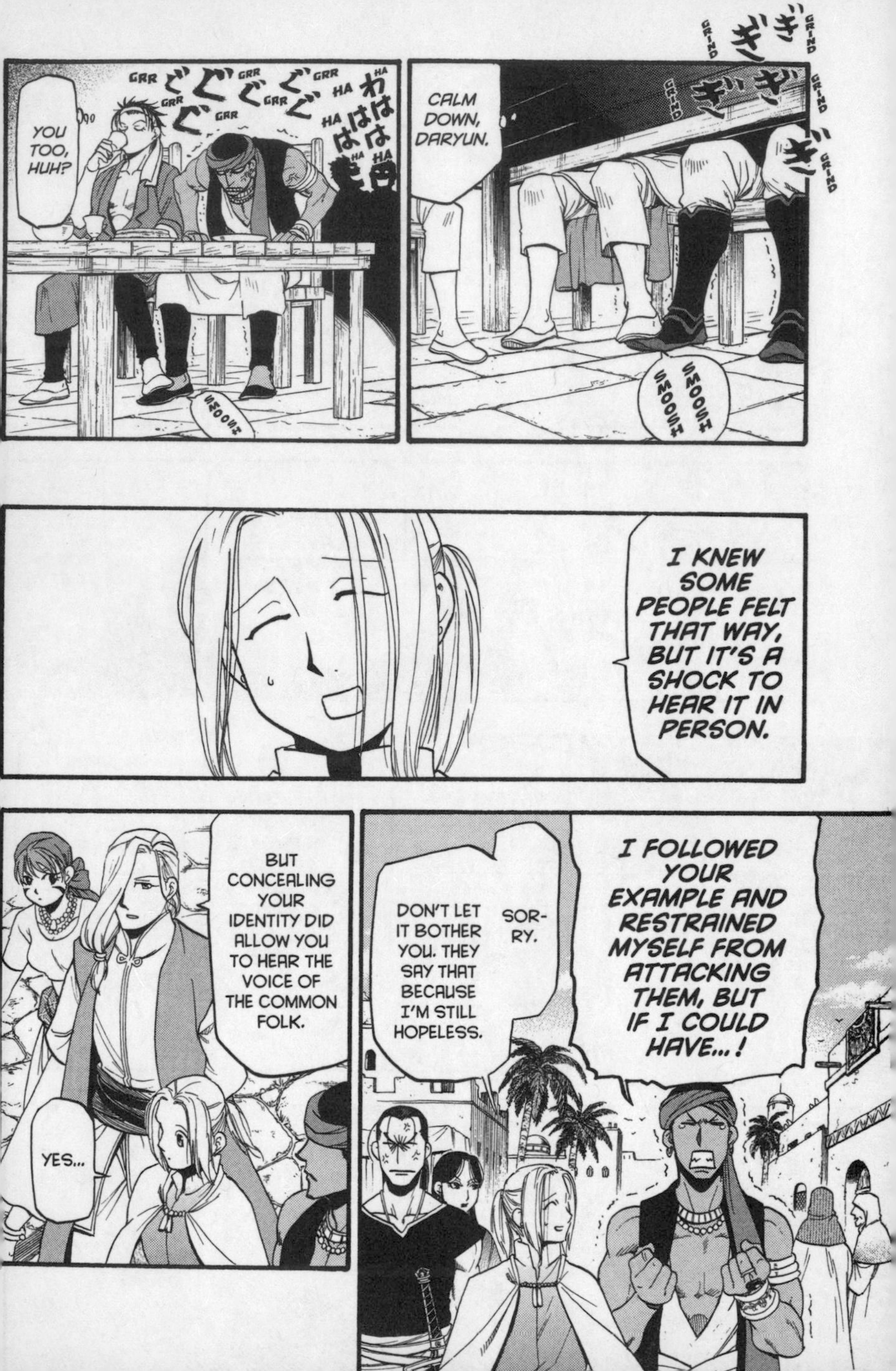
GRIND GRIND GRIND GRIND GRIND
CALM DOWN, DARYUN.
SMOOSH SMOOSH
YOU TOO, HUH?
GRR GRR GRR GRR GRR GRR
HA HA HA HA HA HA
SMOOSH
I KNEW SOME PEOPLE FELT THAT WAY, BUT IT'S A SHOCK TO HEAR IT IN PERSON.
I FOLLOWED YOUR EXAMPLE AND RESTRAINED MYSELF FROM ATTACKING THEM, BUT IF I COULD HAVE...!
SOR-RY.
DON'T LET IT BOTHER YOU. THEY SAY THAT BECAUSE I'M STILL HOPELESS.
BUT CONCEALING YOUR IDENTITY DID ALLOW YOU TO HEAR THE VOICE OF THE COMMON FOLK.
YES...

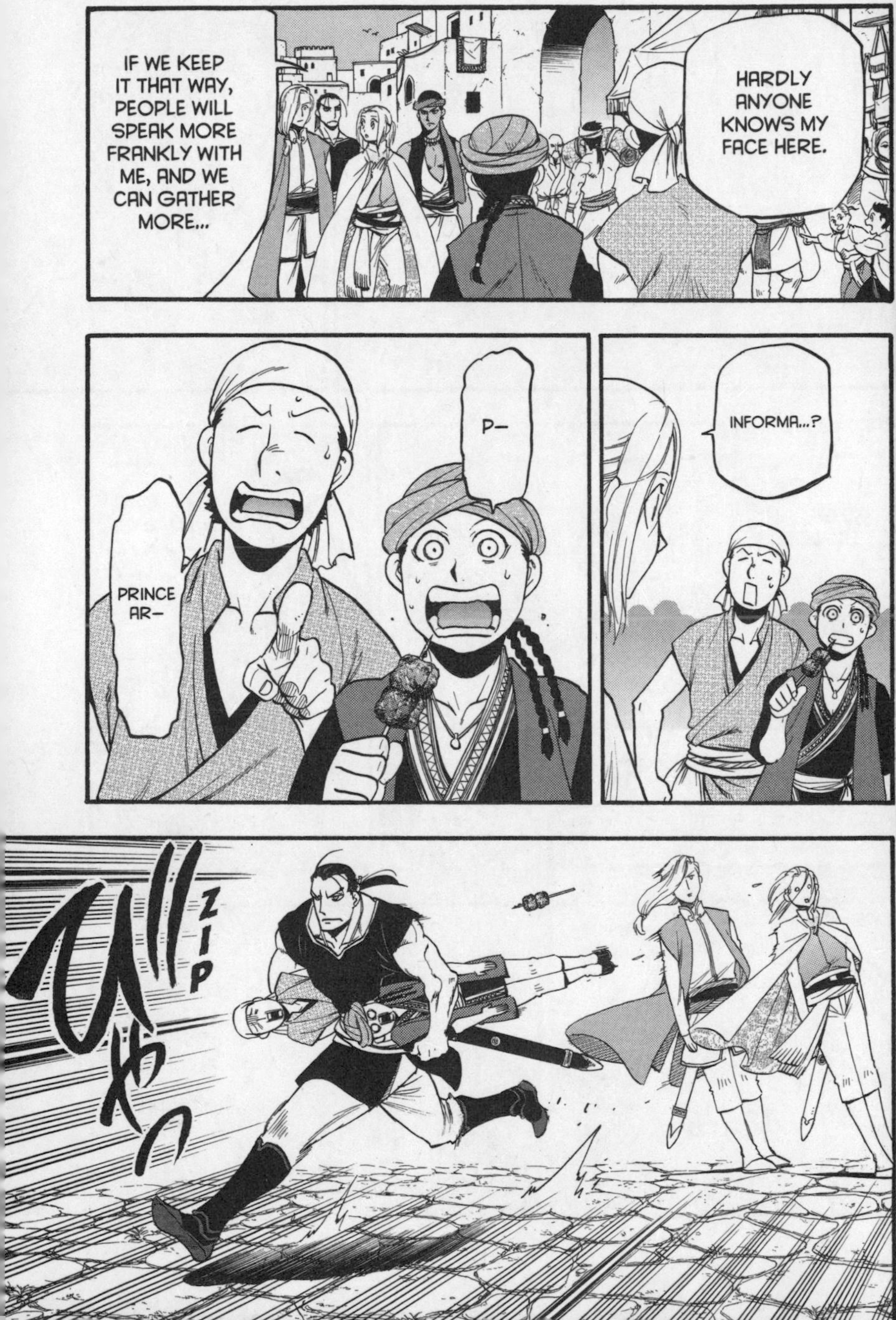
HARDLY ANYONE KNOWS MY FACE HERE.
IF WE KEEP IT THAT WAY, PEOPLE WILL SPEAK MORE FRANKLY WITH ME, AND WE CAN GATHER MORE...
INFORMA...?
P–
PRINCE AR–
ZIP

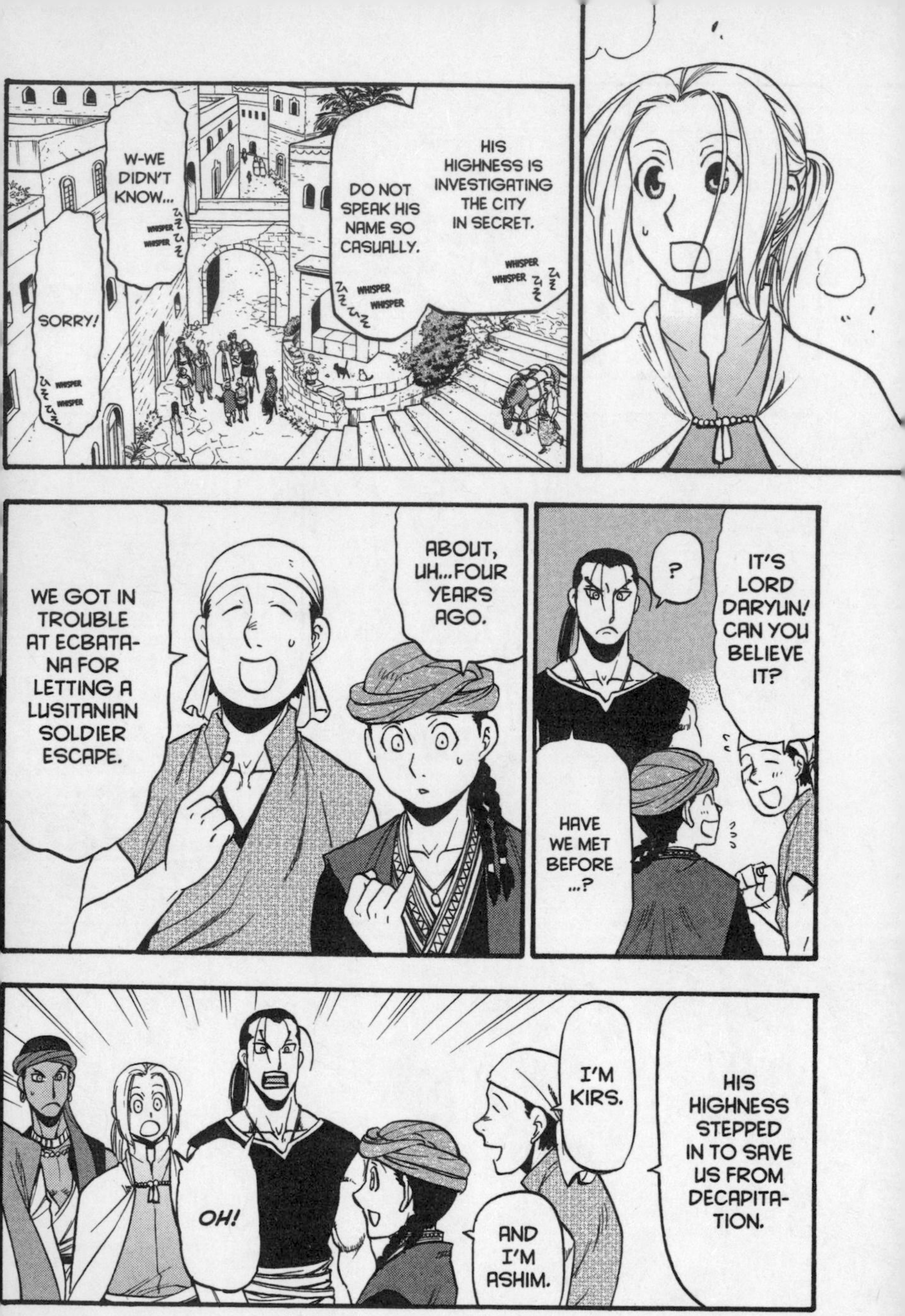
HIS HIGHNESS IS INVESTIGATING THE CITY IN SECRET.
WHISPER WHISPER
DO NOT SPEAK HIS NAME SO CASUALLY.
WHISPER WHISPER
W-WE DIDN'T KNOW...
WHISPER WHISPER
SORRY!
WHISPER WHISPER
IT'S LORD DARYUN! CAN YOU BELIEVE IT?
?
HAVE WE MET BEFORE ...?
ABOUT, UH...FOUR YEARS AGO.
WE GOT IN TROUBLE AT ECBATA-NA FOR LETTING A LUSITANIAN SOLDIER ESCAPE.
HIS HIGHNESS STEPPED IN TO SAVE US FROM DECAPITA-TION.
I'M KIRS.
AND I'M ASHIM.
OH!

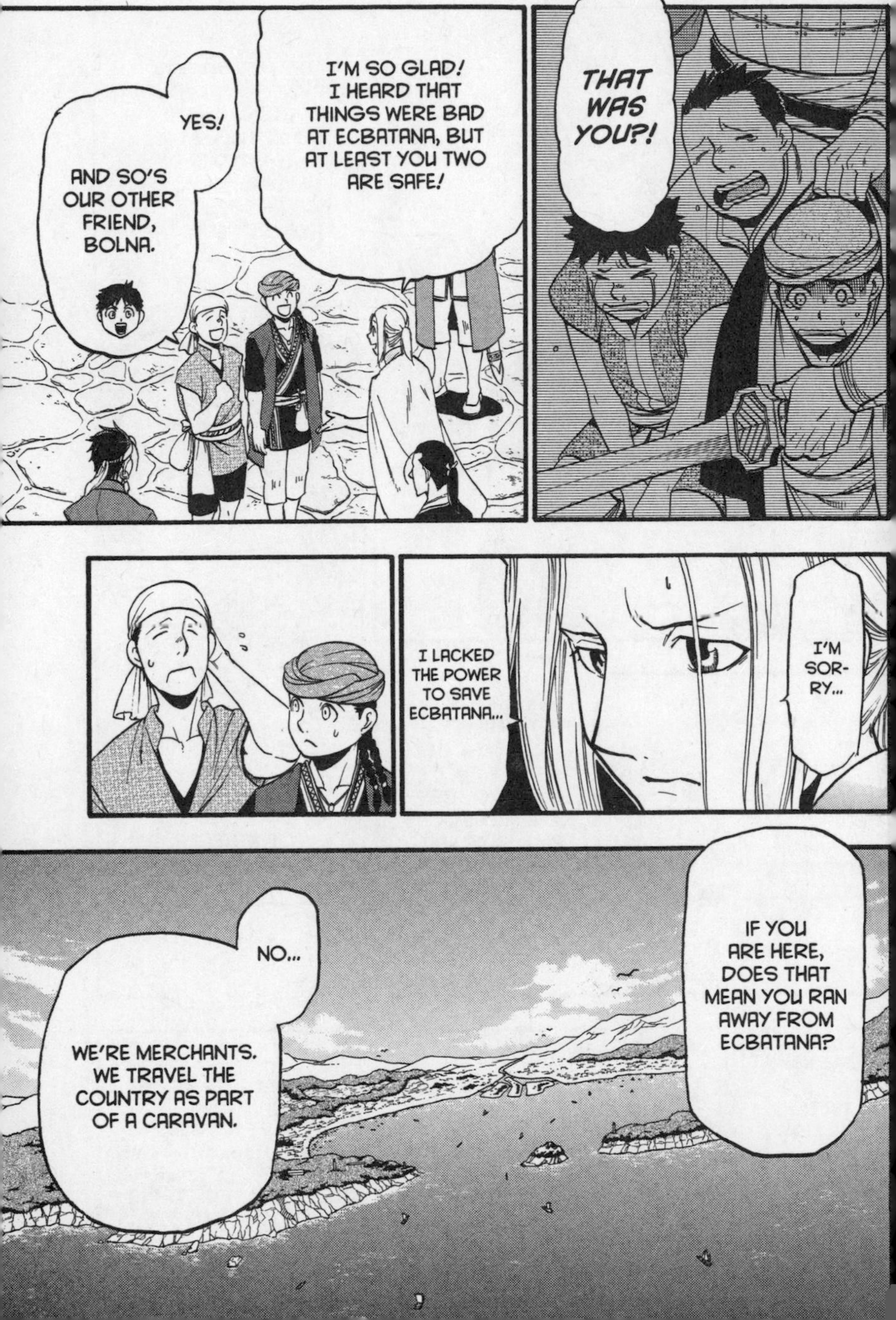
THAT WAS YOU?!
I'M SO GLAD! I HEARD THAT THINGS WERE BAD AT ECBATANA, BUT AT LEAST YOU TWO ARE SAFE!
YES!
AND SO'S OUR OTHER FRIEND, BOLNA.
I'M SORRY...
I LACKED THE POWER TO SAVE ECBATANA...
IF YOU ARE HERE, DOES THAT MEAN YOU RAN AWAY FROM ECBATANA?
NO...
WE'RE MERCHANTS. WE TRAVEL THE COUNTRY AS PART OF A CARAVAN.

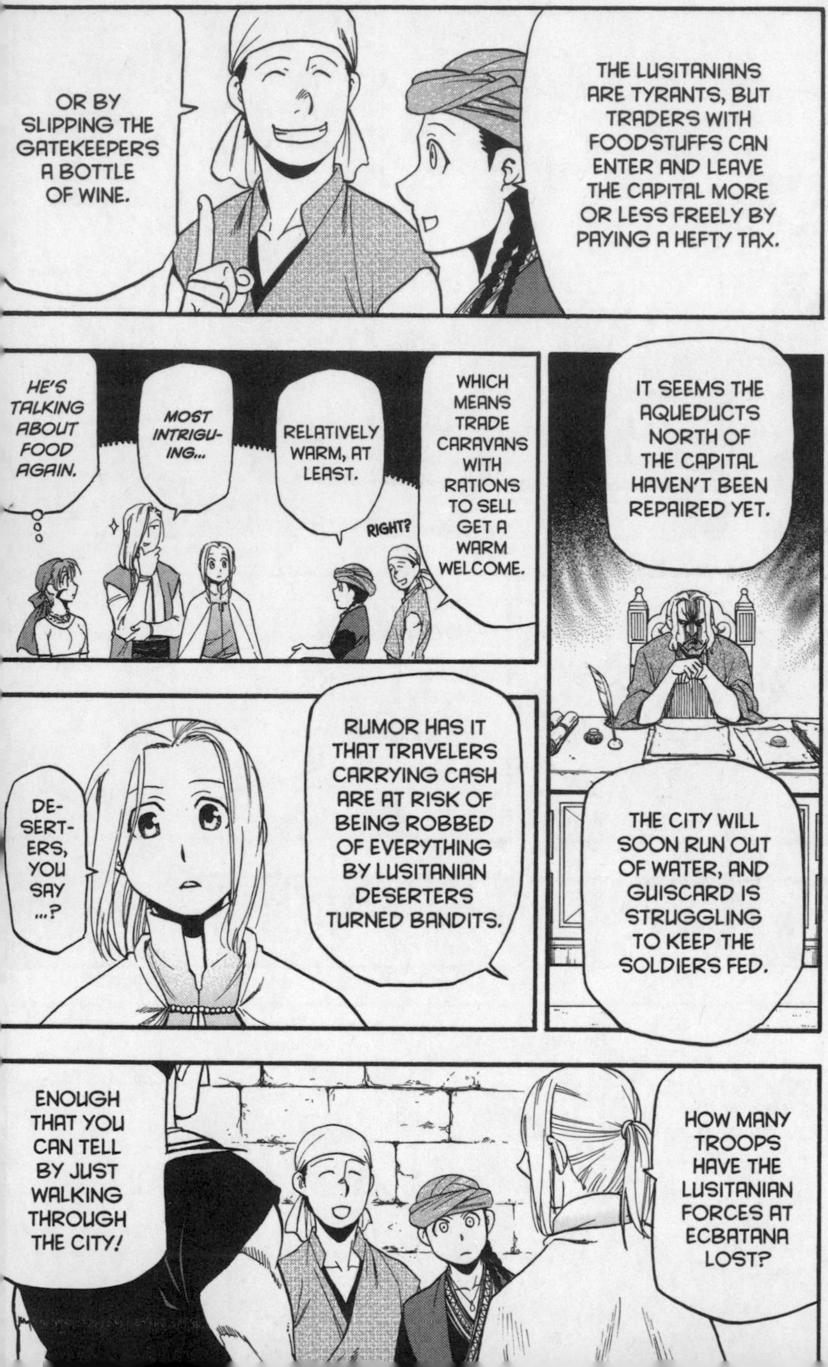
THE LUSITANIANS ARE TYRANTS, BUT TRADERS WITH FOODSTUFFS CAN ENTER AND LEAVE THE CAPITAL MORE OR LESS FREELY BY PAYING A HEFTY TAX.
OR BY SLIPPING THE GATEKEEPERS A BOTTLE OF WINE.
IT SEEMS THE AQUEDUCTS NORTH OF THE CAPITAL HAVEN'T BEEN REPAIRED YET.
THE CITY WILL SOON RUN OUT OF WATER, AND GUISCARD IS STRUGGLING TO KEEP THE SOLDIERS FED.
WHICH MEANS TRADE CARAVANS WITH RATIONS TO SELL GET A WARM WELCOME.
RIGHT?
RELATIVELY WARM, AT LEAST.
MOST INTRIGU-ING...
HE'S TALKING ABOUT FOOD AGAIN.
RUMOR HAS IT THAT TRAVELERS CARRYING CASH ARE AT RISK OF BEING ROBBED OF EVERYTHING BY LUSITANIAN DESERTERS TURNED BANDITS.
DE-SERT-ERS, YOU SAY ...?
HOW MANY TROOPS HAVE THE LUSITANIAN FORCES AT ECBATANA LOST?
ENOUGH THAT YOU CAN TELL BY JUST WALKING THROUGH THE CITY!

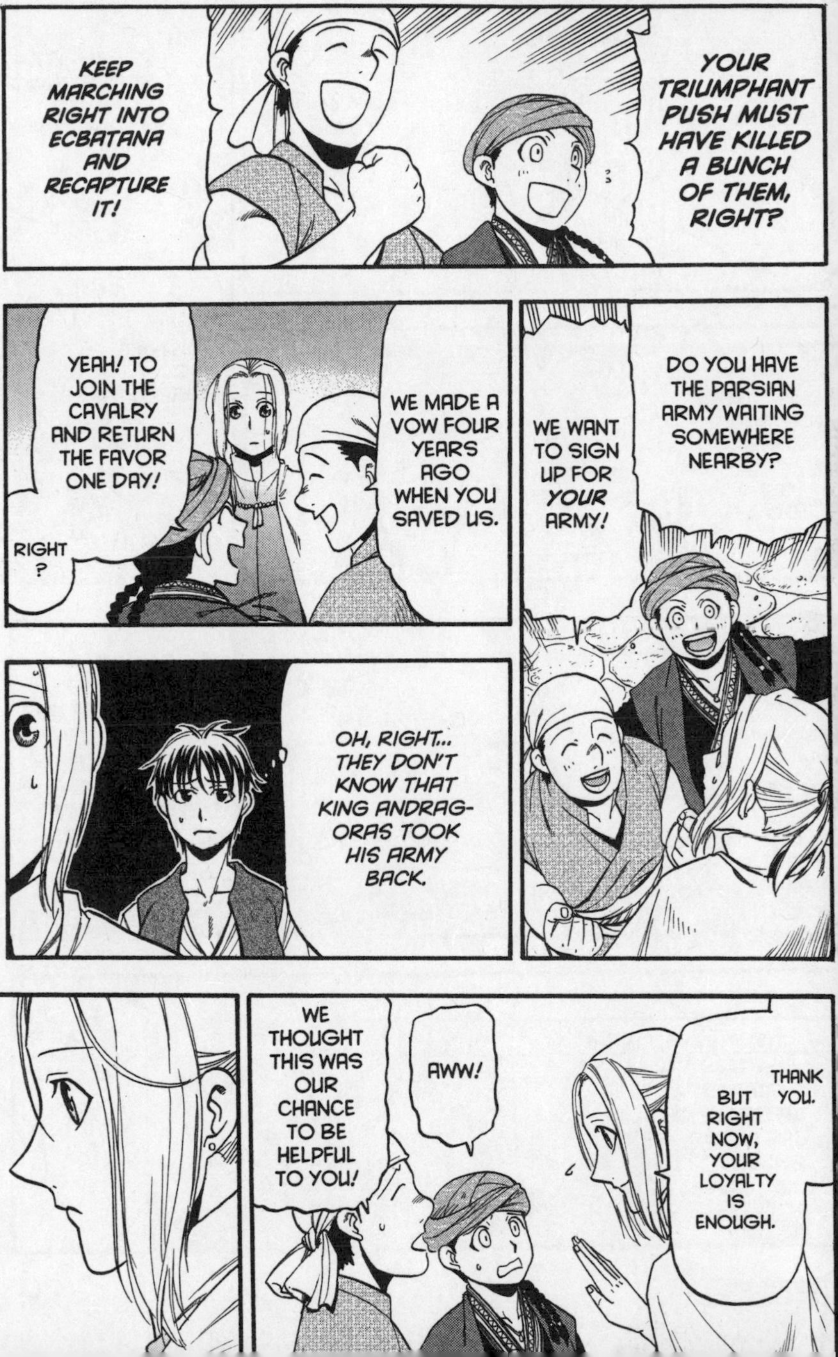
YOUR TRIUMPHANT PUSH MUST HAVE KILLED A BUNCH OF THEM, RIGHT?
KEEP MARCHING RIGHT INTO ECBATANA AND RECAPTURE IT!
DO YOU HAVE THE PARSIAN ARMY WAITING SOMEWHERE NEARBY?
WE WANT TO SIGN UP FOR *YOUR* ARMY!
WE MADE A VOW FOUR YEARS AGO WHEN YOU SAVED US.
YEAH! TO JOIN THE CAVALRY AND RETURN THE FAVOR ONE DAY!
RIGHT?
OH, RIGHT... THEY DON'T KNOW THAT KING ANDRAG-ORAS TOOK HIS ARMY BACK.
THANK YOU.
BUT RIGHT NOW, YOUR LOYALTY IS ENOUGH.
AWW!
WE THOUGHT THIS WAS OUR CHANCE TO BE HELPFUL TO YOU!

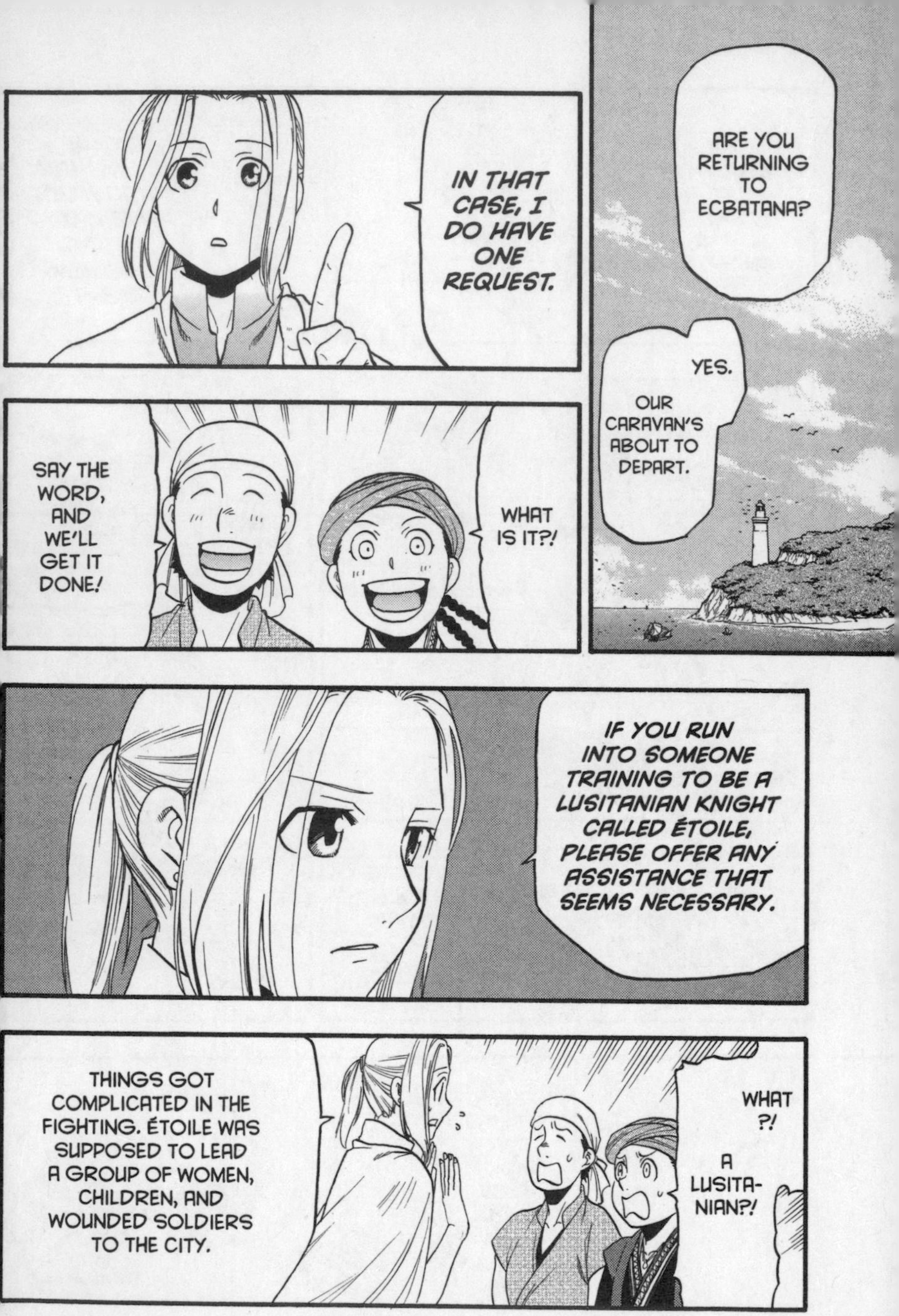
ARE YOU RETURNING TO ECBATANA?
YES.
OUR CARAVAN'S ABOUT TO DEPART.
IN THAT CASE, I DO HAVE ONE REQUEST.
WHAT IS IT?!
SAY THE WORD, AND WE'LL GET IT DONE!
IF YOU RUN INTO SOMEONE TRAINING TO BE A LUSITANIAN KNIGHT CALLED ÉTOILE, PLEASE OFFER ANY ASSISTANCE THAT SEEMS NECESSARY.
WHAT?!
A LUSITANIAN?!
THINGS GOT COMPLICATED IN THE FIGHTING. ÉTOILE WAS SUPPOSED TO LEAD A GROUP OF WOMEN, CHILDREN, AND WOUNDED SOLDIERS TO THE CITY.

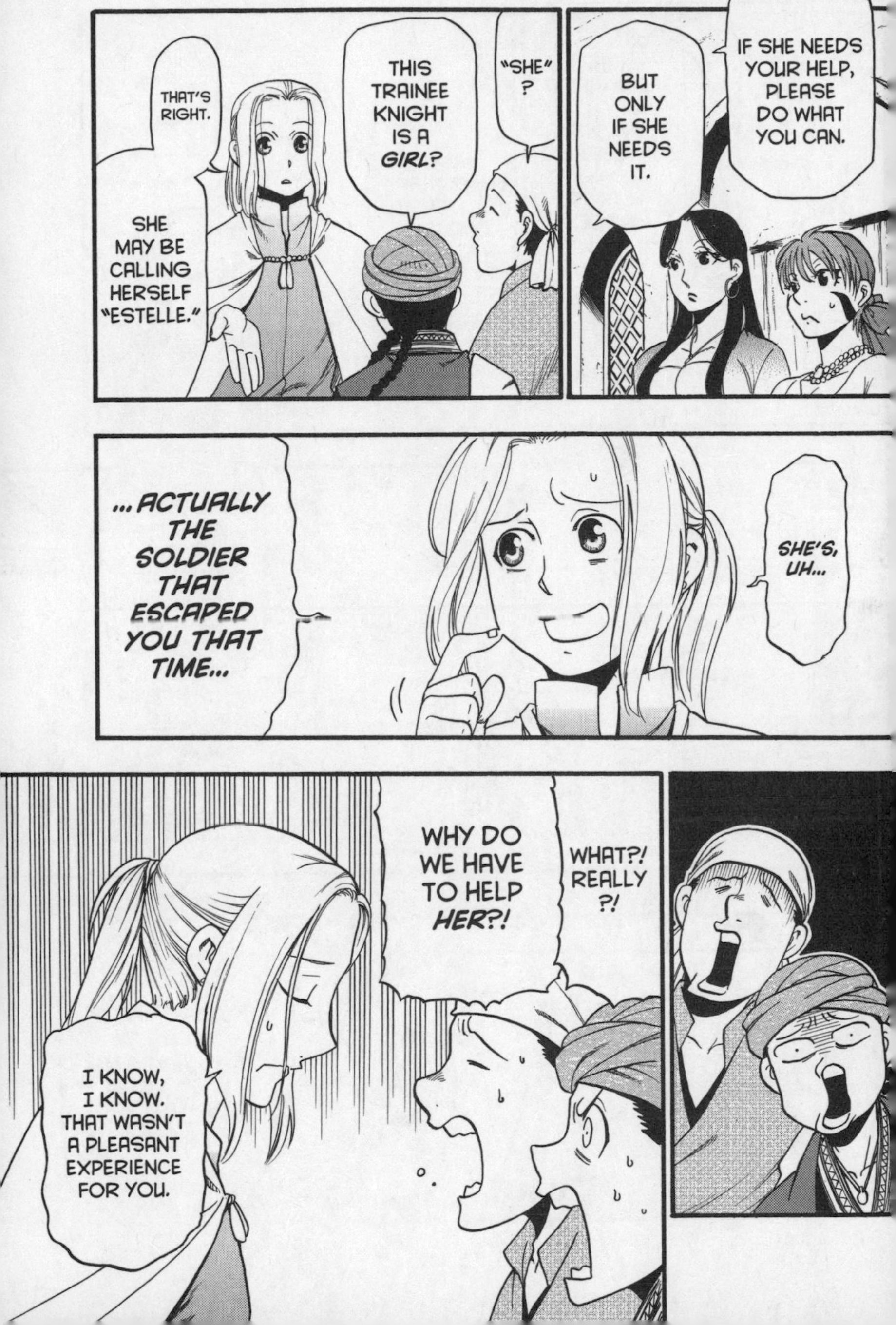
IF SHE NEEDS YOUR HELP, PLEASE DO WHAT YOU CAN.
BUT ONLY IF SHE NEEDS IT.
"SHE"?
THIS TRAINEE KNIGHT IS A *GIRL*?
THAT'S RIGHT.
SHE MAY BE CALLING HERSELF "ESTELLE."
SHE'S, UH...
...ACTUALLY THE SOLDIER THAT ESCAPED YOU THAT TIME...
WHAT?! REALLY?!
WHY DO WE HAVE TO HELP *HER*?!
I KNOW, I KNOW. THAT WASN'T A PLEASANT EXPERIENCE FOR YOU.

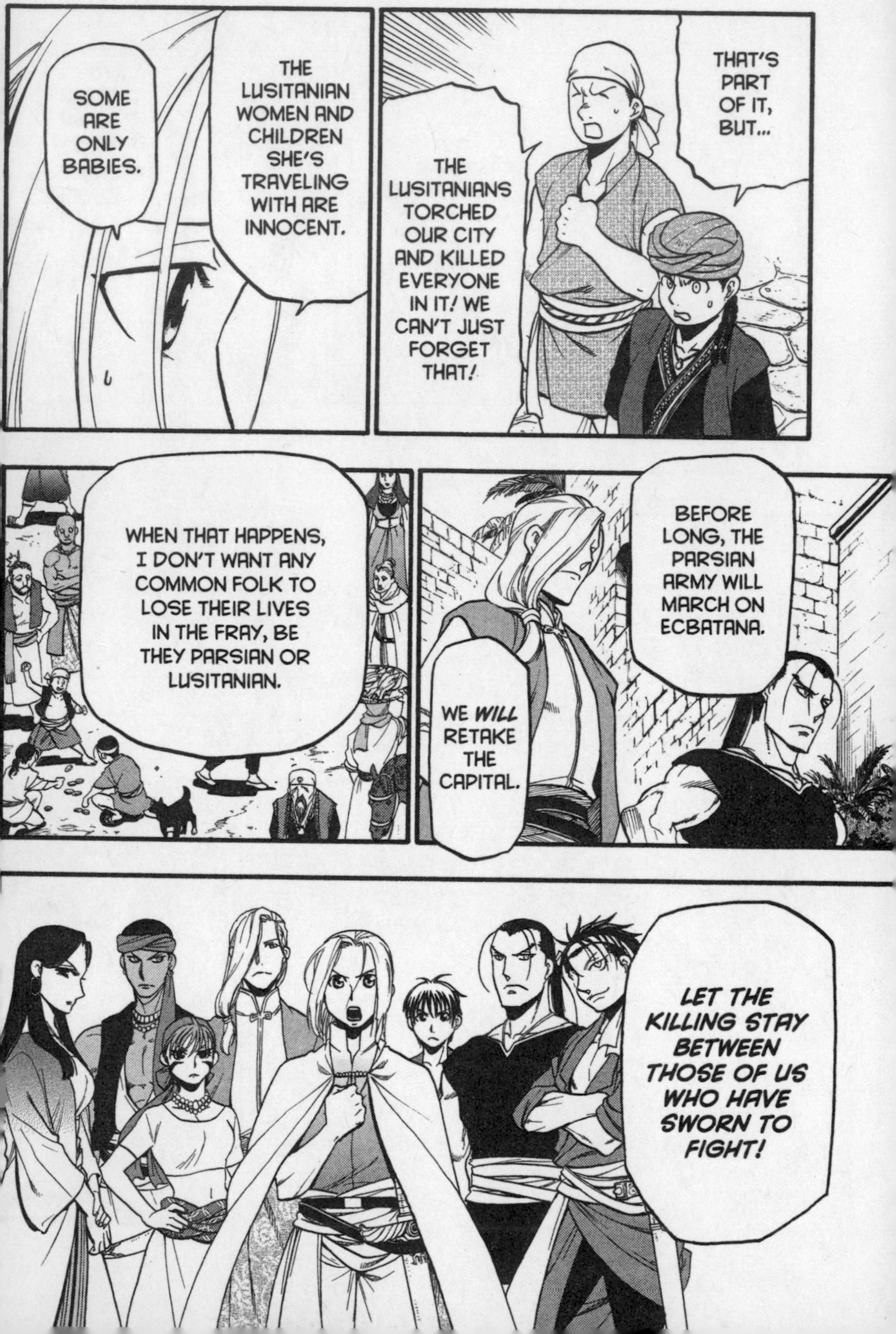
THAT'S PART OF IT, BUT...
THE LUSITANIANS TORCHED OUR CITY AND KILLED EVERYONE IN IT! WE CAN'T JUST FORGET THAT!
THE LUSITANIAN WOMEN AND CHILDREN SHE'S TRAVELING WITH ARE INNOCENT.
SOME ARE ONLY BABIES.
BEFORE LONG, THE PARSIAN ARMY WILL MARCH ON ECBATANA.
WE *WILL* RETAKE THE CAPITAL.
WHEN THAT HAPPENS, I DON'T WANT ANY COMMON FOLK TO LOSE THEIR LIVES IN THE FRAY, BE THEY PARSIAN OR LUSITANIAN.
LET THE KILLING STAY BETWEEN THOSE OF US WHO HAVE SWORN TO FIGHT!

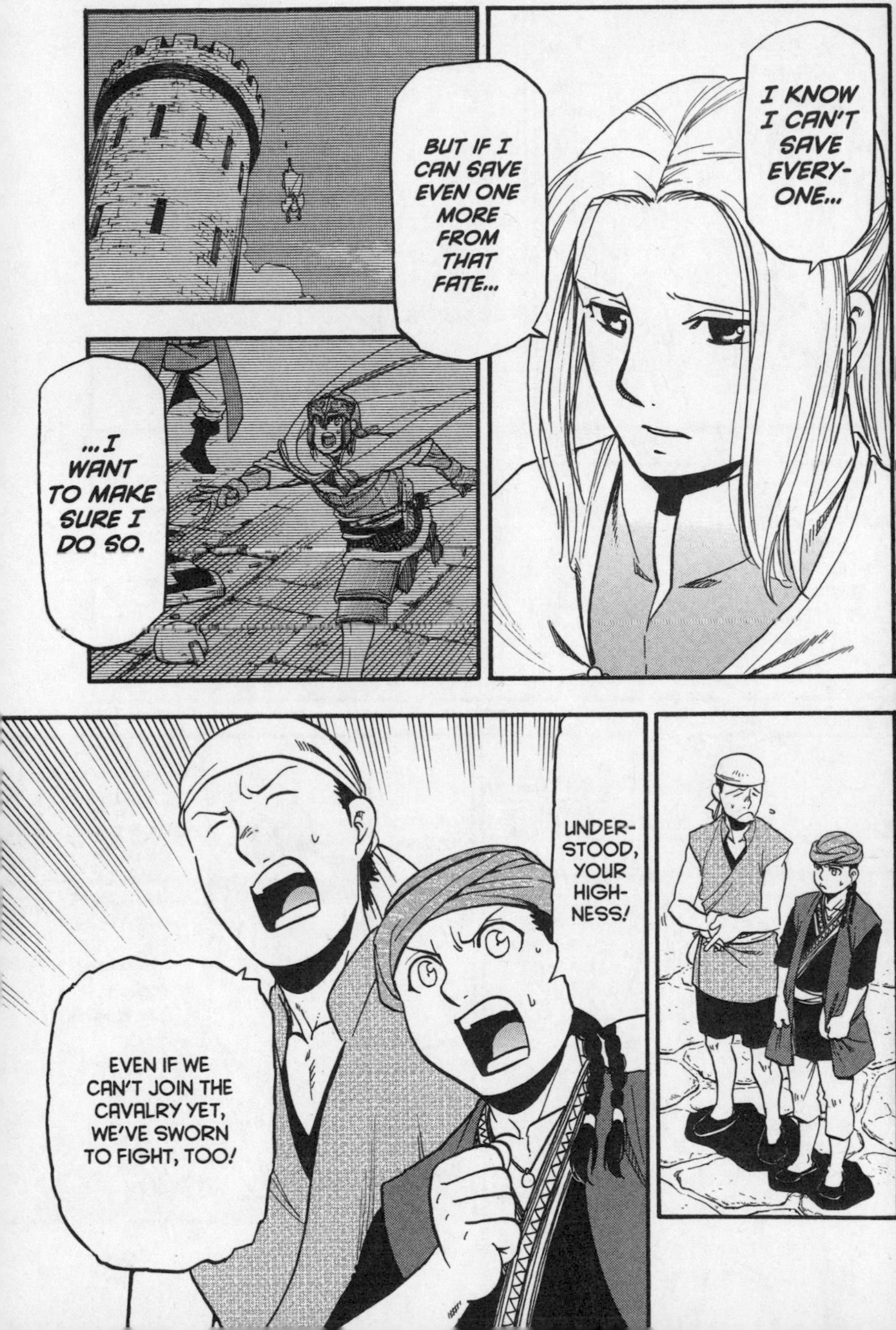
I KNOW I CAN'T SAVE EVERY-ONE...
BUT IF I CAN SAVE EVEN ONE MORE FROM THAT FATE...
...I WANT TO MAKE SURE I DO SO.
UNDER-STOOD, YOUR HIGH-NESS!
EVEN IF WE CAN'T JOIN THE CAVALRY YET, WE'VE SWORN TO FIGHT, TOO!

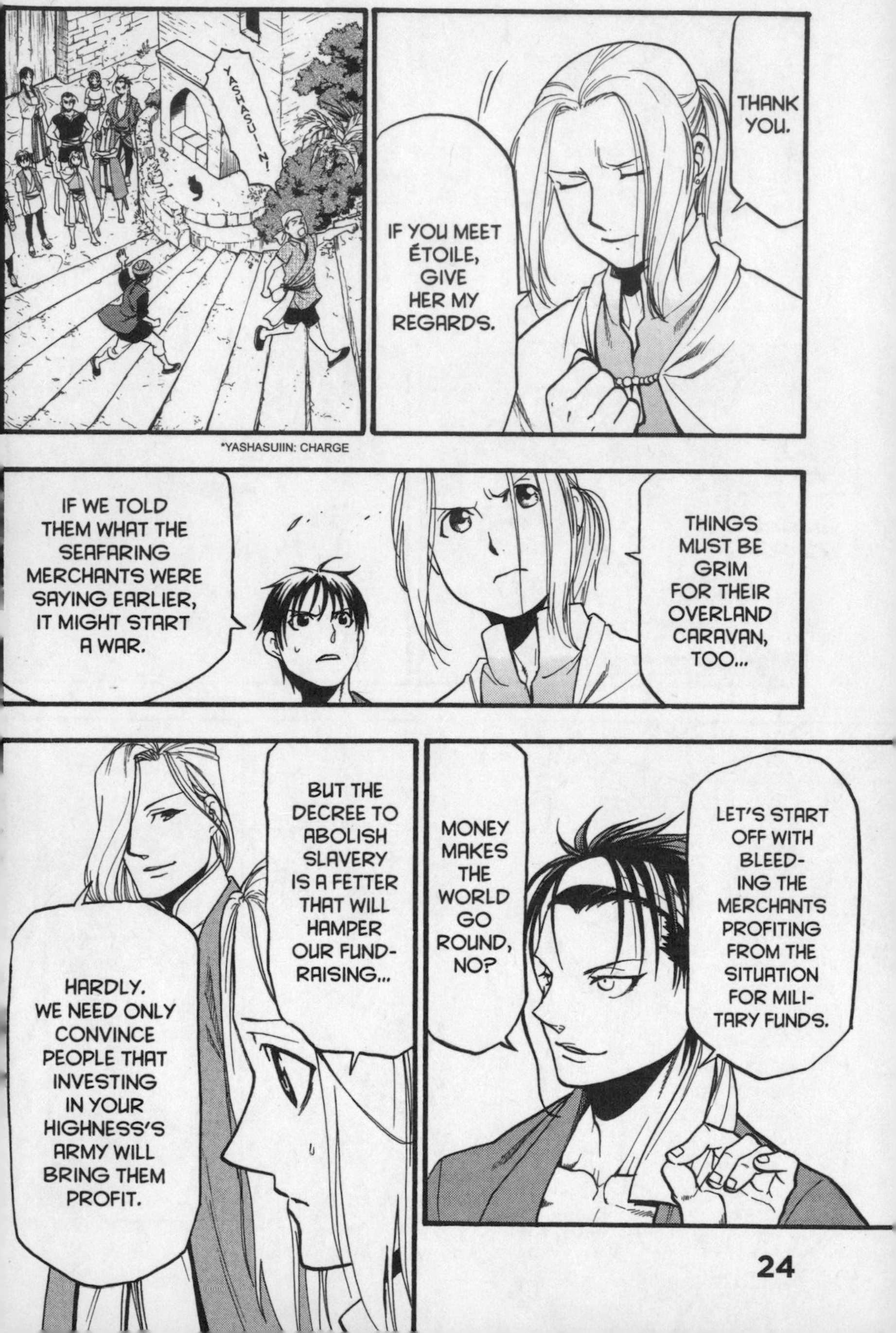
THANK YOU.
IF YOU MEET ÉTOILE, GIVE HER MY REGARDS.
YASHASUIIN!
THINGS MUST BE GRIM FOR THEIR OVERLAND CARAVAN, TOO...
IF WE TOLD THEM WHAT THE SEAFARING MERCHANTS WERE SAYING EARLIER, IT MIGHT START A WAR.
LET'S START OFF WITH BLEED-ING THE MERCHANTS PROFITING FROM THE SITUATION FOR MILI-TARY FUNDS.
MONEY MAKES THE WORLD GO ROUND, NO?
BUT THE DECREE TO ABOLISH SLAVERY IS A FETTER THAT WILL HAMPER OUR FUND-RAISING...
HARDLY. WE NEED ONLY CONVINCE PEOPLE THAT INVESTING IN YOUR HIGHNESS'S ARMY WILL BRING THEM PROFIT.
*YASHASUIIN: CHARGE

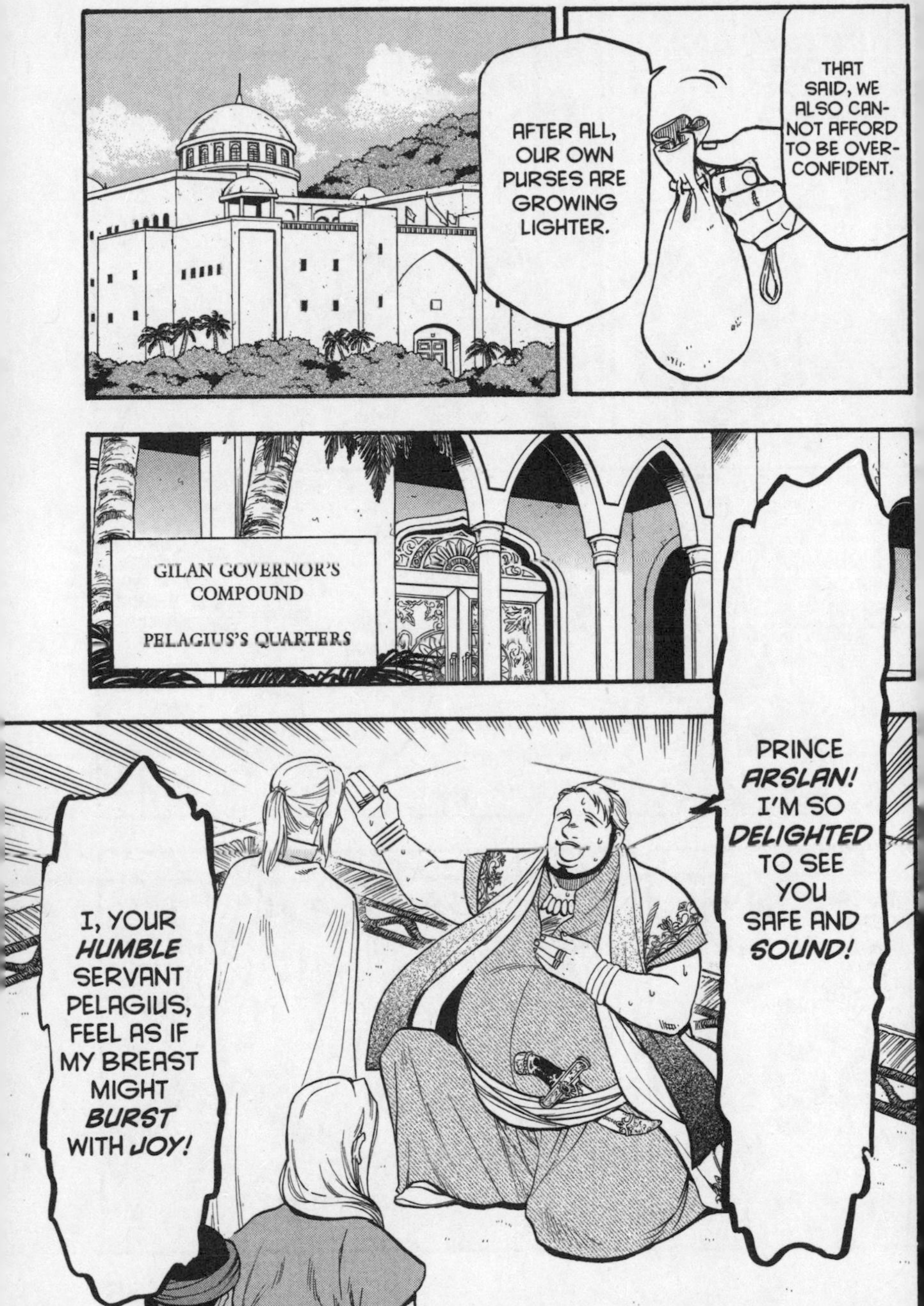
THAT SAID, WE ALSO CAN-NOT AFFORD TO BE OVER-CONFIDENT.
AFTER ALL, OUR OWN PURSES ARE GROWING LIGHTER.
GILAN GOVERNOR'S COMPOUND
PELAGIUS'S QUARTERS
PRINCE ARSLAN! I'M SO DELIGHTED TO SEE YOU SAFE AND SOUND!
I, YOUR HUMBLE SERVANT PELAGIUS, FEEL AS IF MY BREAST MIGHT BURST WITH JOY!

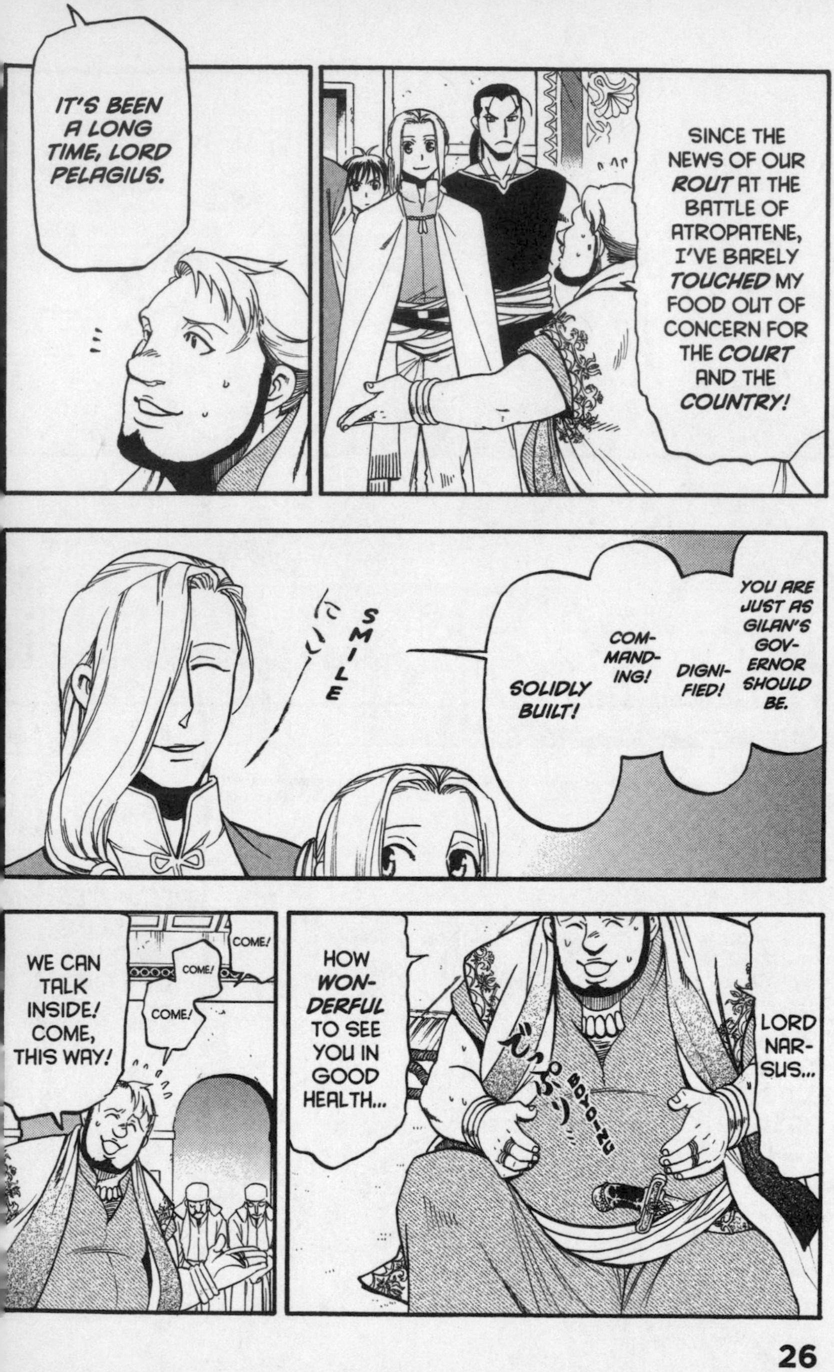

SINCE THE NEWS OF OUR ROUT AT THE BATTLE OF ATROPATENE, I'VE BARELY TOUCHED MY FOOD OUT OF CONCERN FOR THE COURT AND THE COUNTRY!
IT'S BEEN A LONG TIME, LORD PELAGIUS.
YOU ARE JUST AS GILAN'S GOVERNOR SHOULD BE.
DIGNIFIED!
COMMANDING!
SOLIDLY BUILT!
SMILE
LORD NARSUS...
BOYO-NN
HOW WONDERFUL TO SEE YOU IN GOOD HEALTH...
COME!
COME!
COME!
WE CAN TALK INSIDE! COME, THIS WAY!

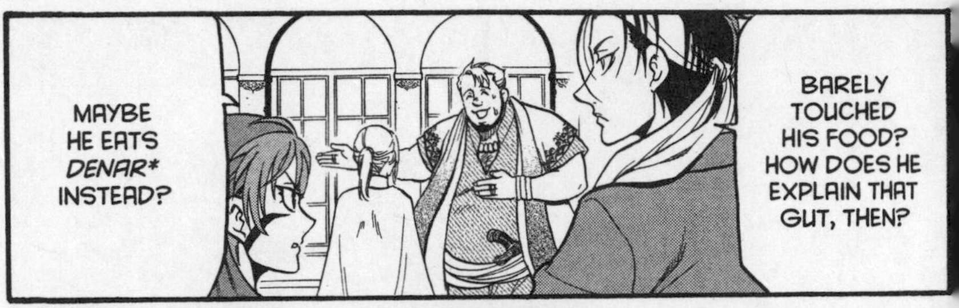
BARELY TOUCHED HIS FOOD? HOW DOES HE EXPLAIN THAT GUT, THEN?
MAYBE HE EATS *DENAR** INSTEAD?

*GOLD COINS

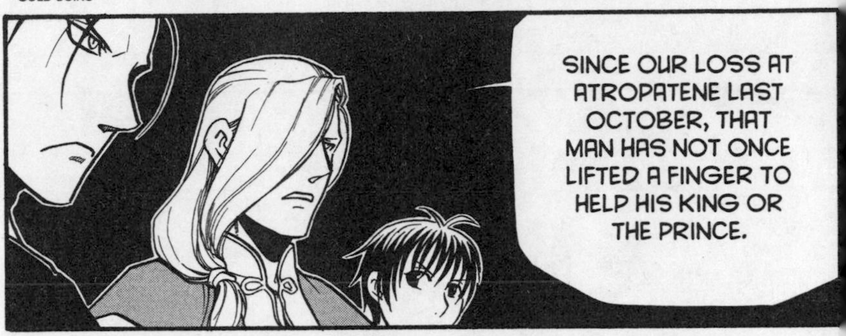
SINCE OUR LOSS AT ATROPATENE LAST OCTOBER, THAT MAN HAS NOT ONCE LIFTED A FINGER TO HELP HIS KING OR THE PRINCE.

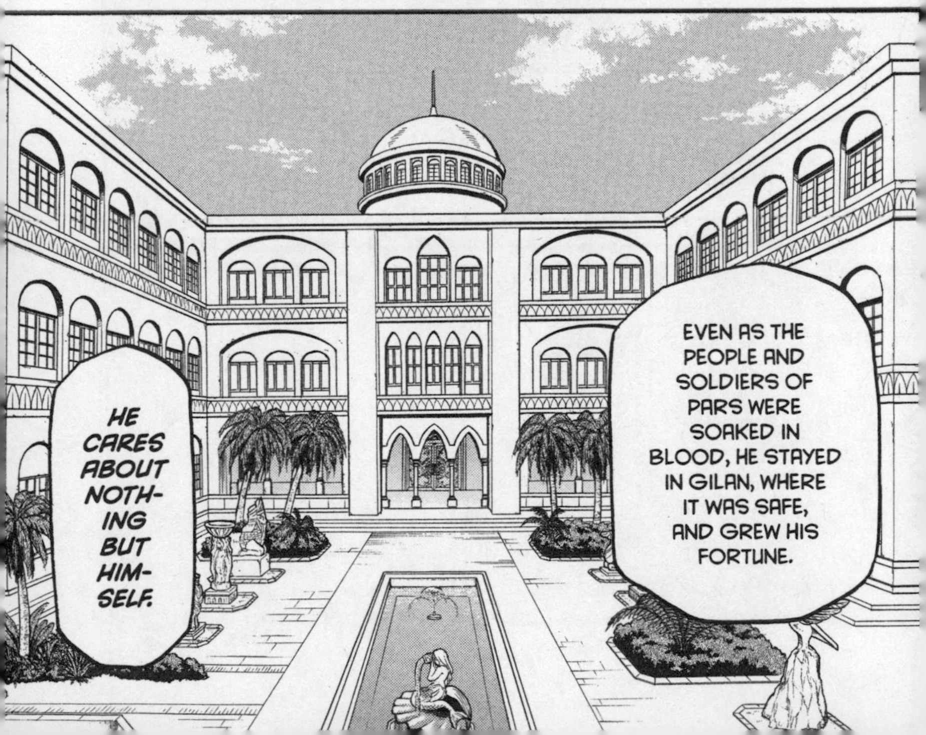
EVEN AS THE PEOPLE AND SOLDIERS OF PARS WERE SOAKED IN BLOOD, HE STAYED IN GILAN, WHERE IT WAS SAFE, AND GREW HIS FORTUNE.
HE CARES ABOUT NOTHING BUT HIMSELF.

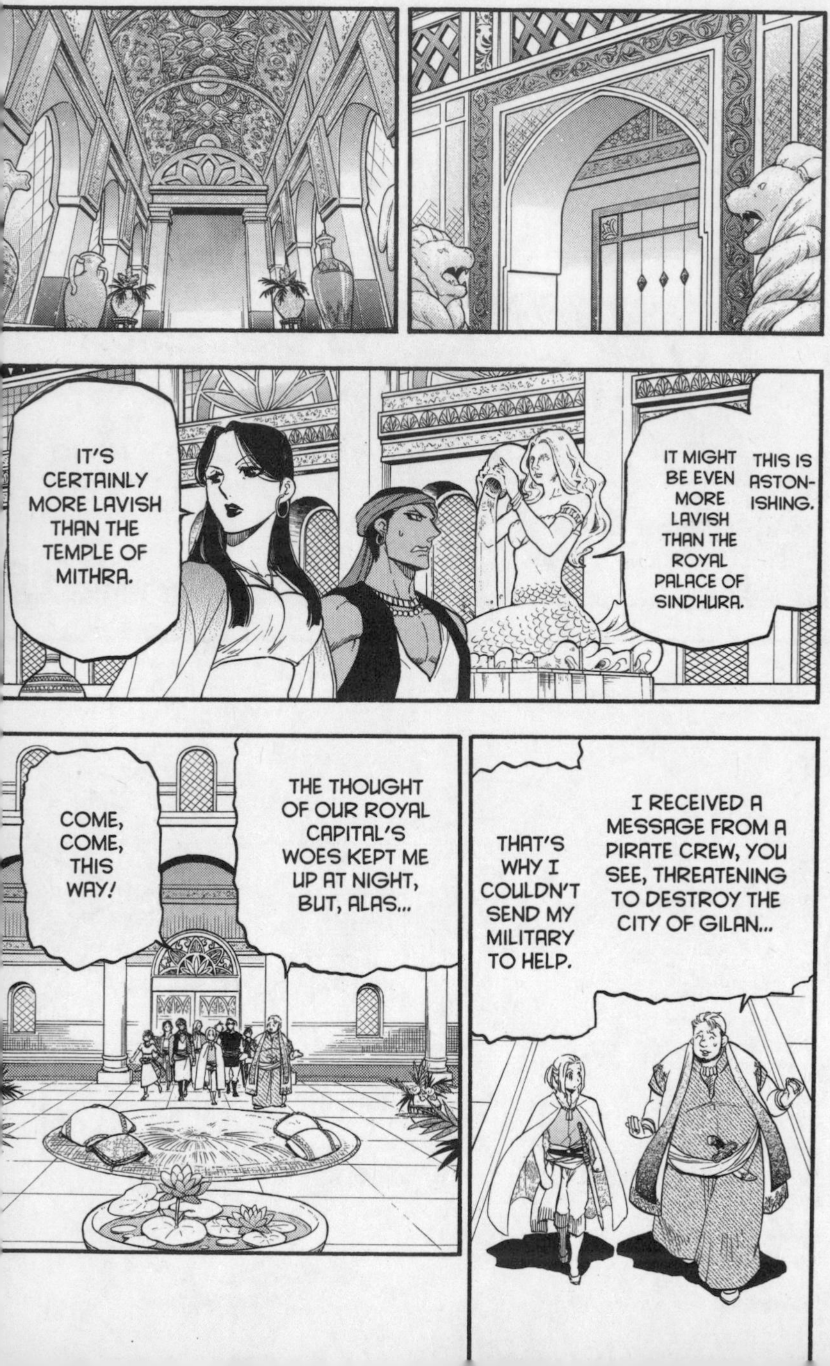
THIS IS ASTONISHING.
IT MIGHT BE EVEN MORE LAVISH THAN THE ROYAL PALACE OF SINDHURA.
IT'S CERTAINLY MORE LAVISH THAN THE TEMPLE OF MITHRA.
I RECEIVED A MESSAGE FROM A PIRATE CREW, YOU SEE, THREATENING TO DESTROY THE CITY OF GILAN...
THAT'S WHY I COULDN'T SEND MY MILITARY TO HELP.
THE THOUGHT OF OUR ROYAL CAPITAL'S WOES KEPT ME UP AT NIGHT, BUT, ALAS...
COME, COME, THIS WAY!

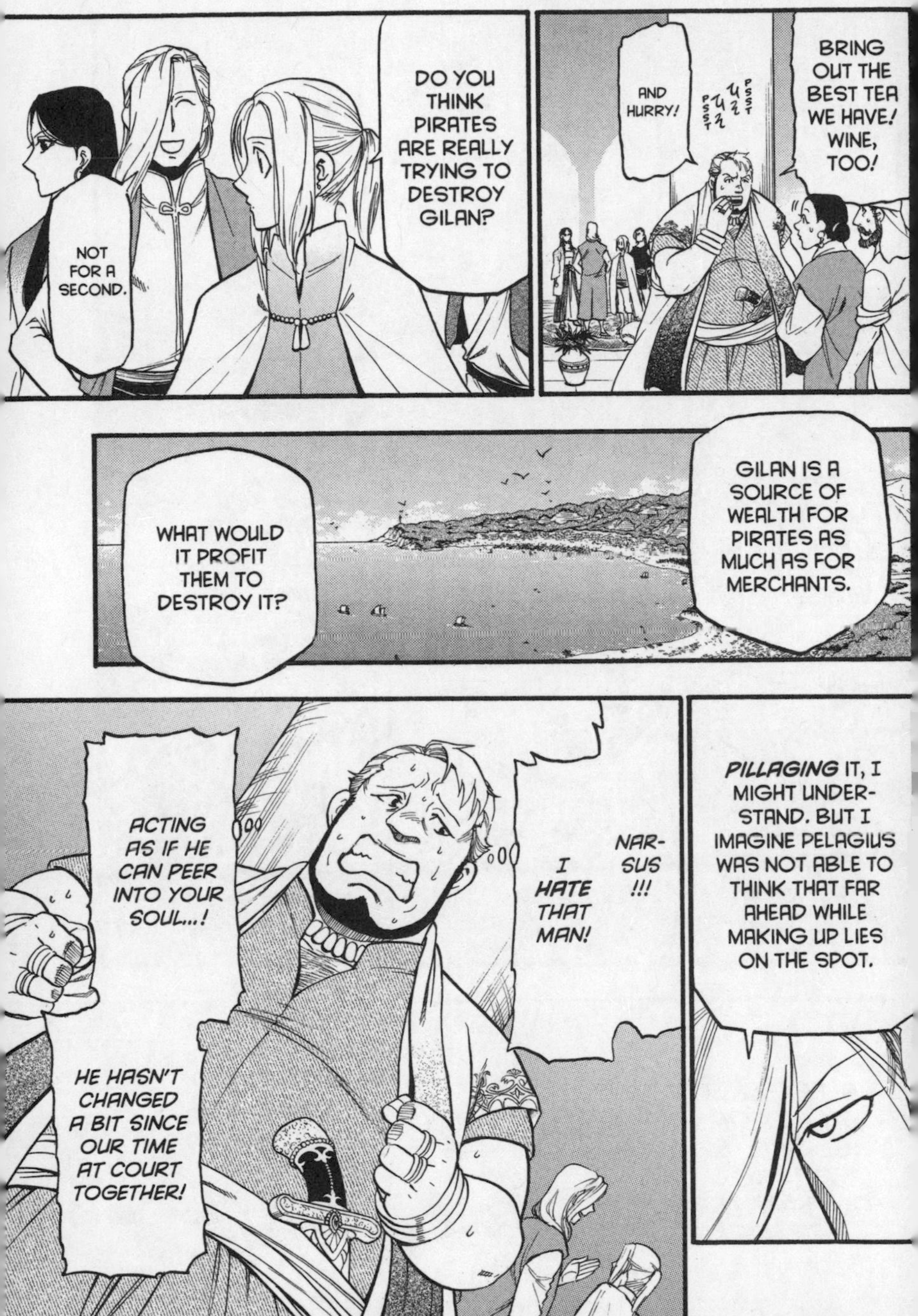
BRING OUT THE BEST TEA WE HAVE! WINE, TOO!
PSST PSST
AND HURRY!
DO YOU THINK PIRATES ARE REALLY TRYING TO DESTROY GILAN?
NOT FOR A SECOND.
GILAN IS A SOURCE OF WEALTH FOR PIRATES AS MUCH AS FOR MERCHANTS.
WHAT WOULD IT PROFIT THEM TO DESTROY IT?
PILLAGING IT, I MIGHT UNDERSTAND. BUT I IMAGINE PELAGIUS WAS NOT ABLE TO THINK THAT FAR AHEAD WHILE MAKING UP LIES ON THE SPOT.
NARSUS!!!
I *HATE* THAT MAN!
ACTING AS IF HE CAN PEER INTO YOUR SOUL...!
HE HASN'T CHANGED A BIT SINCE OUR TIME AT COURT TOGETHER!

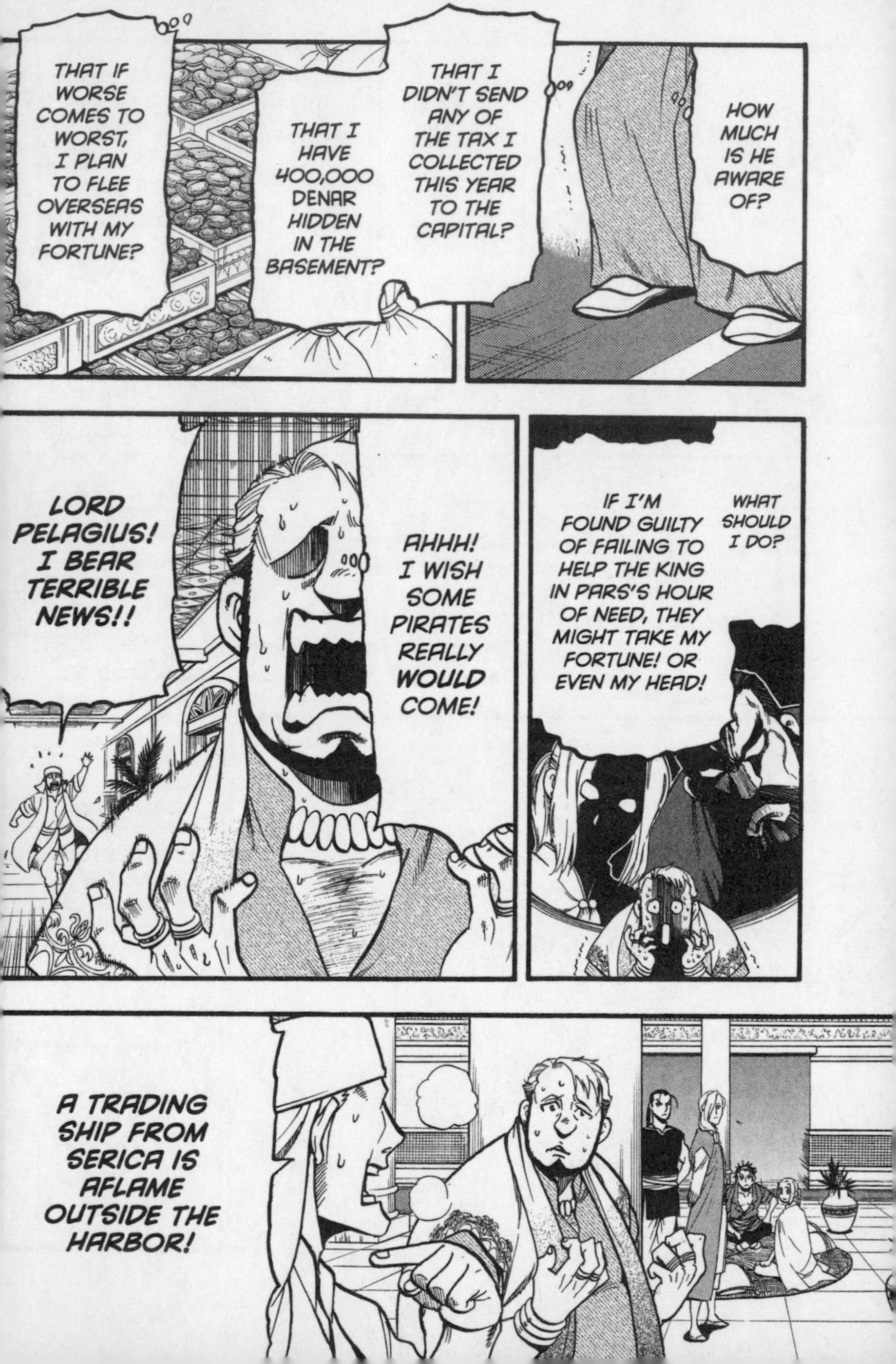
HOW MUCH IS HE AWARE OF?
THAT I DIDN'T SEND ANY OF THE TAX I COLLECTED THIS YEAR TO THE CAPITAL?
THAT I HAVE 400,000 DENAR HIDDEN IN THE BASEMENT?
THAT IF WORSE COMES TO WORST, I PLAN TO FLEE OVERSEAS WITH MY FORTUNE?
WHAT SHOULD I DO?
IF I'M FOUND GUILTY OF FAILING TO HELP THE KING IN PARS'S HOUR OF NEED, THEY MIGHT TAKE MY FORTUNE! OR EVEN MY HEAD!
AHHH! I WISH SOME PIRATES REALLY WOULD COME!
LORD PELAGIUS! I BEAR TERRIBLE NEWS!!
A TRADING SHIP FROM SERICA IS AFLAME OUTSIDE THE HARBOR!

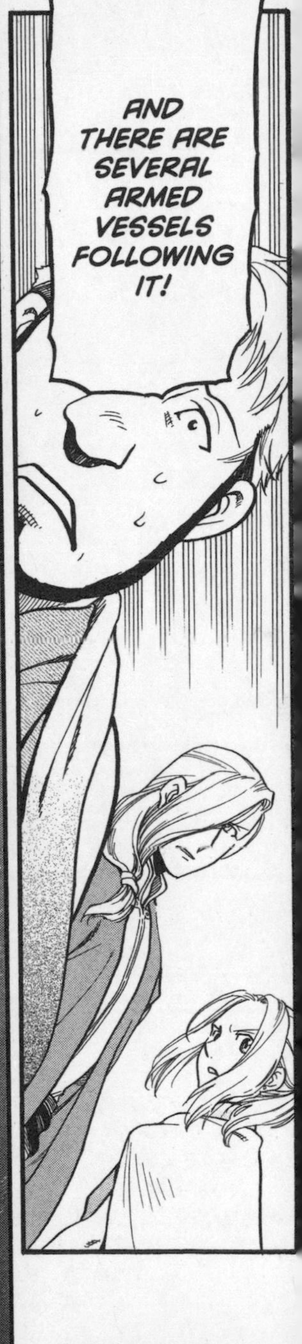
AND THERE ARE SEVERAL ARMED VESSELS FOLLOWING IT!

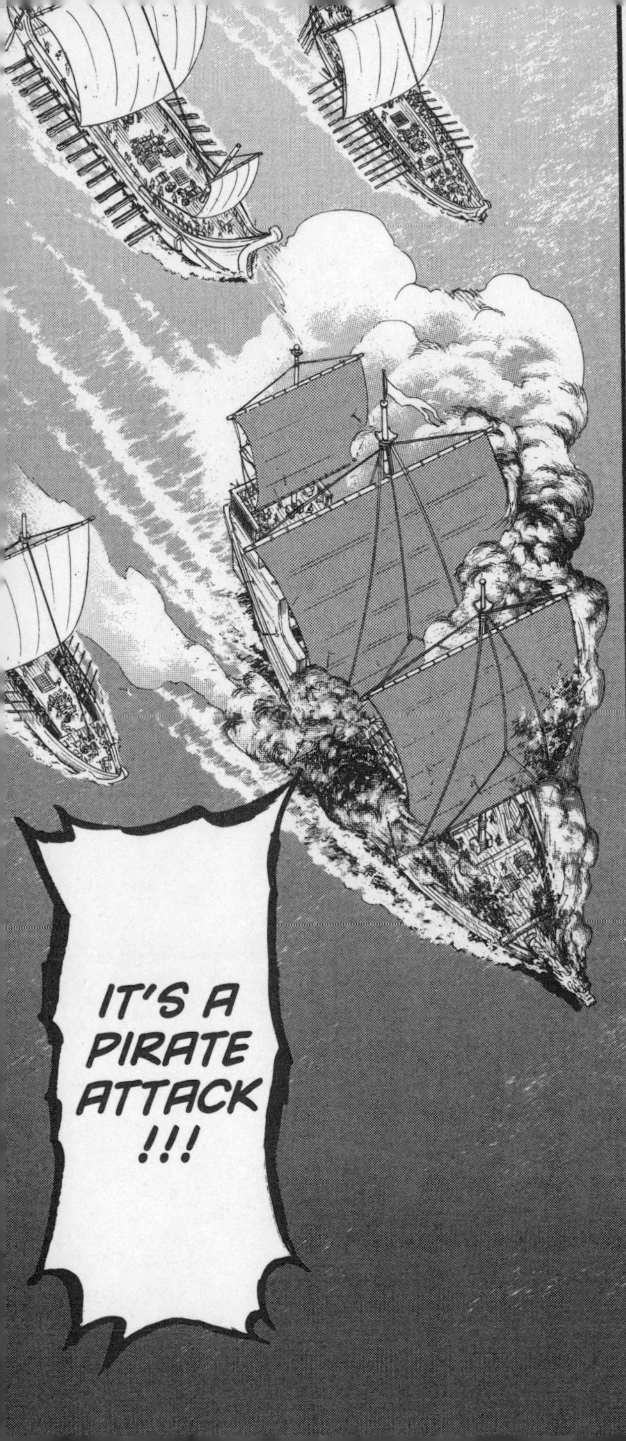
IT'S A PIRATE ATTACK!!!

THE HEROIC LEGEND OF
ARSLAN

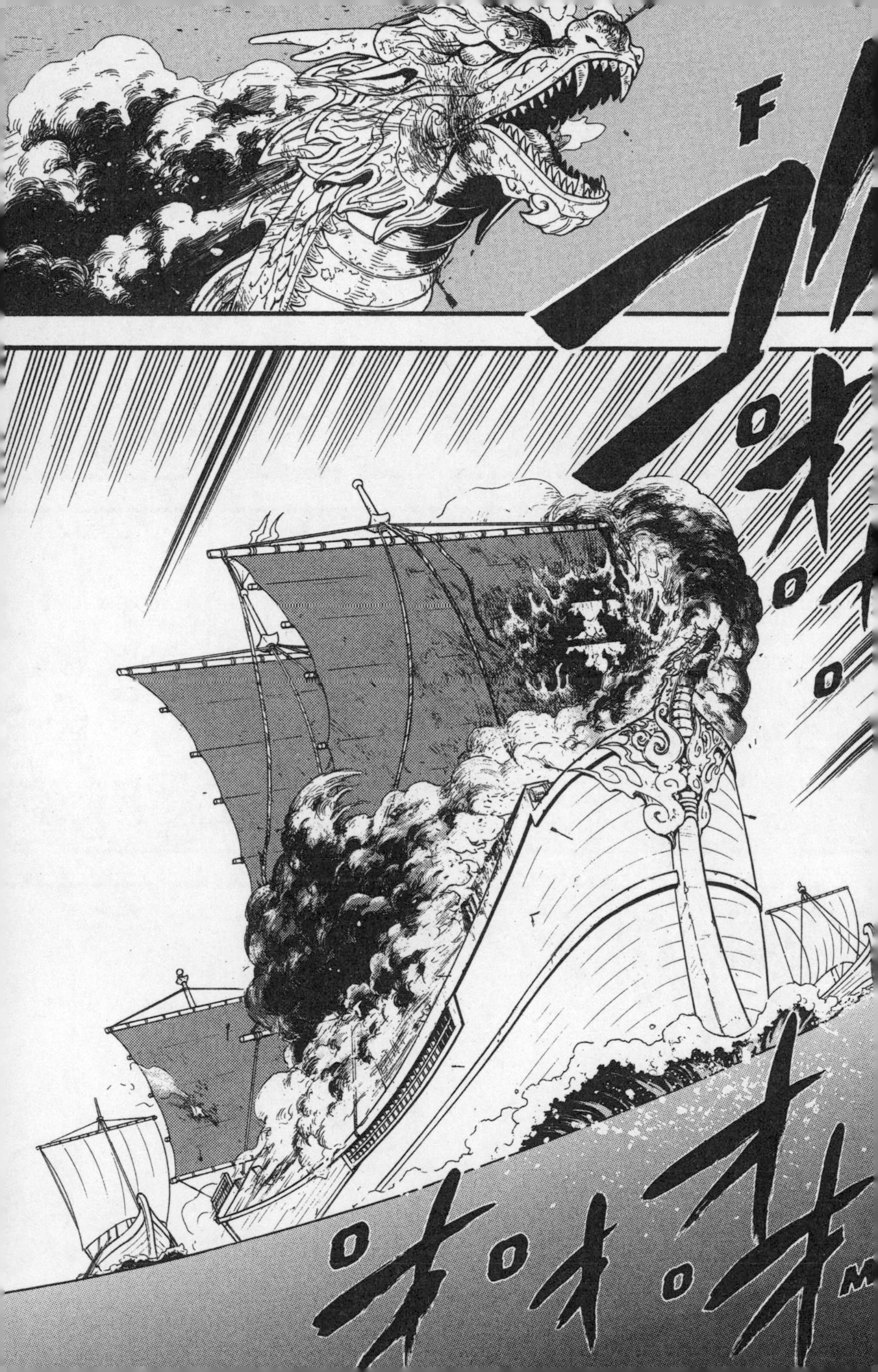
F
M

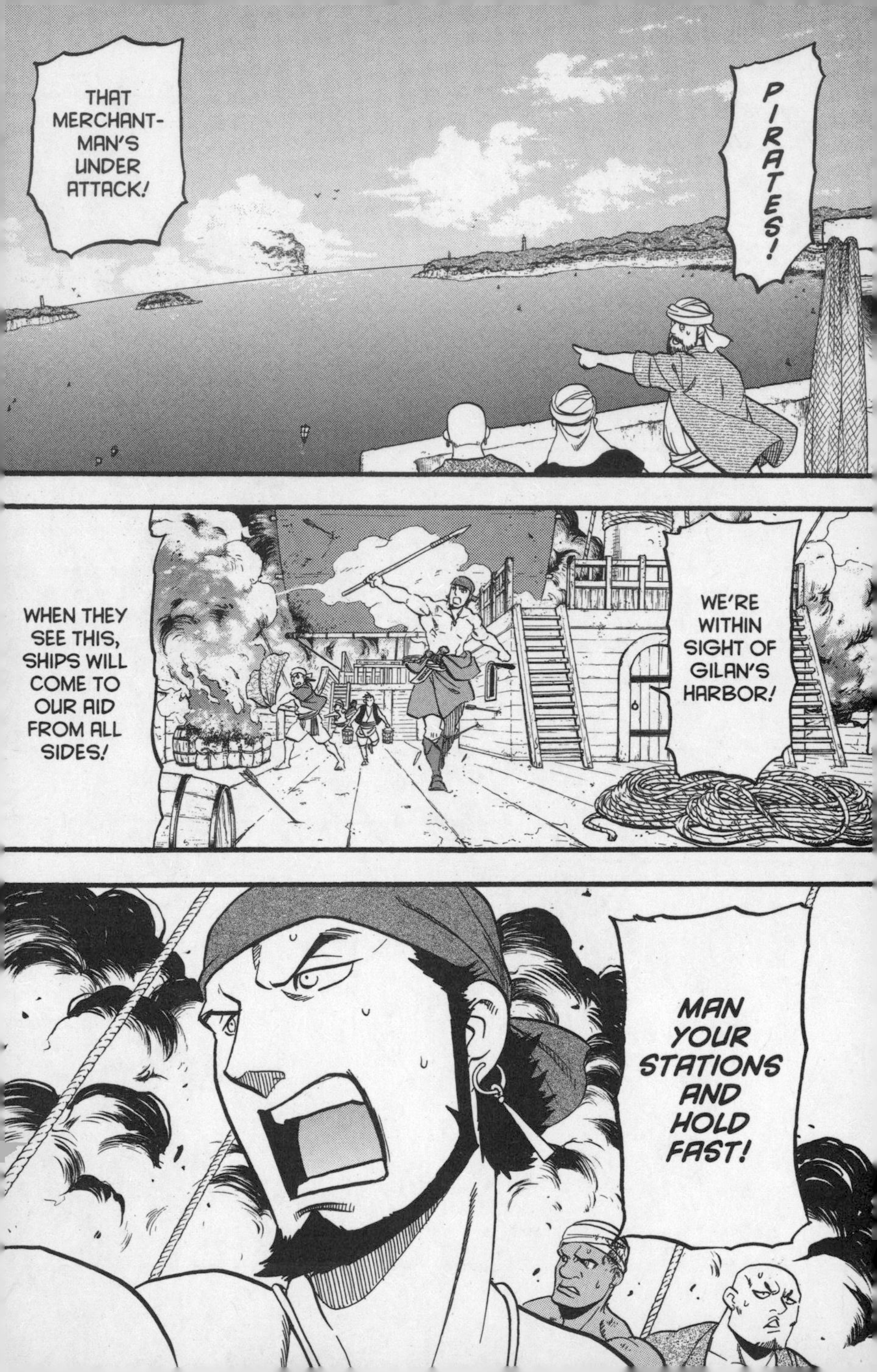
PIRATES!
THAT MERCHANT-MAN'S UNDER ATTACK!
WE'RE WITHIN SIGHT OF GILAN'S HARBOR!
WHEN THEY SEE THIS, SHIPS WILL COME TO OUR AID FROM ALL SIDES!
MAN YOUR STATIONS AND HOLD FAST!

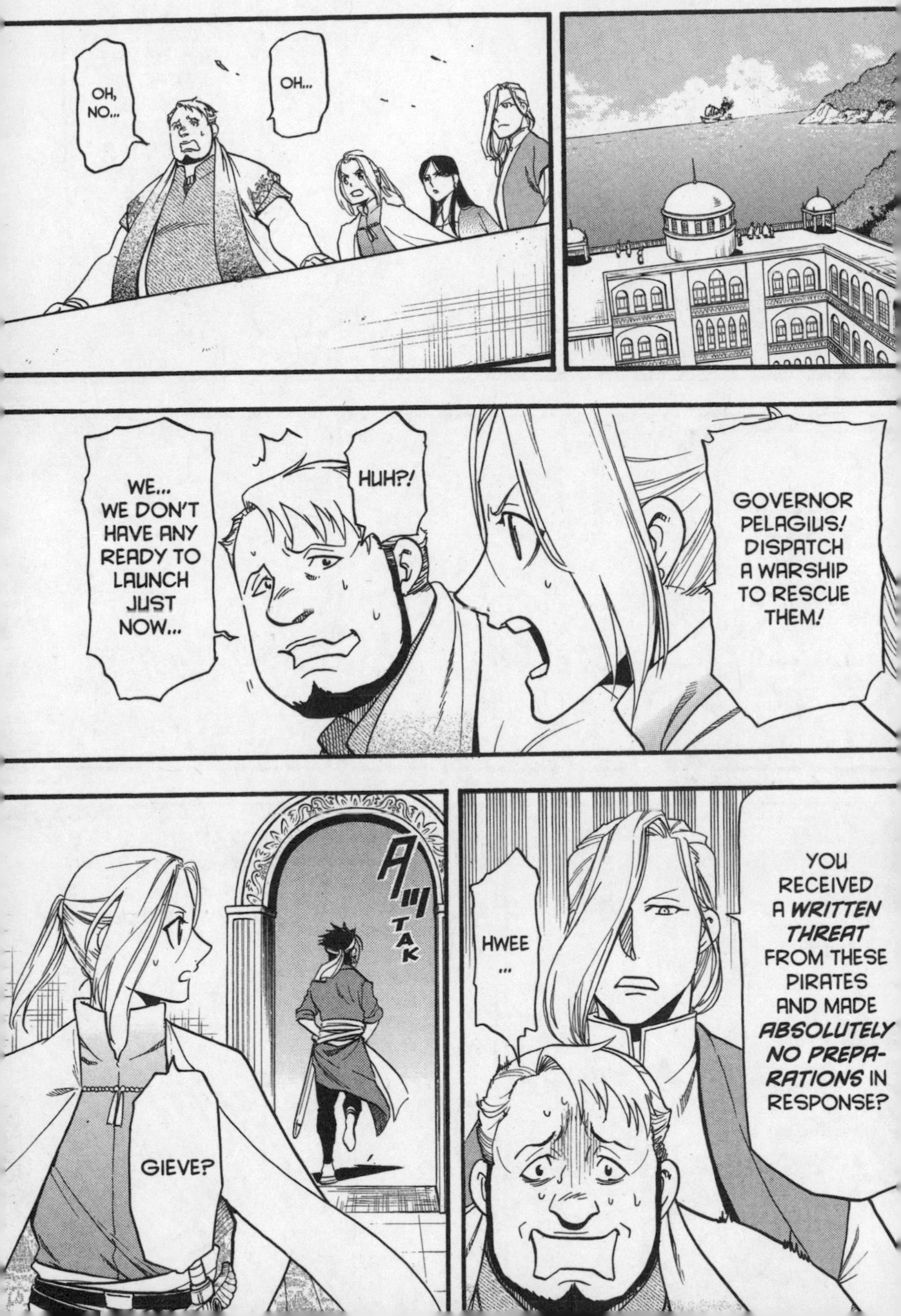
OH...
OH, NO...
GOVERNOR PELAGIUS! DISPATCH A WARSHIP TO RESCUE THEM!
HUH?!
WE... WE DON'T HAVE ANY READY TO LAUNCH JUST NOW...
YOU RECEIVED A WRITTEN THREAT FROM THESE PIRATES AND MADE ABSOLUTELY NO PREPARATIONS IN RESPONSE?
HWEE ...
TAK
GIEVE?

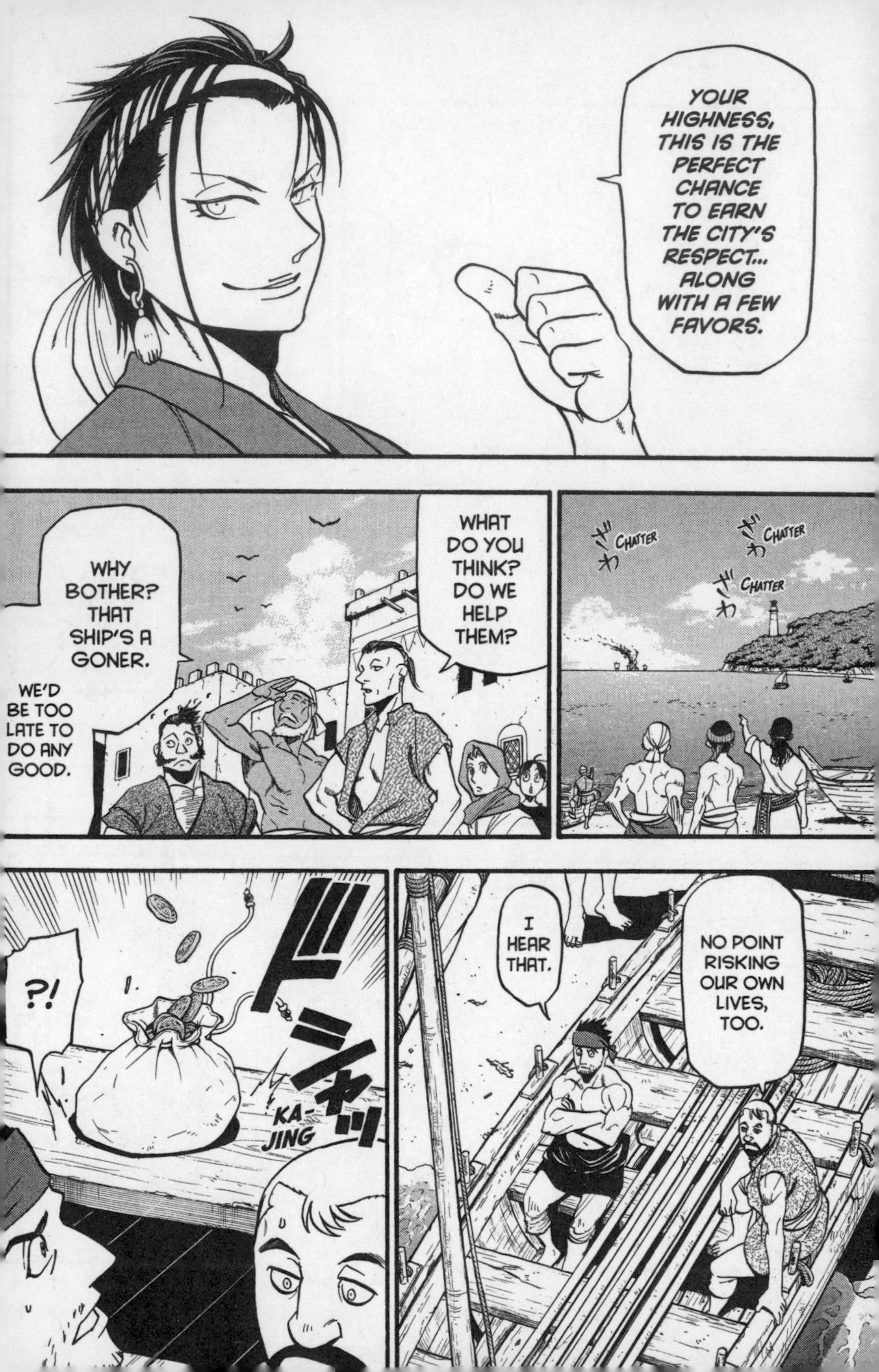
YOUR HIGHNESS, THIS IS THE PERFECT CHANCE TO EARN THE CITY'S RESPECT... ALONG WITH A FEW FAVORS.
ざわ CHATTER
ざわ CHATTER
ざわ CHATTER
WHAT DO YOU THINK? DO WE HELP THEM?
WHY BOTHER? THAT SHIP'S A GONER.
WE'D BE TOO LATE TO DO ANY GOOD.
NO POINT RISKING OUR OWN LIVES, TOO.
I HEAR THAT.
KA-JING
?!

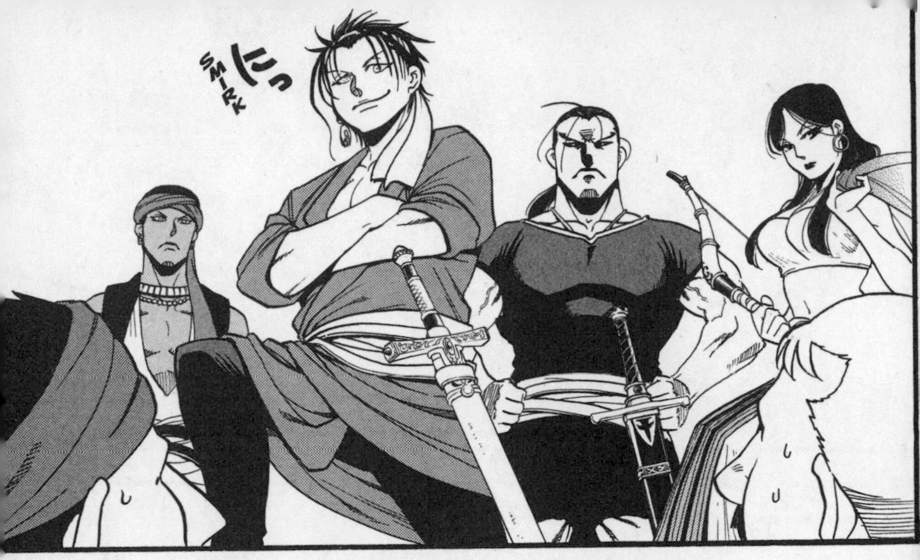
にっ
SMIRK

Chapter 96: Men of the Sea

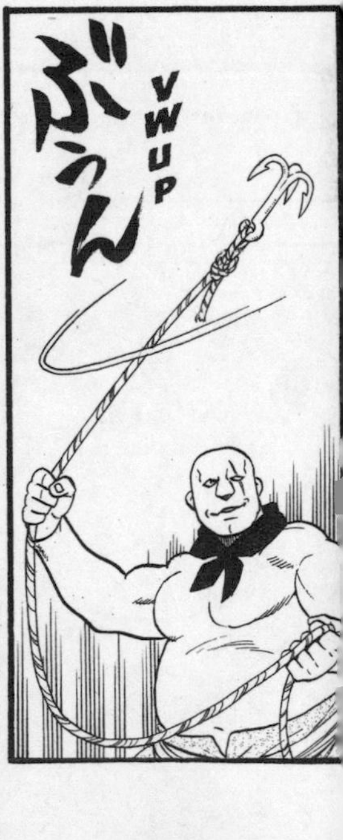
ぶうん
VWUP

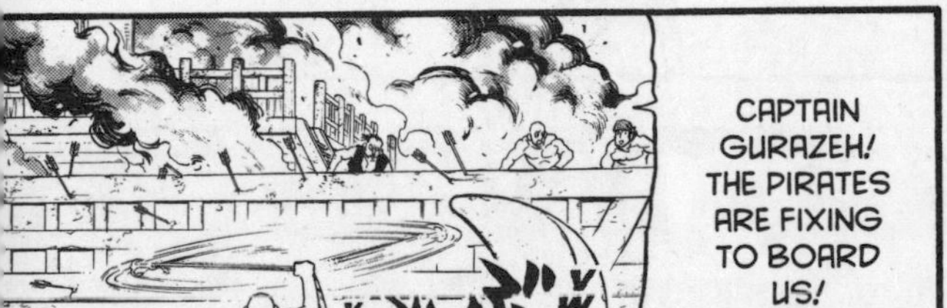
CAPTAIN GURAZEH! THE PIRATES ARE FIXING TO BOARD US!
ぶん
VWUP
ぶん
VWUP
ザザザザザザ
ZOOOOSH

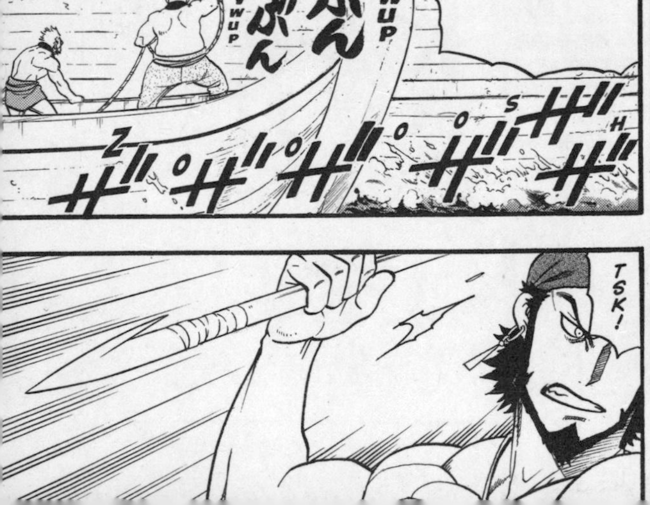
TSK!

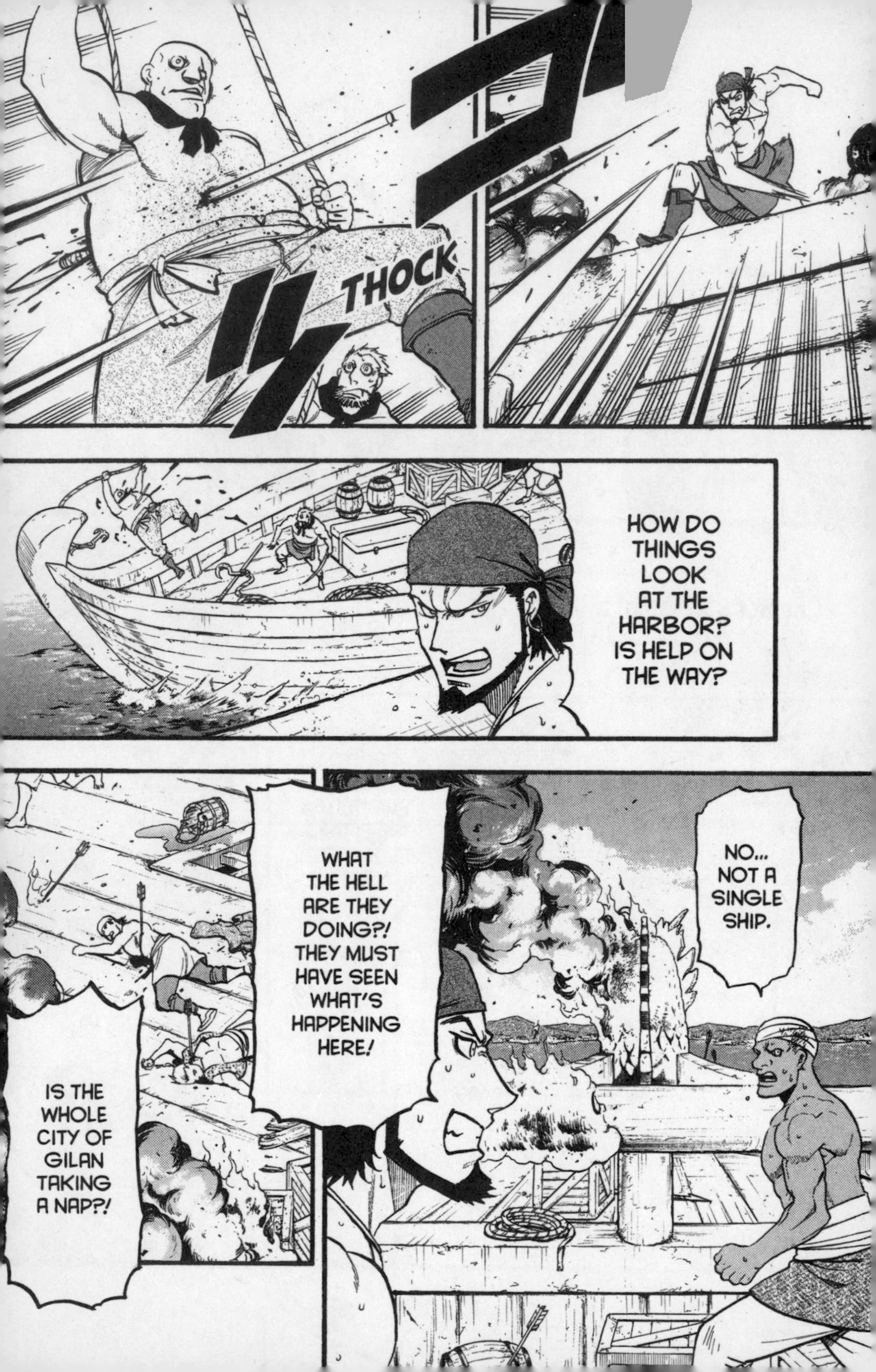
THOCK
HOW DO THINGS LOOK AT THE HARBOR? IS HELP ON THE WAY?
NO... NOT A SINGLE SHIP.
WHAT THE HELL ARE THEY DOING?! THEY MUST HAVE SEEN WHAT'S HAPPENING HERE!
IS THE WHOLE CITY OF GILAN TAKING A NAP?!

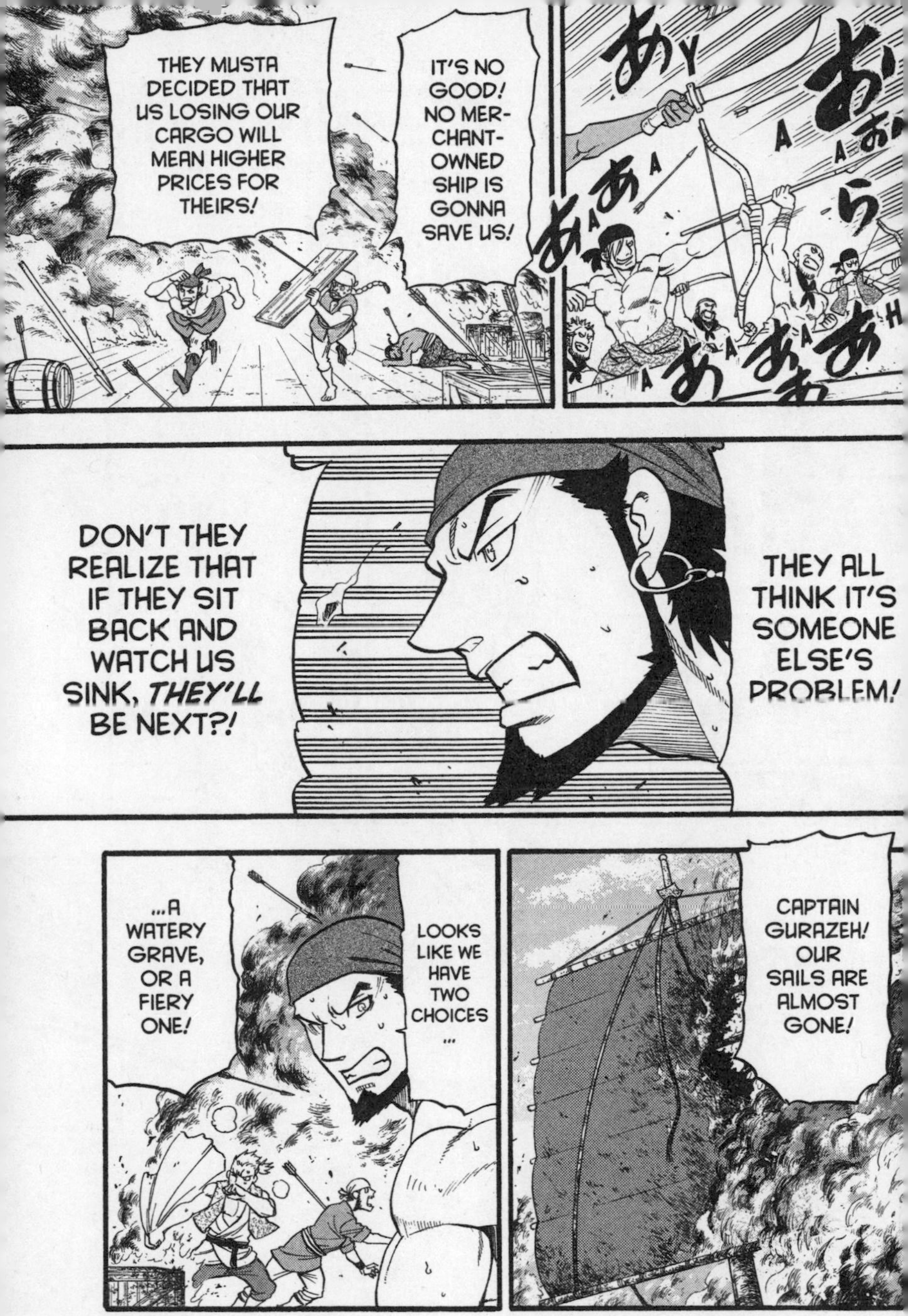
IT'S NO GOOD! NO MERCHANT-OWNED SHIP IS GONNA SAVE US!
THEY MUSTA DECIDED THAT US LOSING OUR CARGO WILL MEAN HIGHER PRICES FOR THEIRS!
THEY ALL THINK IT'S SOMEONE ELSE'S PROBLEM!
DON'T THEY REALIZE THAT IF THEY SIT BACK AND WATCH US SINK, *THEY'LL* BE NEXT?!
CAPTAIN GURAZEH! OUR SAILS ARE ALMOST GONE!
LOOKS LIKE WE HAVE TWO CHOICES ...
...A WATERY GRAVE, OR A FIERY ONE!

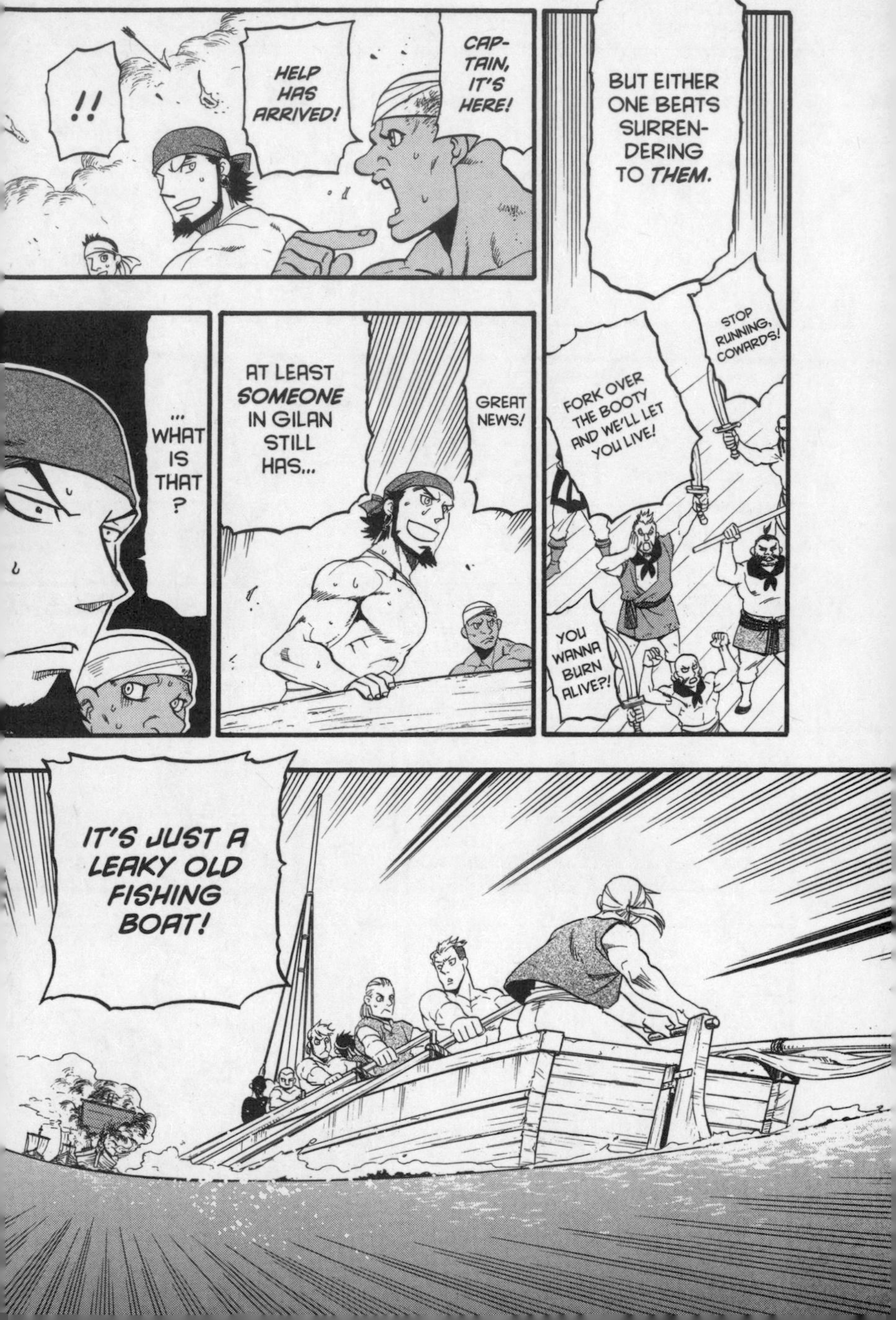
BUT EITHER ONE BEATS SURREN-DERING TO THEM.
STOP RUNNING, COWARDS!
FORK OVER THE BOOTY AND WE'LL LET YOU LIVE!
YOU WANNA BURN ALIVE?!
CAP-TAIN, IT'S HERE!
HELP HAS ARRIVED!
!!
GREAT NEWS!
AT LEAST SOMEONE IN GILAN STILL HAS...
... WHAT IS THAT?
IT'S JUST A LEAKY OLD FISHING BOAT!

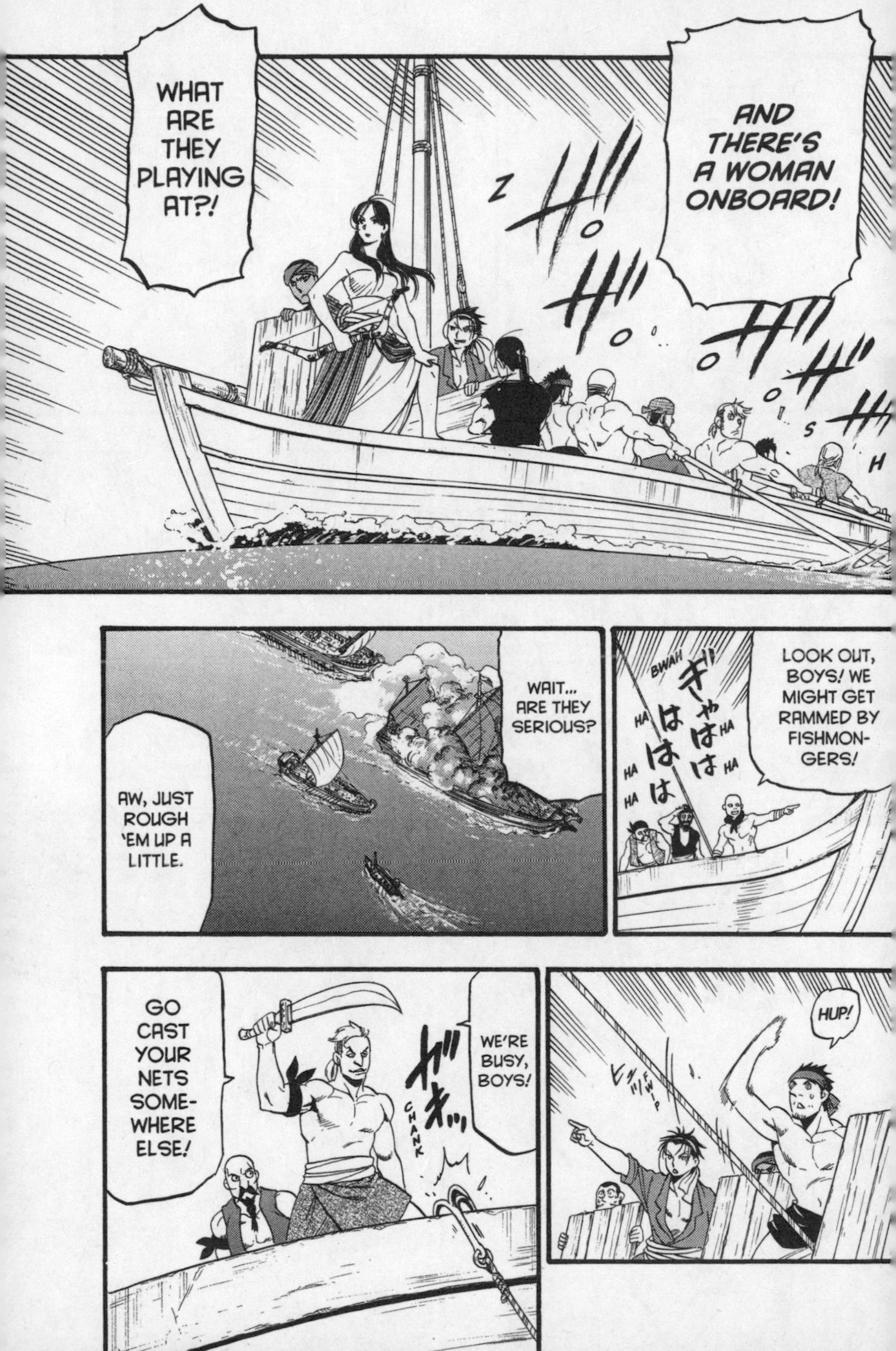
AND THERE'S A WOMAN ONBOARD!
WHAT ARE THEY PLAYING AT?!
LOOK OUT, BOYS! WE MIGHT GET RAMMED BY FISHMONGERS!
BWAH HA HA HA HA HA
WAIT... ARE THEY SERIOUS?
AW, JUST ROUGH 'EM UP A LITTLE.
HUP!
FWIP
WE'RE BUSY, BOYS!
CHANK
GO CAST YOUR NETS SOME-WHERE ELSE!

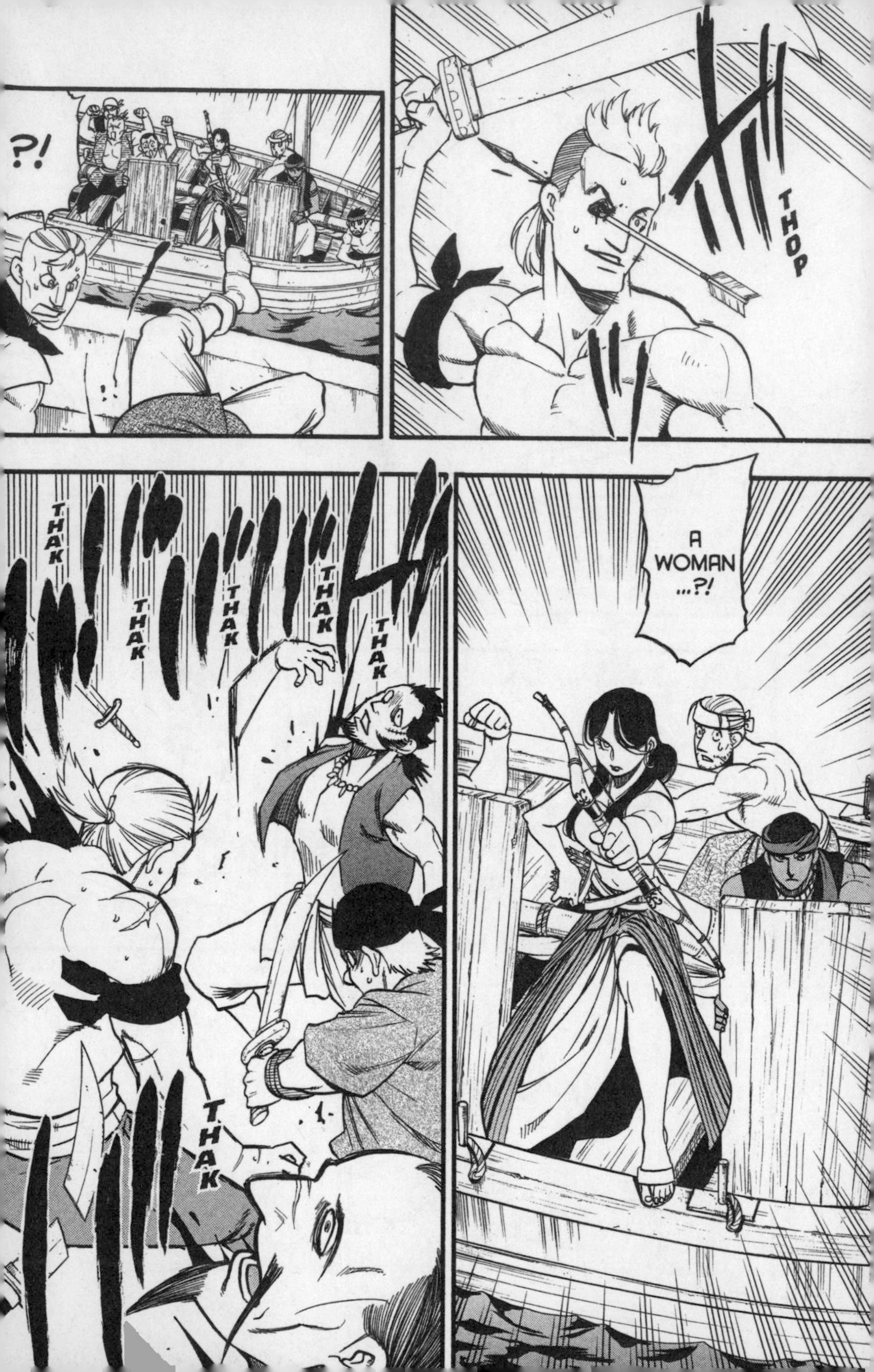
THOP
?!
A WOMAN ...?!
THAK
THAK
THAK
THAK
THAK
THAK

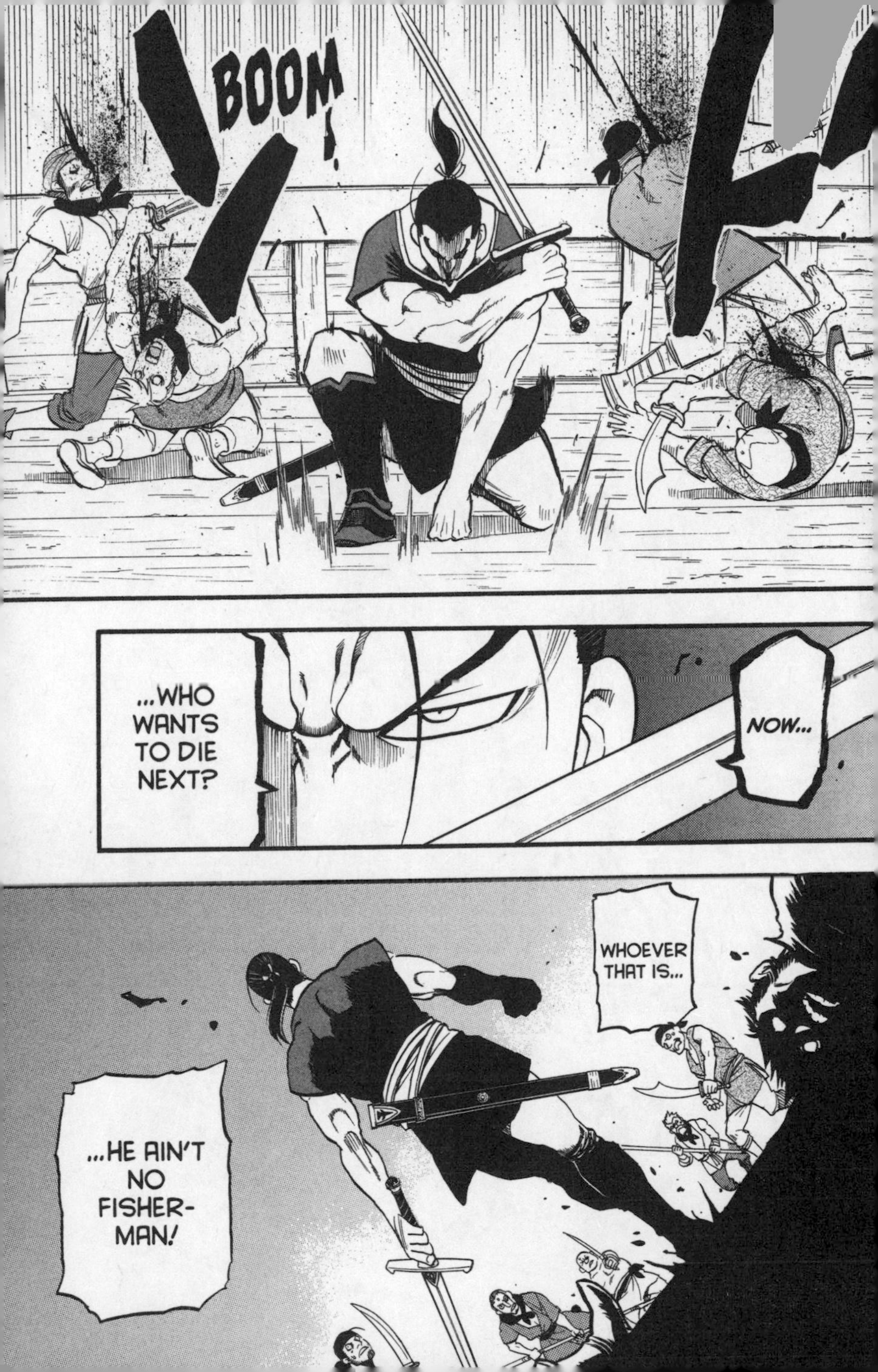
BOOM
NOW...
...WHO WANTS TO DIE NEXT?
WHOEVER THAT IS...
...HE AIN'T NO FISHER-MAN!

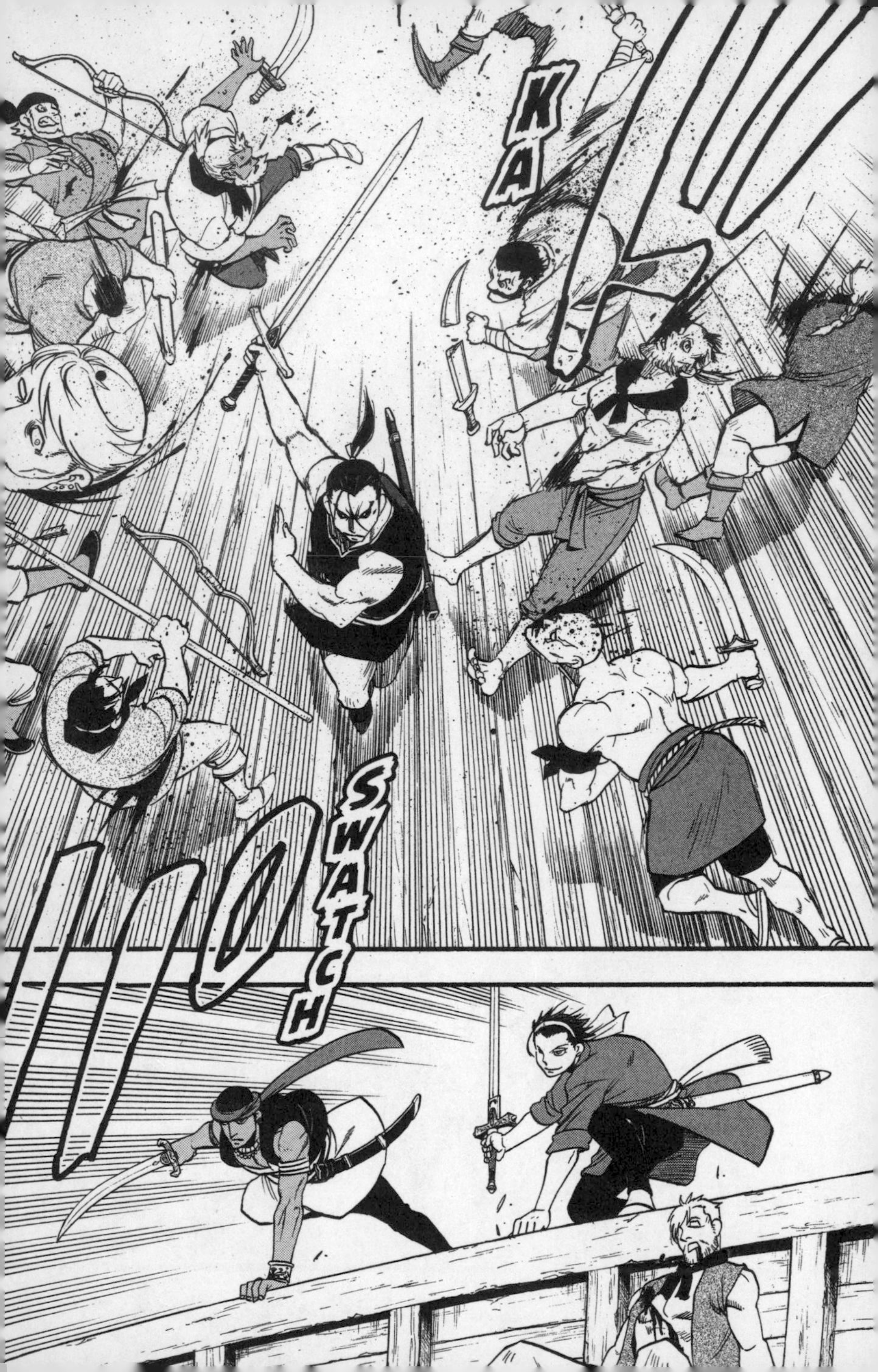
KA
SWATCH

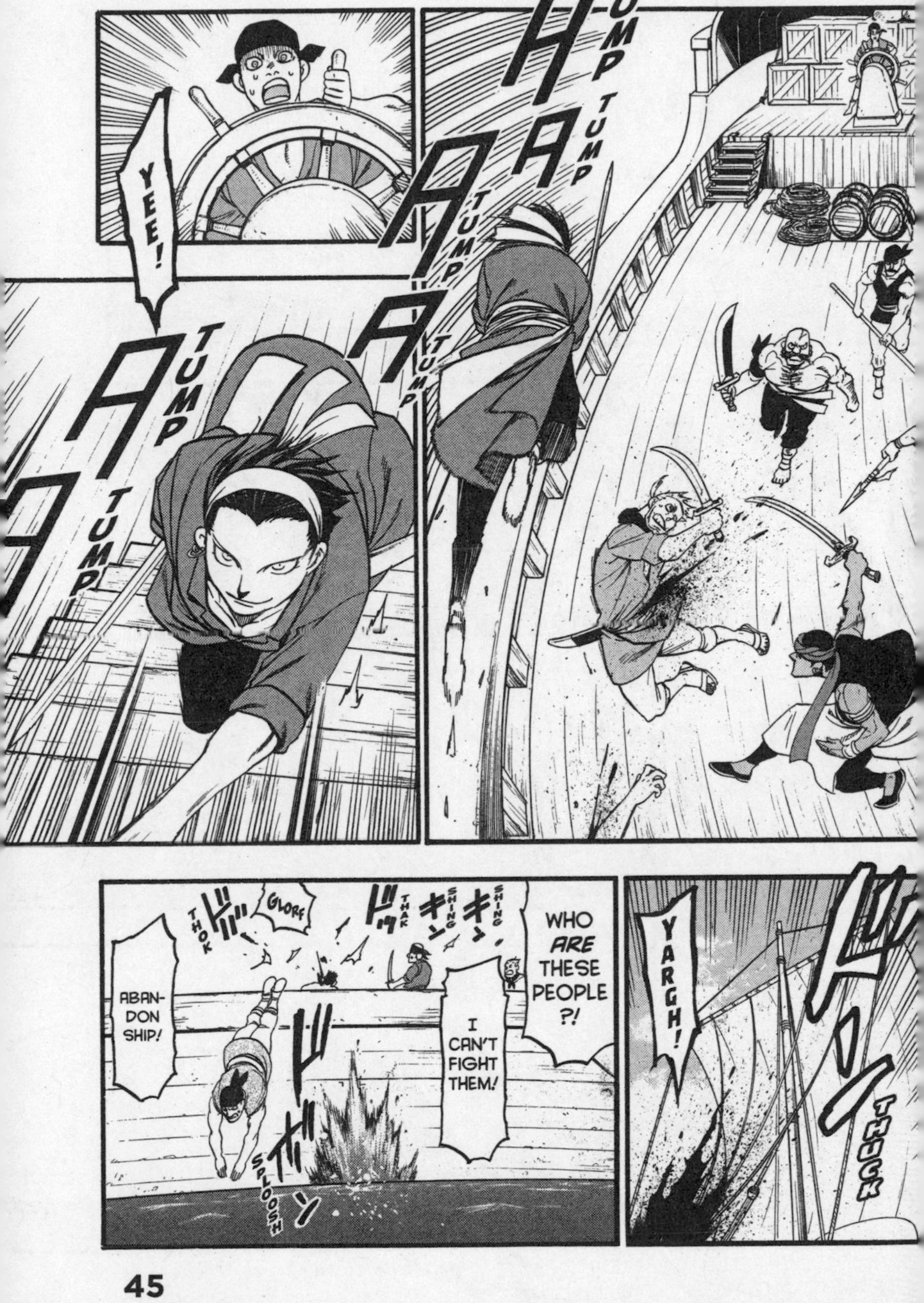
AAAA
TUMP TUMP TUMP
TUMP TUMP
YEE!
TUMP TUMP
YARGH!
THUCK
WHO *ARE* THESE PEOPLE?!
I CAN'T FIGHT THEM!
SHING
SHING
THAK
GLORF
THOK
ABAN-DON SHIP!
SPLOOSH

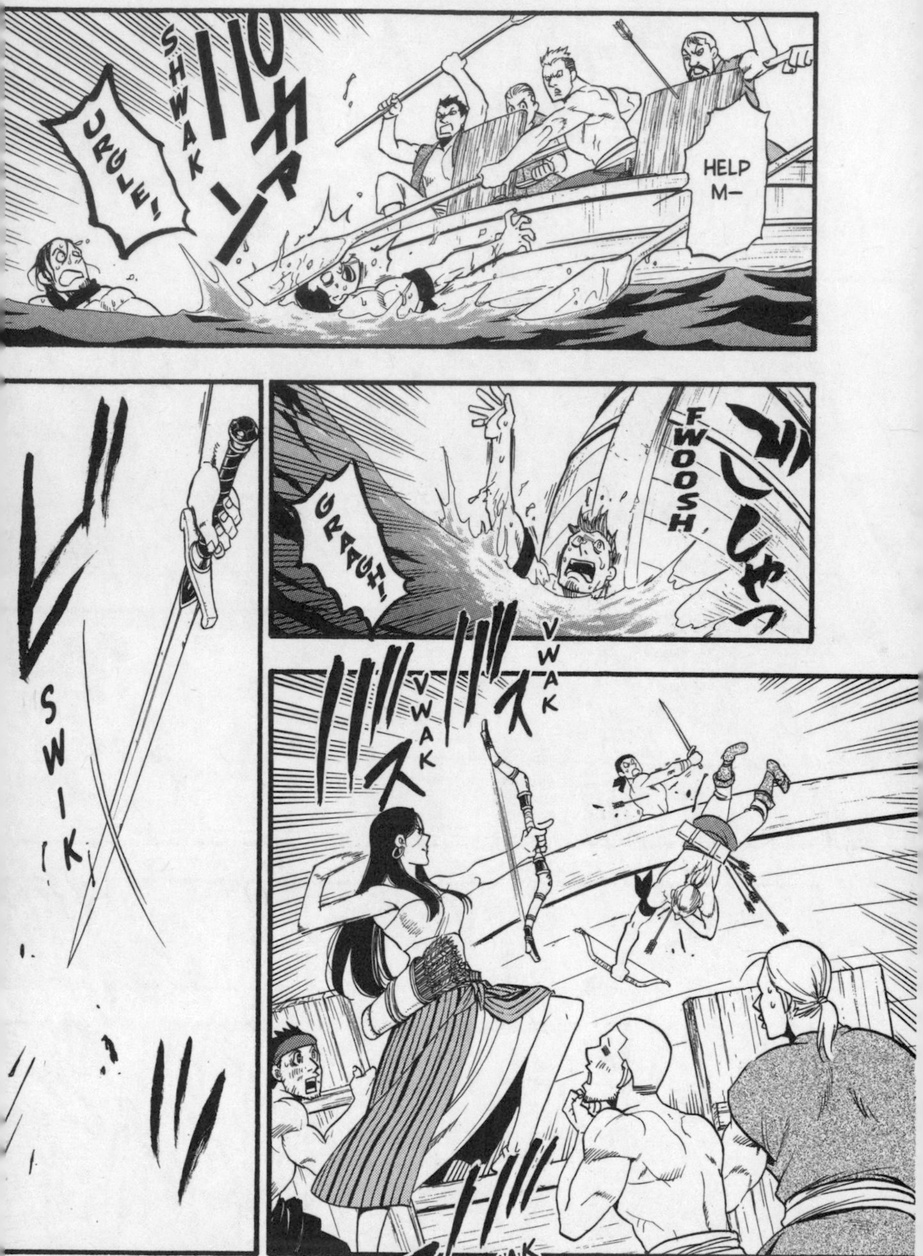
HELP M—
SHWAK
URGLE!
FWOOSH
GRAAGH!
VWAK
VWAK
VWAK
SWIK

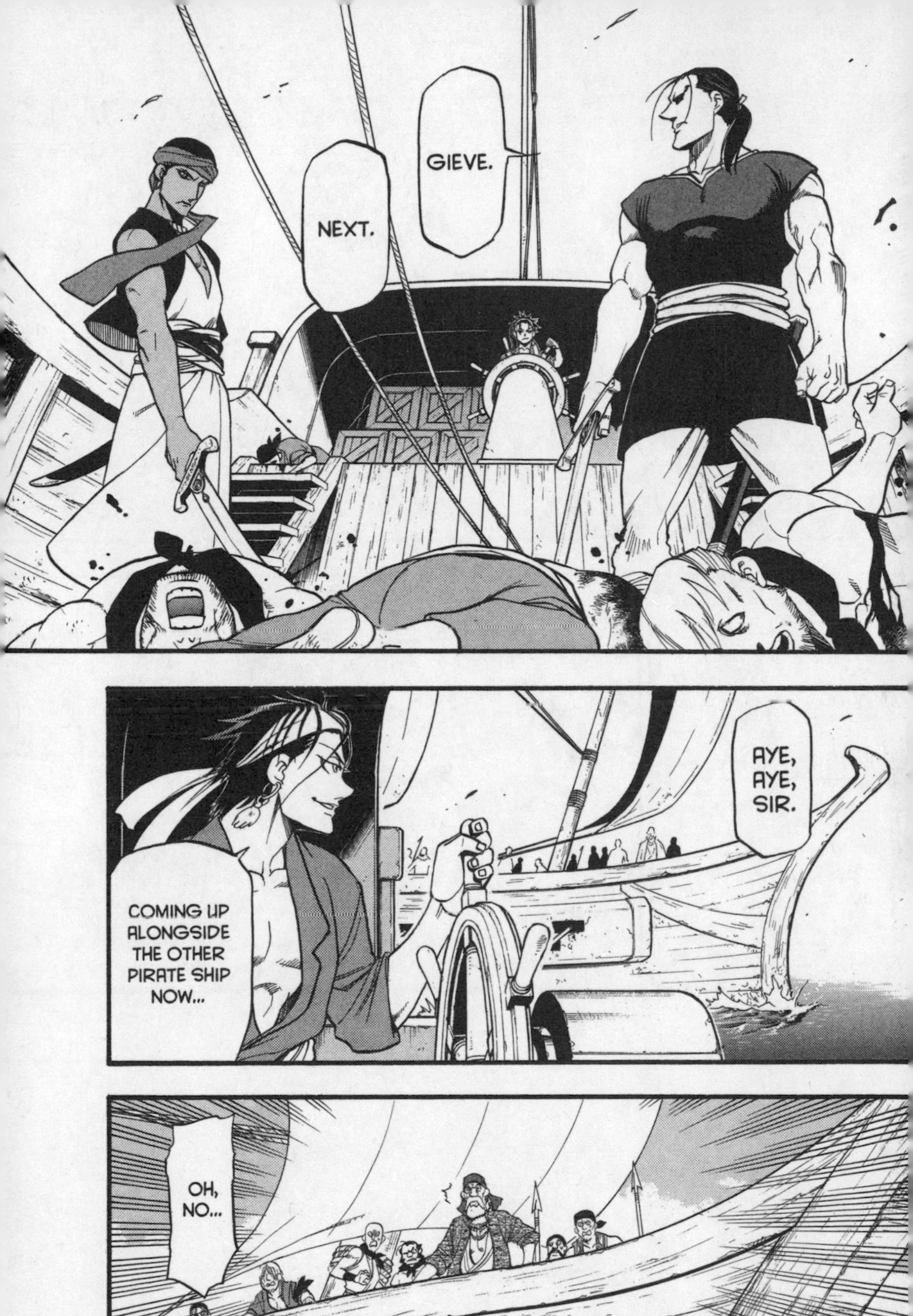
GIEVE.
NEXT.
AYE, AYE, SIR.
COMING UP ALONGSIDE THE OTHER PIRATE SHIP NOW...
OH, NO...

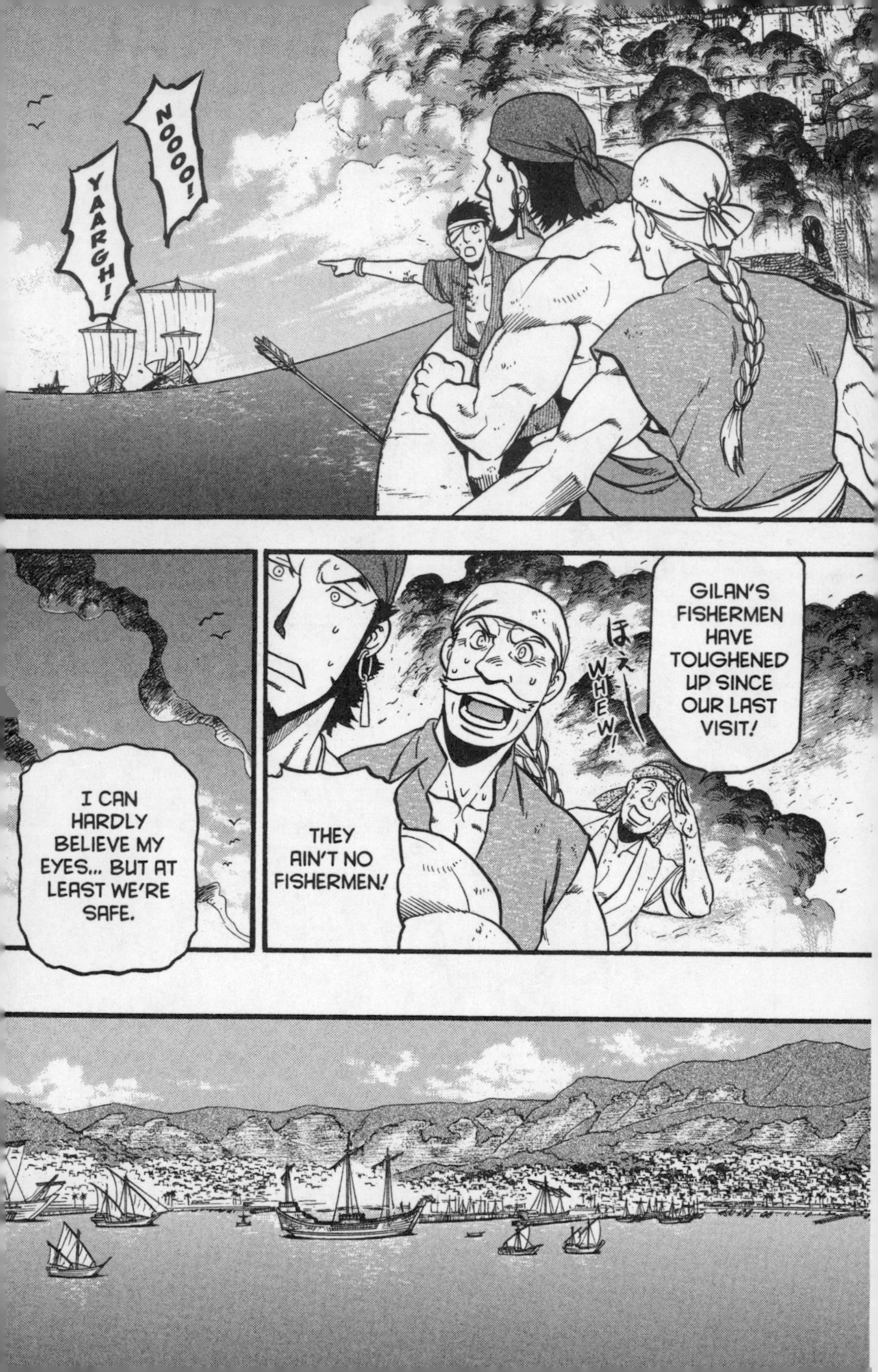
NOOOO!
YAARGH!
GILAN'S FISHERMEN HAVE TOUGHENED UP SINCE OUR LAST VISIT!
ほえ
WHEW!
THEY AIN'T NO FISHERMEN!
I CAN HARDLY BELIEVE MY EYES... BUT AT LEAST WE'RE SAFE.

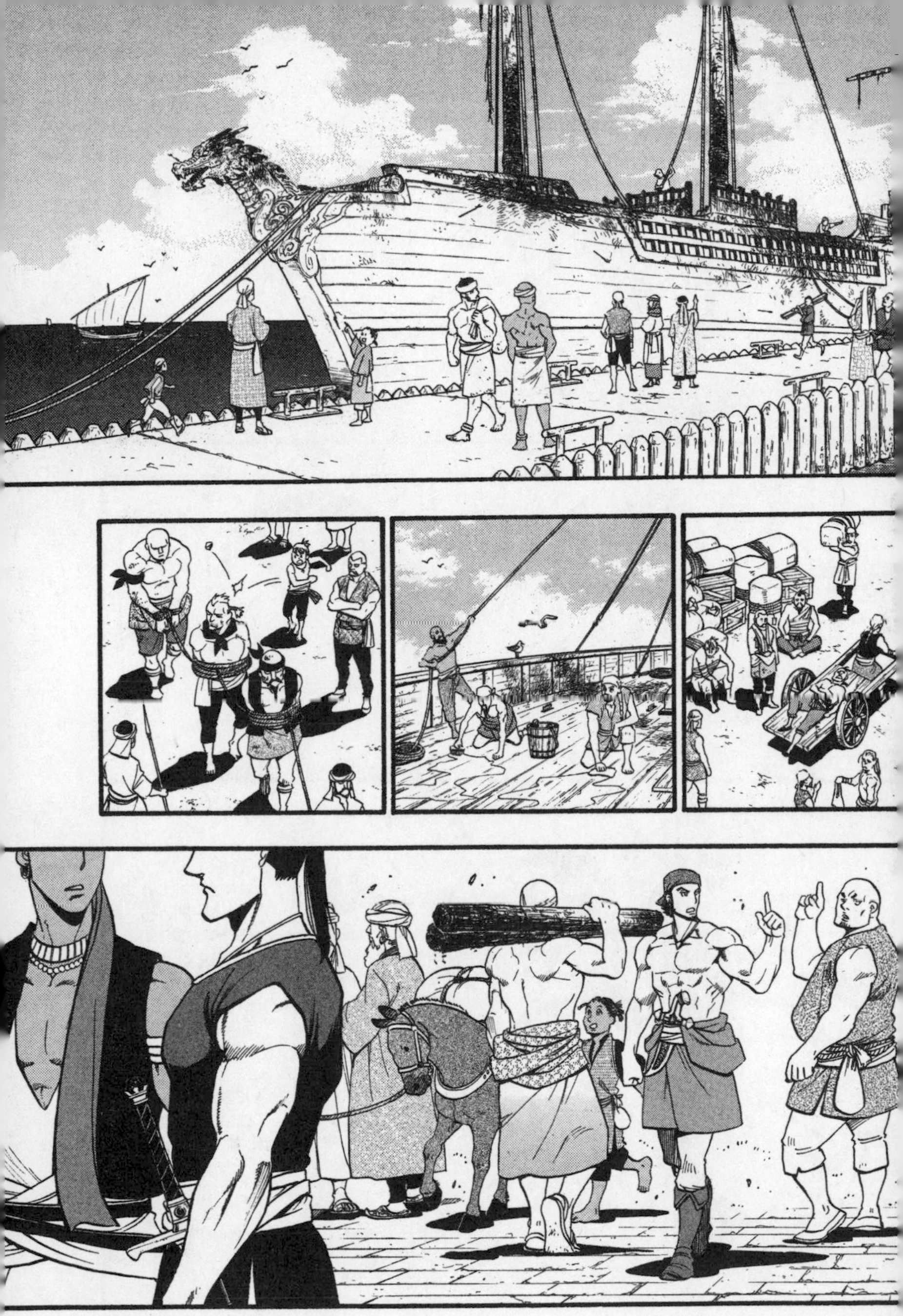

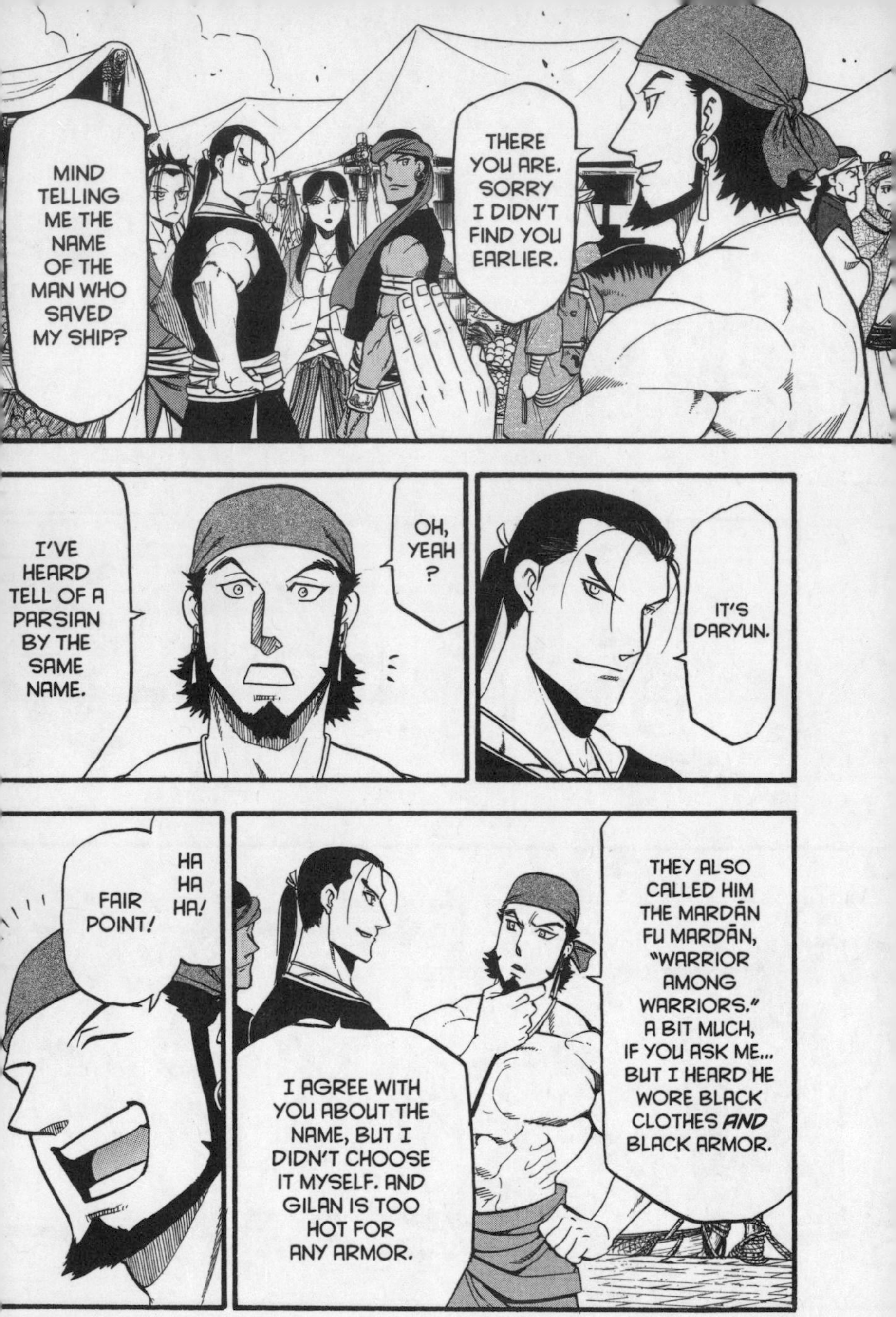
THERE YOU ARE. SORRY I DIDN'T FIND YOU EARLIER.
MIND TELLING ME THE NAME OF THE MAN WHO SAVED MY SHIP?
IT'S DARYUN.
OH, YEAH?
I'VE HEARD TELL OF A PARSIAN BY THE SAME NAME.
THEY ALSO CALLED HIM THE MARDĀN FU MARDĀN, "WARRIOR AMONG WARRIORS." A BIT MUCH, IF YOU ASK ME... BUT I HEARD HE WORE BLACK CLOTHES *AND* BLACK ARMOR.
I AGREE WITH YOU ABOUT THE NAME, BUT I DIDN'T CHOOSE IT MYSELF. AND GILAN IS TOO HOT FOR ANY ARMOR.
HA HA HA!
FAIR POINT!

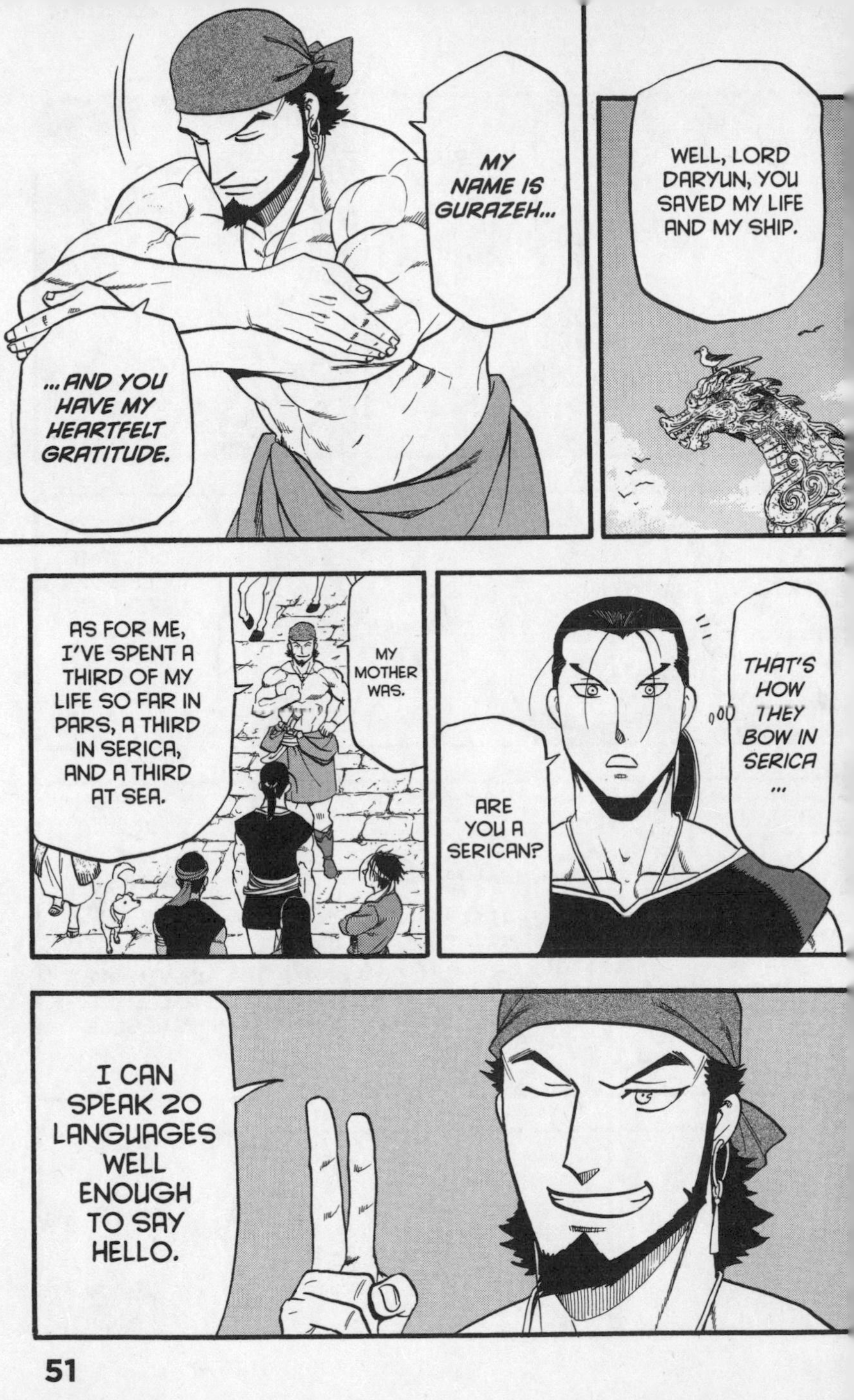
WELL, LORD DARYUN, YOU SAVED MY LIFE AND MY SHIP.
MY NAME IS GURAZEH...
...AND YOU HAVE MY HEARTFELT GRATITUDE.
THAT'S HOW THEY BOW IN SERICA ...
ARE YOU A SERICAN?
MY MOTHER WAS.
AS FOR ME, I'VE SPENT A THIRD OF MY LIFE SO FAR IN PARS, A THIRD IN SERICA, AND A THIRD AT SEA.
I CAN SPEAK 20 LANGUAGES WELL ENOUGH TO SAY HELLO.

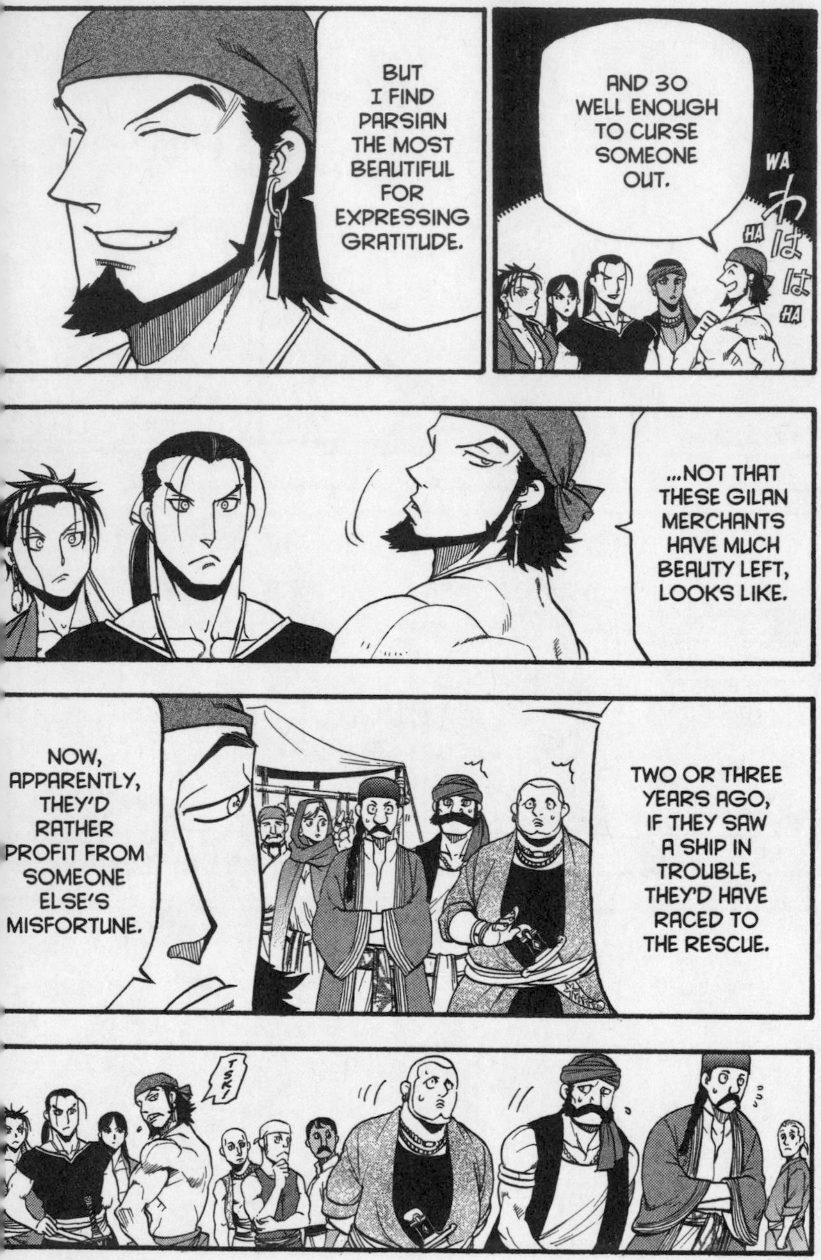
AND 30 WELL ENOUGH TO CURSE SOMEONE OUT.
WA わ HA は HA は
BUT I FIND PARSIAN THE MOST BEAUTIFUL FOR EXPRESSING GRATITUDE.
...NOT THAT THESE GILAN MERCHANTS HAVE MUCH BEAUTY LEFT, LOOKS LIKE.
TWO OR THREE YEARS AGO, IF THEY SAW A SHIP IN TROUBLE, THEY'D HAVE RACED TO THE RESCUE.
NOW, APPARENTLY, THEY'D RATHER PROFIT FROM SOMEONE ELSE'S MISFORTUNE.
TSK!

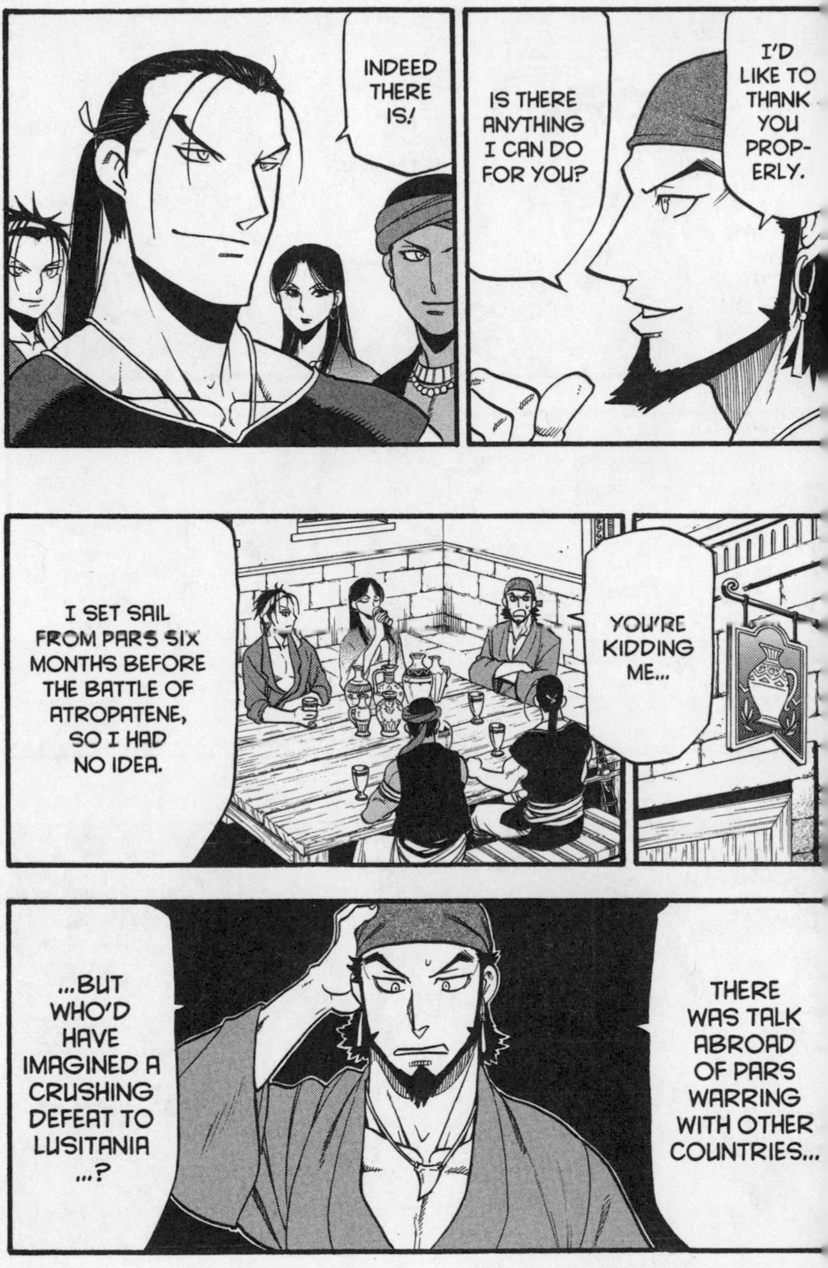
I'D LIKE TO THANK YOU PROPERLY.
IS THERE ANYTHING I CAN DO FOR YOU?
INDEED THERE IS!
YOU'RE KIDDING ME...
I SET SAIL FROM PARS SIX MONTHS BEFORE THE BATTLE OF ATROPATENE, SO I HAD NO IDEA.
THERE WAS TALK ABROAD OF PARS WARRING WITH OTHER COUNTRIES...
...BUT WHO'D HAVE IMAGINED A CRUSHING DEFEAT TO LUSITANIA ...?

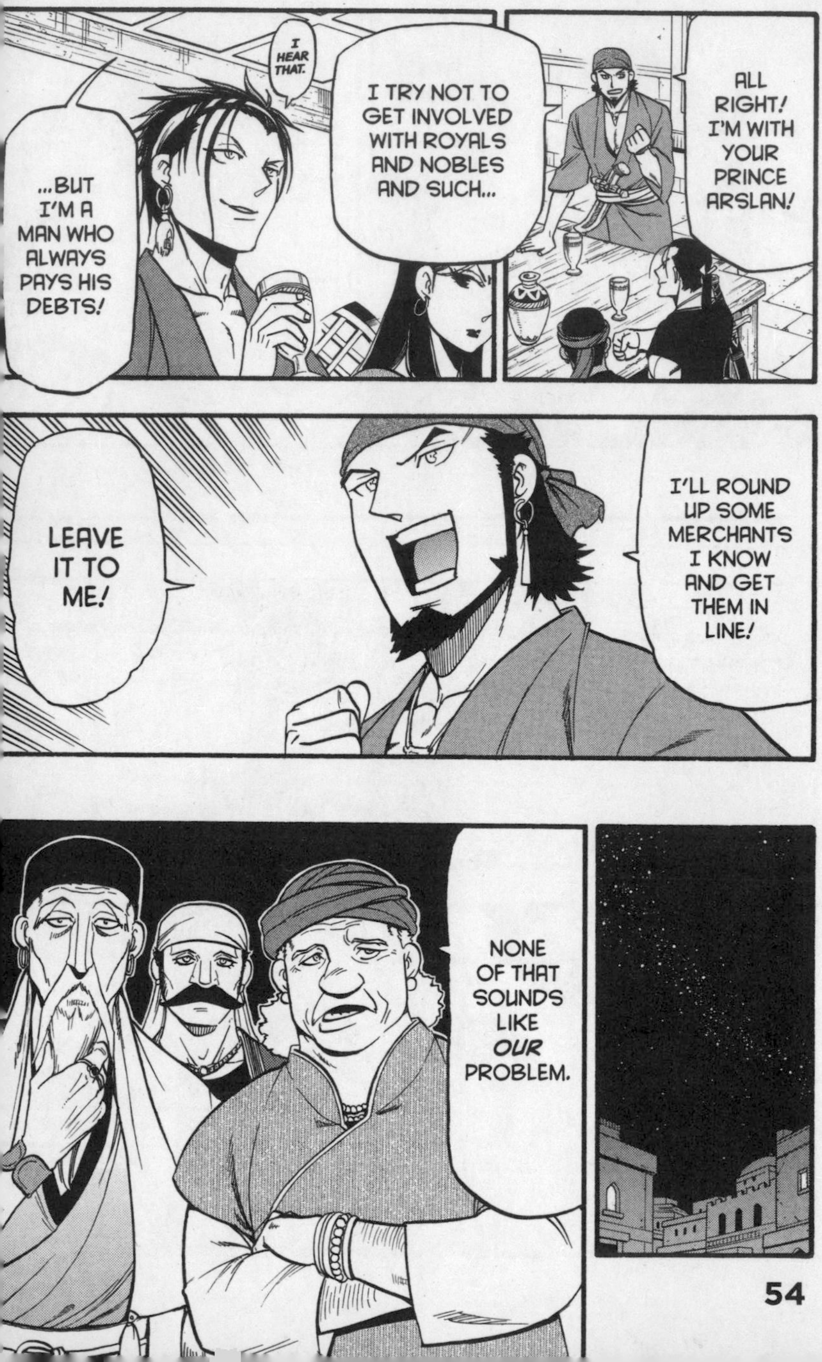
ALL RIGHT! I'M WITH YOUR PRINCE ARSLAN!
I TRY NOT TO GET INVOLVED WITH ROYALS AND NOBLES AND SUCH...
I HEAR THAT.
...BUT I'M A MAN WHO ALWAYS PAYS HIS DEBTS!
I'LL ROUND UP SOME MERCHANTS I KNOW AND GET THEM IN LINE!
LEAVE IT TO ME!
NONE OF THAT SOUNDS LIKE *OUR* PROBLEM.

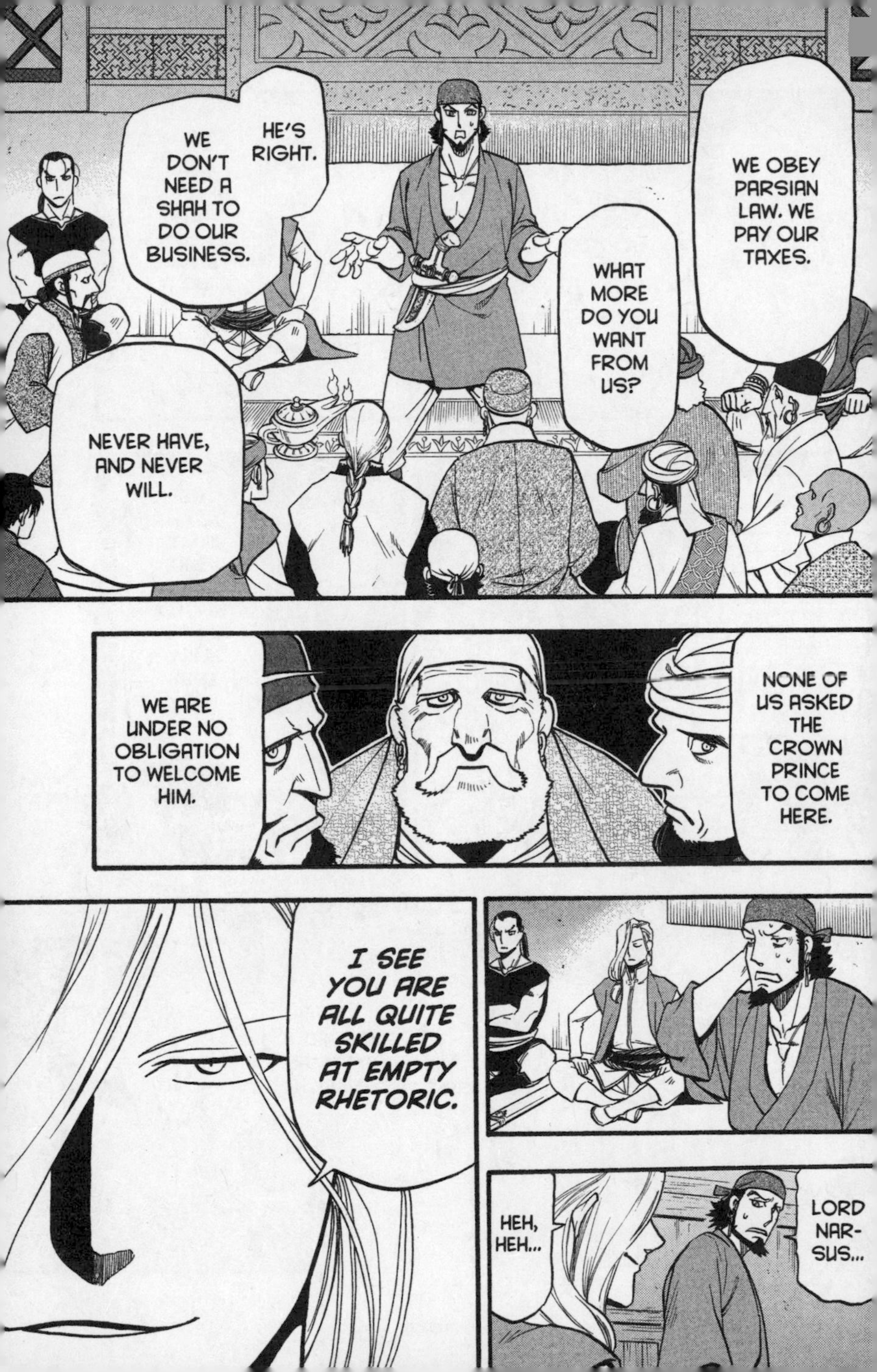
WE OBEY PARSIAN LAW. WE PAY OUR TAXES.
WHAT MORE DO YOU WANT FROM US?
HE'S RIGHT.
WE DON'T NEED A SHAH TO DO OUR BUSINESS.
NEVER HAVE, AND NEVER WILL.
NONE OF US ASKED THE CROWN PRINCE TO COME HERE.
WE ARE UNDER NO OBLIGATION TO WELCOME HIM.
LORD NAR-SUS...
HEH, HEH...
I SEE YOU ARE ALL QUITE SKILLED AT EMPTY RHETORIC.

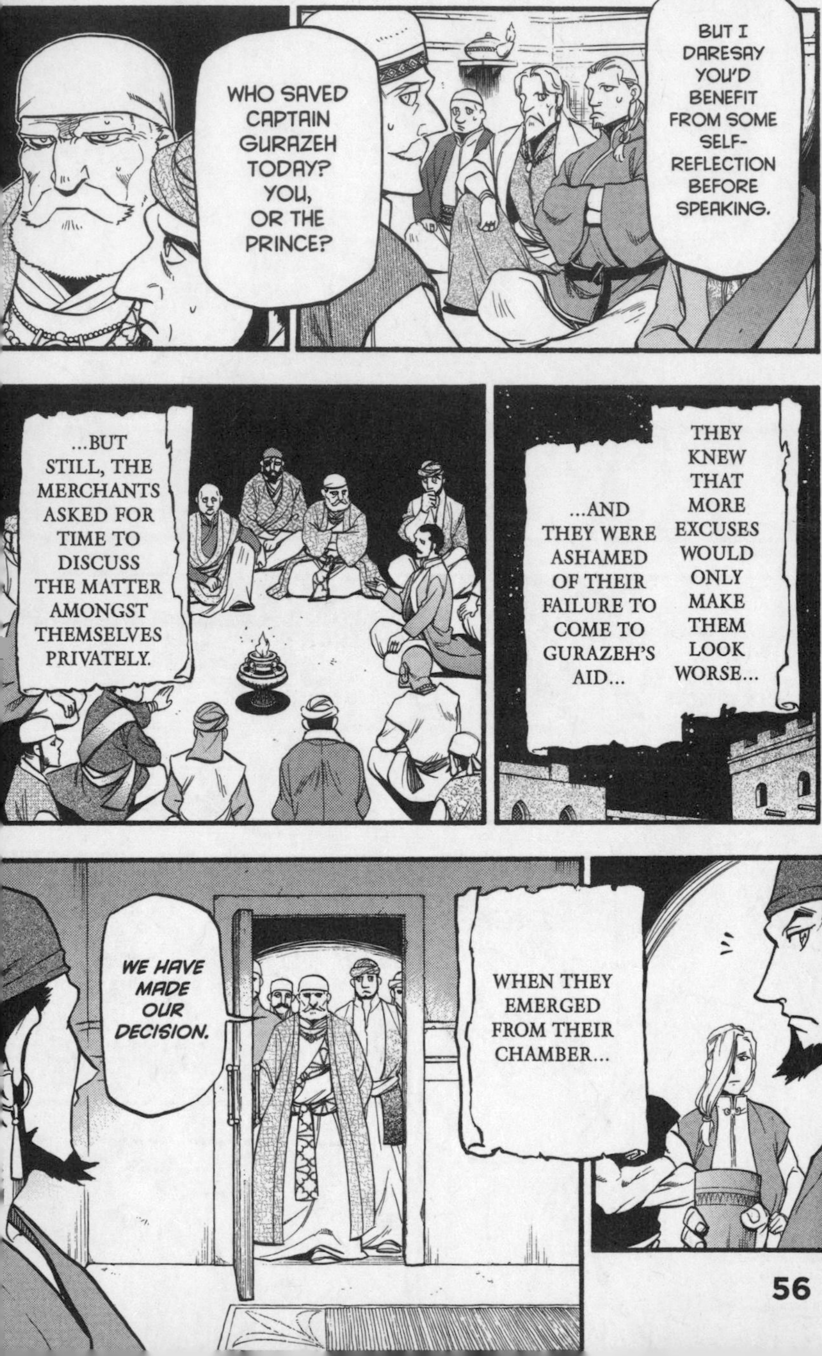
WHO SAVED CAPTAIN GURAZEH TODAY? YOU, OR THE PRINCE?
BUT I DARESAY YOU'D BENEFIT FROM SOME SELF-REFLECTION BEFORE SPEAKING.
THEY KNEW THAT MORE EXCUSES WOULD ONLY MAKE THEM LOOK WORSE...
...AND THEY WERE ASHAMED OF THEIR FAILURE TO COME TO GURAZEH'S AID...
...BUT STILL, THE MERCHANTS ASKED FOR TIME TO DISCUSS THE MATTER AMONGST THEMSELVES PRIVATELY.
WHEN THEY EMERGED FROM THEIR CHAMBER...
WE HAVE MADE OUR DECISION.

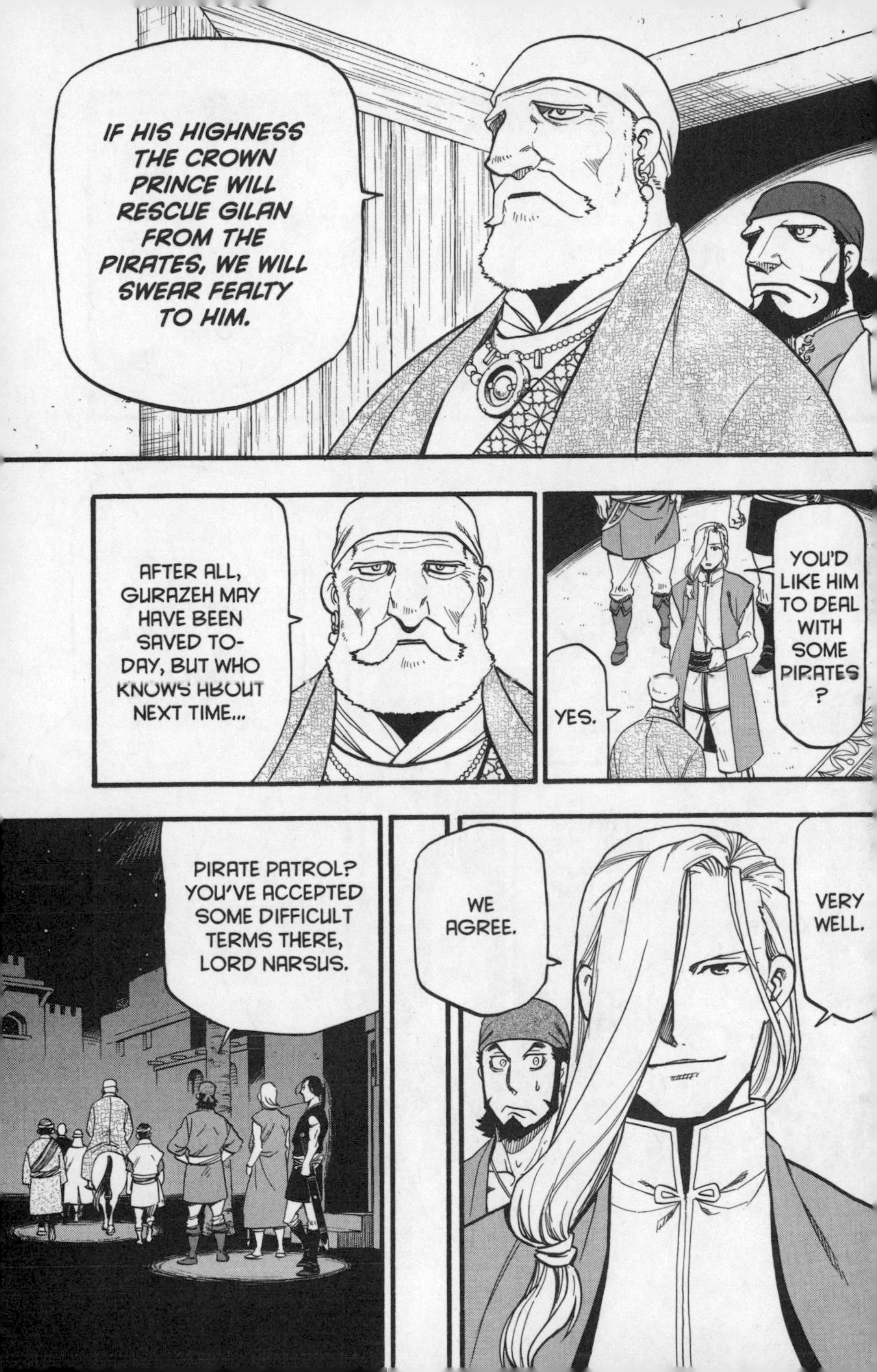
IF HIS HIGHNESS THE CROWN PRINCE WILL RESCUE GILAN FROM THE PIRATES, WE WILL SWEAR FEALTY TO HIM.
YOU'D LIKE HIM TO DEAL WITH SOME PIRATES?
YES.
AFTER ALL, GURAZEH MAY HAVE BEEN SAVED TO-DAY, BUT WHO KNOWS ABOUT NEXT TIME...
VERY WELL.
WE AGREE.
PIRATE PATROL? YOU'VE ACCEPTED SOME DIFFICULT TERMS THERE, LORD NARSUS.

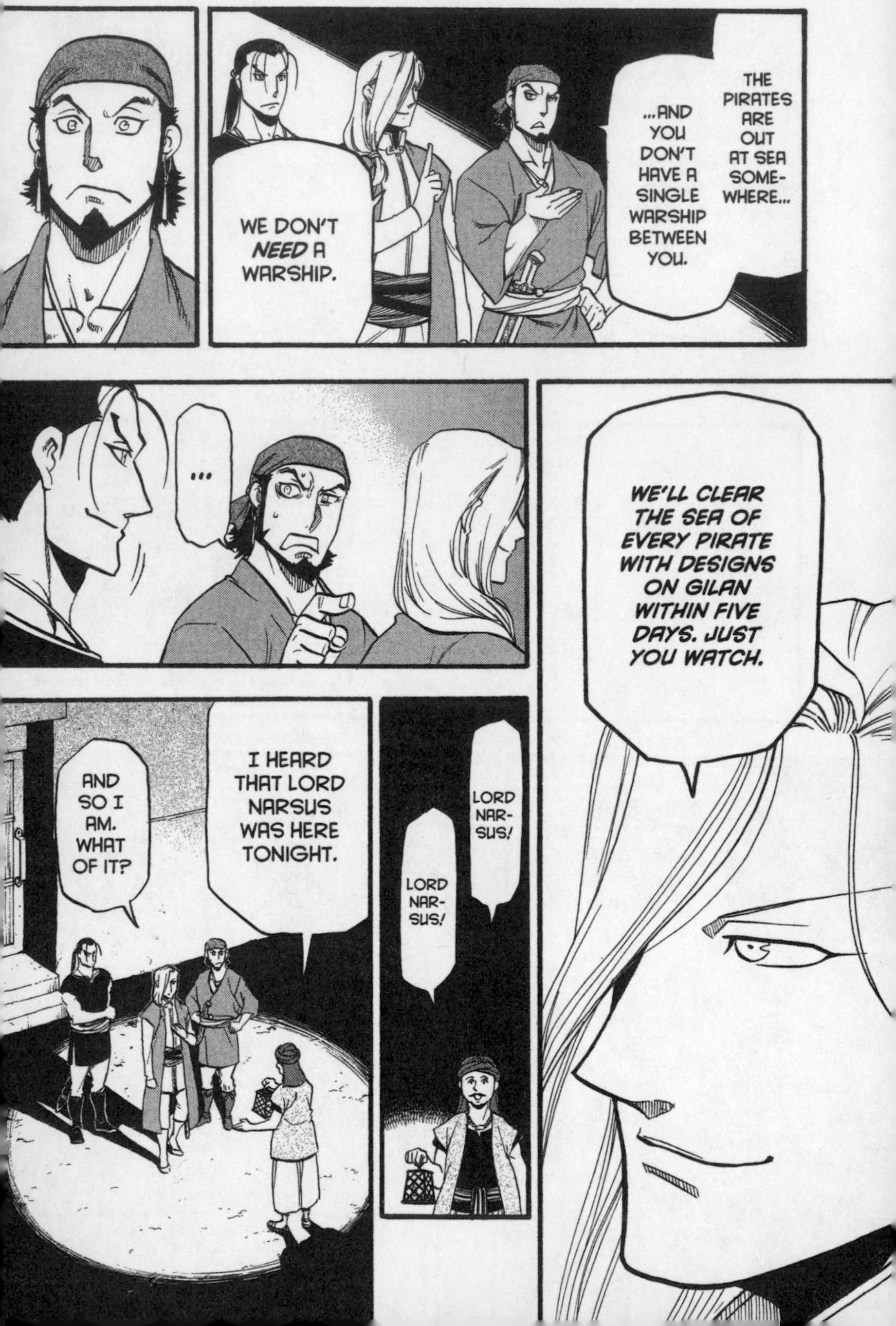
THE PIRATES ARE OUT AT SEA SOME-WHERE...
...AND YOU DON'T HAVE A SINGLE WARSHIP BETWEEN YOU.
WE DON'T *NEED* A WARSHIP.
WE'LL CLEAR THE SEA OF EVERY PIRATE WITH DESIGNS ON GILAN WITHIN FIVE DAYS. JUST YOU WATCH.
...
LORD NAR-SUS!
LORD NAR-SUS!
I HEARD THAT LORD NARSUS WAS HERE TONIGHT.
AND SO I AM. WHAT OF IT?

I AM A MESSENGER FROM CIRCIAS.

LORD SHAGHAD SENT ME TO INFORM YOU THAT HE WILL RETURN HOME TOMORROW.

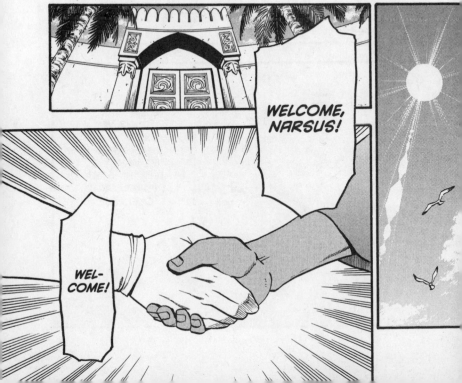

WELCOME, NARSUS!

WEL-COME!

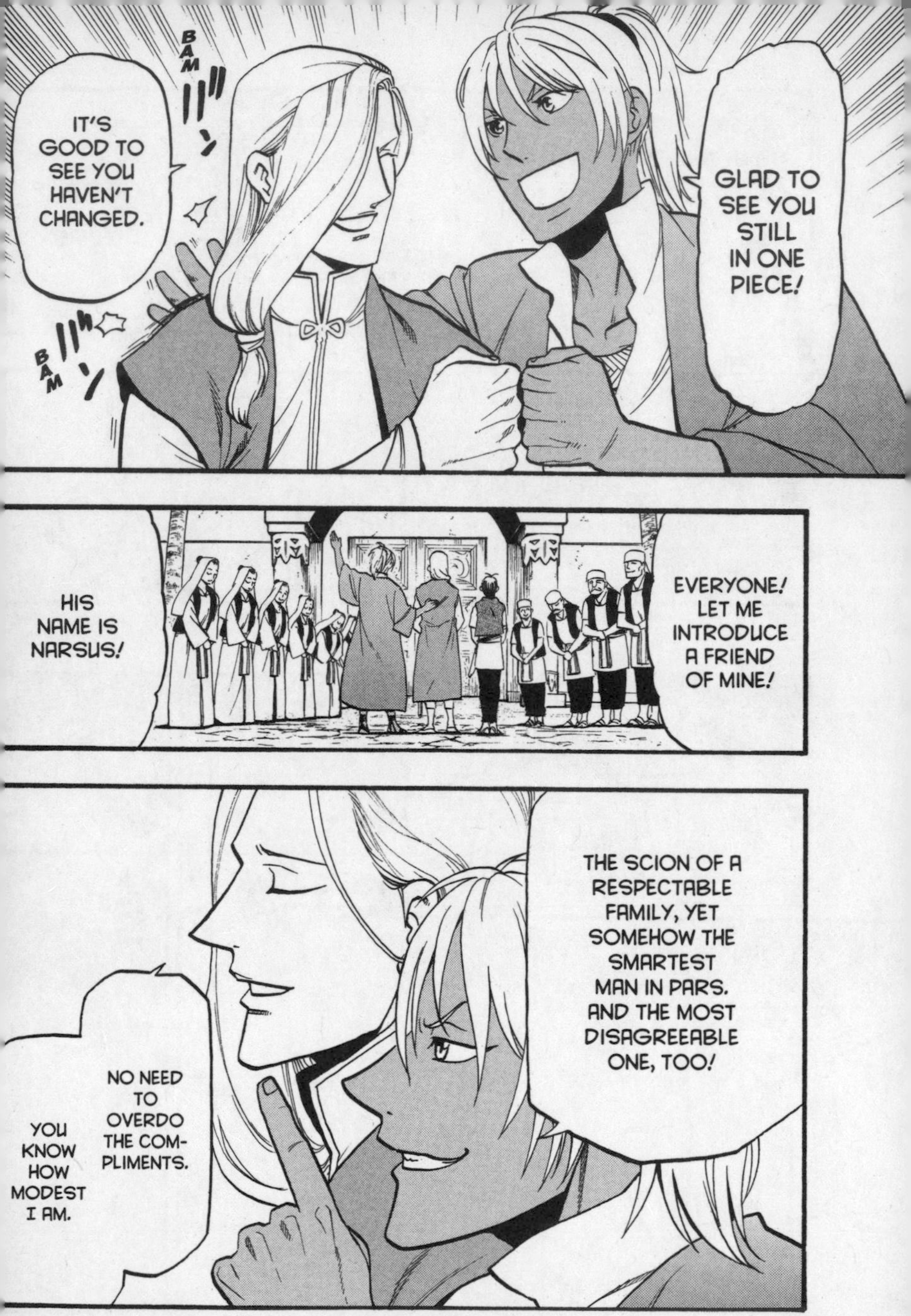
GLAD TO SEE YOU STILL IN ONE PIECE!
BAM
BAM
IT'S GOOD TO SEE YOU HAVEN'T CHANGED.
EVERYONE! LET ME INTRODUCE A FRIEND OF MINE!
HIS NAME IS NARSUS!
THE SCION OF A RESPECTABLE FAMILY, YET SOMEHOW THE SMARTEST MAN IN PARS. AND THE MOST DISAGREEABLE ONE, TOO!
NO NEED TO OVERDO THE COMPLIMENTS.
YOU KNOW HOW MODEST I AM.

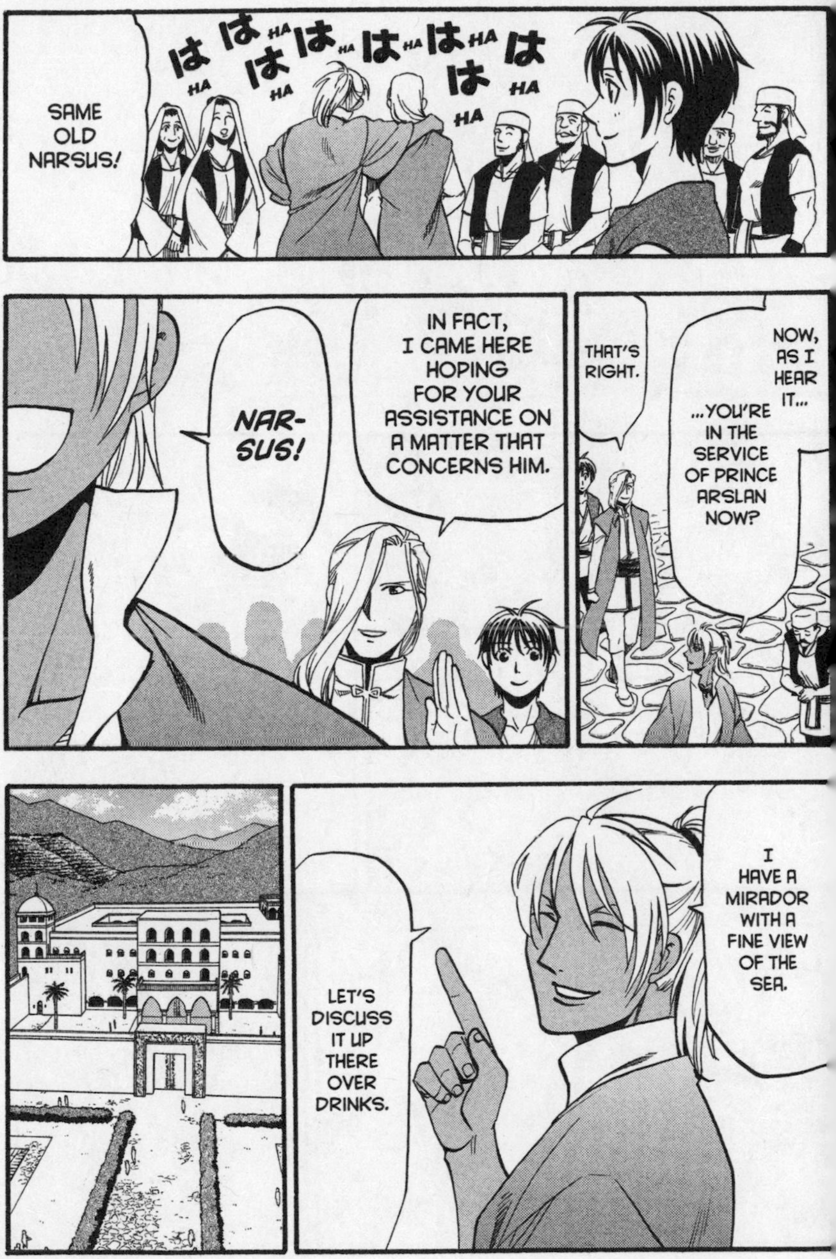

ははははははは
HA HA HA HA HA HA HA HA HA
SAME OLD NARSUS!
NOW, AS I HEAR IT...
...YOU'RE IN THE SERVICE OF PRINCE ARSLAN NOW?
THAT'S RIGHT.
IN FACT, I CAME HERE HOPING FOR YOUR ASSISTANCE ON A MATTER THAT CONCERNS HIM.
NAR-SUS!
I HAVE A MIRADOR WITH A FINE VIEW OF THE SEA.
LET'S DISCUSS IT UP THERE OVER DRINKS.

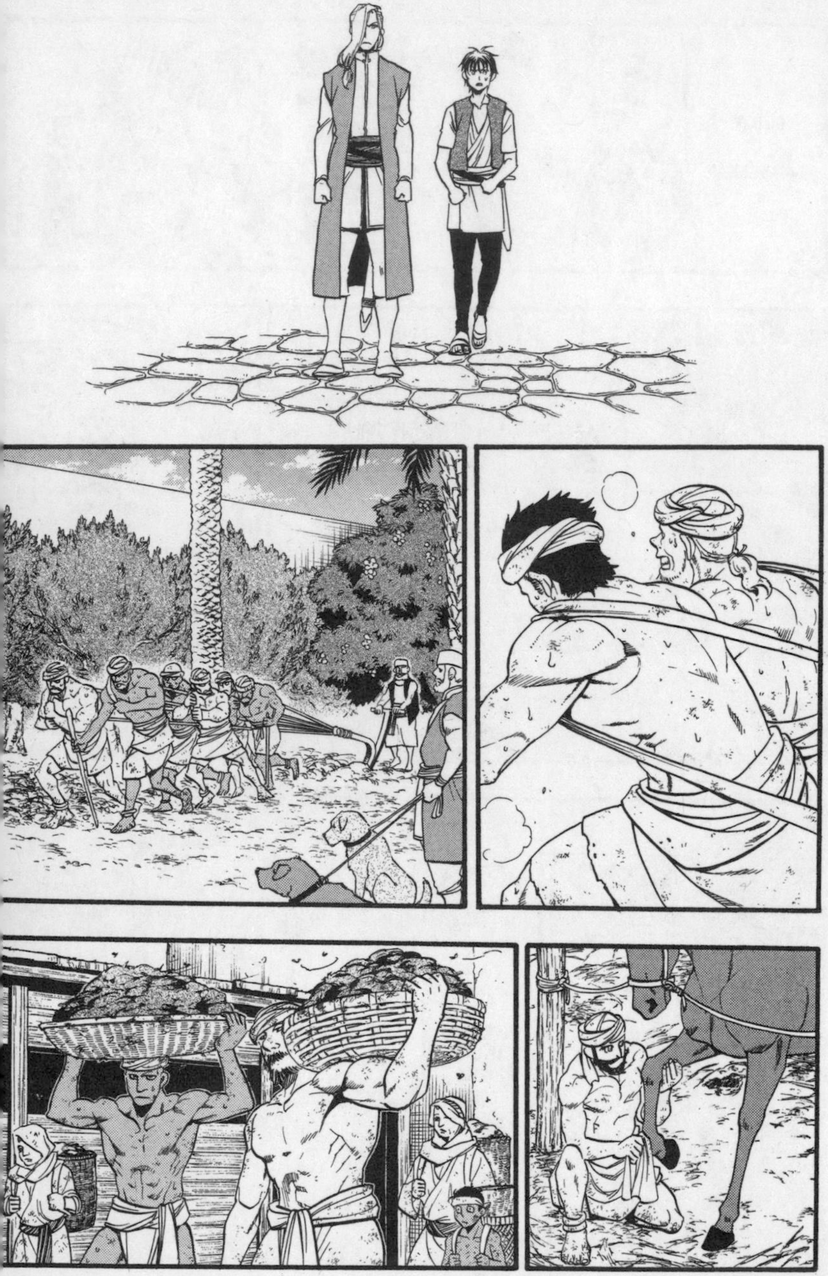

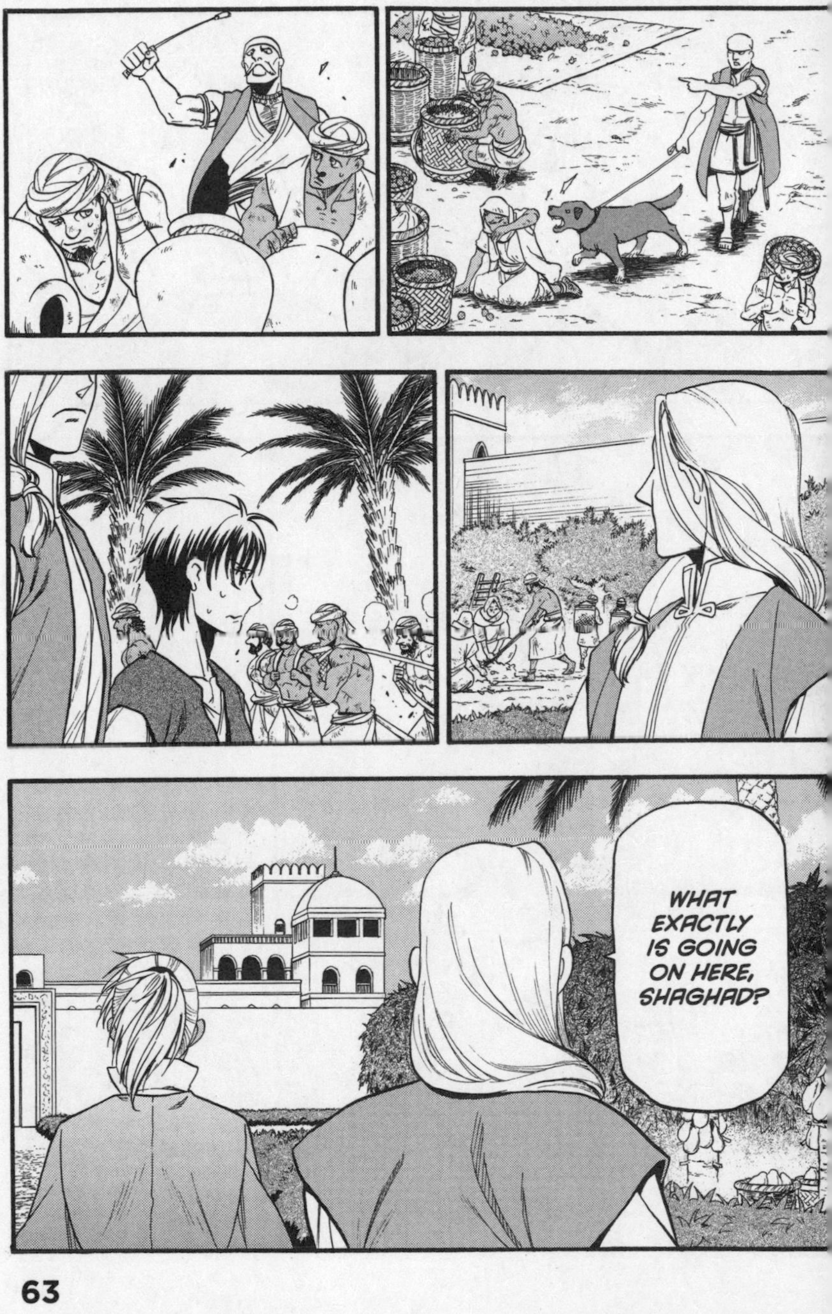
WHAT EXACTLY IS GOING ON HERE, SHAGHAD?

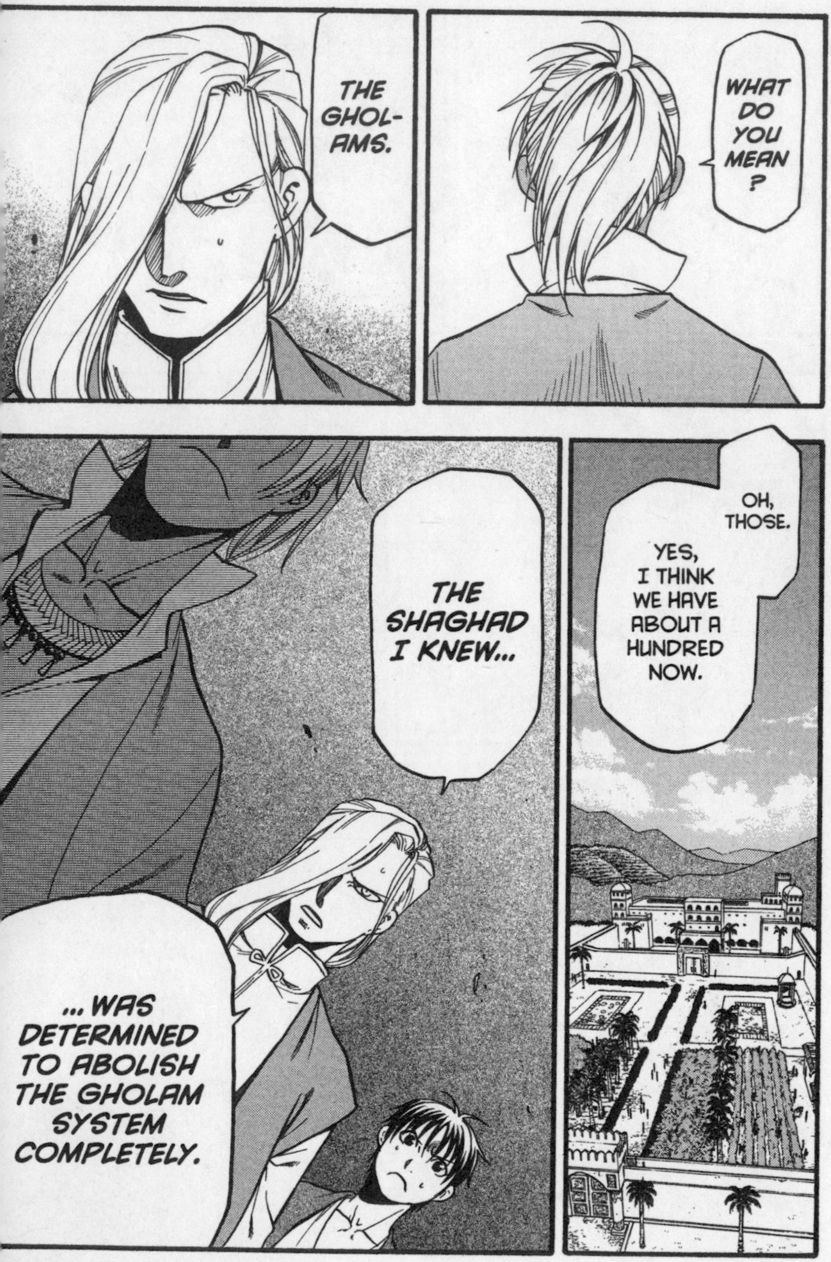
WHAT DO YOU MEAN?
THE GHOL-AMS.
OH, THOSE.
YES, I THINK WE HAVE ABOUT A HUNDRED NOW.
THE SHAGHAD I KNEW...
...WAS DETERMINED TO ABOLISH THE GHOLAM SYSTEM COMPLETELY.

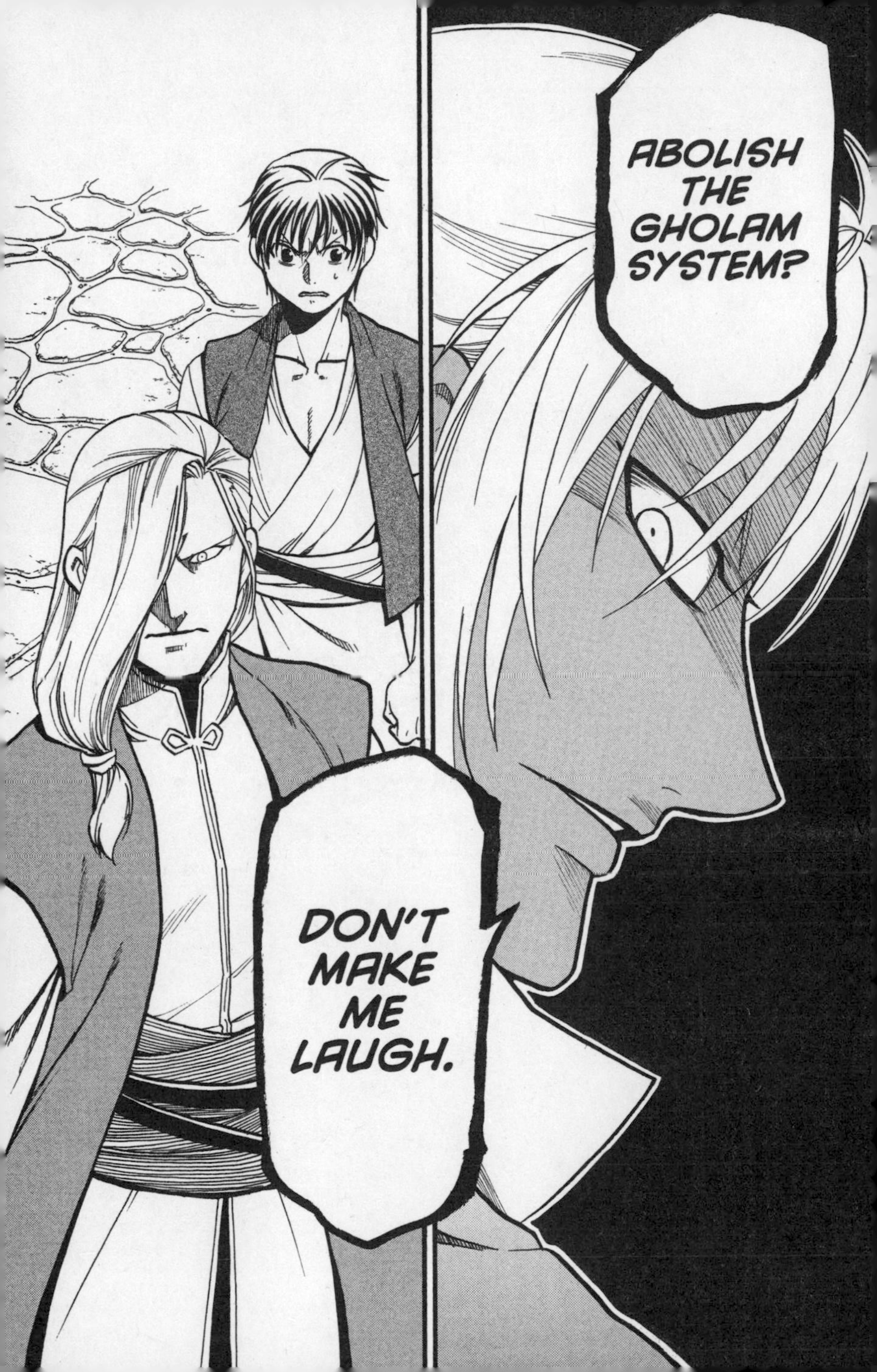
ABOLISH THE GHOLAM SYSTEM?
DON'T MAKE ME LAUGH.

THE HEROIC LEGEND OF
ARSLAN

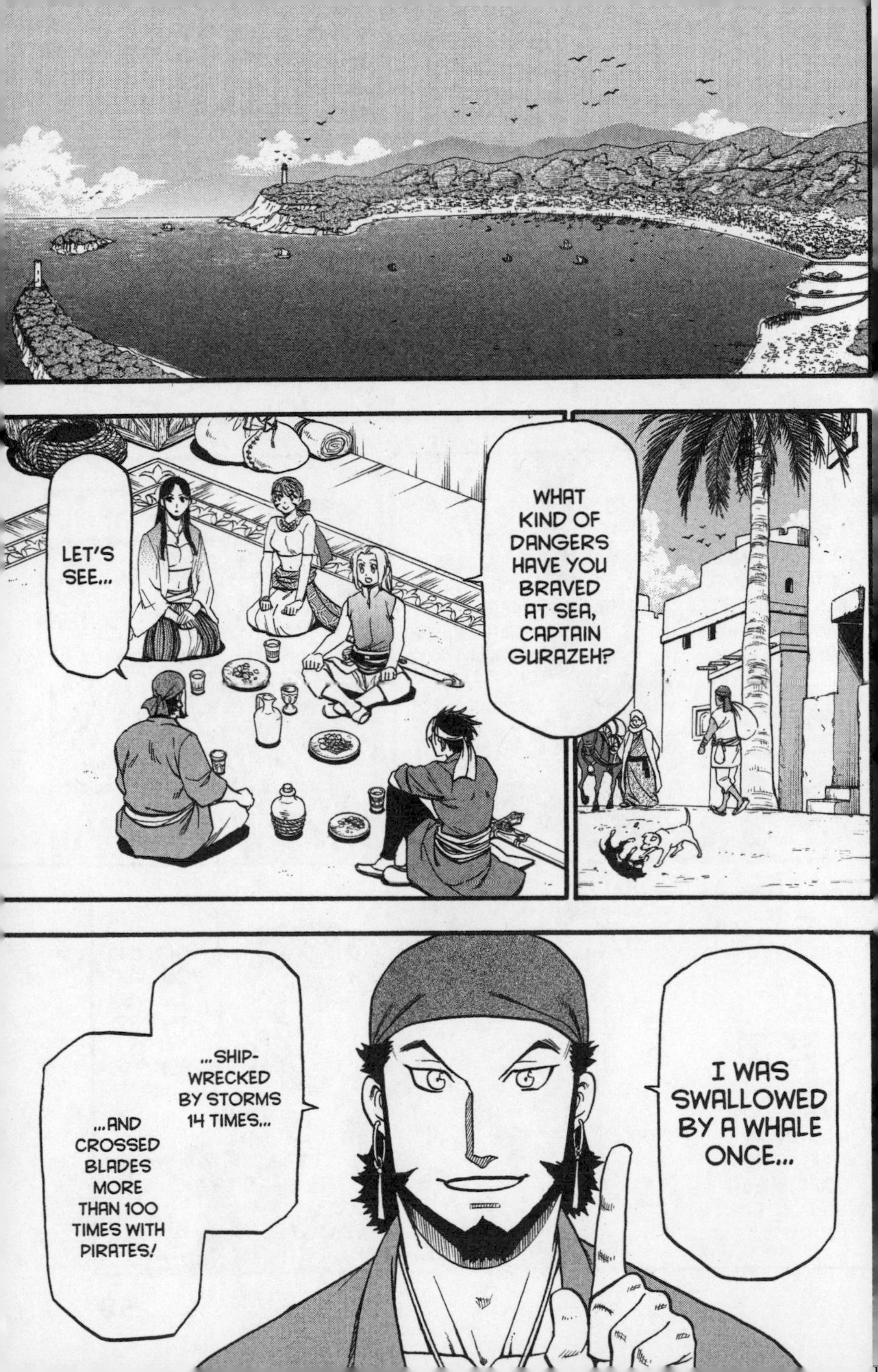
WHAT KIND OF DANGERS HAVE YOU BRAVED AT SEA, CAPTAIN GURAZEH?
LET'S SEE...
I WAS SWALLOWED BY A WHALE ONCE...
...SHIP-WRECKED BY STORMS 14 TIMES...
...AND CROSSED BLADES MORE THAN 100 TIMES WITH PIRATES!

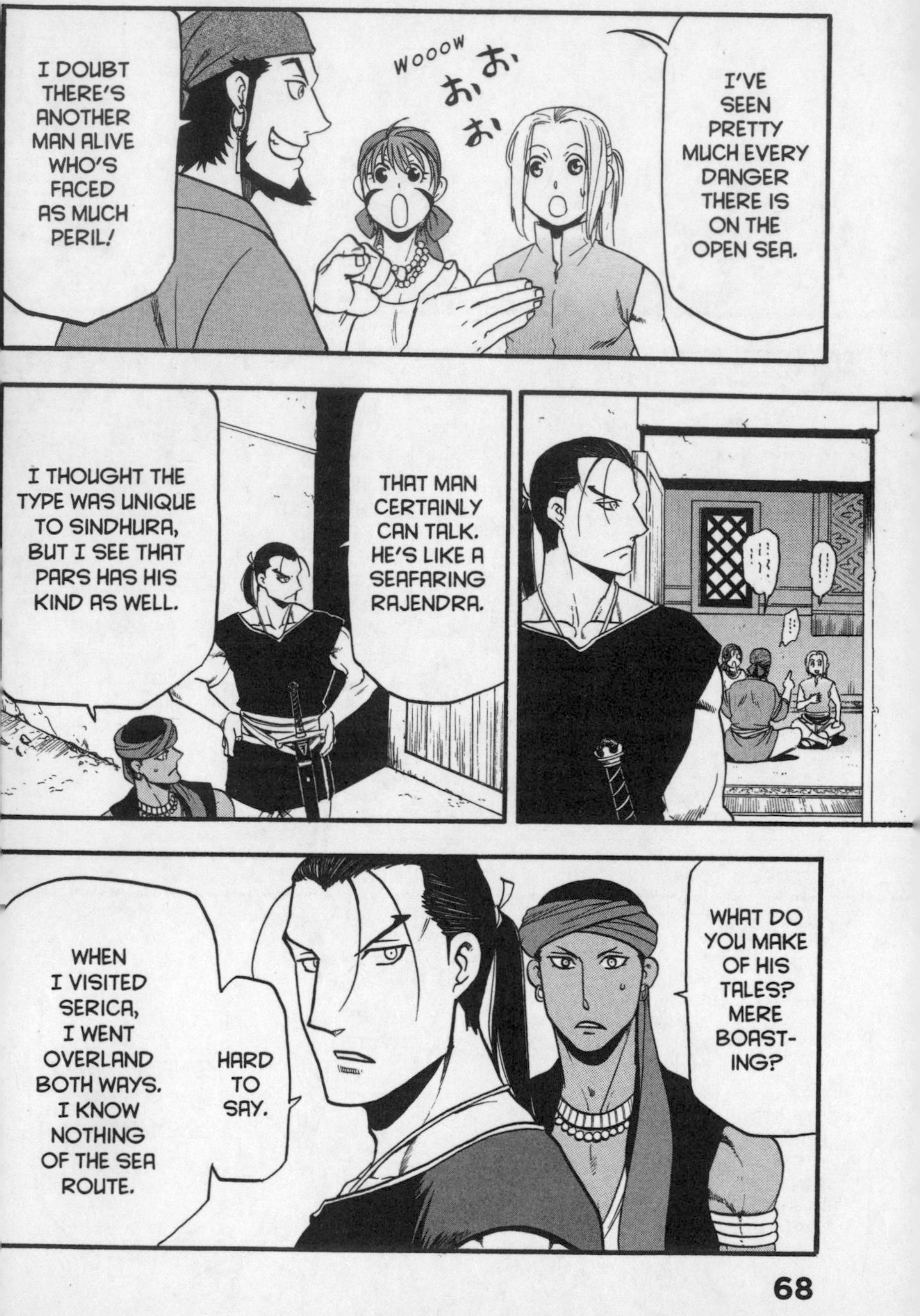
I'VE SEEN PRETTY MUCH EVERY DANGER THERE IS ON THE OPEN SEA.
WOOOW
おおお
I DOUBT THERE'S ANOTHER MAN ALIVE WHO'S FACED AS MUCH PERIL!
THAT MAN CERTAINLY CAN TALK. HE'S LIKE A SEAFARING RAJENDRA.
I THOUGHT THE TYPE WAS UNIQUE TO SINDHURA, BUT I SEE THAT PARS HAS HIS KIND AS WELL.
WHAT DO YOU MAKE OF HIS TALES? MERE BOAST-ING?
HARD TO SAY.
WHEN I VISITED SERICA, I WENT OVERLAND BOTH WAYS. I KNOW NOTHING OF THE SEA ROUTE.

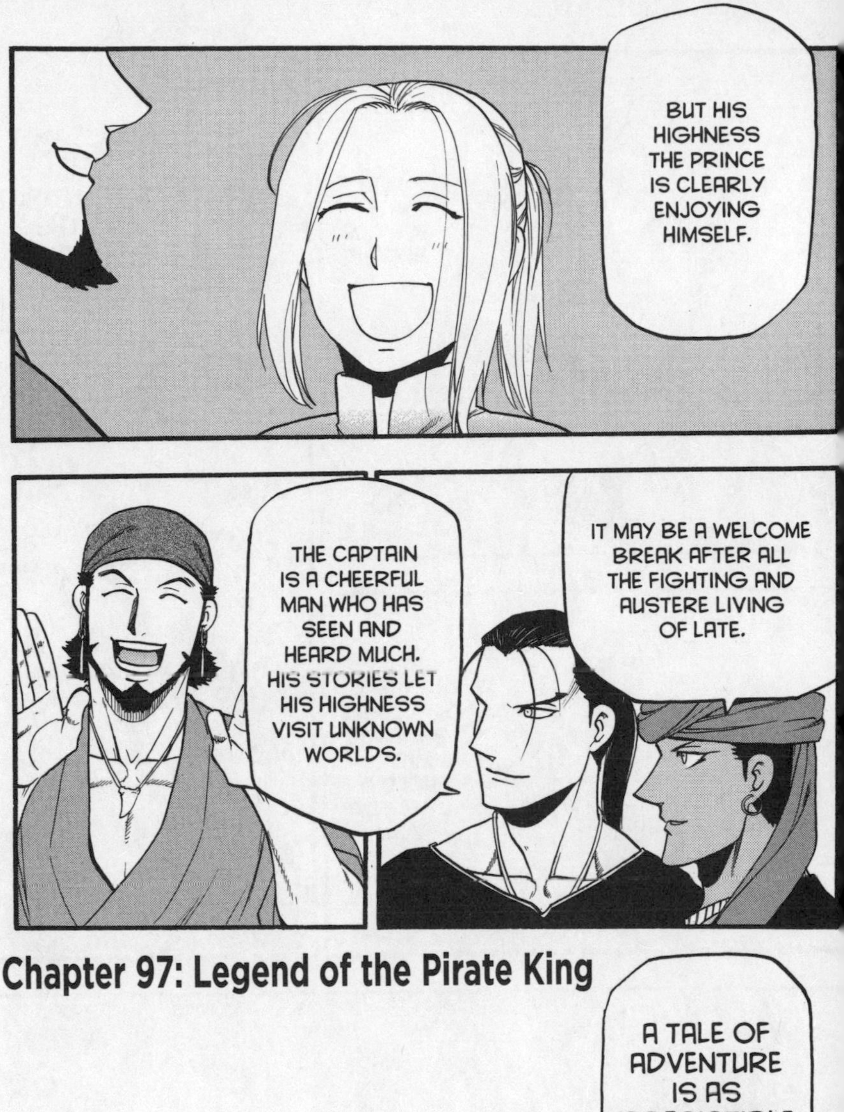
BUT HIS HIGHNESS THE PRINCE IS CLEARLY ENJOYING HIMSELF.
IT MAY BE A WELCOME BREAK AFTER ALL THE FIGHTING AND AUSTERE LIVING OF LATE.
THE CAPTAIN IS A CHEERFUL MAN WHO HAS SEEN AND HEARD MUCH. HIS STORIES LET HIS HIGHNESS VISIT UNKNOWN WORLDS.

Chapter 97: Legend of the Pirate King

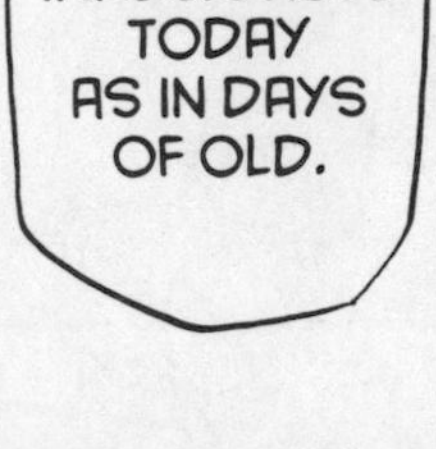
A TALE OF ADVENTURE IS AS IRRESISTIBLE TODAY AS IN DAYS OF OLD.

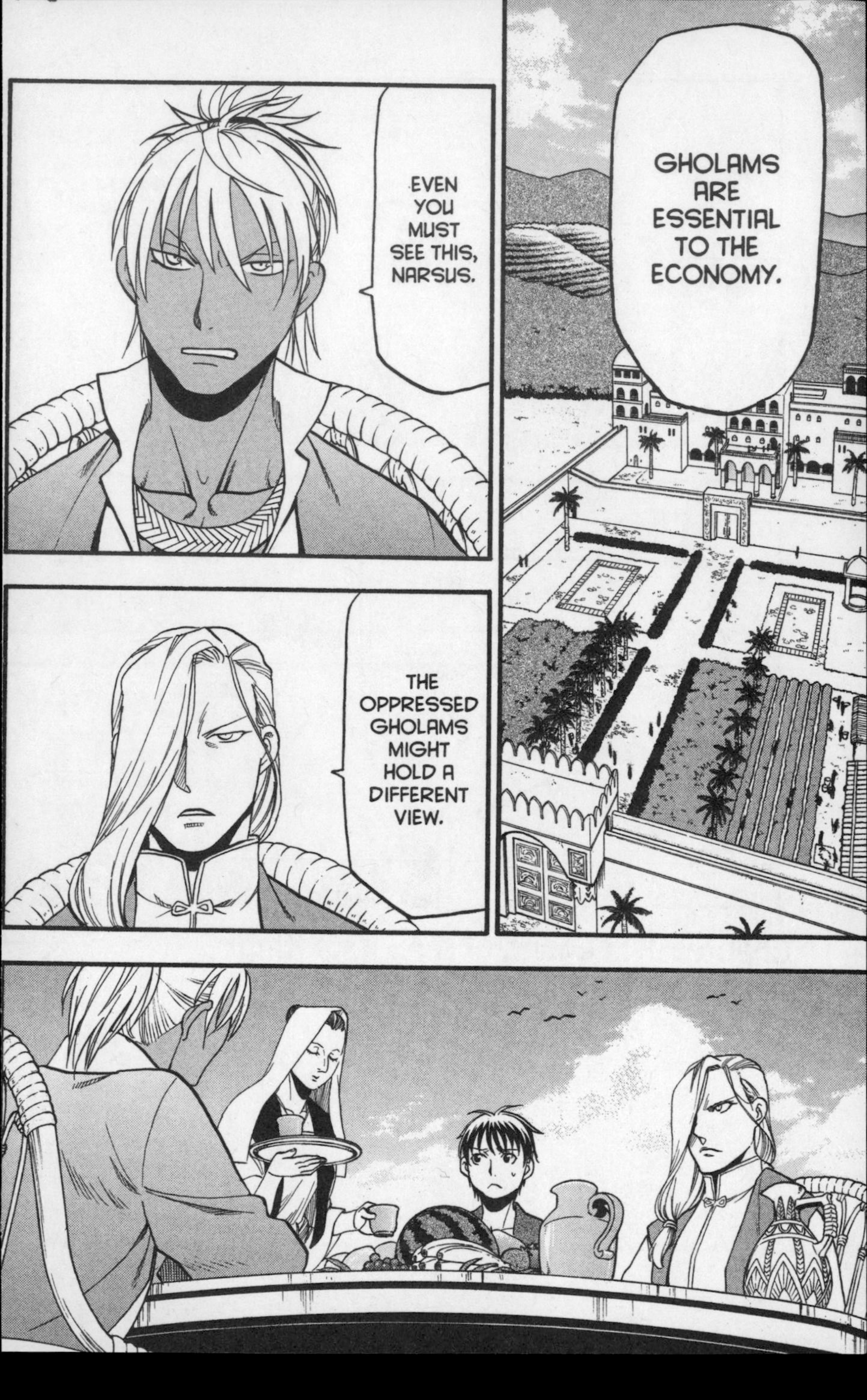
GHOLAMS ARE ESSENTIAL TO THE ECONOMY.
EVEN YOU MUST SEE THIS, NARSUS.
THE OPPRESSED GHOLAMS MIGHT HOLD A DIFFERENT VIEW.

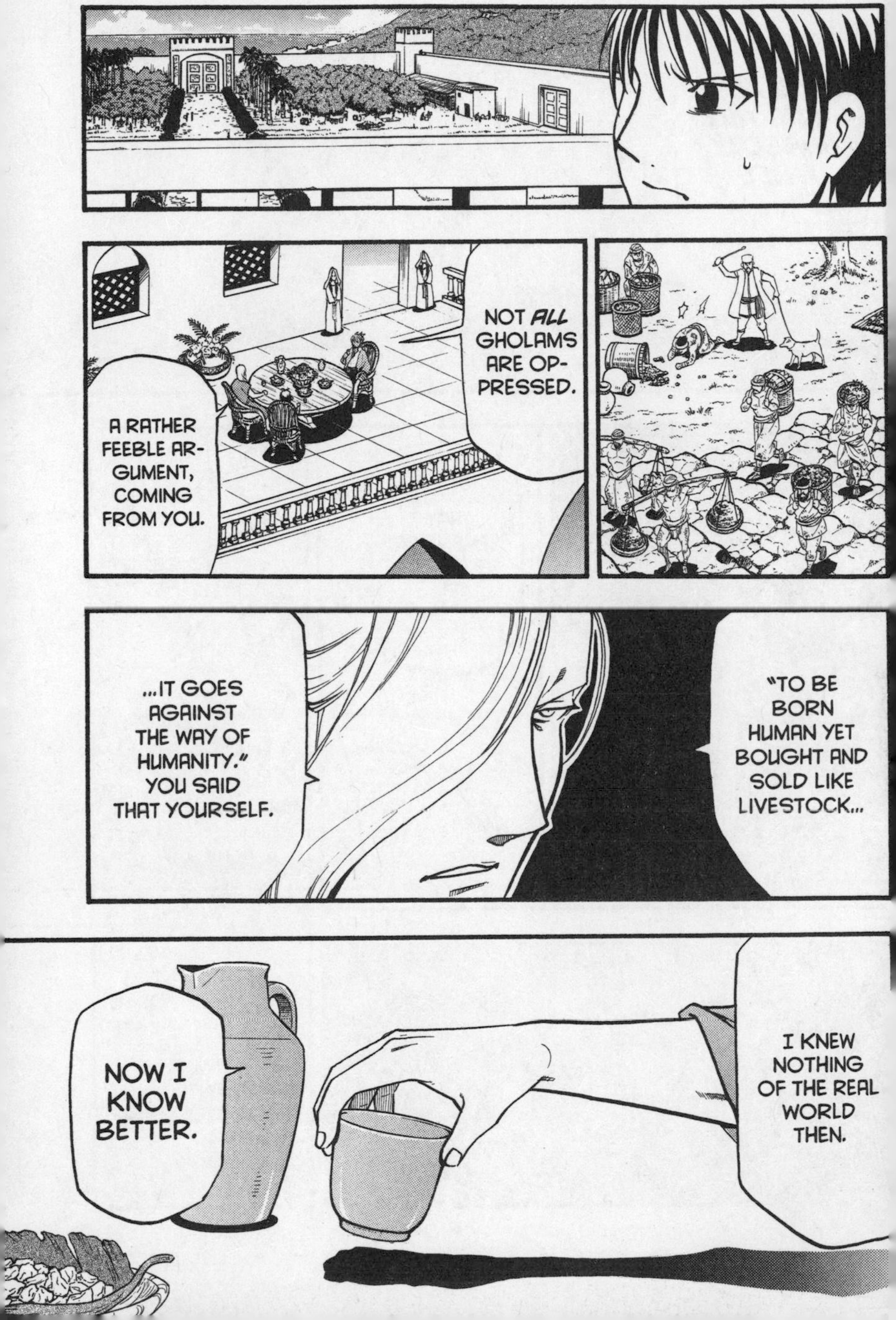
NOT *ALL* GHOLAMS ARE OPPRESSED.
A RATHER FEEBLE ARGUMENT, COMING FROM YOU.
"TO BE BORN HUMAN YET BOUGHT AND SOLD LIKE LIVESTOCK...
...IT GOES AGAINST THE WAY OF HUMANITY." YOU SAID THAT YOURSELF.
I KNEW NOTHING OF THE REAL WORLD THEN.
NOW I KNOW BETTER.

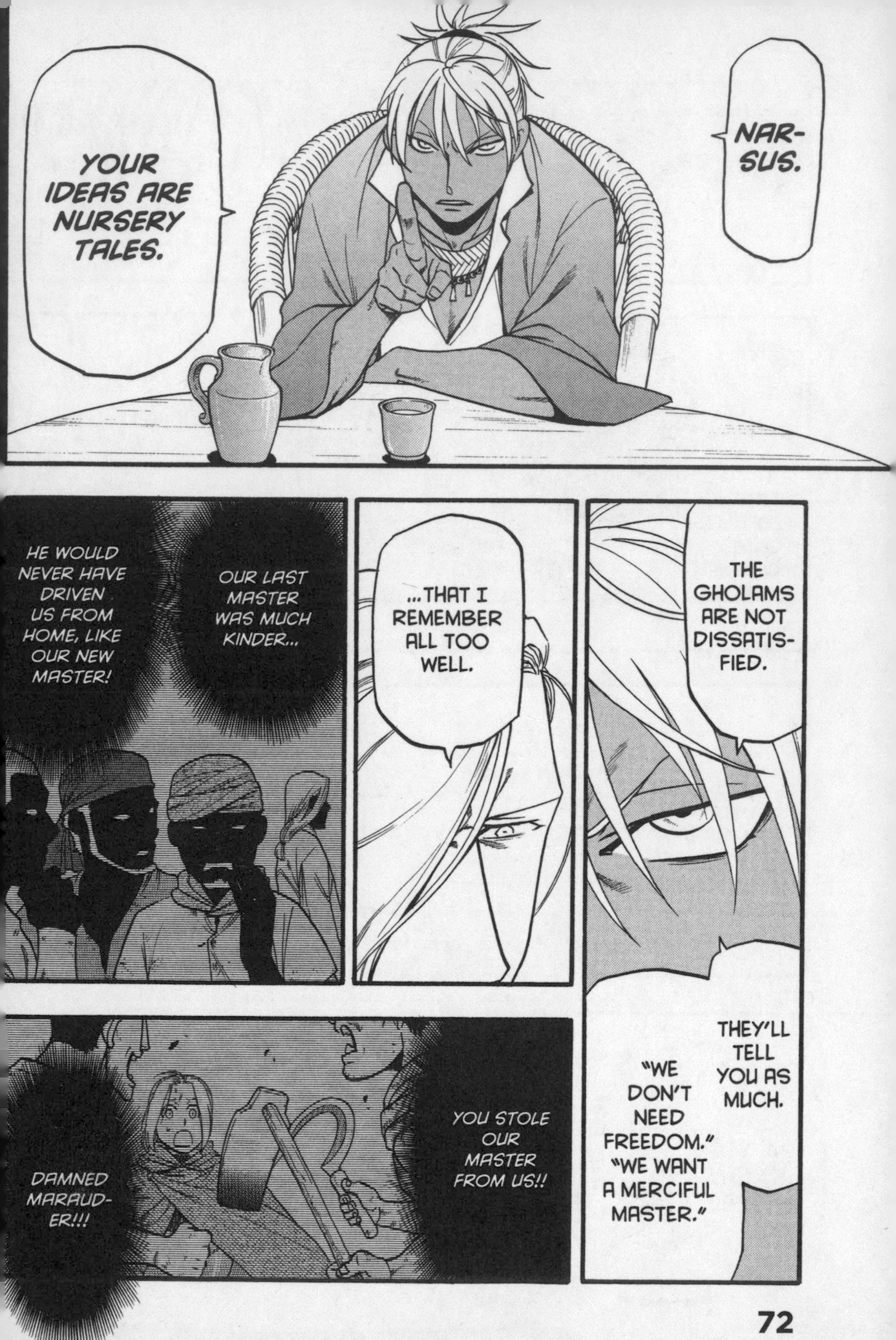
NARSUS.
YOUR IDEAS ARE NURSERY TALES.
THE GHOLAMS ARE NOT DISSATISFIED.
THEY'LL TELL YOU AS MUCH.
“WE DON'T NEED FREEDOM.” “WE WANT A MERCIFUL MASTER.”
...THAT I REMEMBER ALL TOO WELL.
OUR LAST MASTER WAS MUCH KINDER...
HE WOULD NEVER HAVE DRIVEN US FROM HOME, LIKE OUR NEW MASTER!
YOU STOLE OUR MASTER FROM US!!
DAMNED MARAUDER!!!

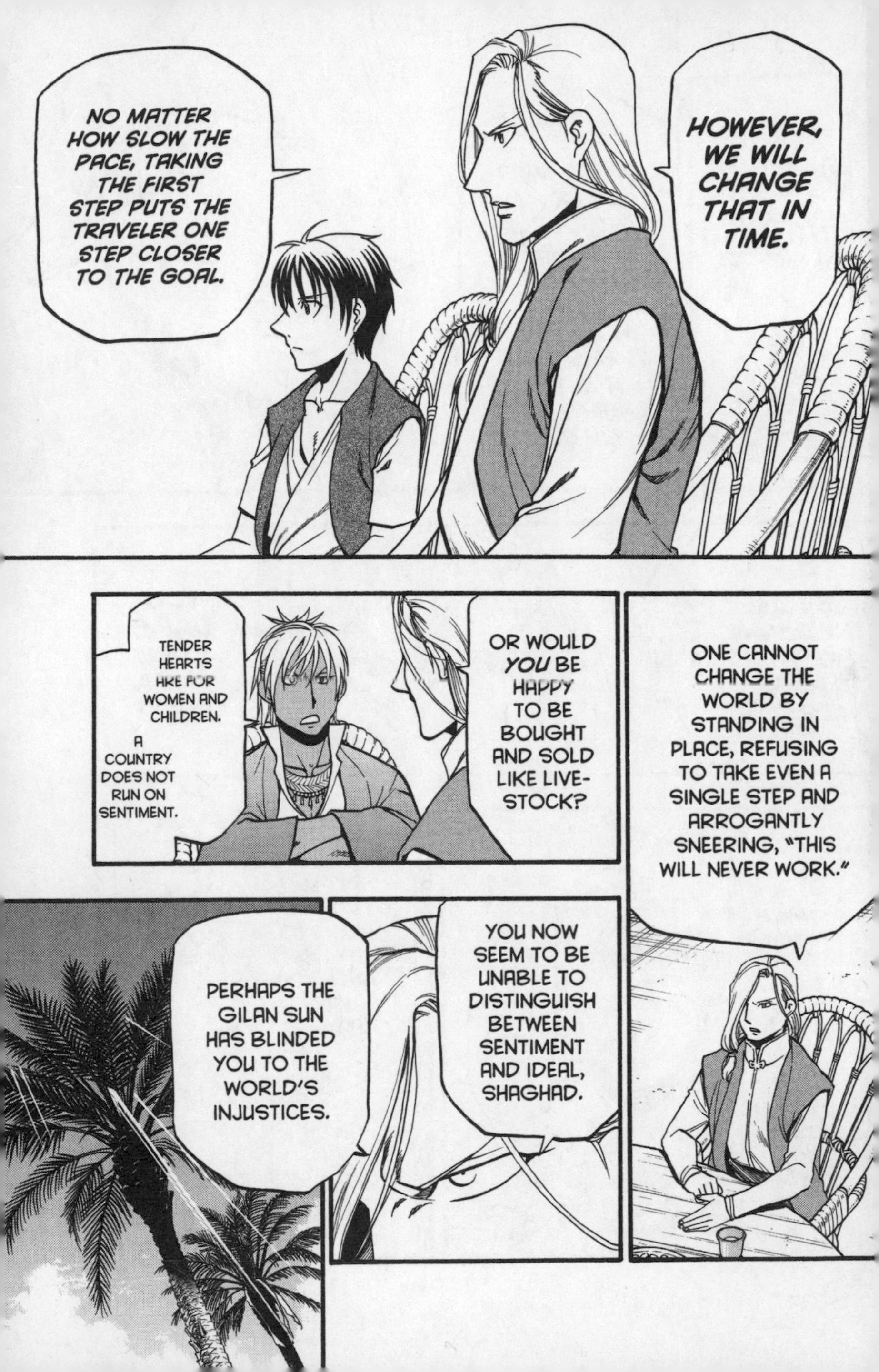
HOWEVER, WE WILL CHANGE THAT IN TIME.
NO MATTER HOW SLOW THE PACE, TAKING THE FIRST STEP PUTS THE TRAVELER ONE STEP CLOSER TO THE GOAL.
ONE CANNOT CHANGE THE WORLD BY STANDING IN PLACE, REFUSING TO TAKE EVEN A SINGLE STEP AND ARROGANTLY SNEERING, "THIS WILL NEVER WORK."
OR WOULD *YOU* BE HAPPY TO BE BOUGHT AND SOLD LIKE LIVE-STOCK?
TENDER HEARTS ARE FOR WOMEN AND CHILDREN.
A COUNTRY DOES NOT RUN ON SENTIMENT.
YOU NOW SEEM TO BE UNABLE TO DISTINGUISH BETWEEN SENTIMENT AND IDEAL, SHAGHAD.
PERHAPS THE GILAN SUN HAS BLINDED YOU TO THE WORLD'S INJUSTICES.

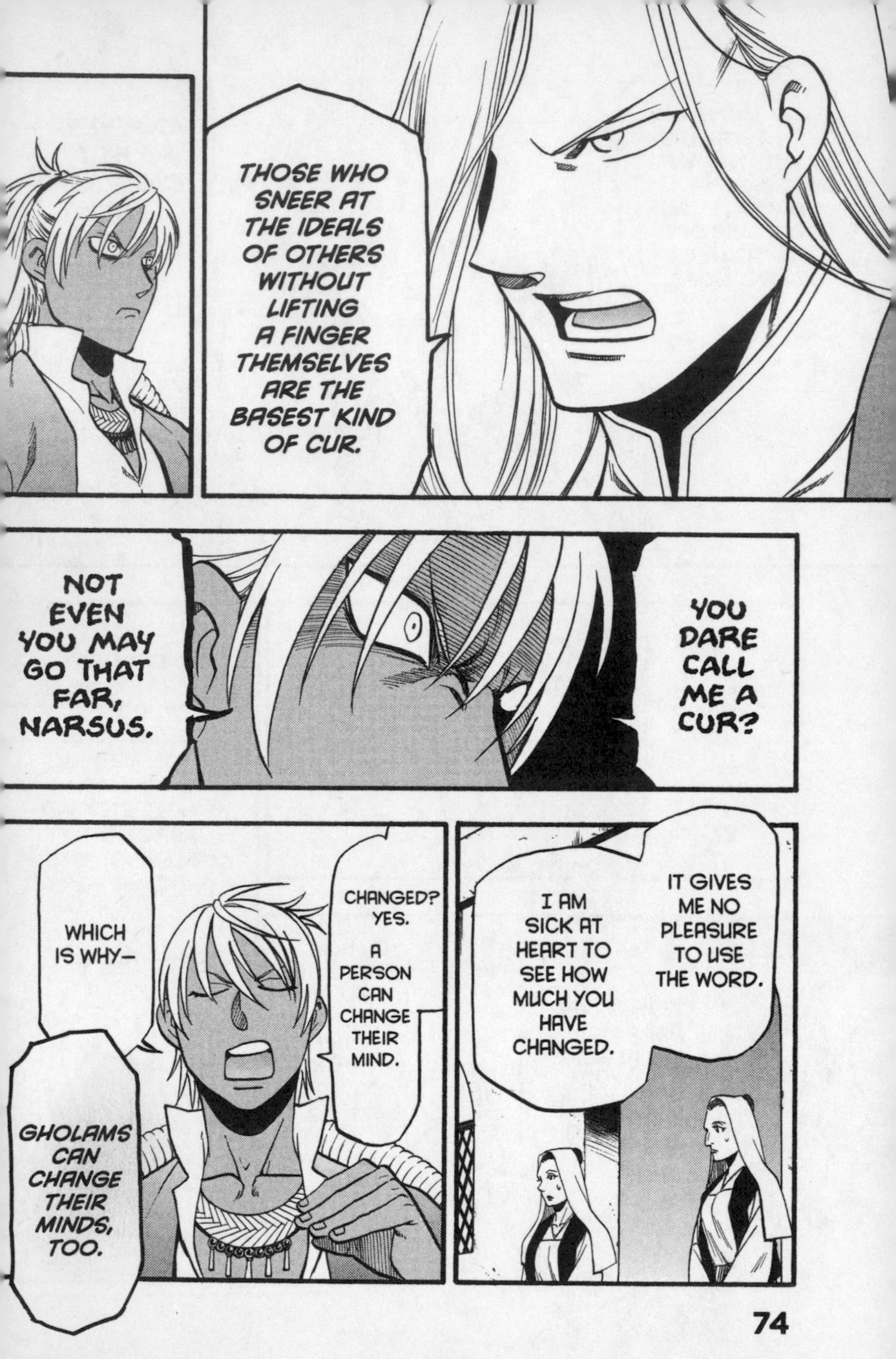
THOSE WHO SNEER AT THE IDEALS OF OTHERS WITHOUT LIFTING A FINGER THEMSELVES ARE THE BASEST KIND OF CUR.
YOU DARE CALL ME A CUR?
NOT EVEN YOU MAY GO THAT FAR, NARSUS.
IT GIVES ME NO PLEASURE TO USE THE WORD.
I AM SICK AT HEART TO SEE HOW MUCH YOU HAVE CHANGED.
CHANGED? YES.
A PERSON CAN CHANGE THEIR MIND.
WHICH IS WHY—
GHOLAMS CAN CHANGE THEIR MINDS, TOO.

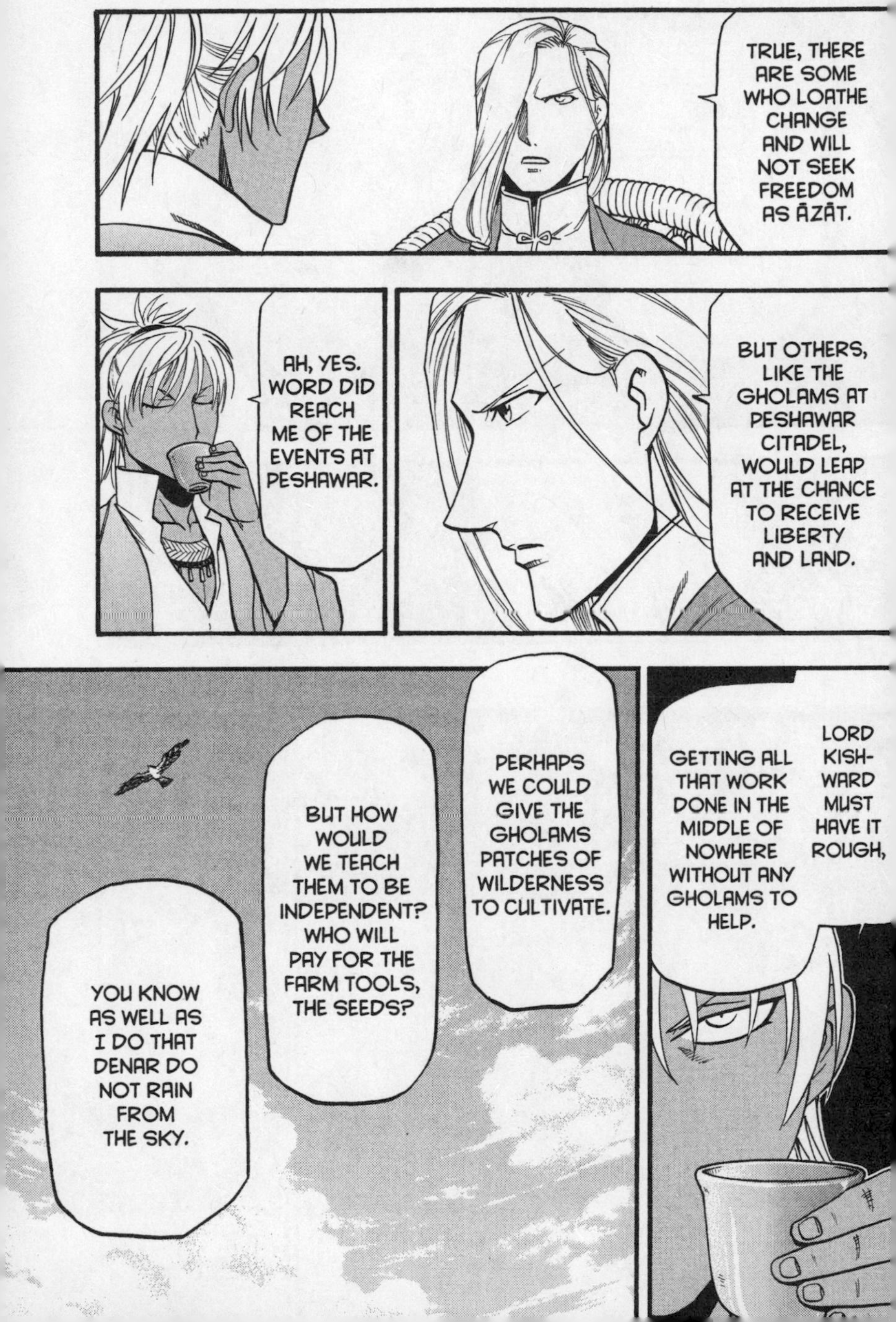
TRUE, THERE ARE SOME WHO LOATHE CHANGE AND WILL NOT SEEK FREEDOM AS ĀZĀT.
BUT OTHERS, LIKE THE GHOLAMS AT PESHAWAR CITADEL, WOULD LEAP AT THE CHANCE TO RECEIVE LIBERTY AND LAND.
AH, YES. WORD DID REACH ME OF THE EVENTS AT PESHAWAR.
LORD KISH-WARD MUST HAVE IT ROUGH,
GETTING ALL THAT WORK DONE IN THE MIDDLE OF NOWHERE WITHOUT ANY GHOLAMS TO HELP.
PERHAPS WE COULD GIVE THE GHOLAMS PATCHES OF WILDERNESS TO CULTIVATE.
BUT HOW WOULD WE TEACH THEM TO BE INDEPENDENT? WHO WILL PAY FOR THE FARM TOOLS, THE SEEDS?
YOU KNOW AS WELL AS I DO THAT DENAR DO NOT RAIN FROM THE SKY.

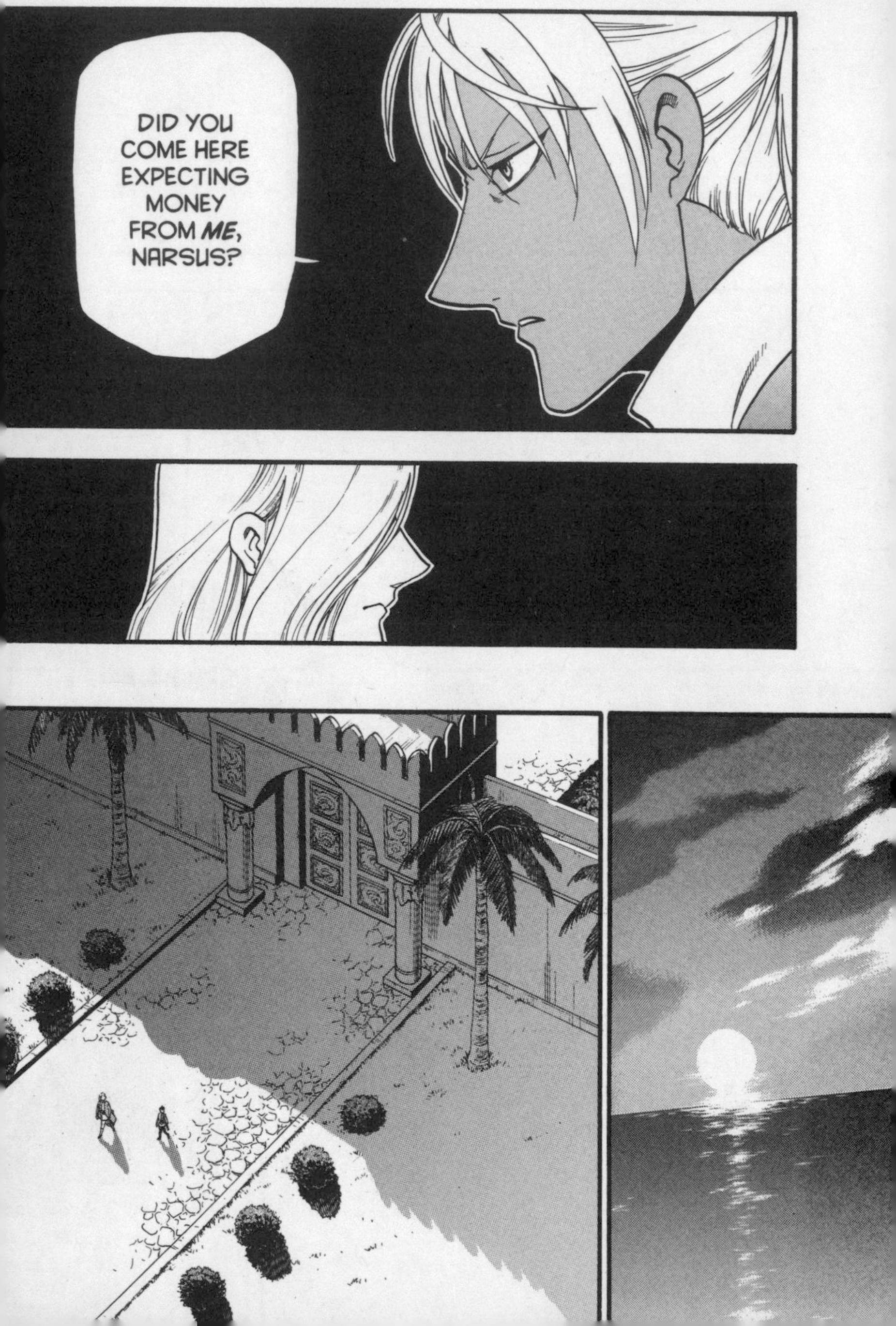
DID YOU
COME HERE
EXPECTING
MONEY
FROM *ME*,
NARSUS?

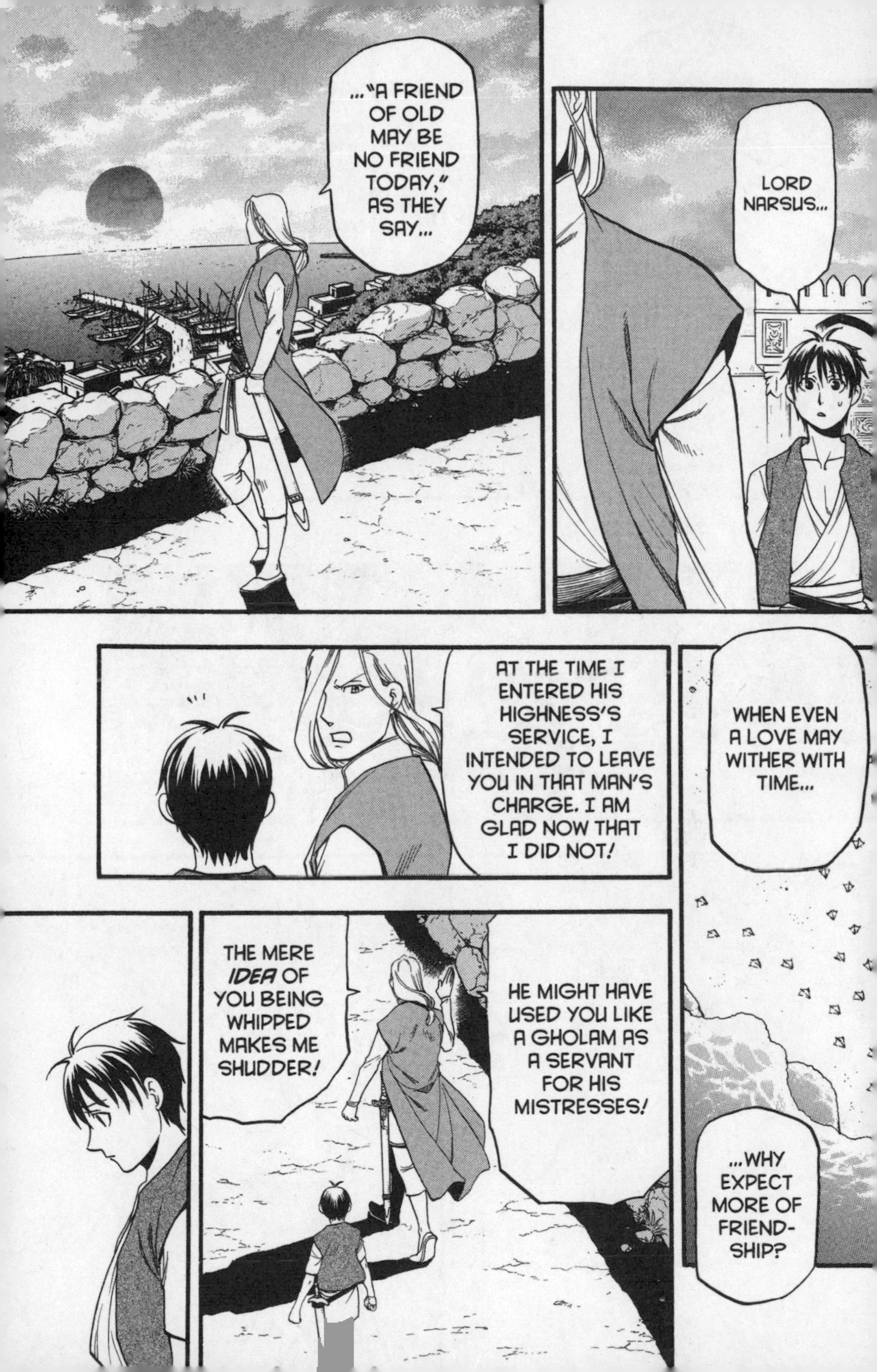
LORD NARSUS...
..."A FRIEND OF OLD MAY BE NO FRIEND TODAY," AS THEY SAY...
WHEN EVEN A LOVE MAY WITHER WITH TIME...
...WHY EXPECT MORE OF FRIEND-SHIP?
AT THE TIME I ENTERED HIS HIGHNESS'S SERVICE, I INTENDED TO LEAVE YOU IN THAT MAN'S CHARGE. I AM GLAD NOW THAT I DID NOT!
HE MIGHT HAVE USED YOU LIKE A GHOLAM AS A SERVANT FOR HIS MISTRESSES!
THE MERE *IDEA* OF YOU BEING WHIPPED MAKES ME SHUDDER!

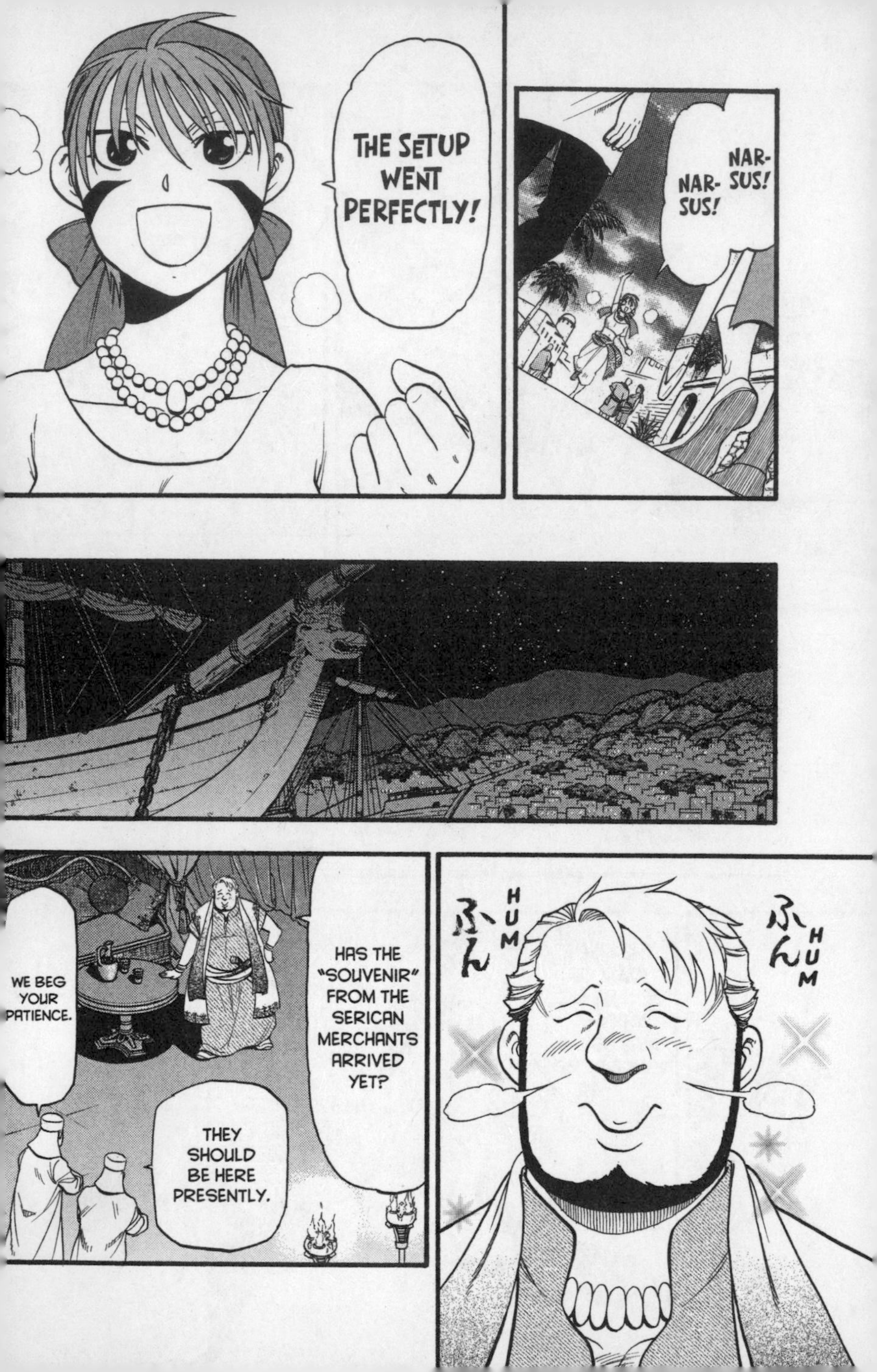
NAR-SUS!
NAR-SUS!
THE SETUP WENT PERFECTLY!
ふん HUM
ふん HUM
HAS THE "SOUVENIR" FROM THE SERICAN MERCHANTS ARRIVED YET?
THEY SHOULD BE HERE PRESENTLY.
WE BEG YOUR PATIENCE.

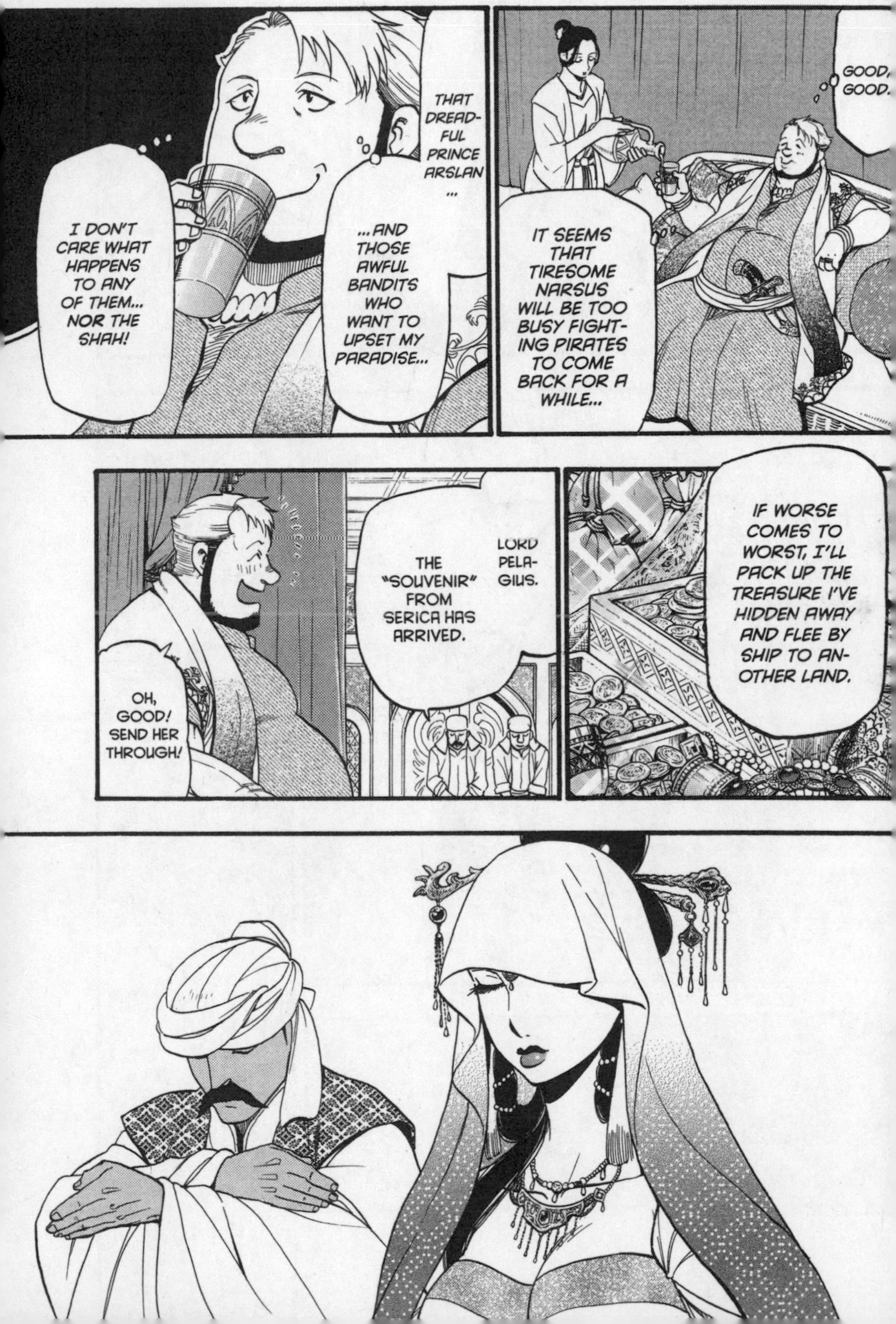
GOOD, GOOD.
IT SEEMS THAT TIRESOME NARSUS WILL BE TOO BUSY FIGHTING PIRATES TO COME BACK FOR A WHILE...
THAT DREADFUL PRINCE ARSLAN ...
...AND THOSE AWFUL BANDITS WHO WANT TO UPSET MY PARADISE...
I DON'T CARE WHAT HAPPENS TO ANY OF THEM... NOR THE SHAH!
IF WORSE COMES TO WORST, I'LL PACK UP THE TREASURE I'VE HIDDEN AWAY AND FLEE BY SHIP TO ANOTHER LAND.
LORD PELAGIUS.
THE "SOUVENIR" FROM SERICA HAS ARRIVED.
OH, GOOD! SEND HER THROUGH!

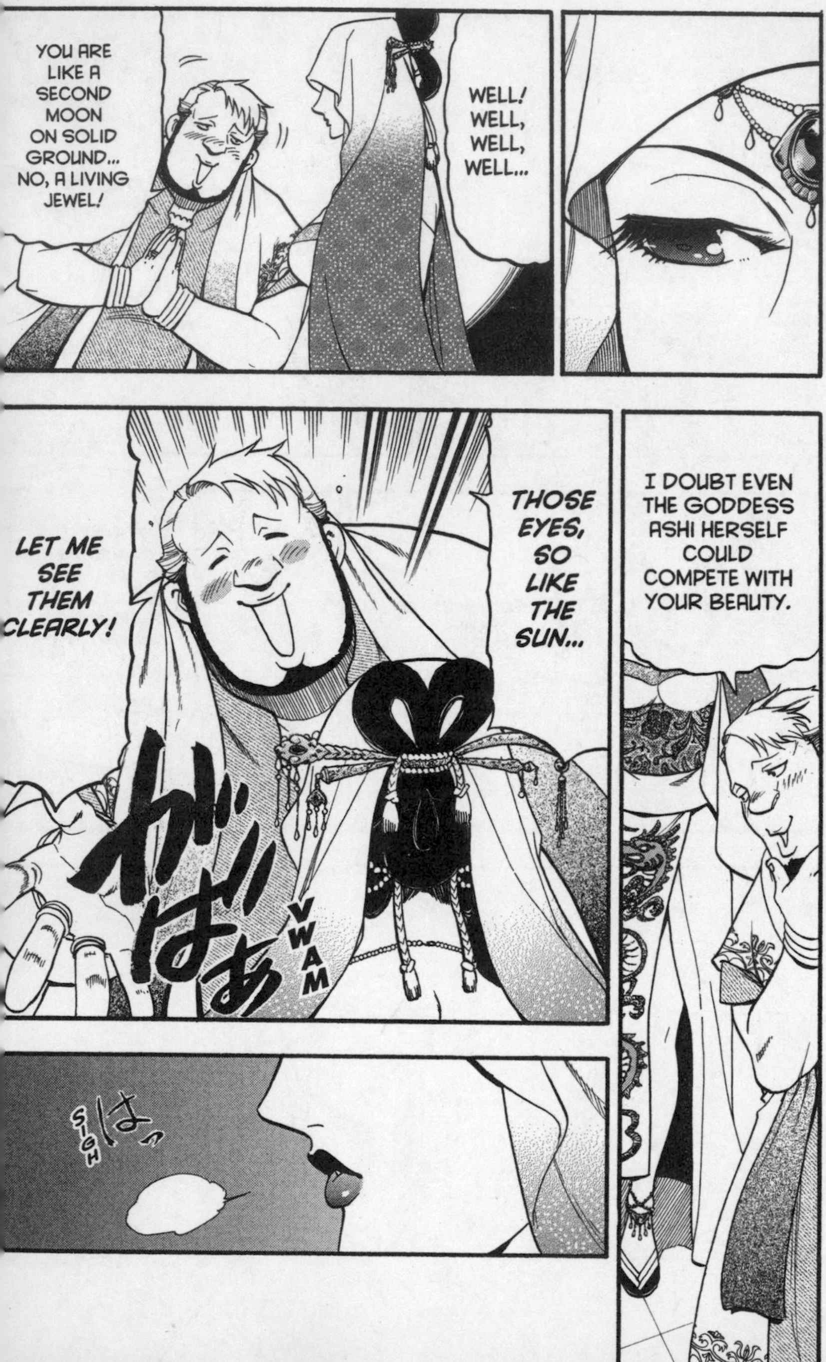
WELL! WELL, WELL, WELL...
YOU ARE LIKE A SECOND MOON ON SOLID GROUND... NO, A LIVING JEWEL!
I DOUBT EVEN THE GODDESS ASHI HERSELF COULD COMPETE WITH YOUR BEAUTY.
THOSE EYES, SO LIKE THE SUN...
LET ME SEE THEM CLEARLY!
がばぁ
VWAM
はっ
SIGH

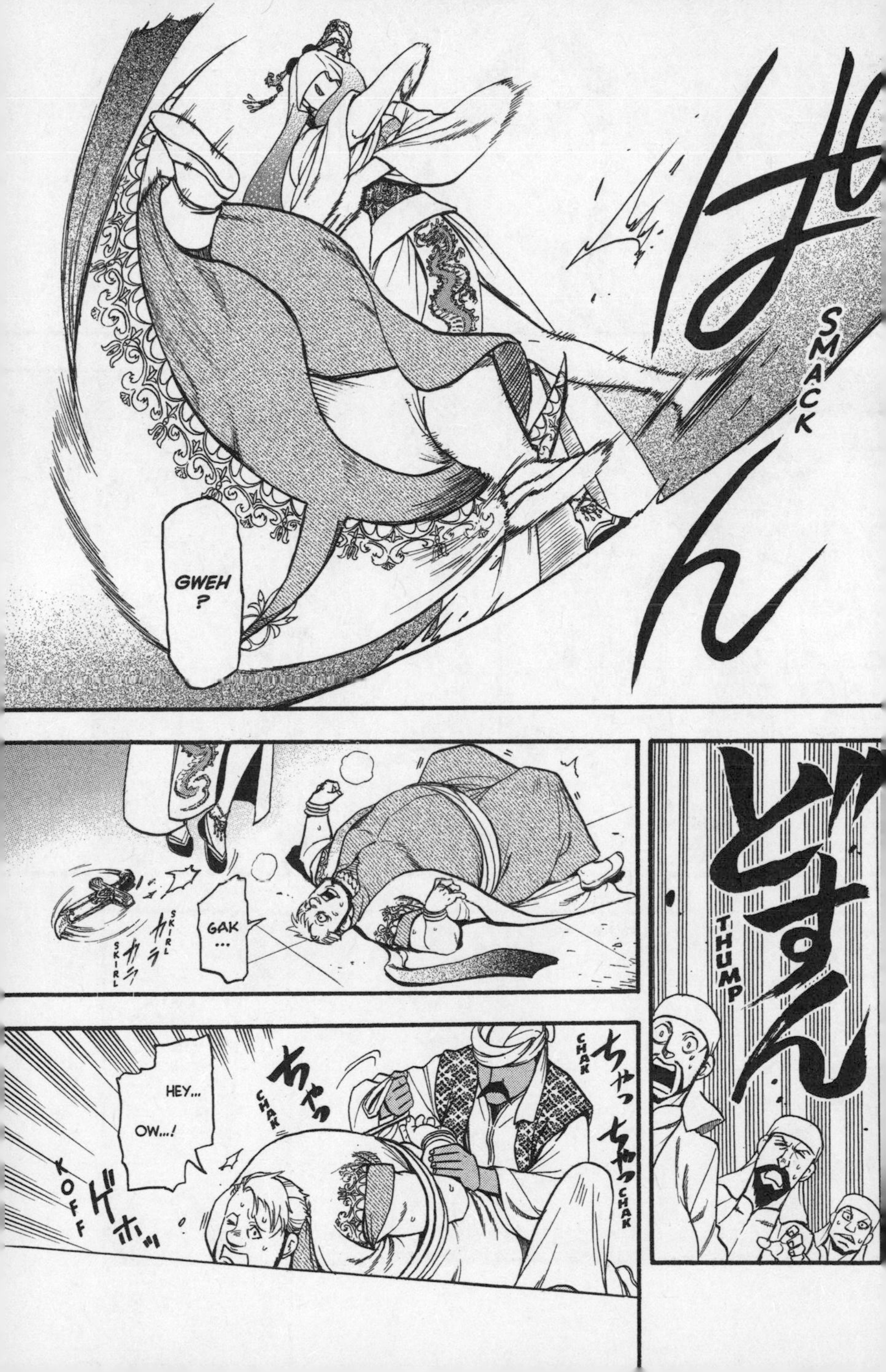
SMACK
GWEH ?
どすん
THUMP
GAK ...
カラ
SKIRL
カラ
SKIRL
ちゃっ
CHAK
ちゃっ
CHAK
ちゃっ
CHAK
HEY...
OW...!
ゲホッ
KOFF

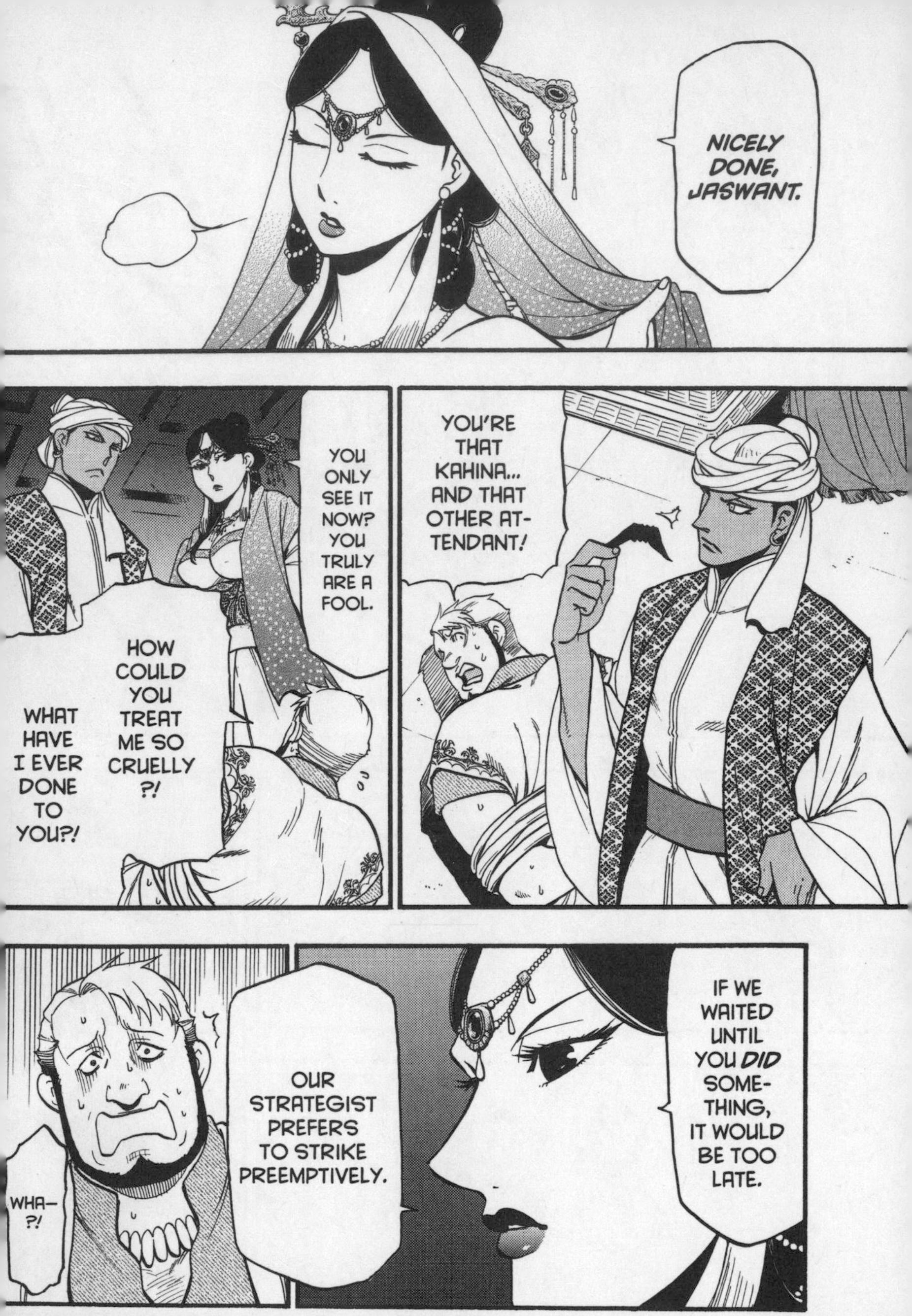
NICELY DONE, JASWANT.
YOU'RE THAT KAHINA... AND THAT OTHER ATTENDANT!
YOU ONLY SEE IT NOW? YOU TRULY ARE A FOOL.
HOW COULD YOU TREAT ME SO CRUELLY?!
WHAT HAVE I EVER DONE TO YOU?!
IF WE WAITED UNTIL YOU *DID* SOMETHING, IT WOULD BE TOO LATE.
OUR STRATEGIST PREFERS TO STRIKE PREEMPTIVELY.
WHA—?!

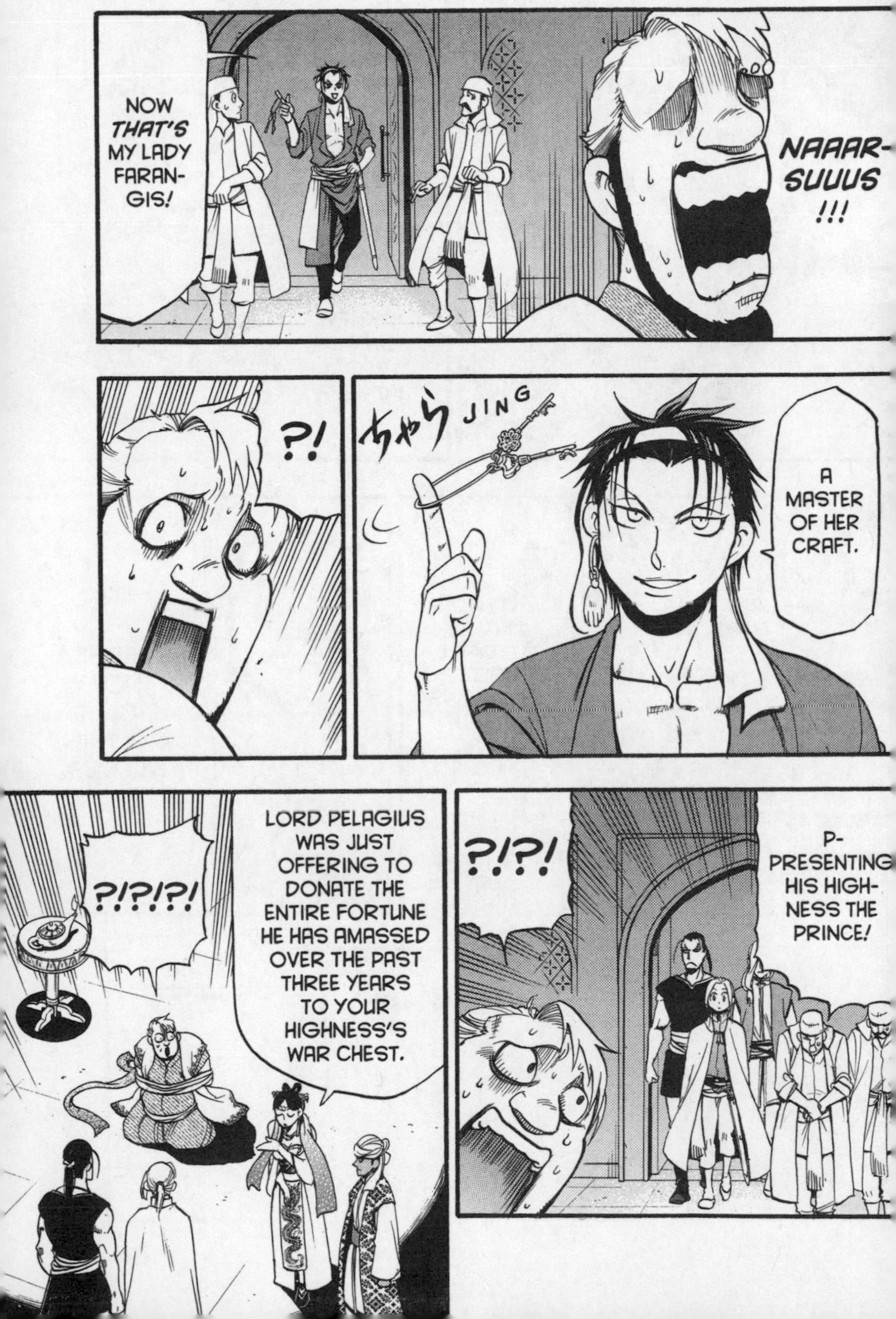
NAAAR-SUUUS!!!
NOW THAT'S MY LADY FARANGIS!
ちゃら JING
A MASTER OF HER CRAFT.
?!
P-PRESENTING HIS HIGHNESS THE PRINCE!
?!?!
LORD PELAGIUS WAS JUST OFFERING TO DONATE THE ENTIRE FORTUNE HE HAS AMASSED OVER THE PAST THREE YEARS TO YOUR HIGHNESS'S WAR CHEST.
?!?!?!

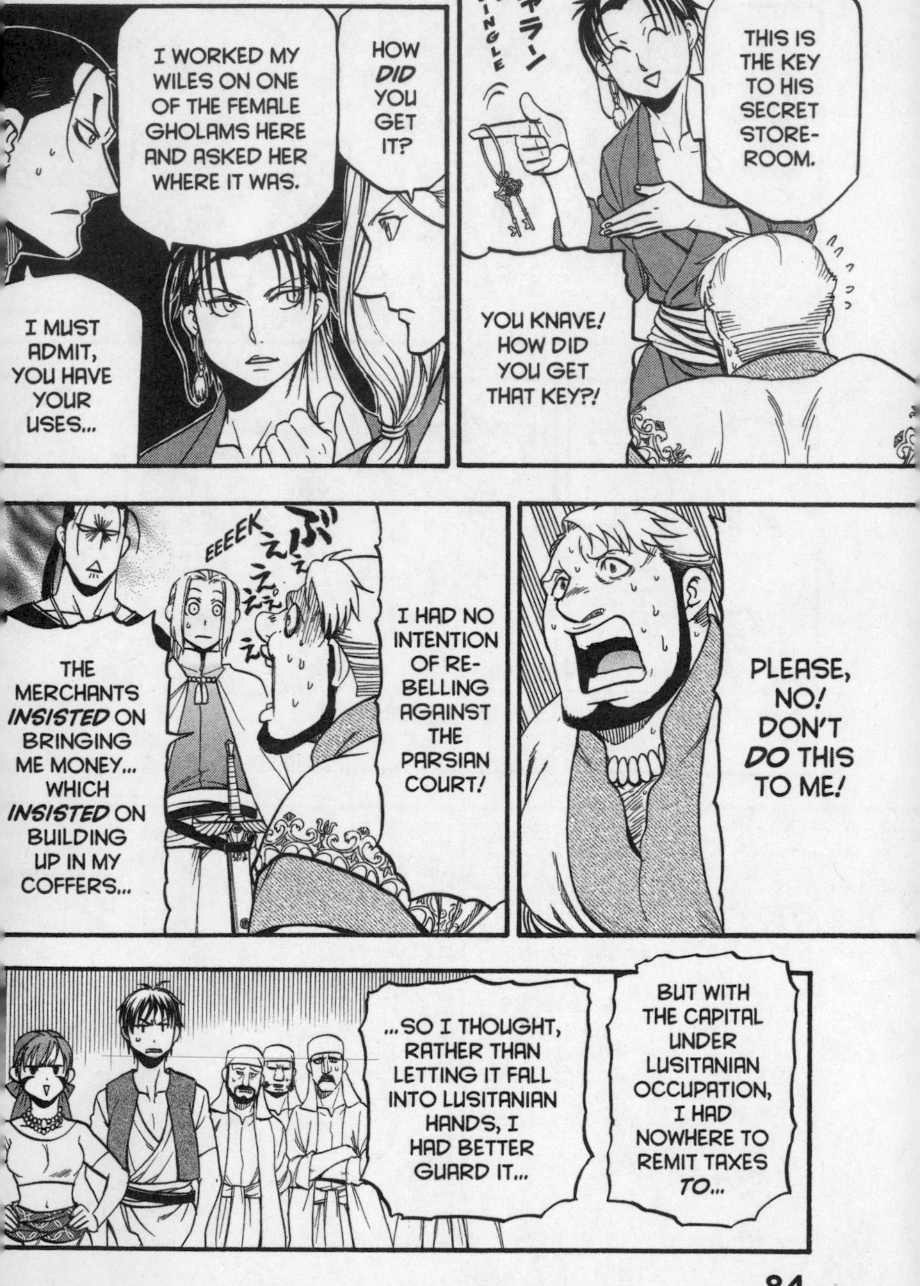
チャラーン
JINGLE
THIS IS THE KEY TO HIS SECRET STORE-ROOM.
YOU KNAVE! HOW DID YOU GET THAT KEY?!
HOW *DID* YOU GET IT?
I WORKED MY WILES ON ONE OF THE FEMALE GHOLAMS HERE AND ASKED HER WHERE IT WAS.
I MUST ADMIT, YOU HAVE YOUR USES...
PLEASE, NO! DON'T *DO* THIS TO ME!
ぶえええええ
EEEEK
I HAD NO INTENTION OF RE-BELLING AGAINST THE PARSIAN COURT!
THE MERCHANTS *INSISTED* ON BRINGING ME MONEY... WHICH *INSISTED* ON BUILDING UP IN MY COFFERS...
BUT WITH THE CAPITAL UNDER LUSITANIAN OCCUPATION, I HAD NOWHERE TO REMIT TAXES *TO*...
...SO I THOUGHT, RATHER THAN LETTING IT FALL INTO LUSITANIAN HANDS, I HAD BETTER GUARD IT...

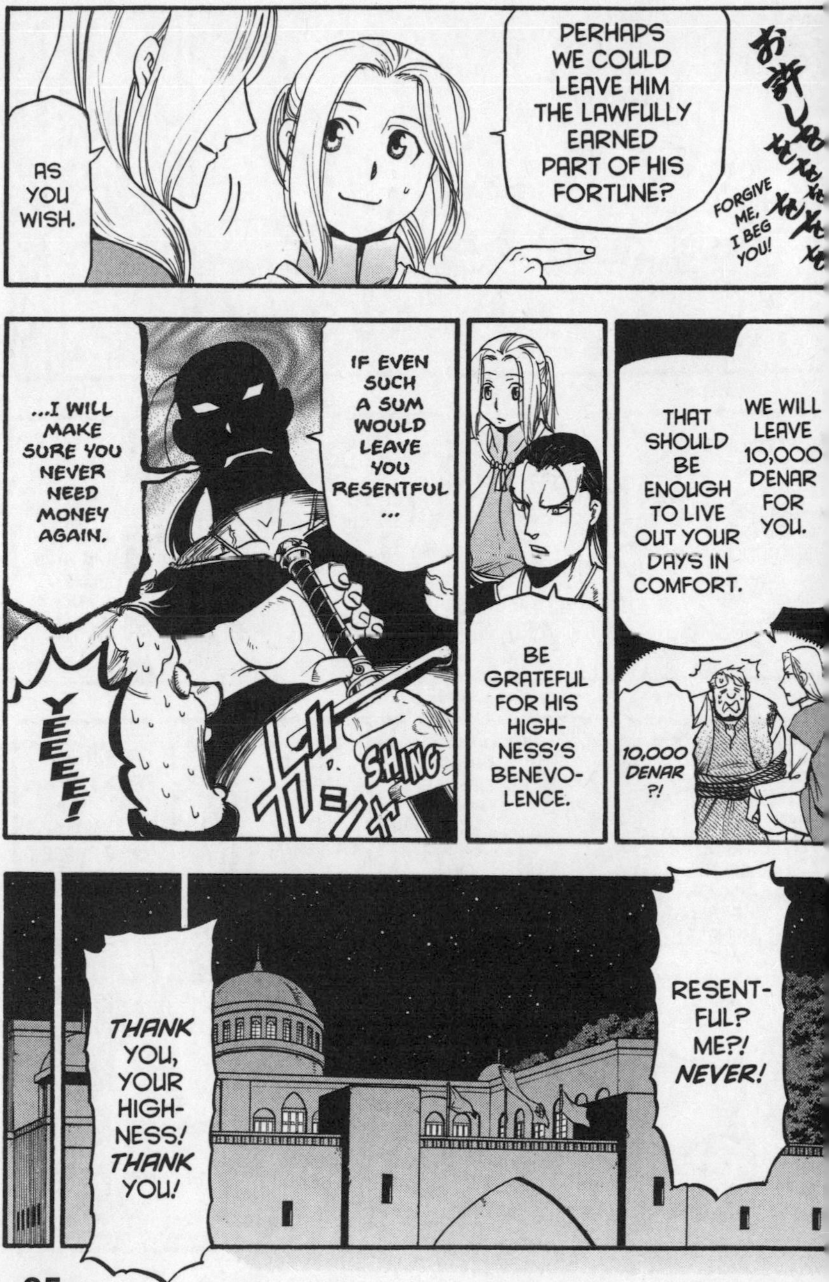

FORGIVE ME, I BEG YOU!
PERHAPS WE COULD LEAVE HIM THE LAWFULLY EARNED PART OF HIS FORTUNE?
AS YOU WISH.
WE WILL LEAVE 10,000 DENAR FOR YOU.
THAT SHOULD BE ENOUGH TO LIVE OUT YOUR DAYS IN COMFORT.
10,000 DENAR?!
BE GRATEFUL FOR HIS HIGH-NESS'S BENEVO-LENCE.
IF EVEN SUCH A SUM WOULD LEAVE YOU RESENTFUL...
...I WILL MAKE SURE YOU NEVER NEED MONEY AGAIN.
SHING
YEEEE!
RESENT-FUL? ME?! NEVER!
THANK YOU, YOUR HIGH-NESS! THANK YOU!

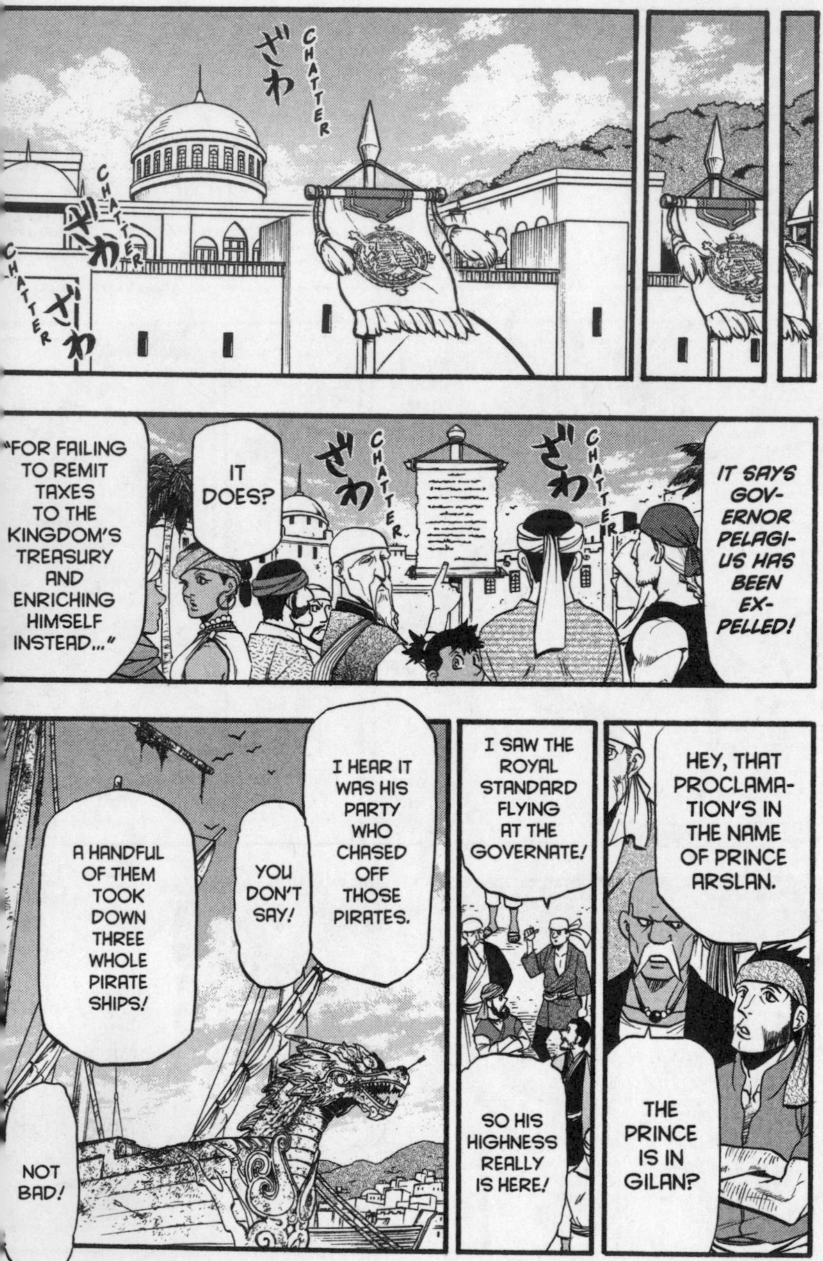

ざわ CHATTER
ざわ CHATTER
ざわ CHATTER
IT SAYS GOVERNOR PELAGIUS HAS BEEN EXPELLED!
ざわ CHATTER
ざわ CHATTER
IT DOES?
"FOR FAILING TO REMIT TAXES TO THE KINGDOM'S TREASURY AND ENRICHING HIMSELF INSTEAD..."
HEY, THAT PROCLAMATION'S IN THE NAME OF PRINCE ARSLAN.
THE PRINCE IS IN GILAN?
I SAW THE ROYAL STANDARD FLYING AT THE GOVERNATE!
SO HIS HIGHNESS REALLY IS HERE!
I HEAR IT WAS HIS PARTY WHO CHASED OFF THOSE PIRATES.
YOU DON'T SAY!
A HANDFUL OF THEM TOOK DOWN THREE WHOLE PIRATE SHIPS!
NOT BAD!

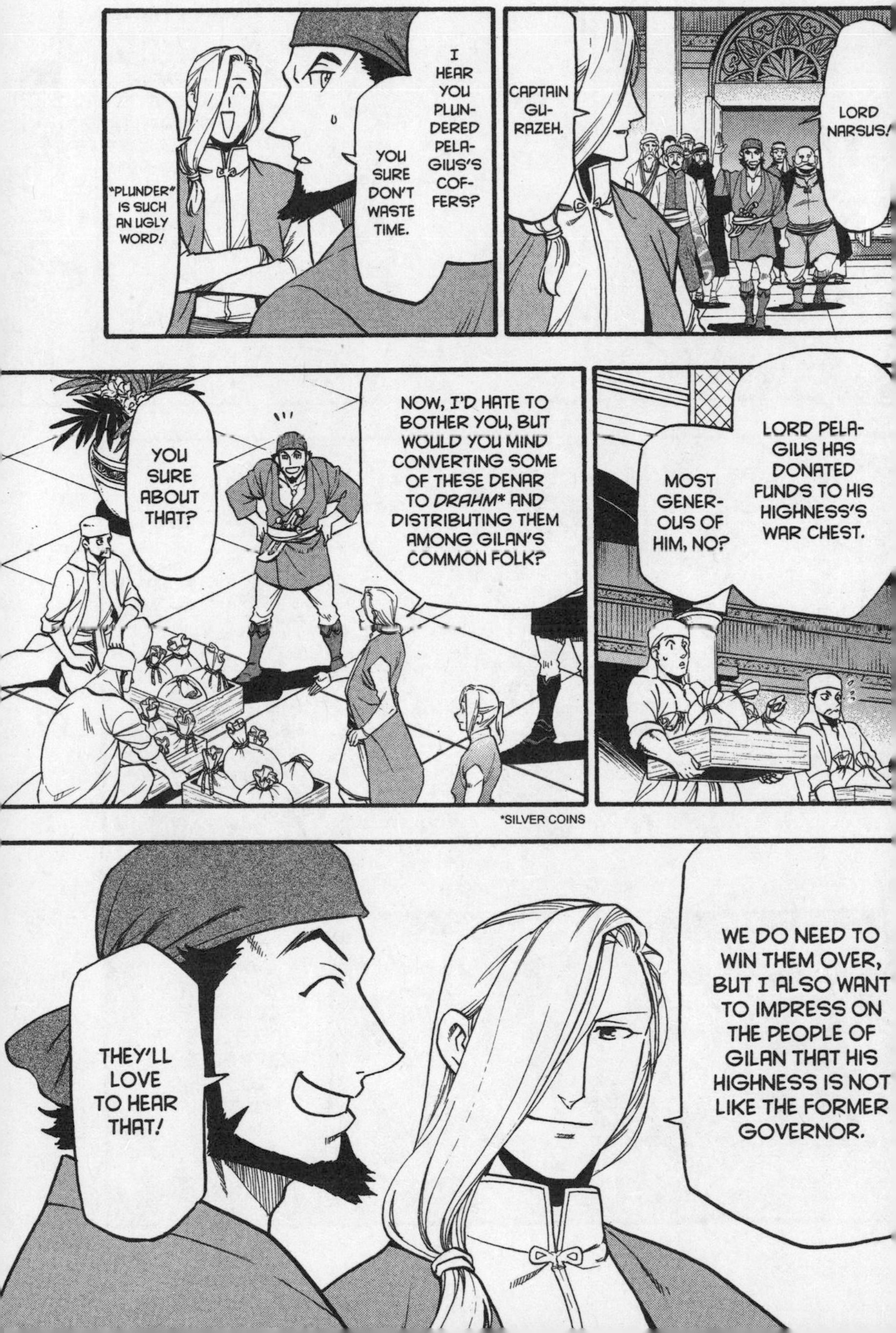
LORD NARSUS!
CAPTAIN GURAZEH.
I HEAR YOU PLUNDERED PELAGIUS'S COFFERS?
YOU SURE DON'T WASTE TIME.
"PLUNDER" IS SUCH AN UGLY WORD!
LORD PELAGIUS HAS DONATED FUNDS TO HIS HIGHNESS'S WAR CHEST.
MOST GENEROUS OF HIM, NO?
NOW, I'D HATE TO BOTHER YOU, BUT WOULD YOU MIND CONVERTING SOME OF THESE DENAR TO *DRAHM** AND DISTRIBUTING THEM AMONG GILAN'S COMMON FOLK?
YOU SURE ABOUT THAT?
WE DO NEED TO WIN THEM OVER, BUT I ALSO WANT TO IMPRESS ON THE PEOPLE OF GILAN THAT HIS HIGHNESS IS NOT LIKE THE FORMER GOVERNOR.
THEY'LL LOVE TO HEAR THAT!

*SILVER COINS

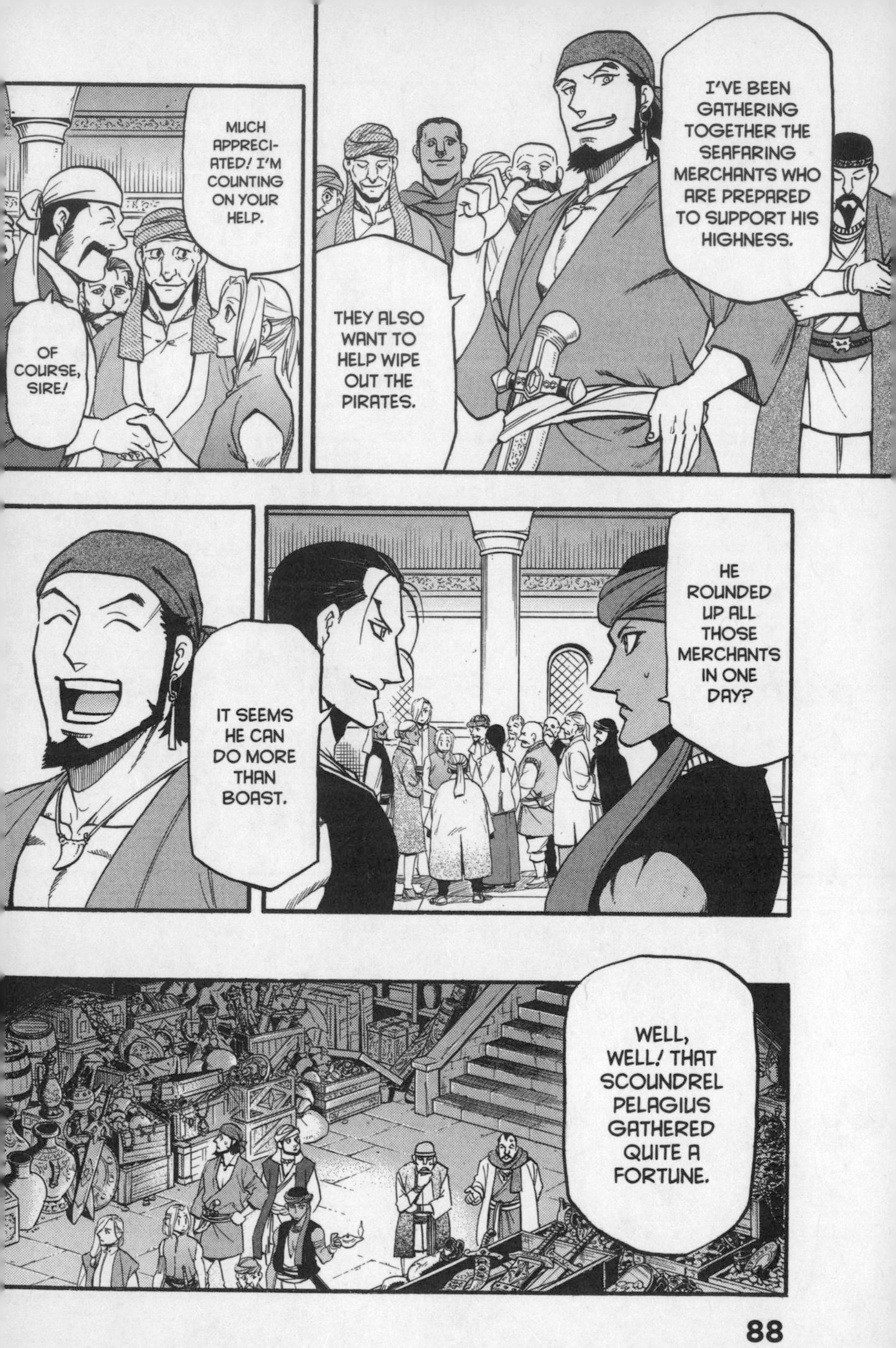
I'VE BEEN GATHERING TOGETHER THE SEAFARING MERCHANTS WHO ARE PREPARED TO SUPPORT HIS HIGHNESS.
THEY ALSO WANT TO HELP WIPE OUT THE PIRATES.
MUCH APPRECIATED! I'M COUNTING ON YOUR HELP.
OF COURSE, SIRE!
HE ROUNDED UP ALL THOSE MERCHANTS IN ONE DAY?
IT SEEMS HE CAN DO MORE THAN BOAST.
WELL, WELL! THAT SCOUNDREL PELAGIUS GATHERED QUITE A FORTUNE.

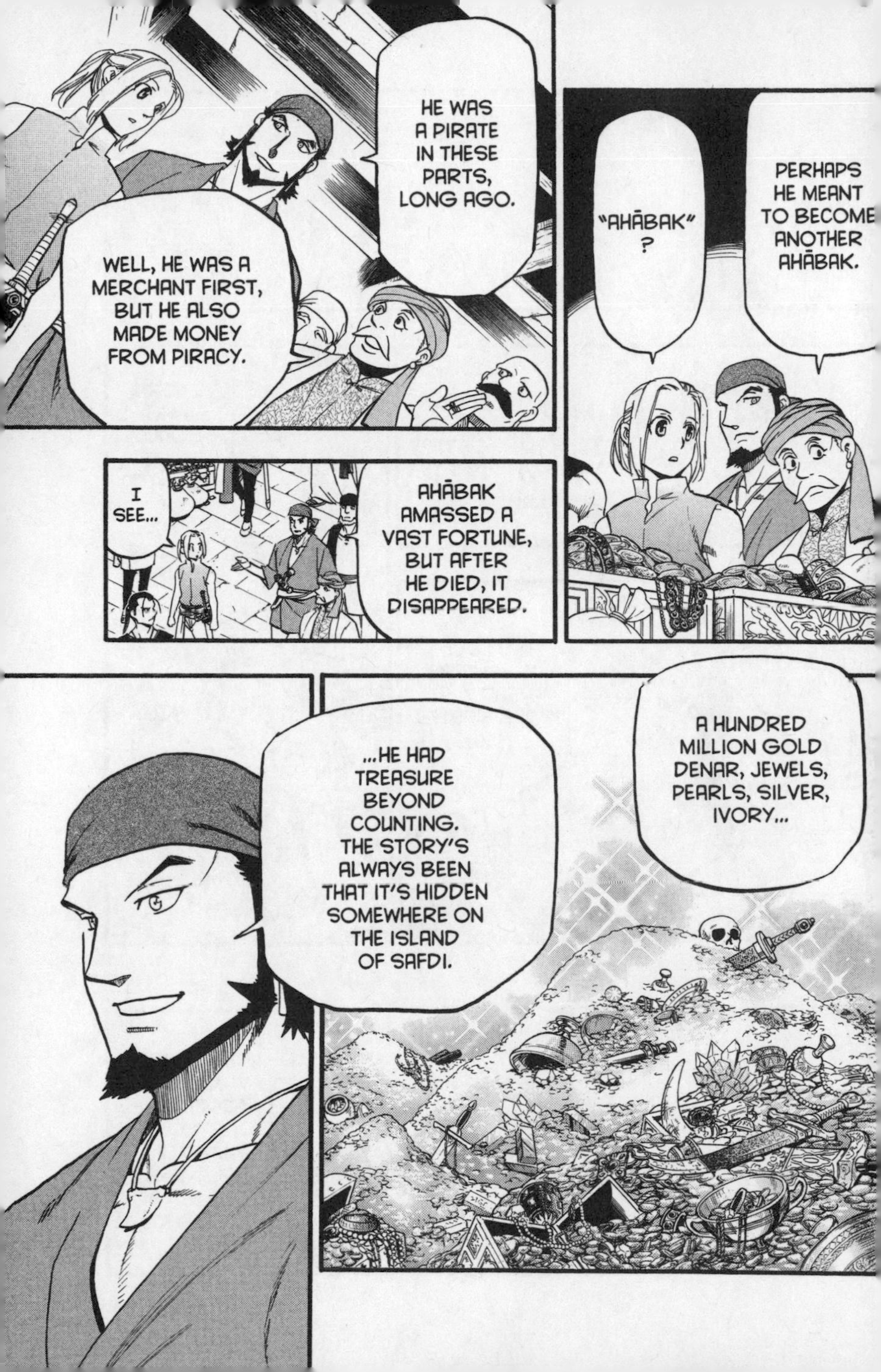
PERHAPS HE MEANT TO BECOME ANOTHER AHĀBAK.
"AHĀBAK"?
HE WAS A PIRATE IN THESE PARTS, LONG AGO.
WELL, HE WAS A MERCHANT FIRST, BUT HE ALSO MADE MONEY FROM PIRACY.
AHĀBAK AMASSED A VAST FORTUNE, BUT AFTER HE DIED, IT DISAPPEARED.
I SEE...
A HUNDRED MILLION GOLD DENAR, JEWELS, PEARLS, SILVER, IVORY...
...HE HAD TREASURE BEYOND COUNTING. THE STORY'S ALWAYS BEEN THAT IT'S HIDDEN SOMEWHERE ON THE ISLAND OF SAFDI.

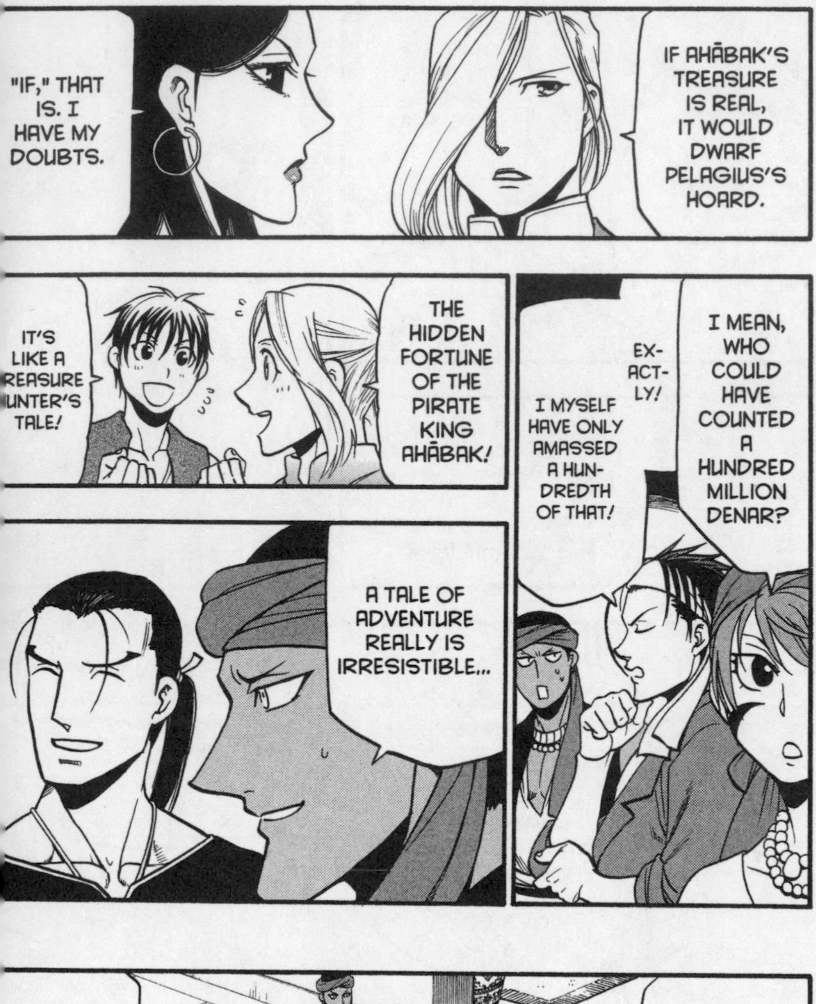
IF AHĀBAK'S TREASURE IS REAL, IT WOULD DWARF PELAGIUS'S HOARD.
"IF," THAT IS. I HAVE MY DOUBTS.
I MEAN, WHO COULD HAVE COUNTED A HUNDRED MILLION DENAR?
EX-ACT-LY!
I MYSELF HAVE ONLY AMASSED A HUN-DREDTH OF THAT!
THE HIDDEN FORTUNE OF THE PIRATE KING AHĀBAK!
IT'S LIKE A REASURE UNTER'S TALE!
A TALE OF ADVENTURE REALLY IS IRRESISTIBLE...
I'M FOND OF AN ADVENTURE STORY MYSELF, BUT THIS ONE IS TOO ABSURD.
NOR DO WE HAVE ANY TIME FOR TREASURE-HUNTING.

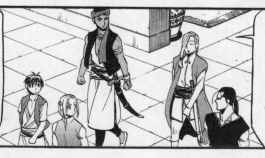

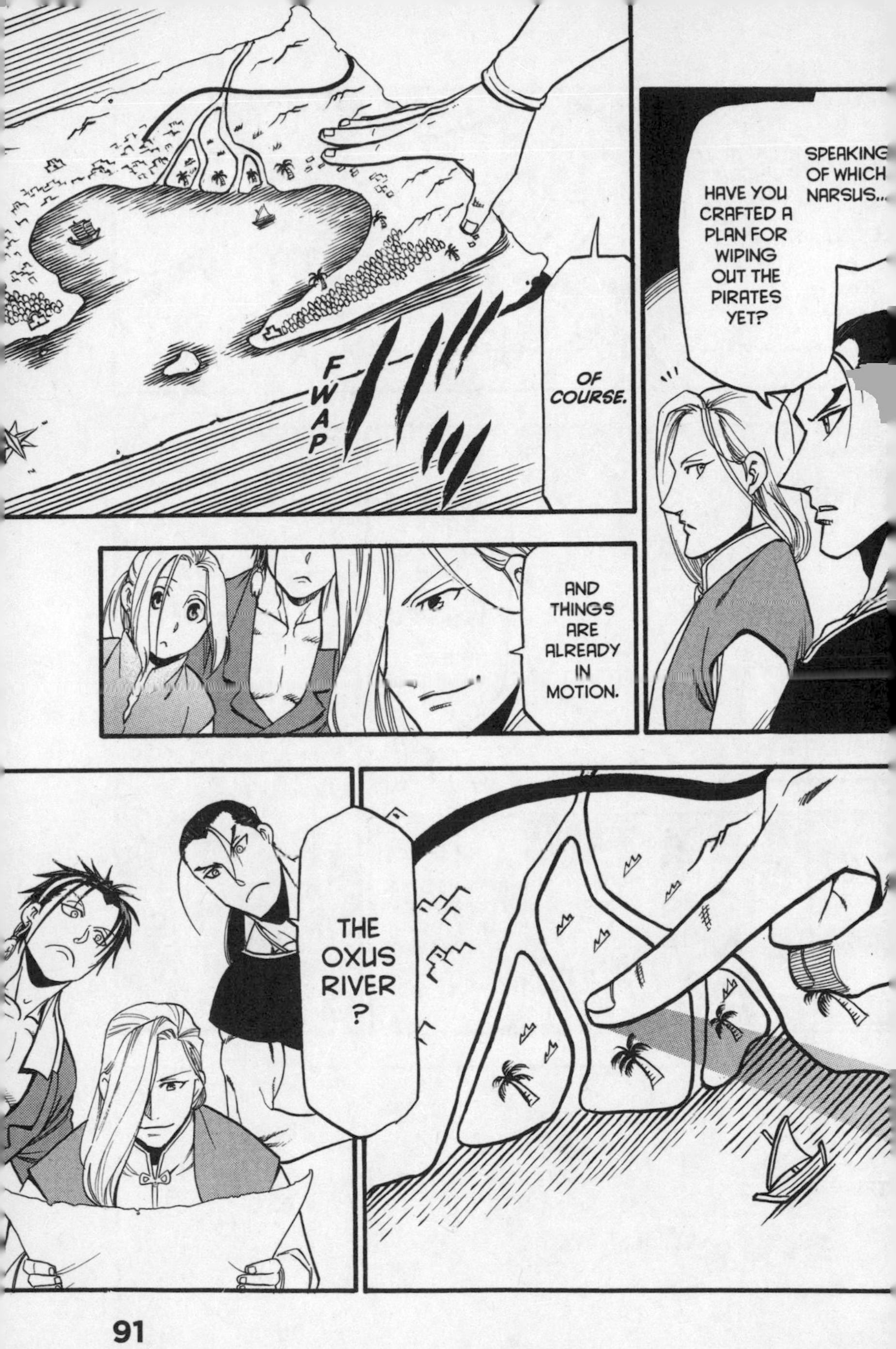
SPEAKING OF WHICH NARSUS...
HAVE YOU CRAFTED A PLAN FOR WIPING OUT THE PIRATES YET?
OF COURSE.
FWAP
AND THINGS ARE ALREADY IN MOTION.
THE OXUS RIVER?

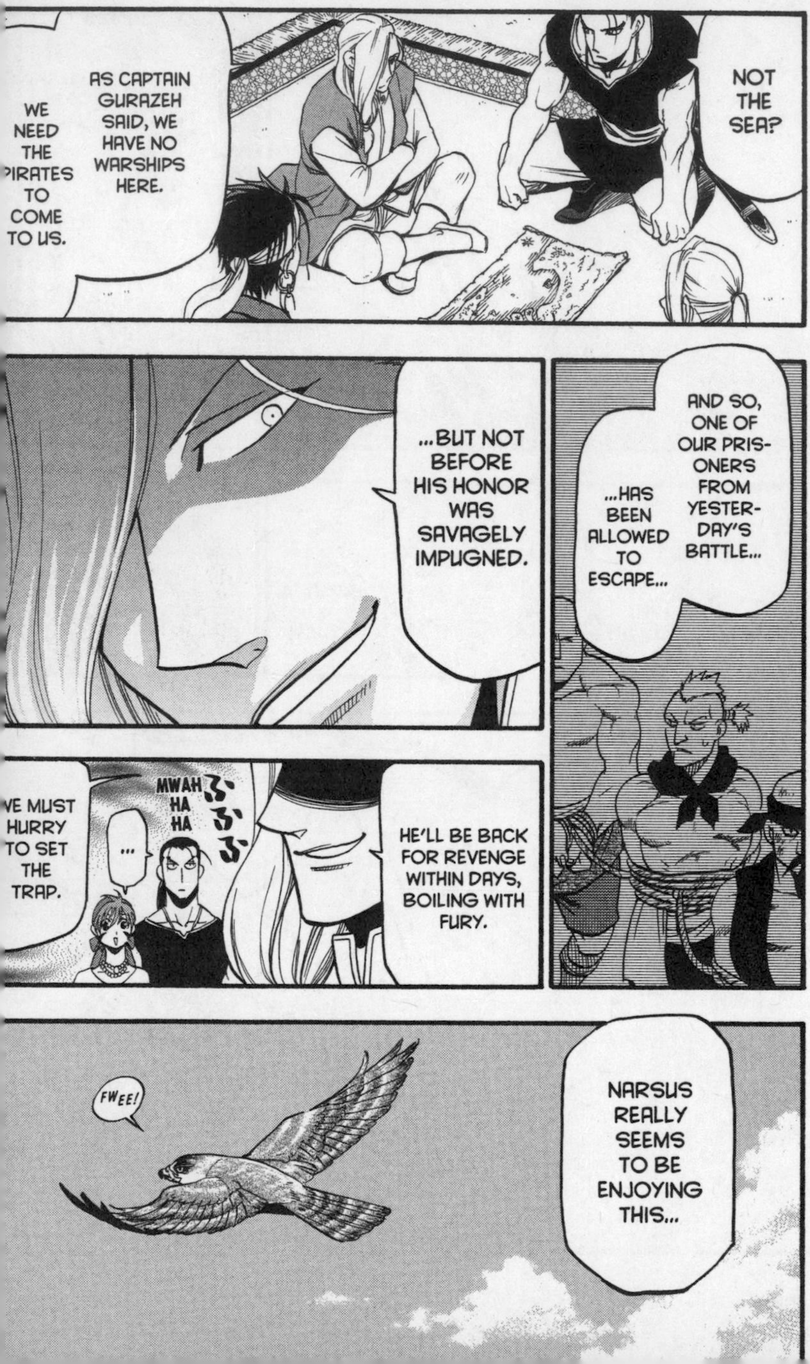
NOT THE SEA?
AS CAPTAIN GURAZEH SAID, WE HAVE NO WARSHIPS HERE.
WE NEED THE PIRATES TO COME TO US.
AND SO, ONE OF OUR PRISONERS FROM YESTERDAY'S BATTLE...
...HAS BEEN ALLOWED TO ESCAPE...
...BUT NOT BEFORE HIS HONOR WAS SAVAGELY IMPUGNED.
HE'LL BE BACK FOR REVENGE WITHIN DAYS, BOILING WITH FURY.
ふふふ
MWAH HA HA
...
WE MUST HURRY TO SET THE TRAP.
NARSUS REALLY SEEMS TO BE ENJOYING THIS...
FWEE!

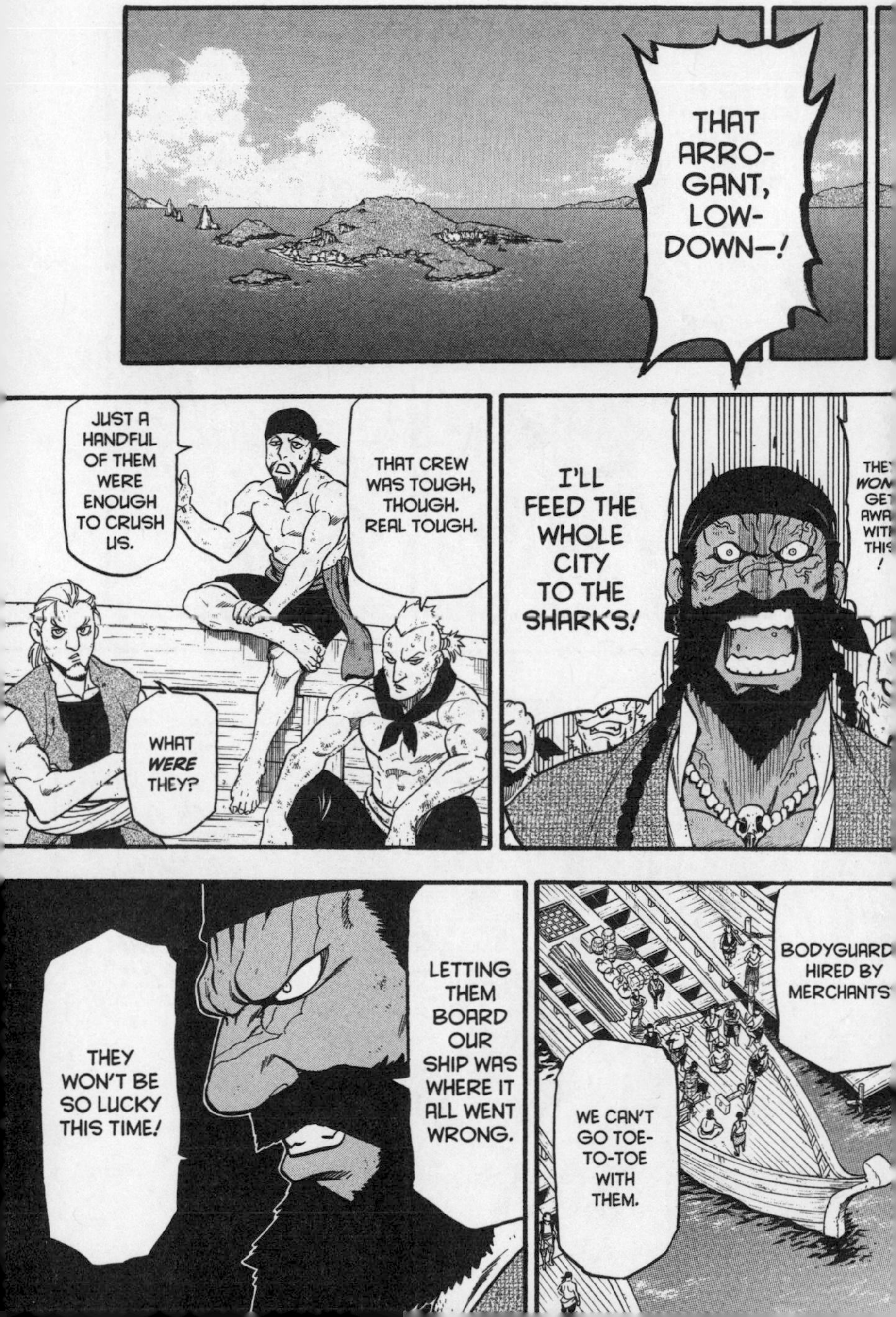
THAT ARRO-GANT, LOW-DOWN—!
I'LL FEED THE WHOLE CITY TO THE SHARKS!
THAT CREW WAS TOUGH, THOUGH. REAL TOUGH.
JUST A HANDFUL OF THEM WERE ENOUGH TO CRUSH US.
WHAT *WERE* THEY?
BODYGUARD HIRED BY MERCHANTS
WE CAN'T GO TOE-TO-TOE WITH THEM.
LETTING THEM BOARD OUR SHIP WAS WHERE IT ALL WENT WRONG.
THEY WON'T BE SO LUCKY THIS TIME!

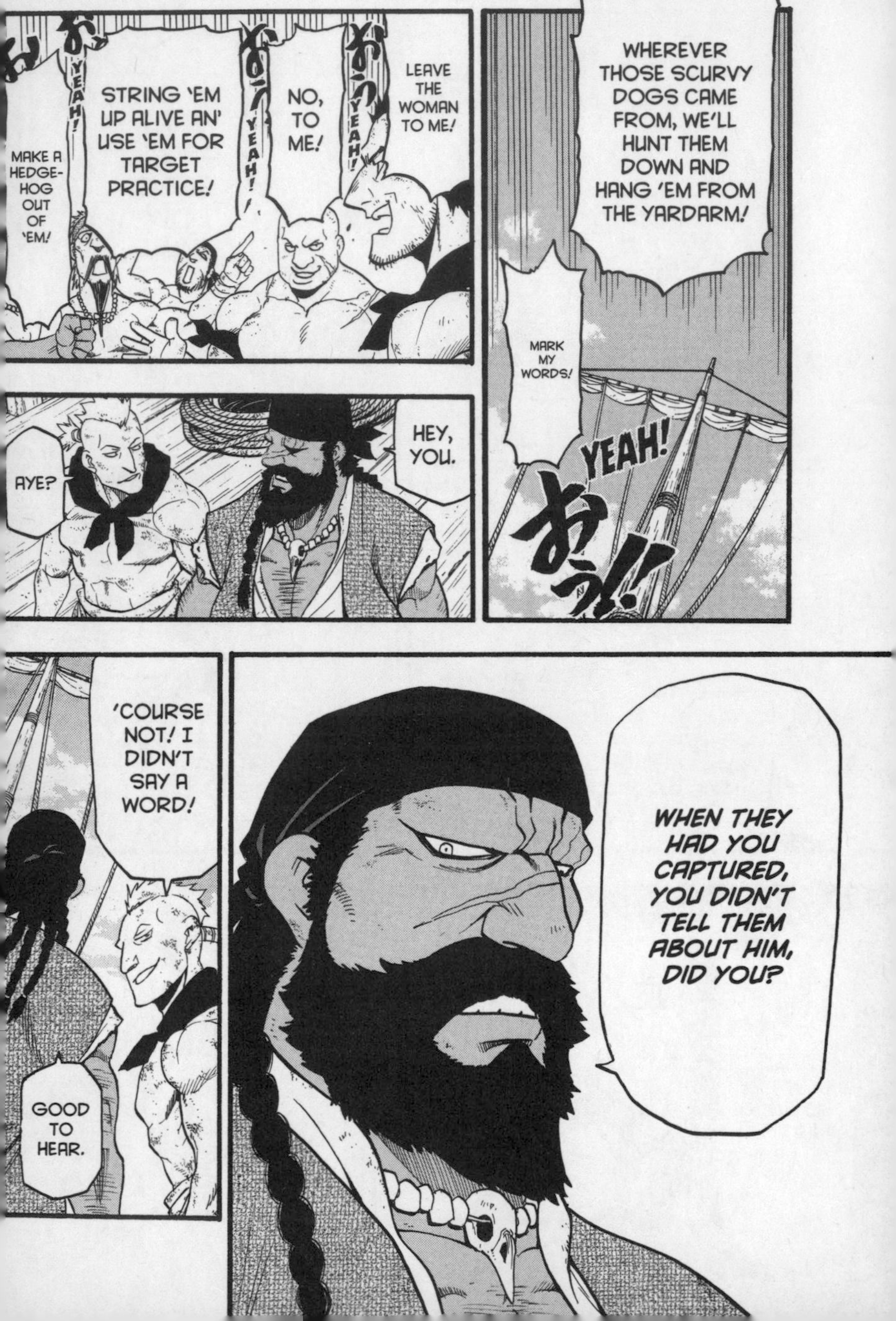
WHEREVER THOSE SCURVY DOGS CAME FROM, WE'LL HUNT THEM DOWN AND HANG 'EM FROM THE YARDARM!
MARK MY WORDS!
YEAH!
おっ!!
LEAVE THE WOMAN TO ME!
YEAH!
NO, TO ME!
YEAH!
STRING 'EM UP ALIVE AN' USE 'EM FOR TARGET PRACTICE!
YEAH!
MAKE A HEDGEHOG OUT OF 'EM!
HEY, YOU.
AYE?
WHEN THEY HAD YOU CAPTURED, YOU DIDN'T TELL THEM ABOUT HIM, DID YOU?
'COURSE NOT! I DIDN'T SAY A WORD!
GOOD TO HEAR.

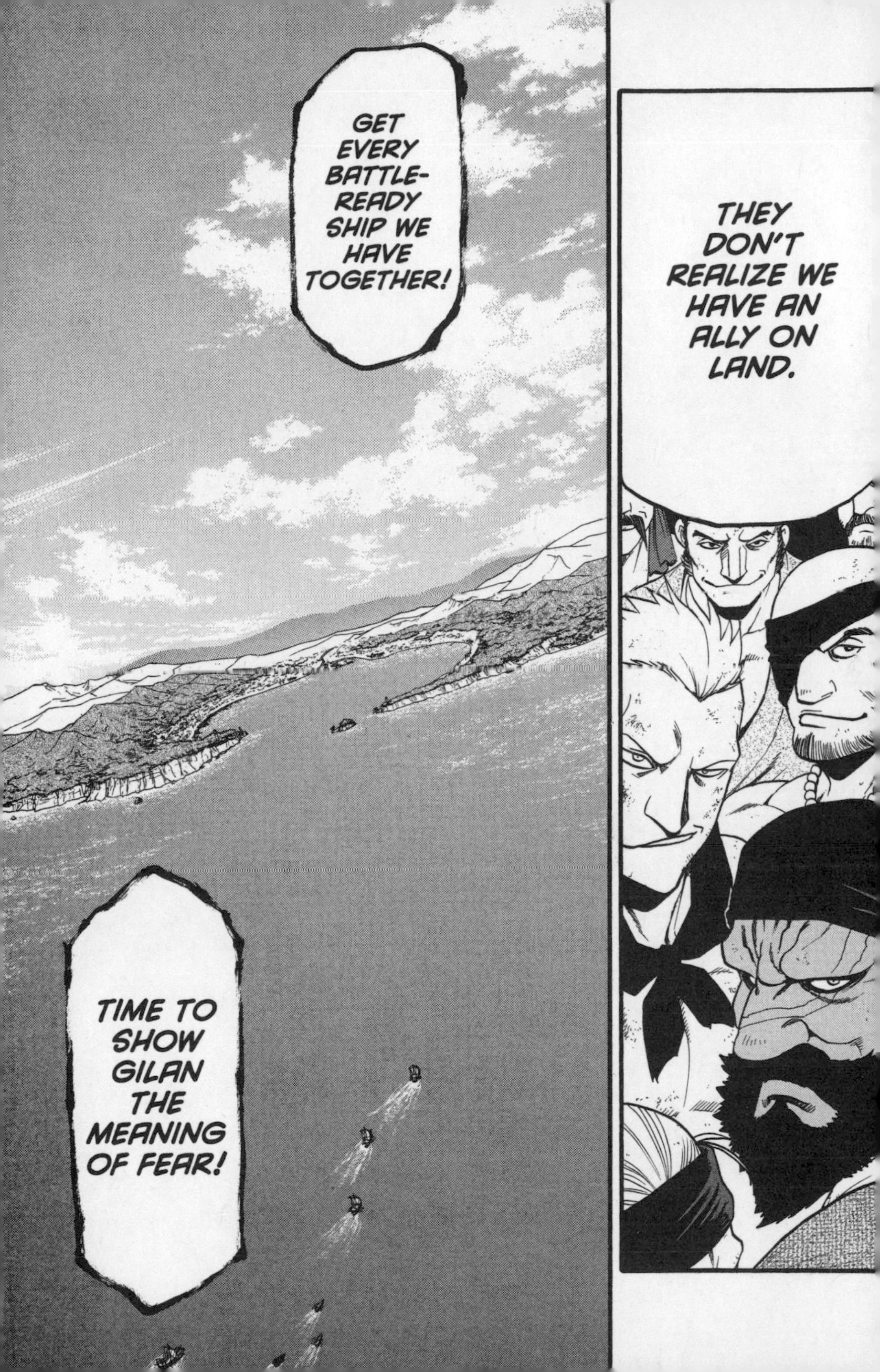
THEY DON'T REALIZE WE HAVE AN ALLY ON LAND.
GET EVERY BATTLE-READY SHIP WE HAVE TOGETHER!
TIME TO SHOW GILAN THE MEANING OF FEAR!

THE HEROIC LEGEND OF
ARSLAN

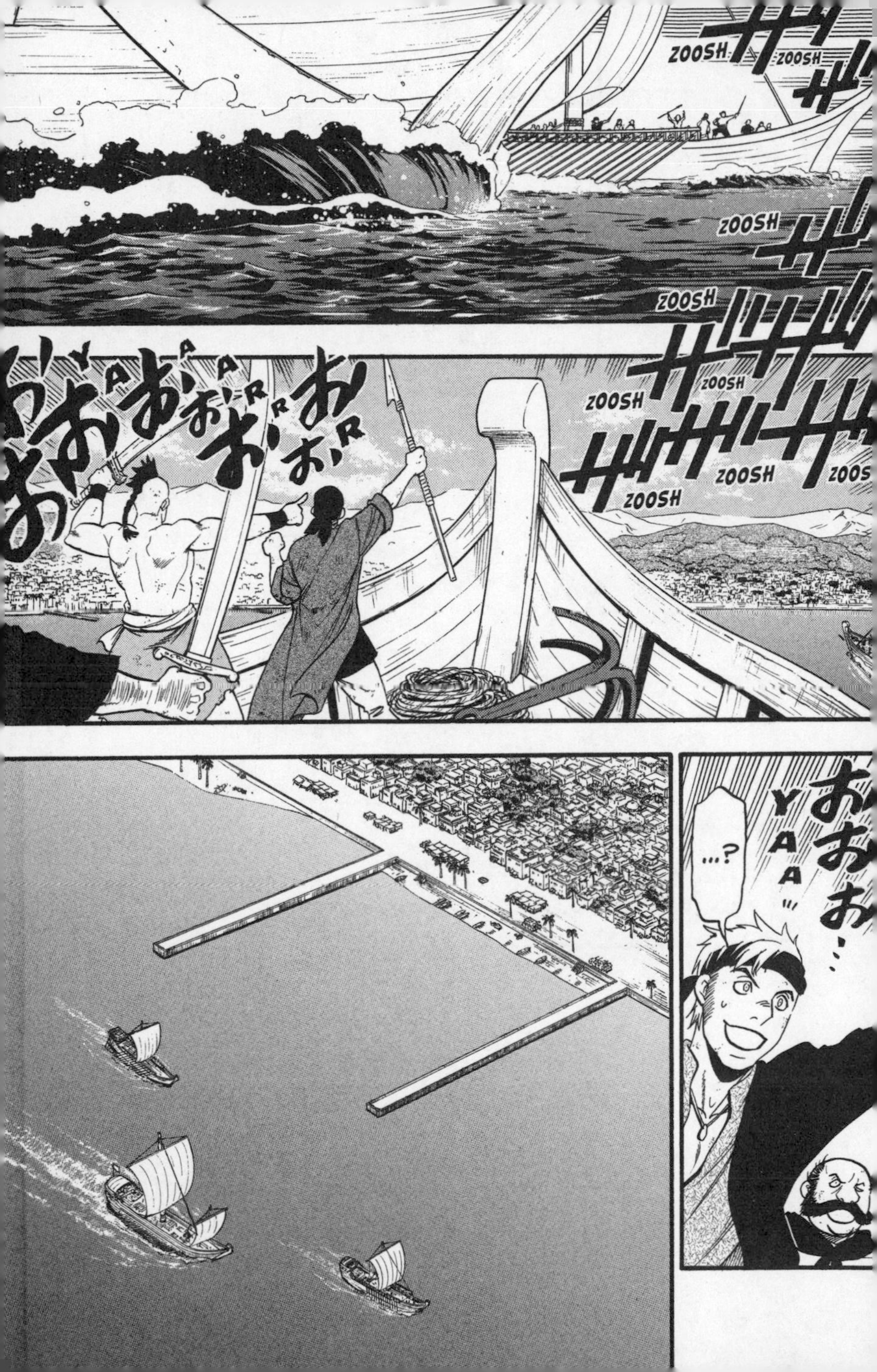
ZOOSH
ZOOSH
ZOOSH
ZOOSH
YAAARRR
ZOOSH
ZOOSH
ZOOSH
ZOOSH
...?
YAAA

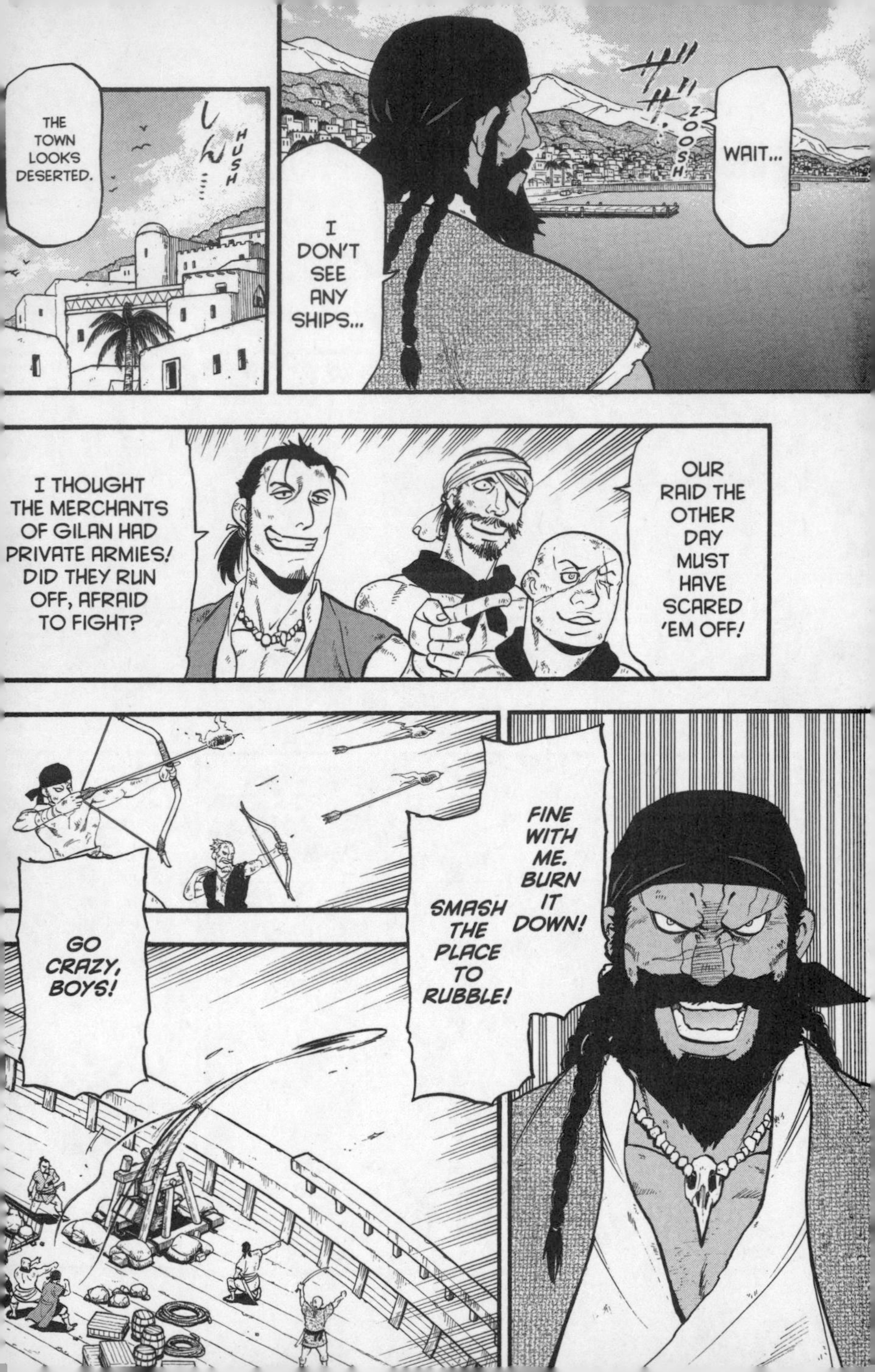
WAIT...
ZOOSH
I DON'T SEE ANY SHIPS...
THE TOWN LOOKS DESERTED.
HUSH
OUR RAID THE OTHER DAY MUST HAVE SCARED 'EM OFF!
I THOUGHT THE MERCHANTS OF GILAN HAD PRIVATE ARMIES! DID THEY RUN OFF, AFRAID TO FIGHT?
FINE WITH ME. BURN IT DOWN!
SMASH THE PLACE TO RUBBLE!
GO CRAZY, BOYS!

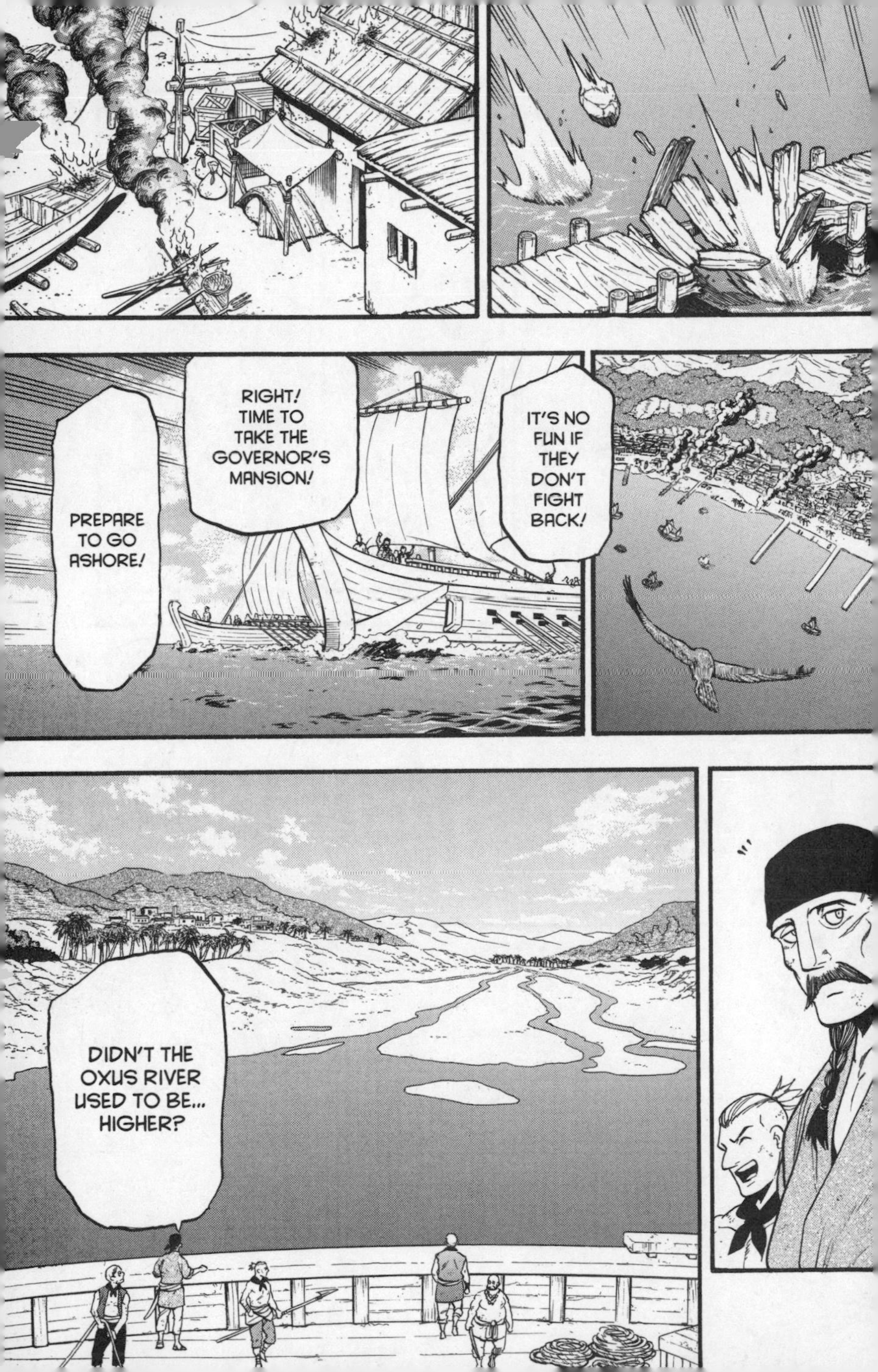
IT'S NO FUN IF THEY DON'T FIGHT BACK!
RIGHT! TIME TO TAKE THE GOVERNOR'S MANSION!
PREPARE TO GO ASHORE!
DIDN'T THE OXUS RIVER USED TO BE... HIGHER?

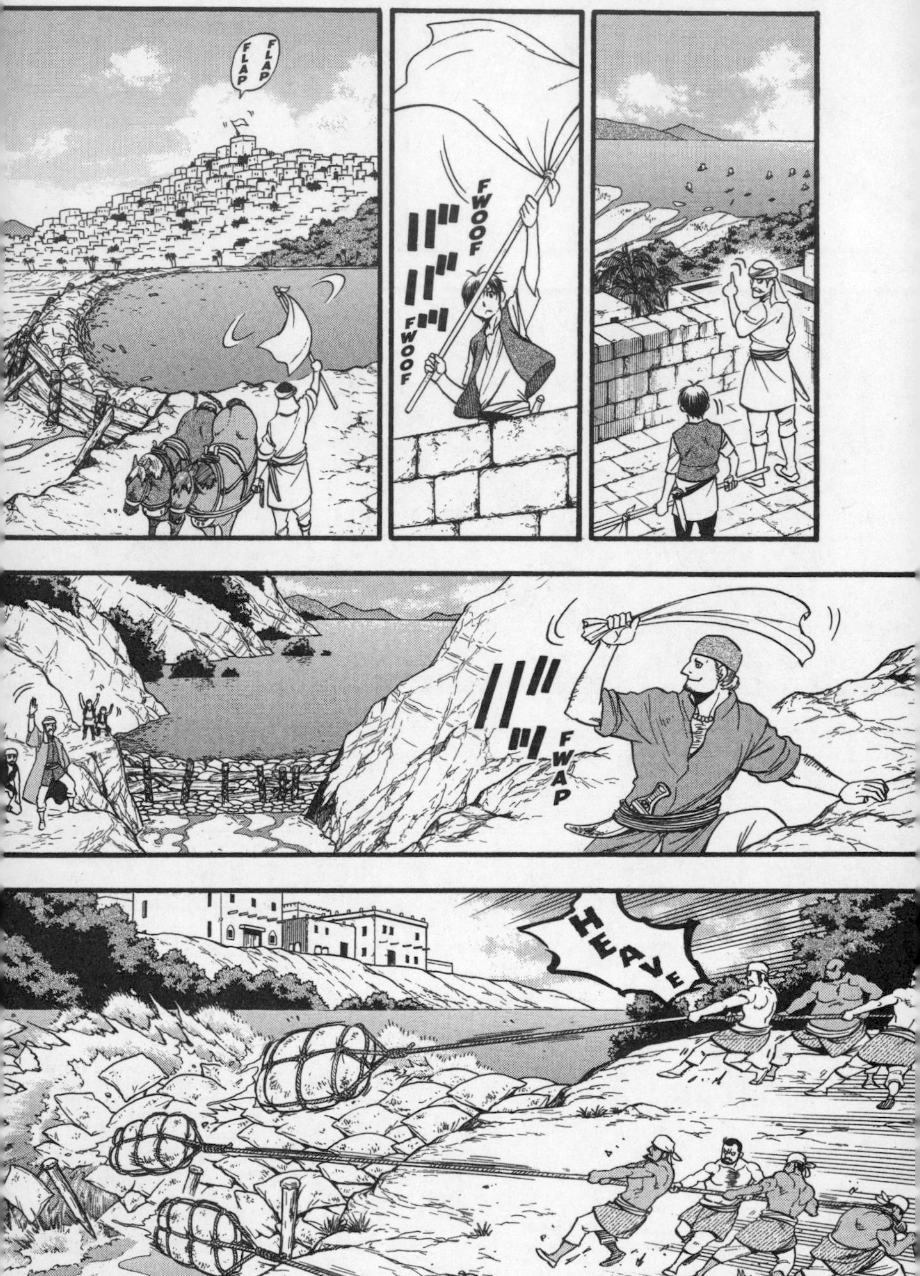
FWOOF
FWOOF
FLAP FLAP
FWAP
HEAVE

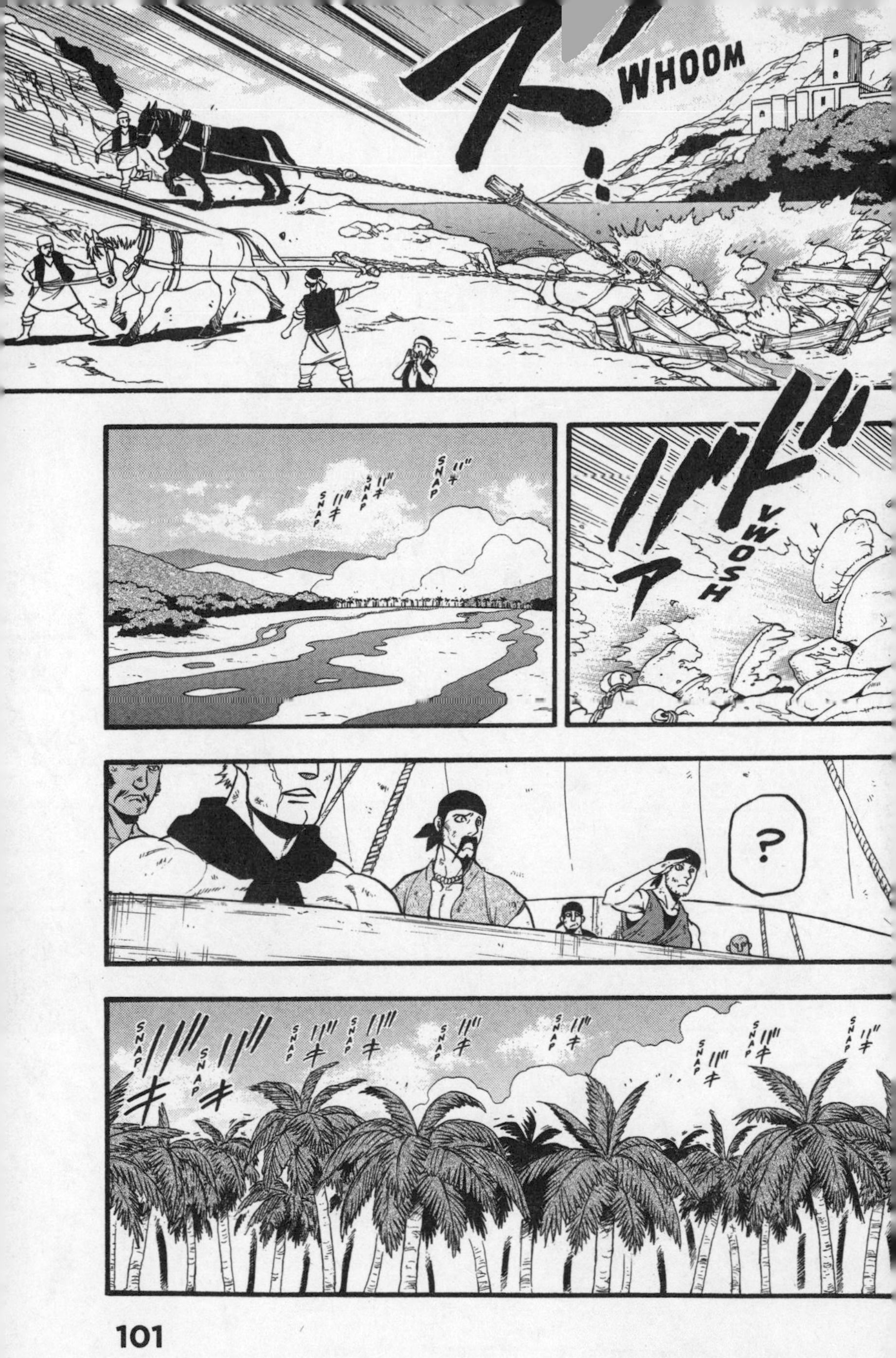
WHOOM
VWOSH
SNAP
SNAP
SNAP
?
SNAP
SNAP
SNAP
SNAP
SNAP
SNAP
SNAP
SNAP
SNAP
SNAP

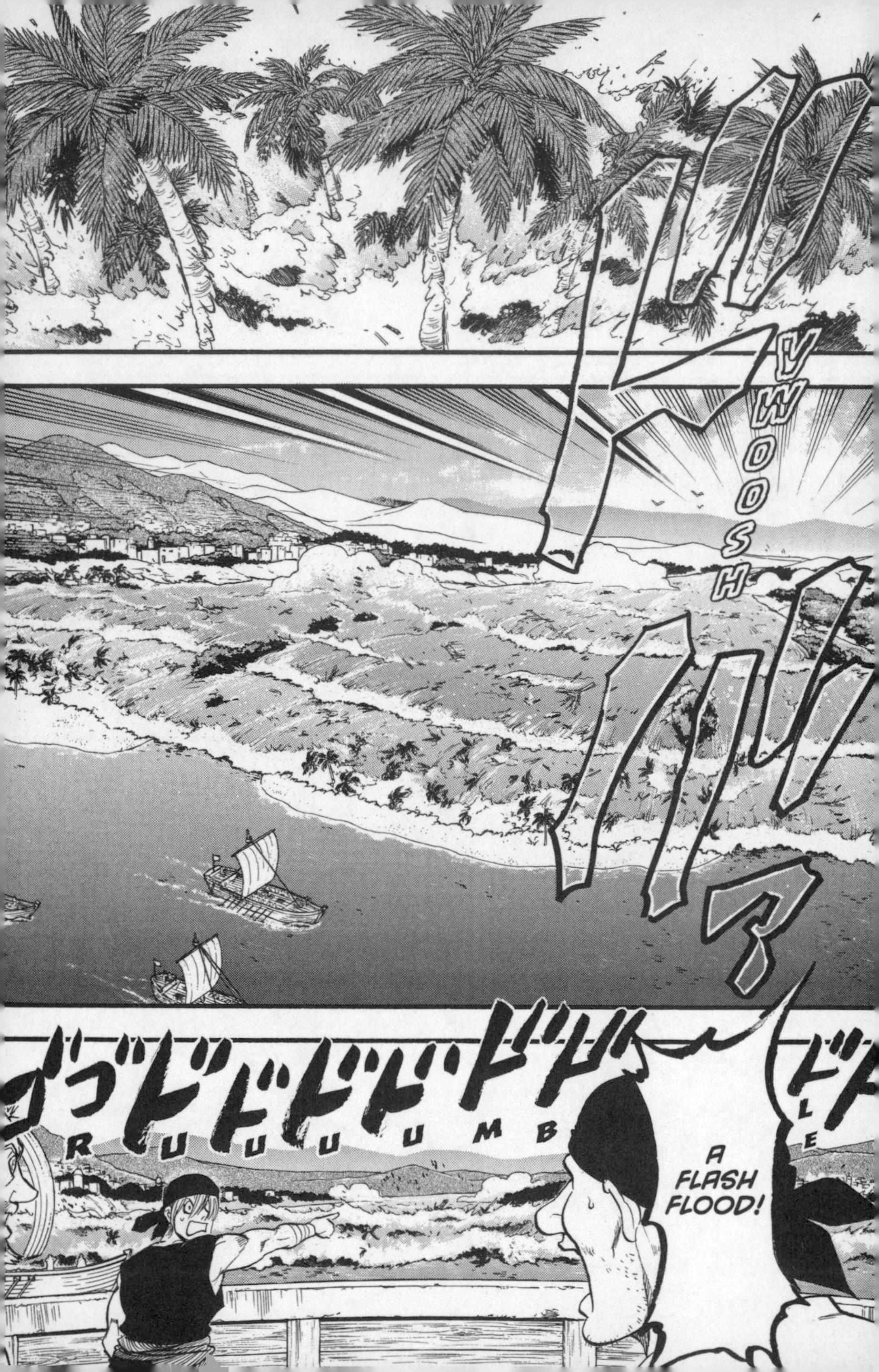
VWOOSH
RUUUUMBLE
A FLASH FLOOD!

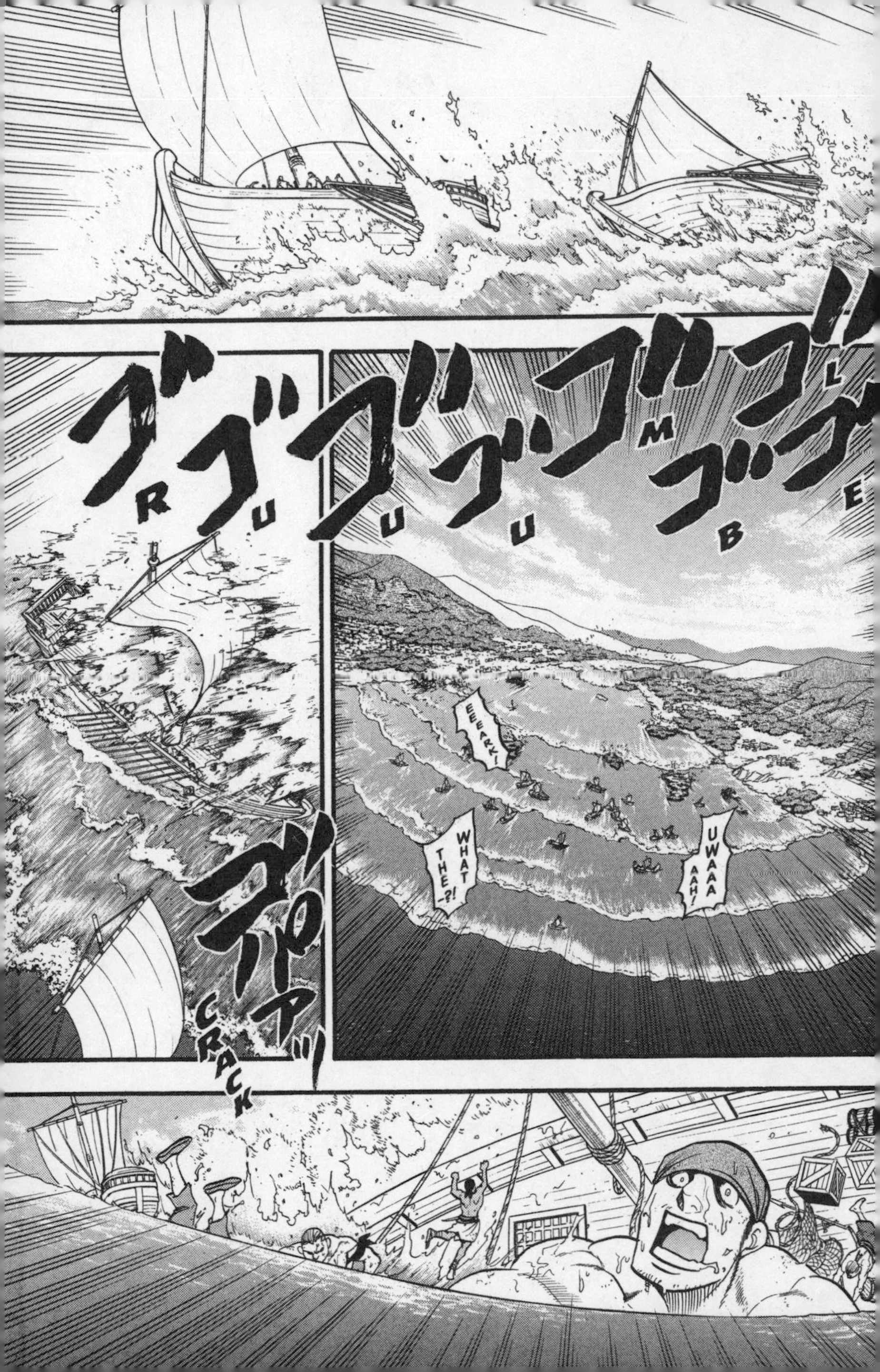
RUUUMBLE
UWAAAAAH!
EEEARK!
WHAT THE-?!
CRACK

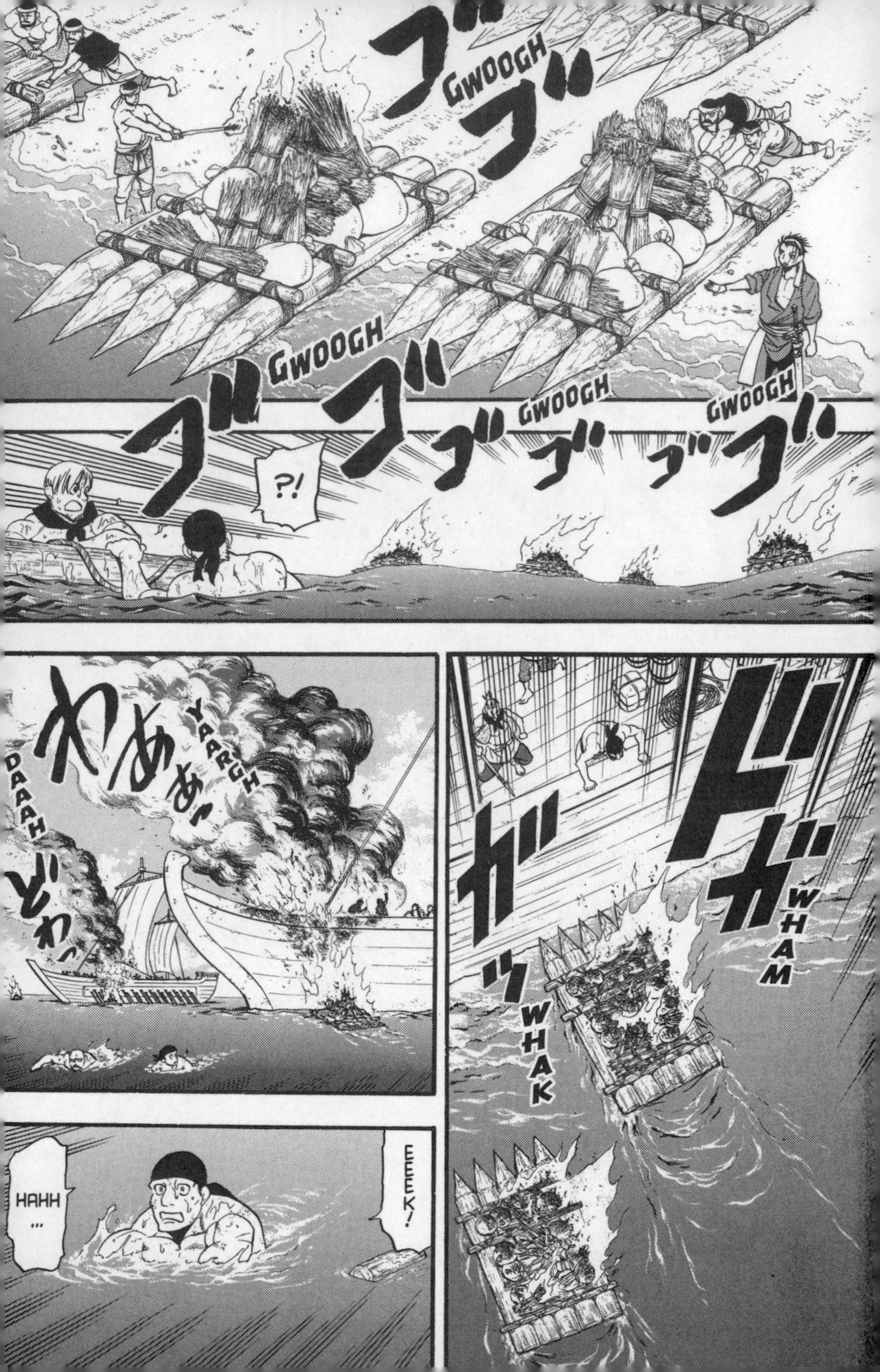
GWOOGH
GWOOGH
GWOOGH
GWOOGH
?!
WHAM
WHAK
YAARGH
DAAAH
EEEK!
HAHH ...

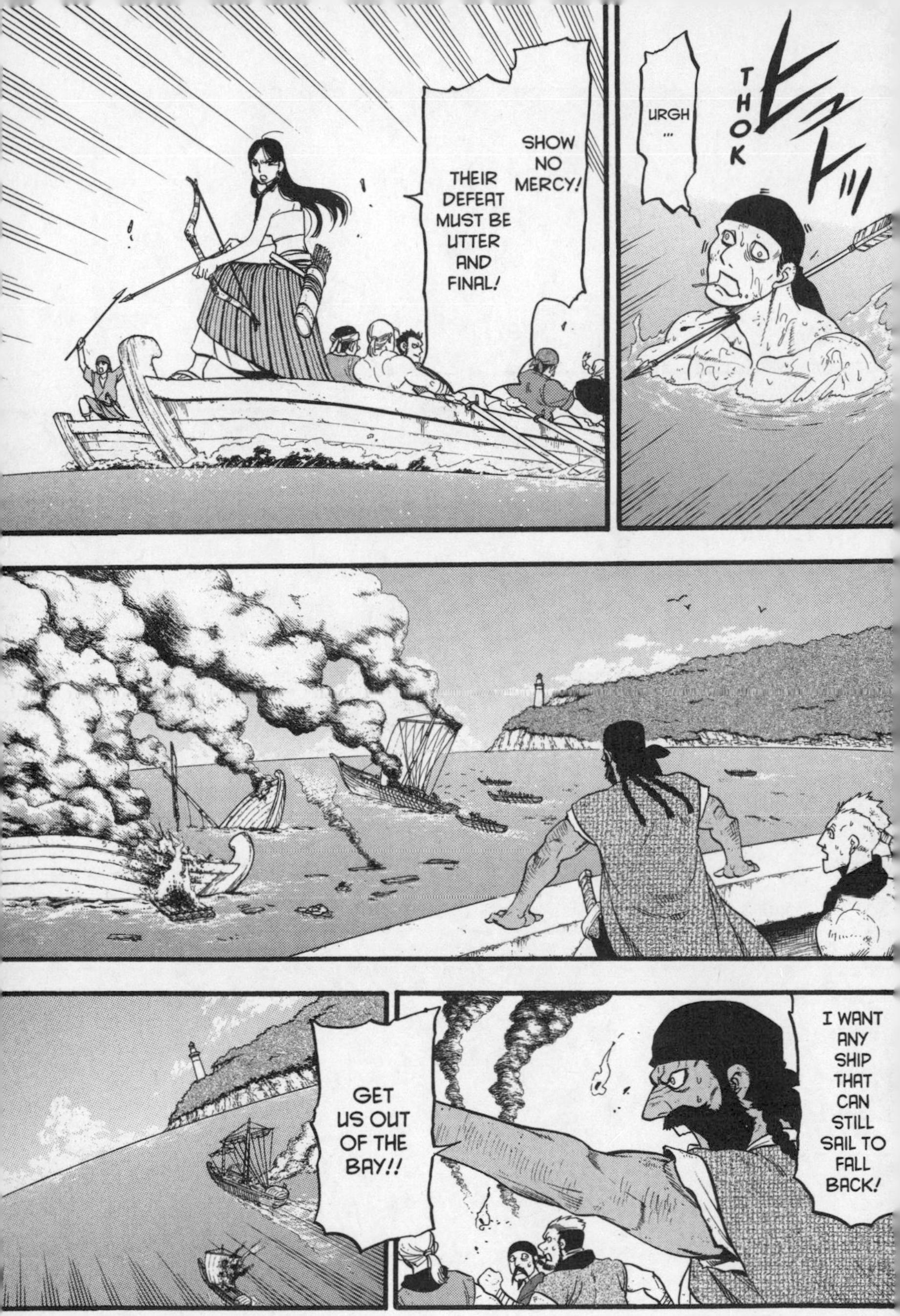
THOK
URGH ...
SHOW NO MERCY!
THEIR DEFEAT MUST BE UTTER AND FINAL!
I WANT ANY SHIP THAT CAN STILL SAIL TO FALL BACK!
GET US OUT OF THE BAY!!

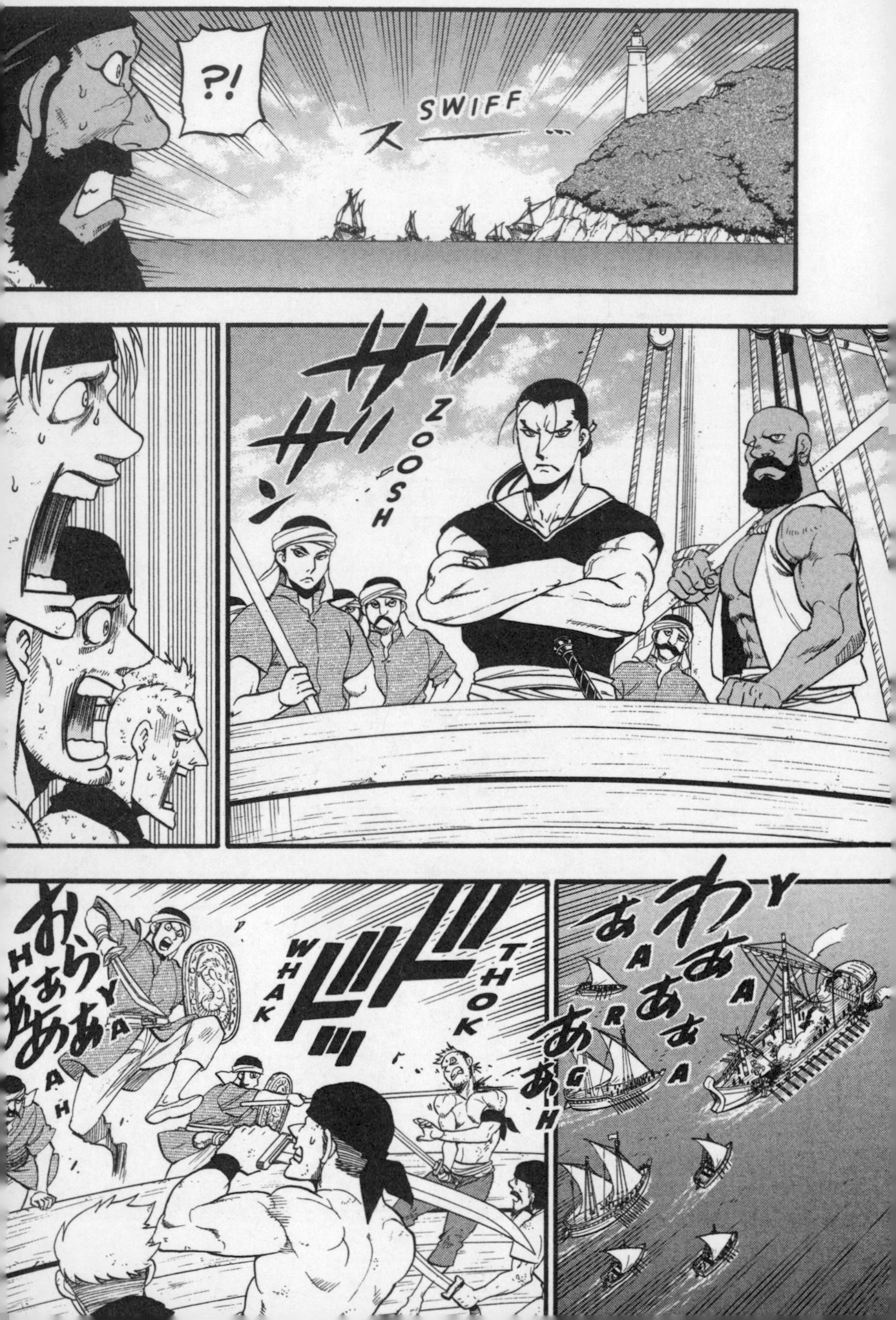
?!
スー…
SWIFF
ザザザン
ZOOOSH
わああああ
YAAARGH
ドドッ
THOK
WHAK
おらあああ
HYAAAH

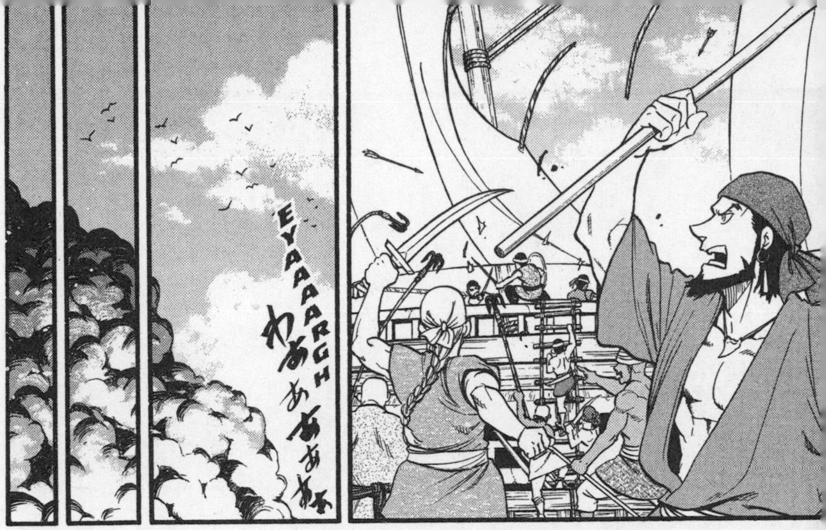
EYAAAARGH

Chapter 98: The Torture of a Civilized Nation

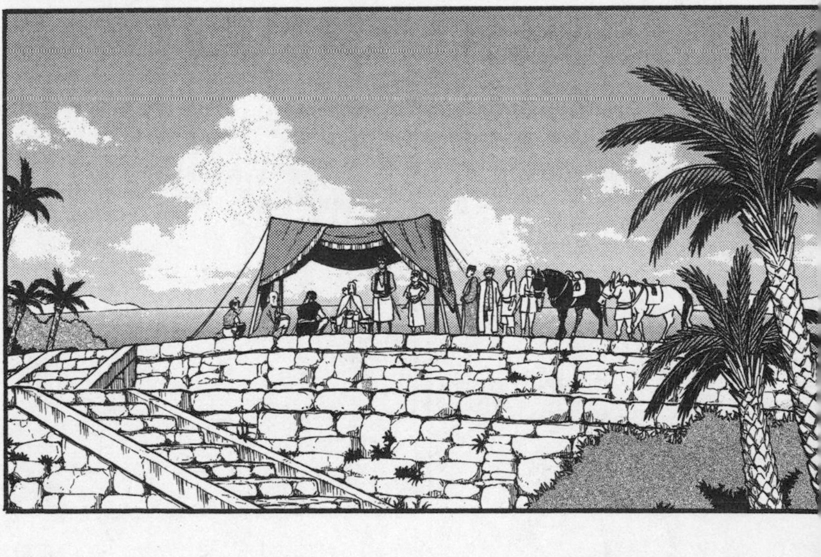

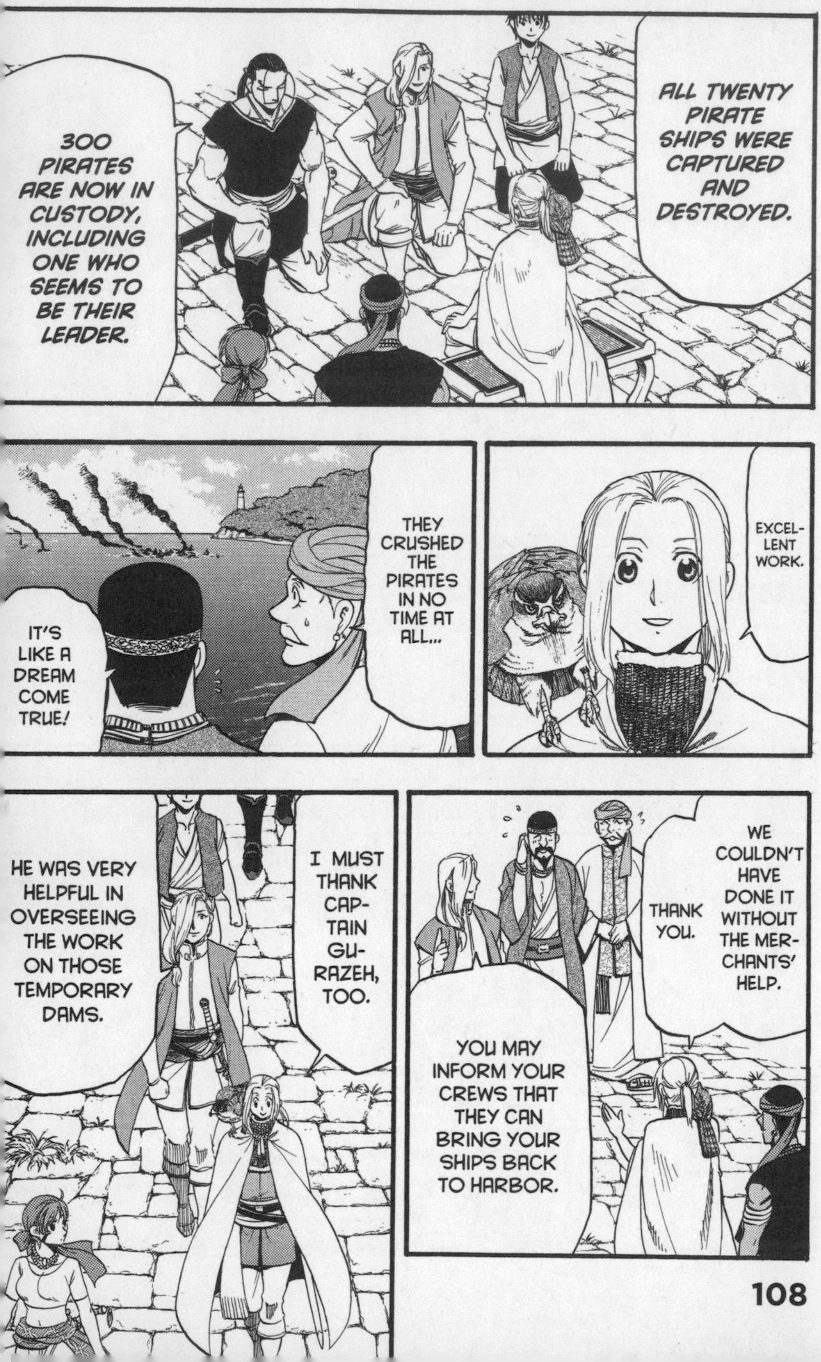
ALL TWENTY PIRATE SHIPS WERE CAPTURED AND DESTROYED.
300 PIRATES ARE NOW IN CUSTODY, INCLUDING ONE WHO SEEMS TO BE THEIR LEADER.
EXCEL-LENT WORK.
THEY CRUSHED THE PIRATES IN NO TIME AT ALL...
IT'S LIKE A DREAM COME TRUE!
WE COULDN'T HAVE DONE IT WITHOUT THE MER-CHANTS' HELP.
THANK YOU.
YOU MAY INFORM YOUR CREWS THAT THEY CAN BRING YOUR SHIPS BACK TO HARBOR.
I MUST THANK CAP-TAIN GU-RAZEH, TOO.
HE WAS VERY HELPFUL IN OVERSEEING THE WORK ON THOSE TEMPORARY DAMS.

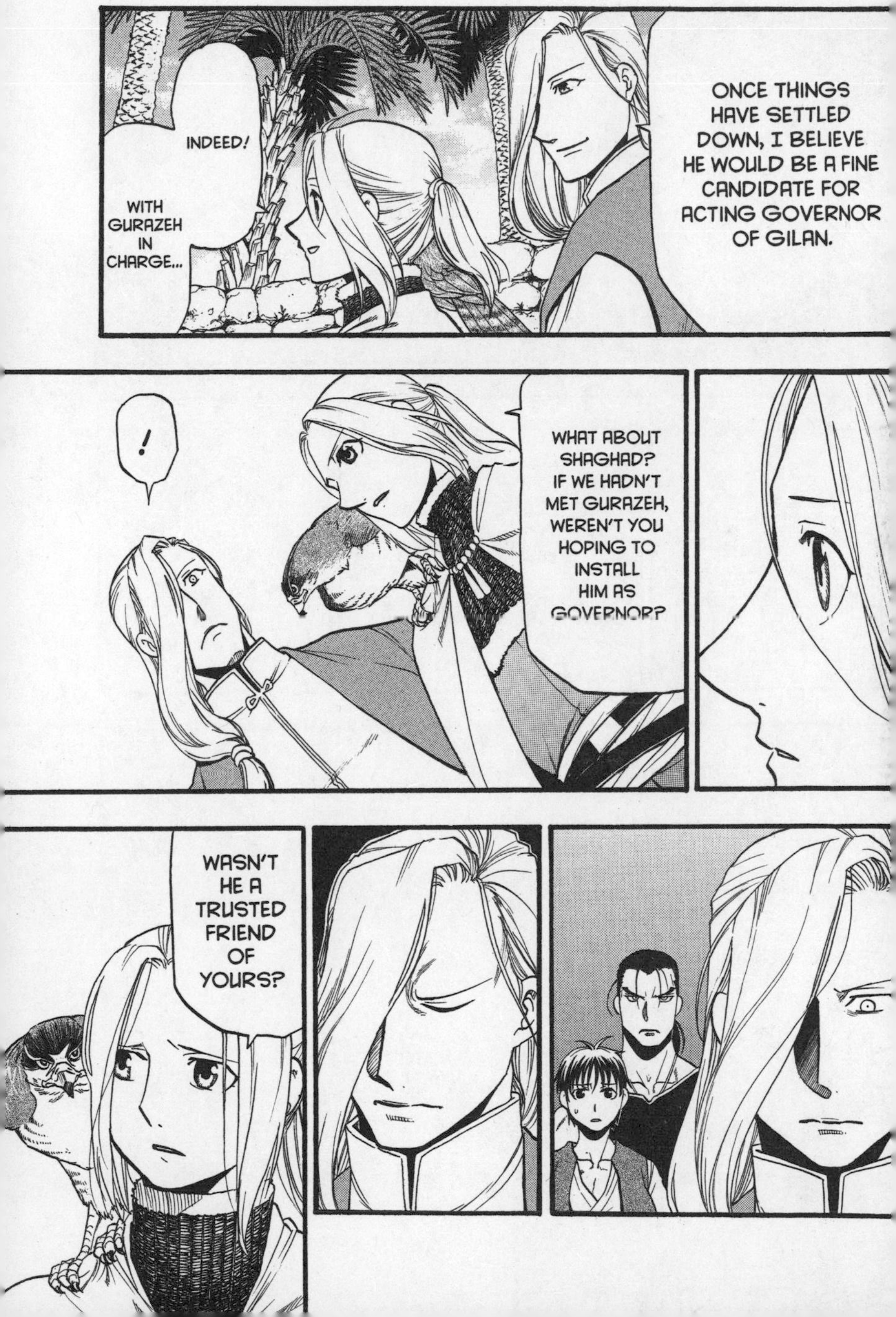
ONCE THINGS HAVE SETTLED DOWN, I BELIEVE HE WOULD BE A FINE CANDIDATE FOR ACTING GOVERNOR OF GILAN.
INDEED!
WITH GURAZEH IN CHARGE...
WHAT ABOUT SHAGHAD? IF WE HADN'T MET GURAZEH, WEREN'T YOU HOPING TO INSTALL HIM AS GOVERNOR?
!
WASN'T HE A TRUSTED FRIEND OF YOURS?

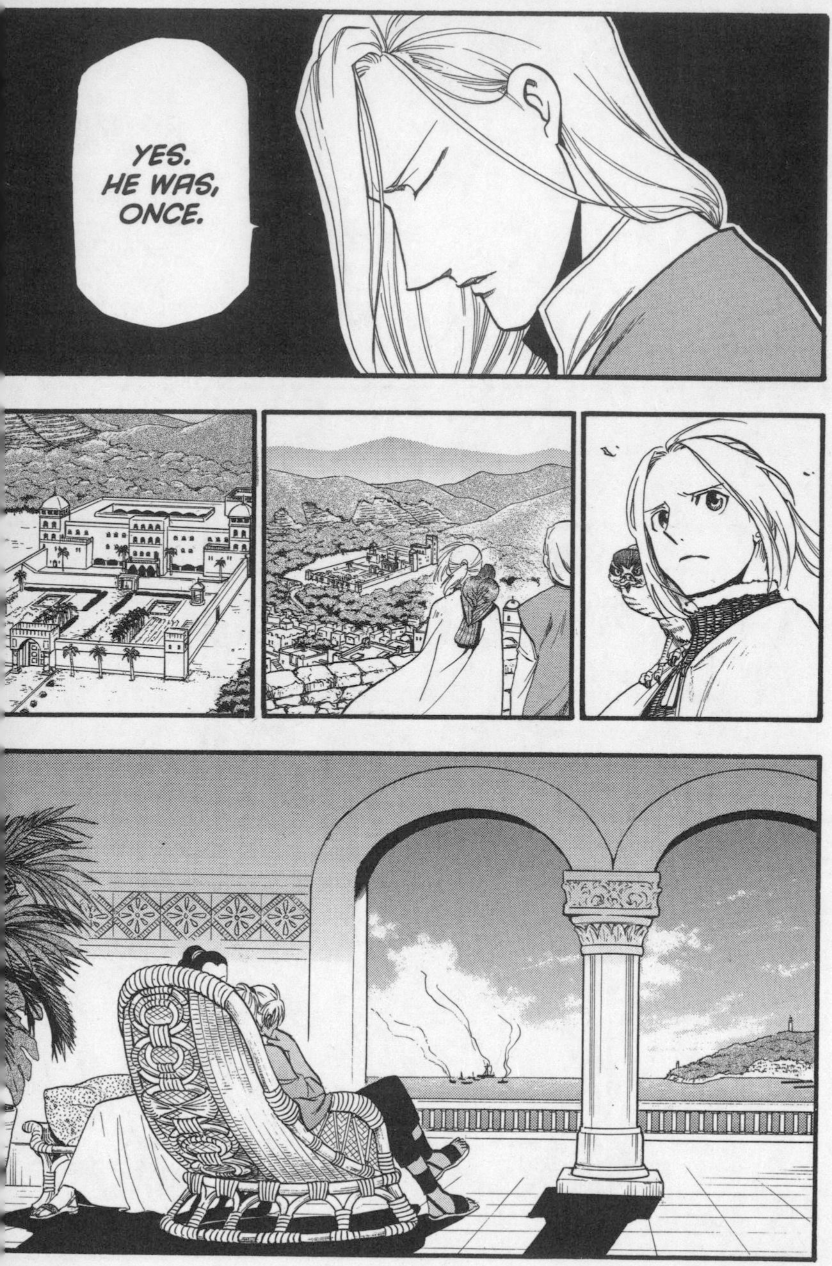
YES. HE WAS, ONCE.

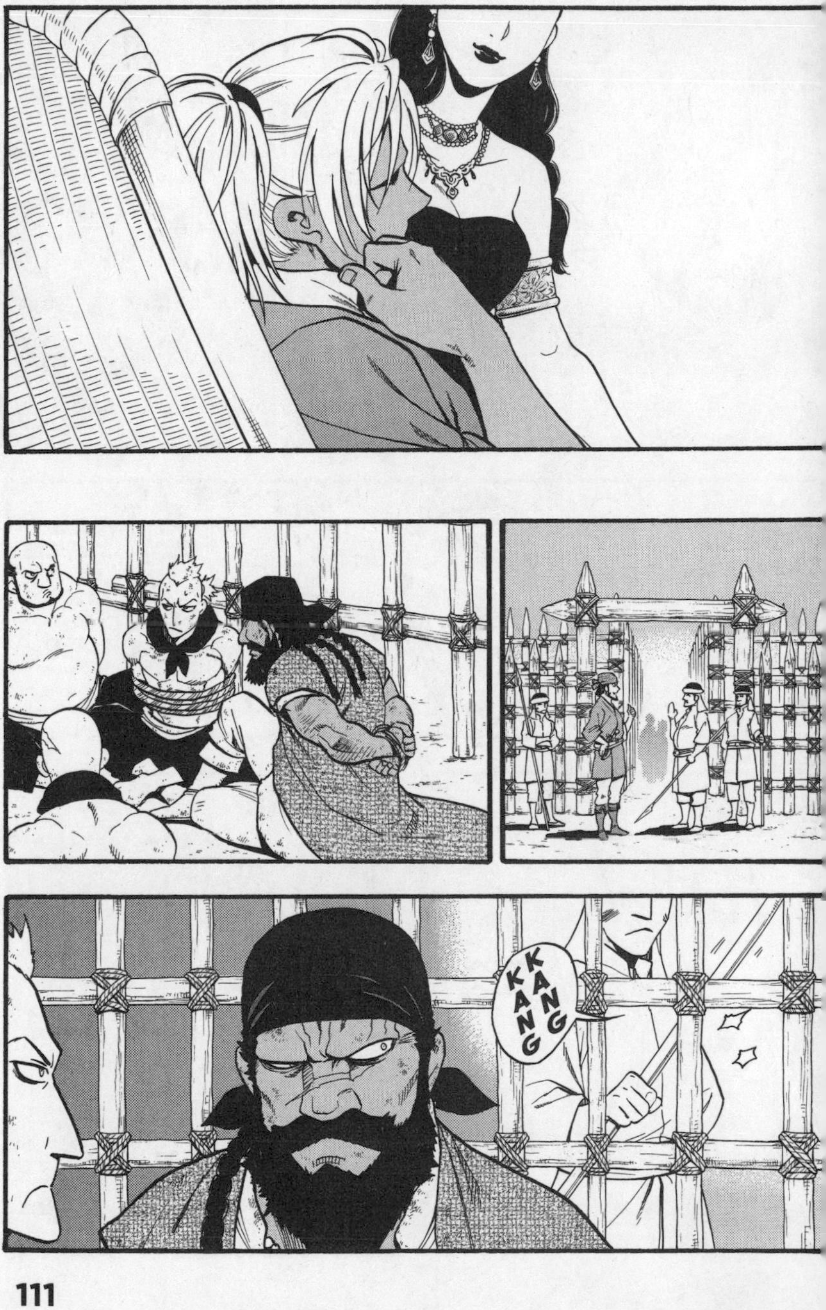
KANG KANG

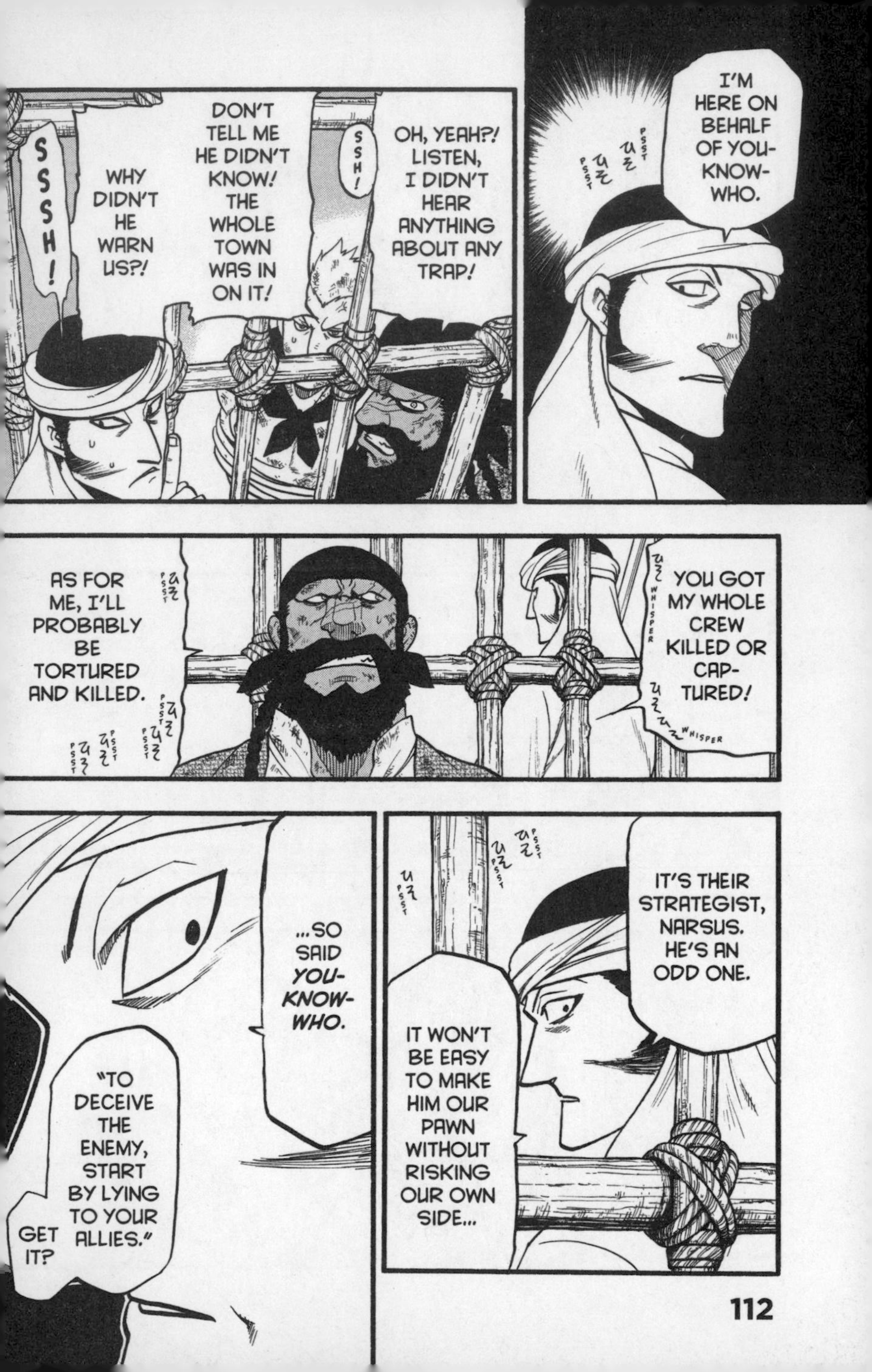
PSST PSST
I'M HERE ON BEHALF OF YOU-KNOW-WHO.
OH, YEAH?! LISTEN, I DIDN'T HEAR ANYTHING ABOUT ANY TRAP!
SSH!
DON'T TELL ME HE DIDN'T KNOW! THE WHOLE TOWN WAS IN ON IT!
WHY DIDN'T HE WARN US?!
SSSH!
WHISPER
YOU GOT MY WHOLE CREW KILLED OR CAPTURED!
WHISPER
PSST
AS FOR ME, I'LL PROBABLY BE TORTURED AND KILLED.
PSST PSST PSST PSST
PSST PSST
IT'S THEIR STRATEGIST, NARSUS. HE'S AN ODD ONE.
PSST
IT WON'T BE EASY TO MAKE HIM OUR PAWN WITHOUT RISKING OUR OWN SIDE...
...SO SAID *YOU-KNOW-WHO.*
"TO DECEIVE THE ENEMY, START BY LYING TO YOUR ALLIES."
GET IT?

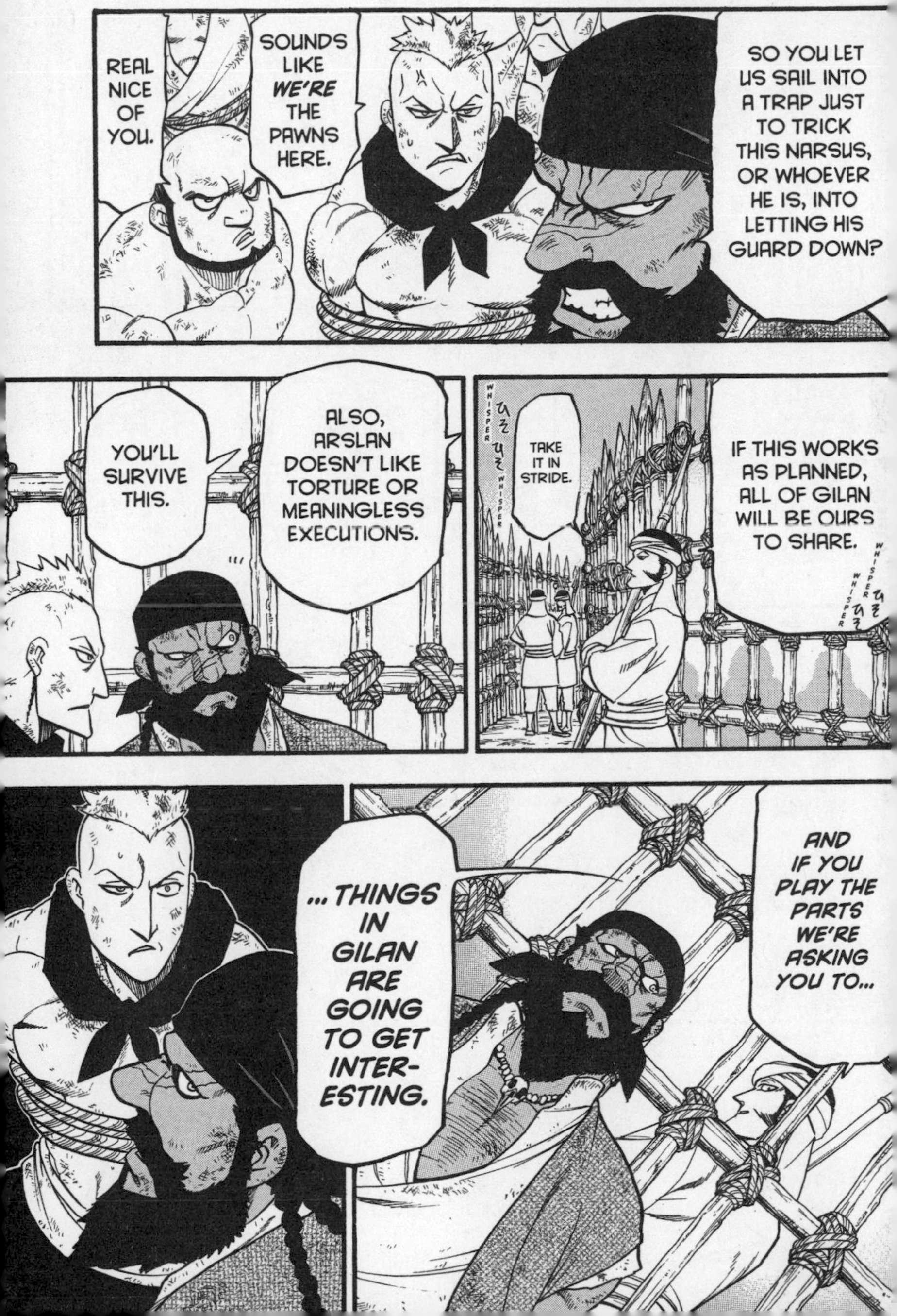
SO YOU LET US SAIL INTO A TRAP JUST TO TRICK THIS NARSUS, OR WHOEVER HE IS, INTO LETTING HIS GUARD DOWN?
SOUNDS LIKE *WE'RE* THE PAWNS HERE.
REAL NICE OF YOU.
IF THIS WORKS AS PLANNED, ALL OF GILAN WILL BE OURS TO SHARE.
WHISPER WHISPER
TAKE IT IN STRIDE.
WHISPER WHISPER
ALSO, ARSLAN DOESN'T LIKE TORTURE OR MEANINGLESS EXECUTIONS.
YOU'LL SURVIVE THIS.
AND IF YOU PLAY THE PARTS WE'RE ASKING YOU TO...
...THINGS IN GILAN ARE GOING TO GET INTER-ESTING.

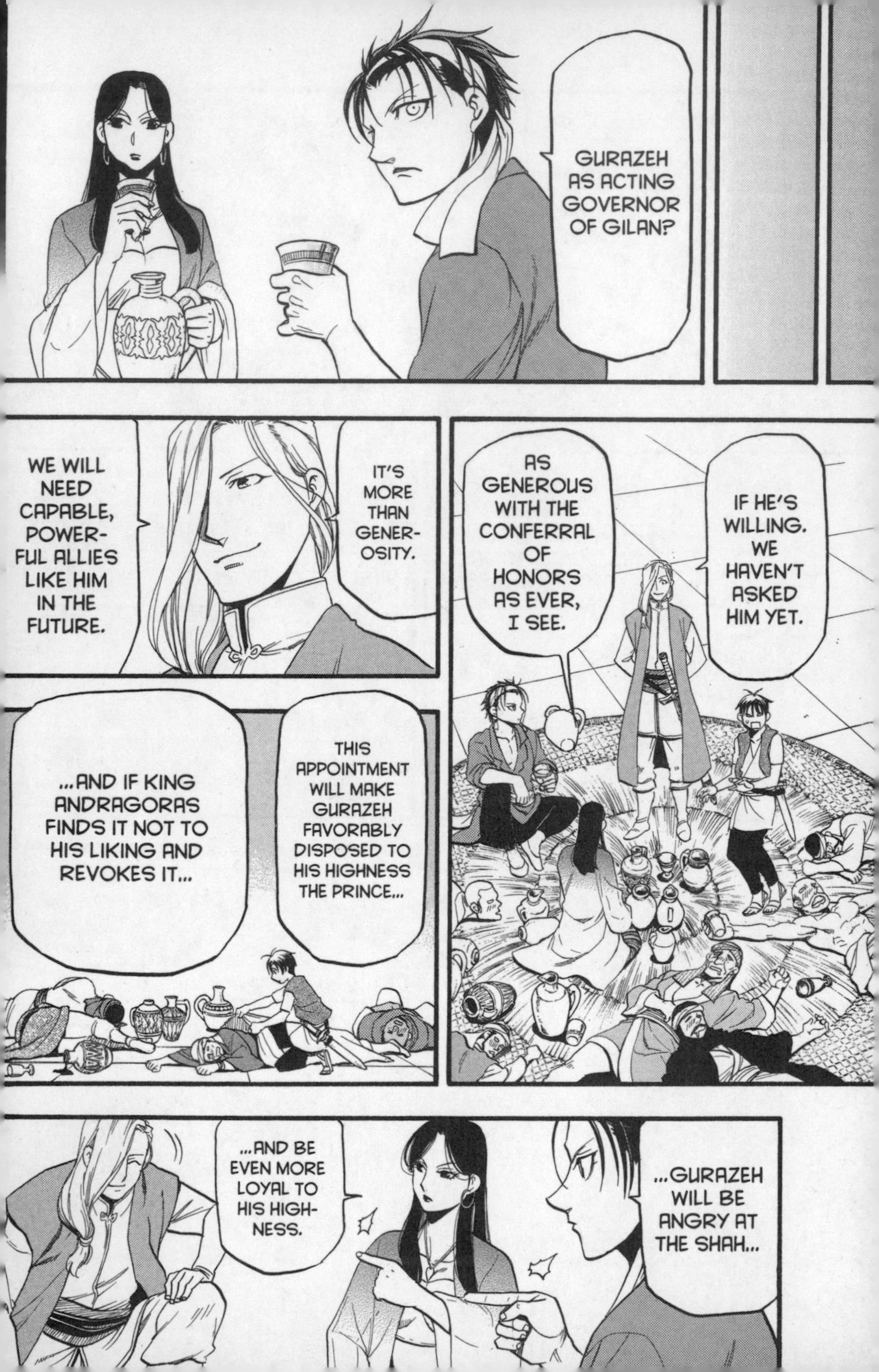
GURAZEH AS ACTING GOVERNOR OF GILAN?
IF HE'S WILLING. WE HAVEN'T ASKED HIM YET.
AS GENEROUS WITH THE CONFERRAL OF HONORS AS EVER, I SEE.
IT'S MORE THAN GENER-OSITY.
WE WILL NEED CAPABLE, POWER-FUL ALLIES LIKE HIM IN THE FUTURE.
THIS APPOINTMENT WILL MAKE GURAZEH FAVORABLY DISPOSED TO HIS HIGHNESS THE PRINCE...
...AND IF KING ANDRAGORAS FINDS IT NOT TO HIS LIKING AND REVOKES IT...
...GURAZEH WILL BE ANGRY AT THE SHAH...
...AND BE EVEN MORE LOYAL TO HIS HIGH-NESS.

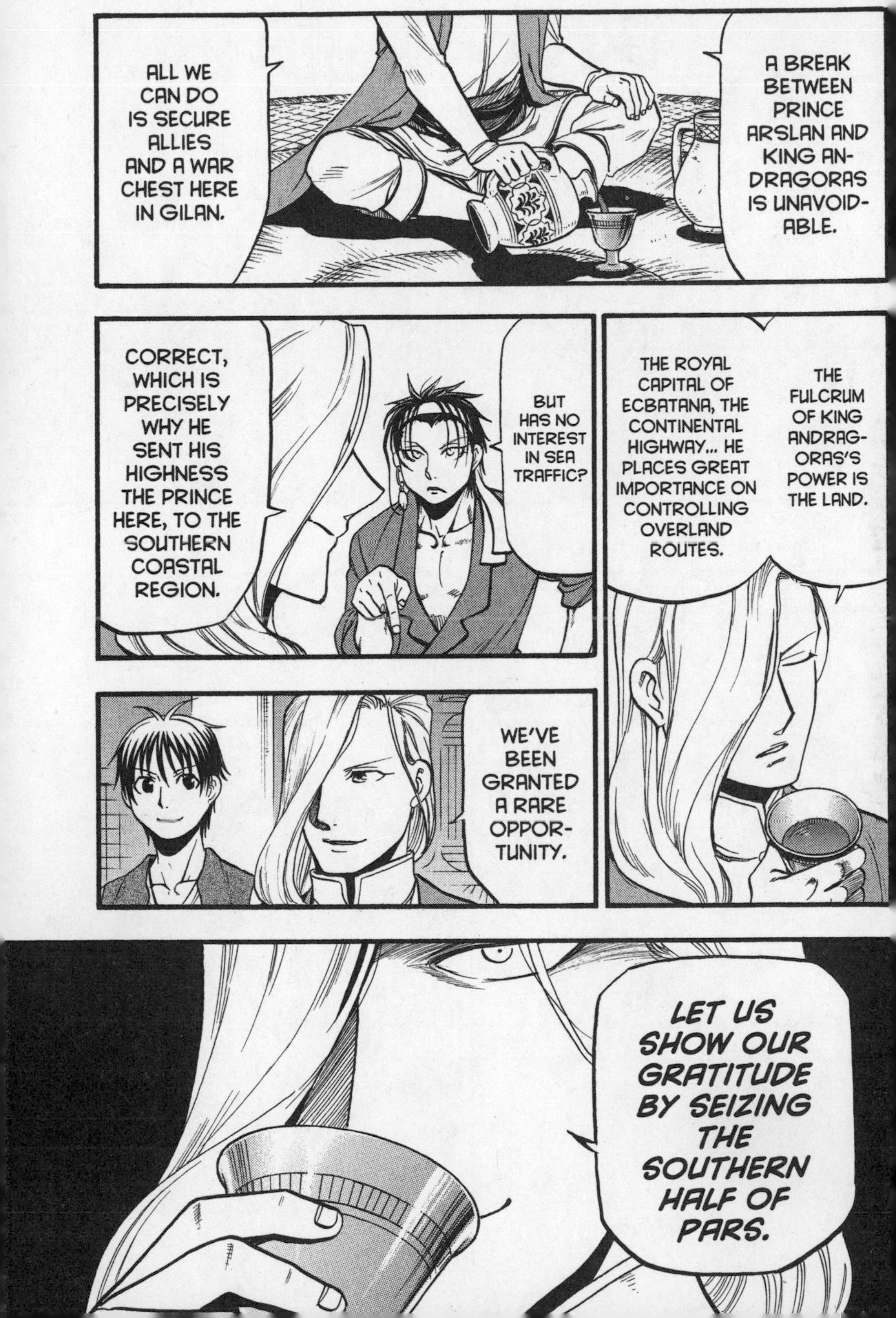
A BREAK BETWEEN PRINCE ARSLAN AND KING ANDRAGORAS IS UNAVOIDABLE.
ALL WE CAN DO IS SECURE ALLIES AND A WAR CHEST HERE IN GILAN.
THE FULCRUM OF KING ANDRAGORAS'S POWER IS THE LAND.
THE ROYAL CAPITAL OF ECBATANA, THE CONTINENTAL HIGHWAY... HE PLACES GREAT IMPORTANCE ON CONTROLLING OVERLAND ROUTES.
BUT HAS NO INTEREST IN SEA TRAFFIC?
CORRECT, WHICH IS PRECISELY WHY HE SENT HIS HIGHNESS THE PRINCE HERE, TO THE SOUTHERN COASTAL REGION.
WE'VE BEEN GRANTED A RARE OPPORTUNITY.
LET US SHOW OUR GRATITUDE BY SEIZING THE SOUTHERN HALF OF PARS.

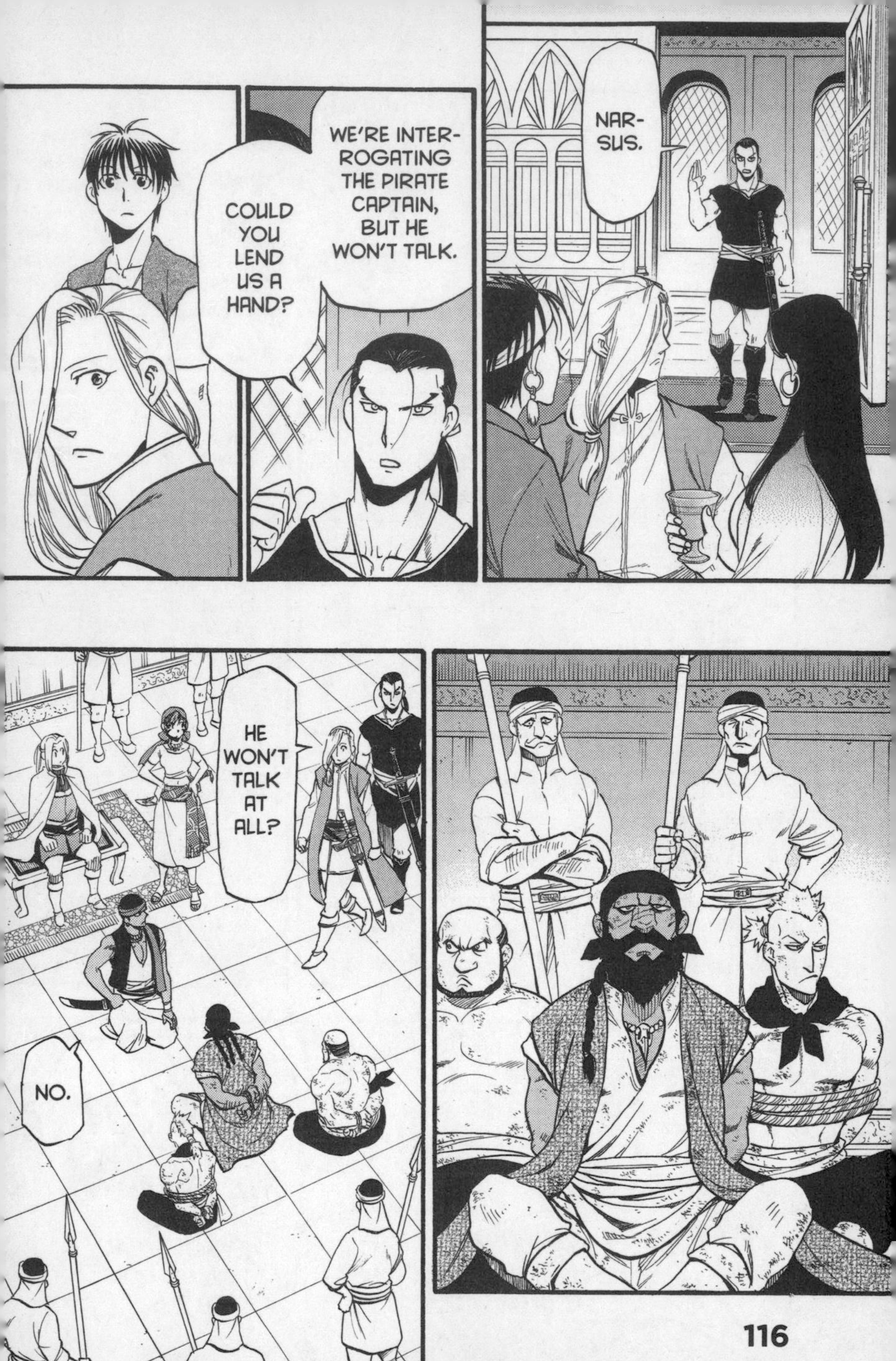
NAR-SUS.
WE'RE INTER-ROGATING THE PIRATE CAPTAIN, BUT HE WON'T TALK.
COULD YOU LEND US A HAND?
HE WON'T TALK AT ALL?
NO.

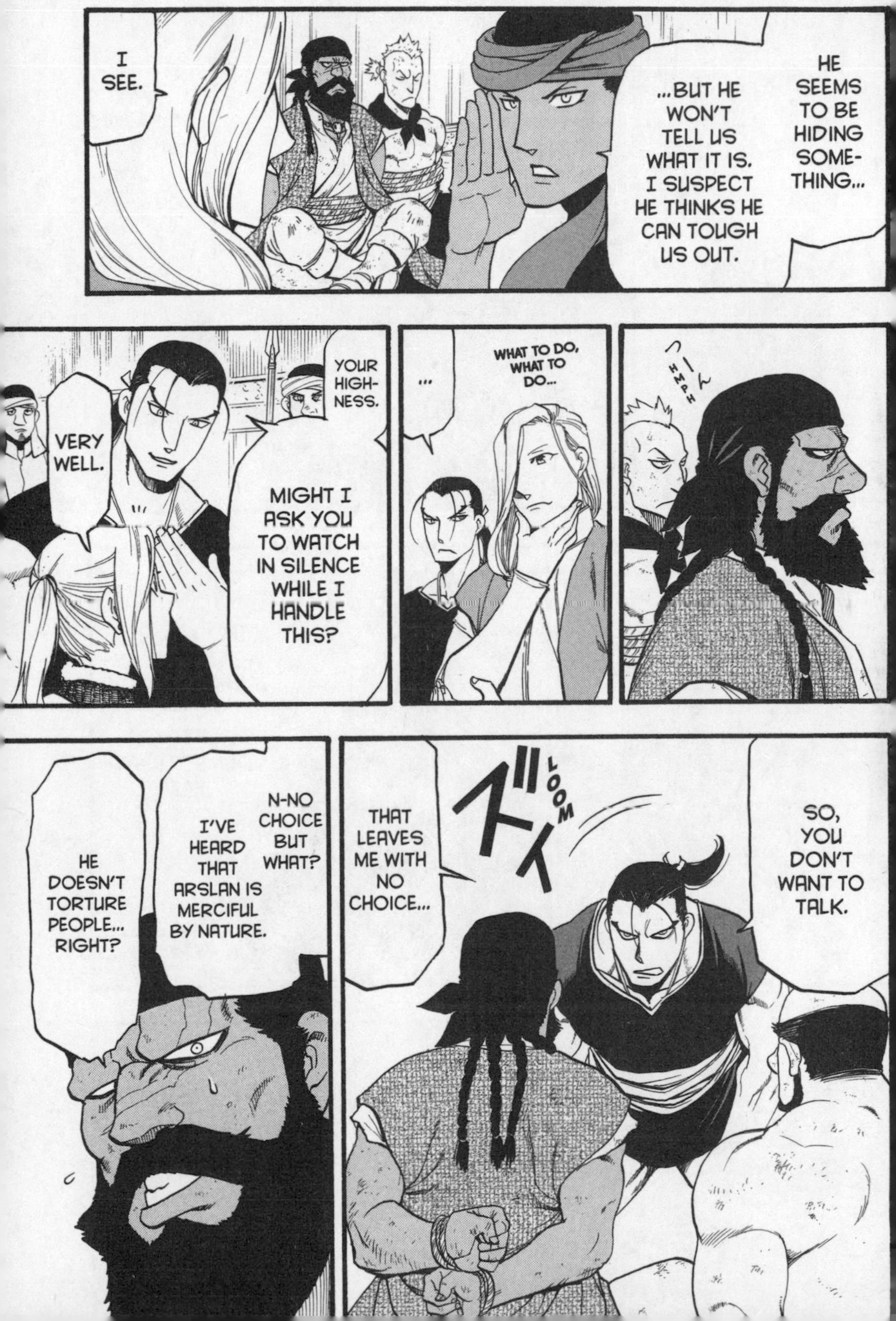
HE SEEMS TO BE HIDING SOME-THING...
...BUT HE WON'T TELL US WHAT IT IS. I SUSPECT HE THINKS HE CAN TOUGH US OUT.
I SEE.
HMPH
WHAT TO DO, WHAT TO DO...
...
YOUR HIGHNESS.
MIGHT I ASK YOU TO WATCH IN SILENCE WHILE I HANDLE THIS?
VERY WELL.
SO, YOU DON'T WANT TO TALK.
LOOM
THAT LEAVES ME WITH NO CHOICE...
N-NO CHOICE BUT WHAT?
I'VE HEARD THAT ARSLAN IS MERCIFUL BY NATURE.
HE DOESN'T TORTURE PEOPLE... RIGHT?

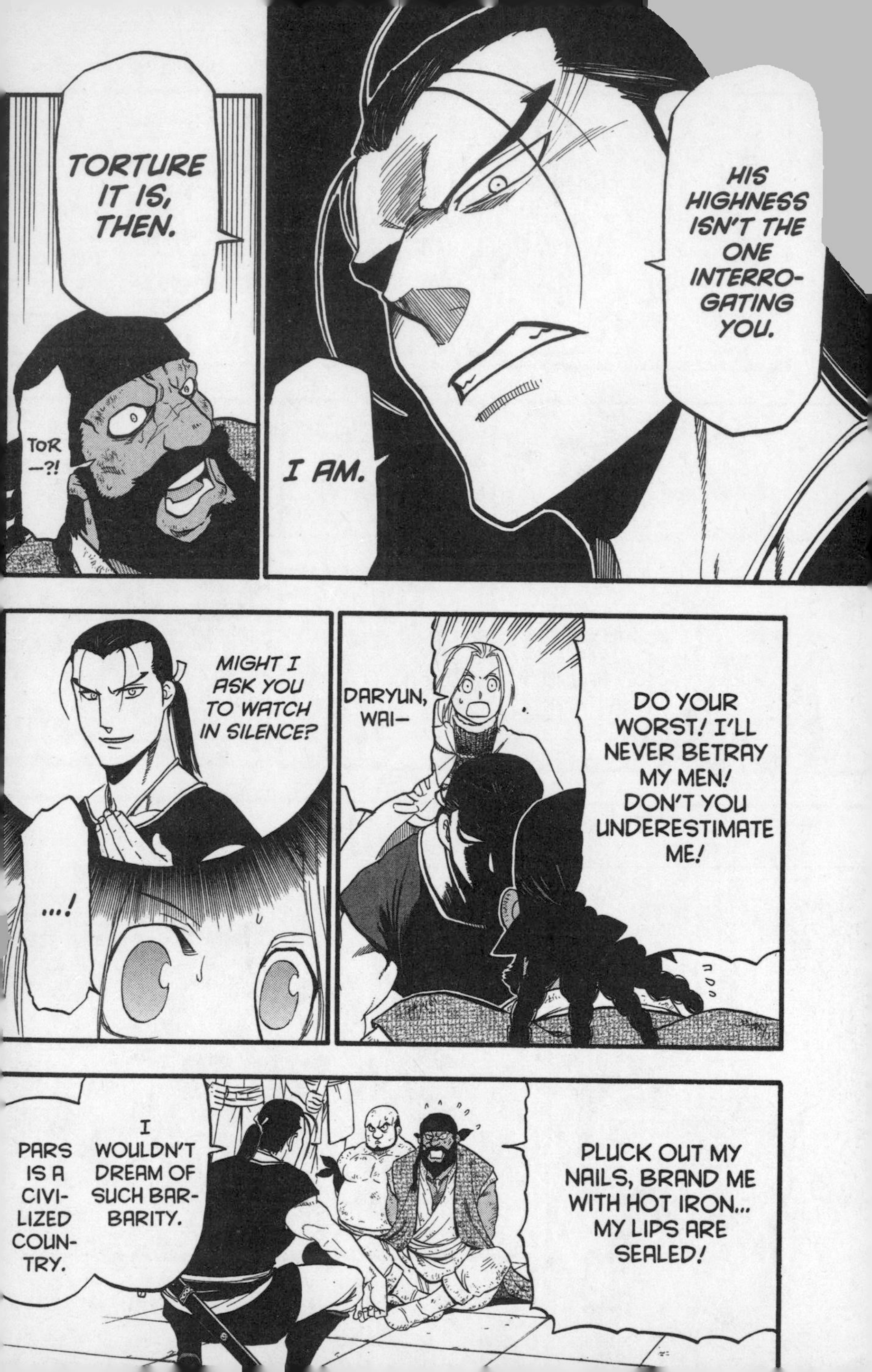
HIS HIGHNESS ISN'T THE ONE INTERROGATING YOU.
I AM.
TORTURE IT IS, THEN.
TOR—?!
DO YOUR WORST! I'LL NEVER BETRAY MY MEN! DON'T YOU UNDERESTIMATE ME!
DARYUN, WAI—
MIGHT I ASK YOU TO WATCH IN SILENCE?
...!
PLUCK OUT MY NAILS, BRAND ME WITH HOT IRON... MY LIPS ARE SEALED!
I WOULDN'T DREAM OF SUCH BARBARITY.
PARS IS A CIVILIZED COUNTRY.

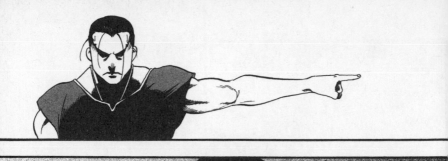

NOW TALK!

OR I'LL HAVE THIS MAN PAINT YOUR PORTRAIT!

HUH?

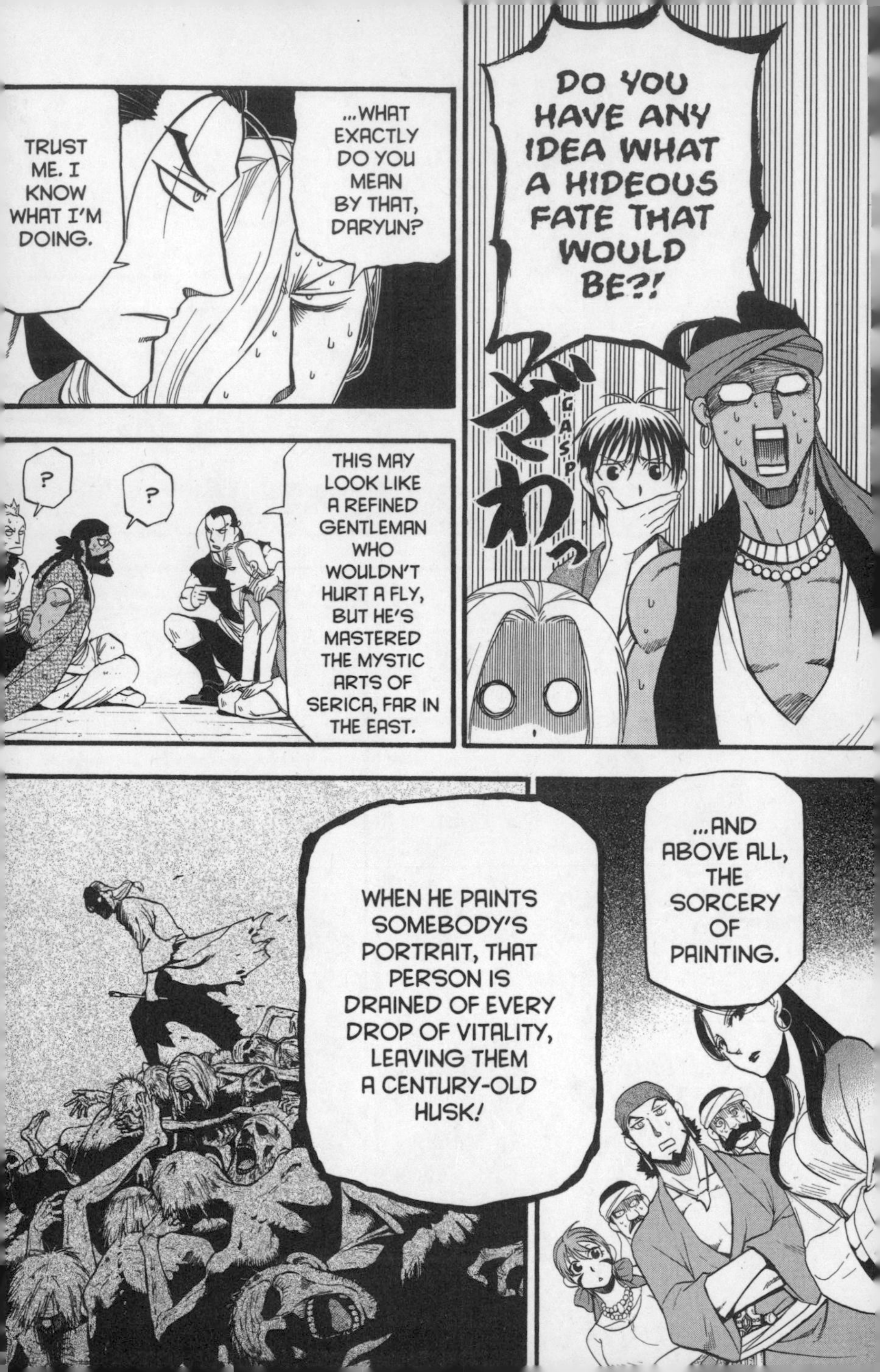
DO YOU HAVE ANY IDEA WHAT A HIDEOUS FATE THAT WOULD BE?!
ざわっ
GASP
...WHAT EXACTLY DO YOU MEAN BY THAT, DARYUN?
TRUST ME. I KNOW WHAT I'M DOING.
THIS MAY LOOK LIKE A REFINED GENTLEMAN WHO WOULDN'T HURT A FLY, BUT HE'S MASTERED THE MYSTIC ARTS OF SERICA, FAR IN THE EAST.
?
?
...AND ABOVE ALL, THE SORCERY OF PAINTING.
WHEN HE PAINTS SOMEBODY'S PORTRAIT, THAT PERSON IS DRAINED OF EVERY DROP OF VITALITY, LEAVING THEM A CENTURY-OLD HUSK!

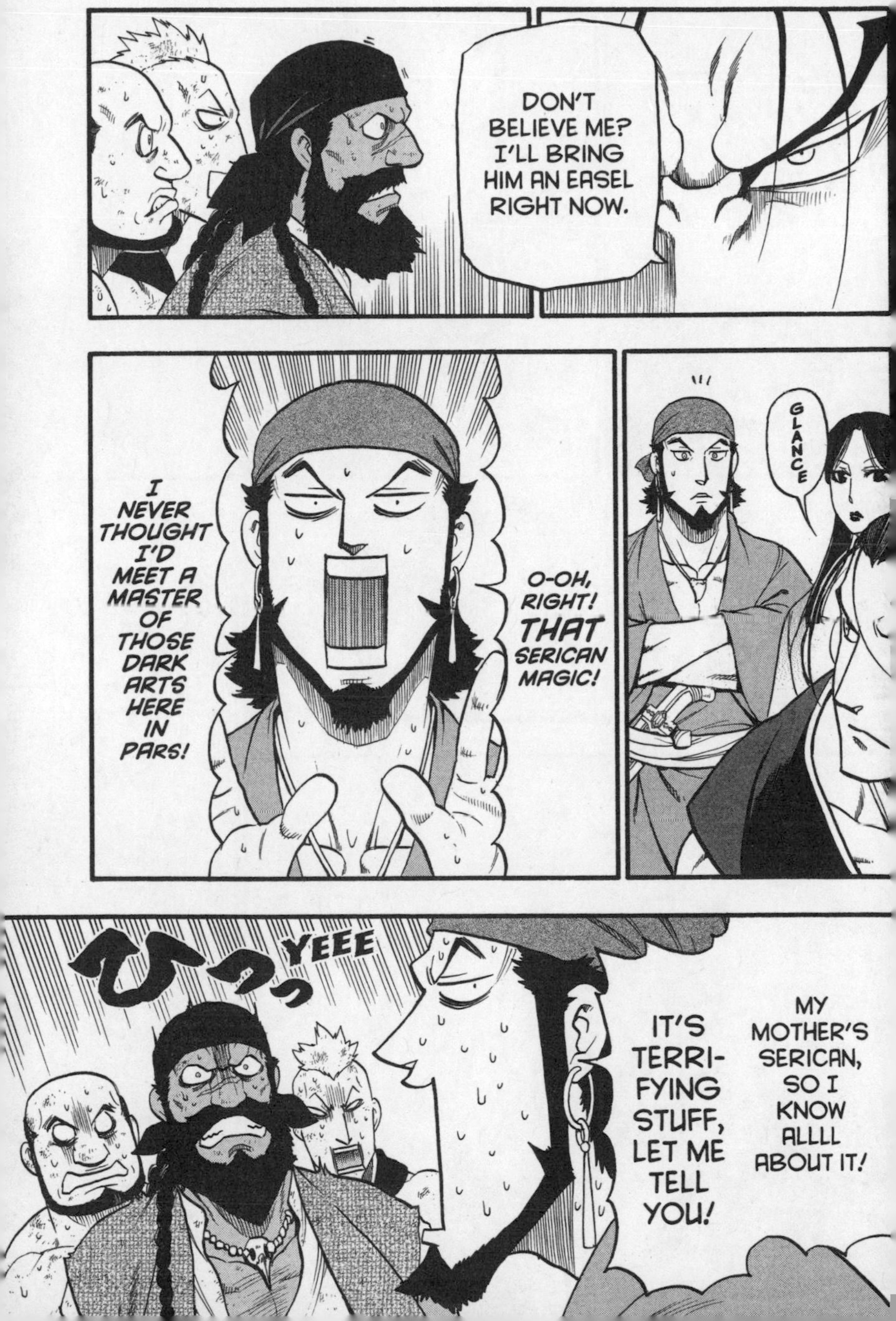
DON'T BELIEVE ME? I'LL BRING HIM AN EASEL RIGHT NOW.
GLANCE
O-OH, RIGHT! THAT SERICAN MAGIC!
I NEVER THOUGHT I'D MEET A MASTER OF THOSE DARK ARTS HERE IN PARS!
MY MOTHER'S SERICAN, SO I KNOW ALLLL ABOUT IT!
IT'S TERRI-FYING STUFF, LET ME TELL YOU!
ひっ
YEEE

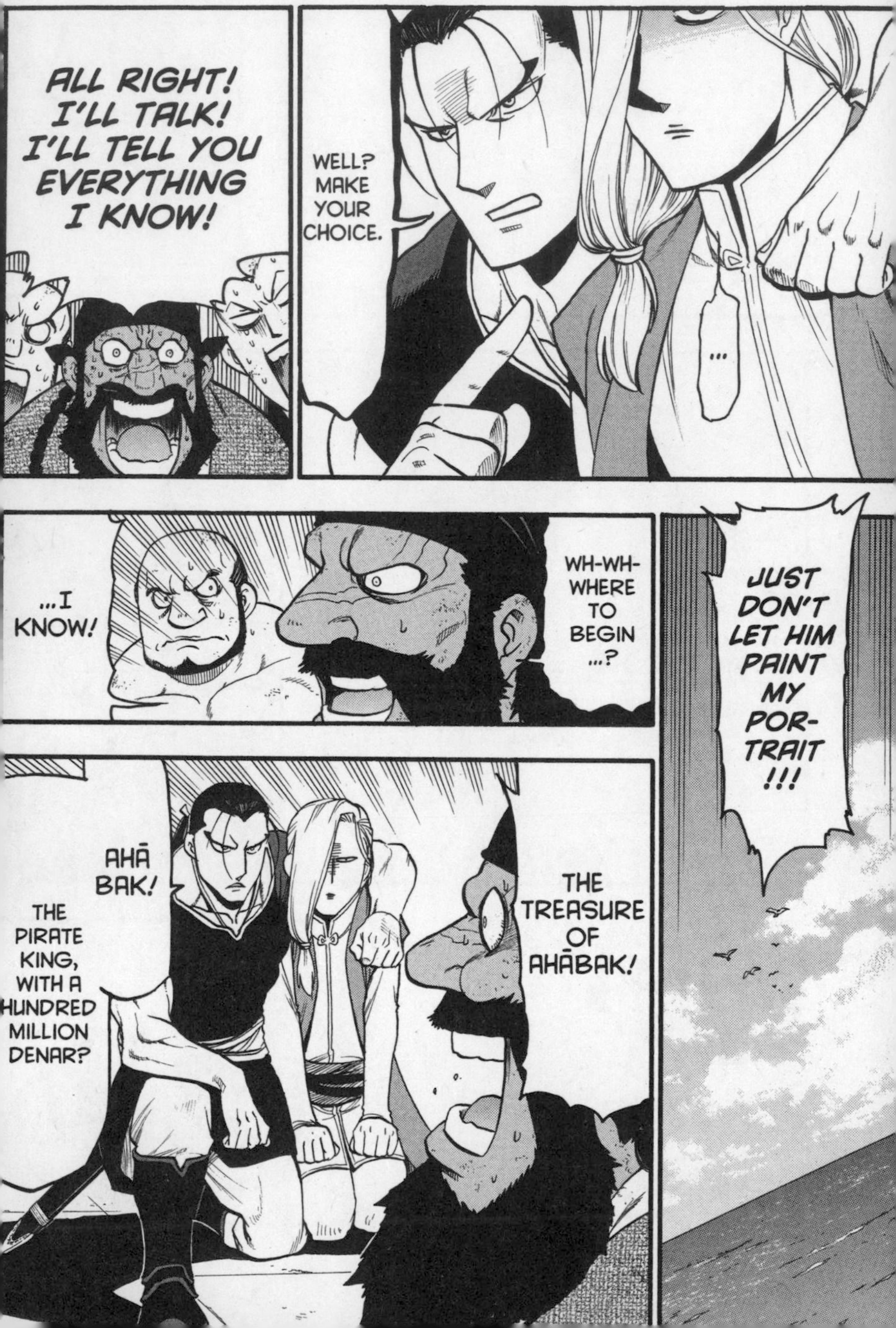
WELL? MAKE YOUR CHOICE.
...
ALL RIGHT! I'LL TALK! I'LL TELL YOU EVERYTHING I KNOW!
JUST DON'T LET HIM PAINT MY POR-TRAIT!!!
WH-WH-WHERE TO BEGIN...?
...I KNOW!
THE TREASURE OF AHĀBAK!
AHĀ BAK!
THE PIRATE KING, WITH A HUNDRED MILLION DENAR?

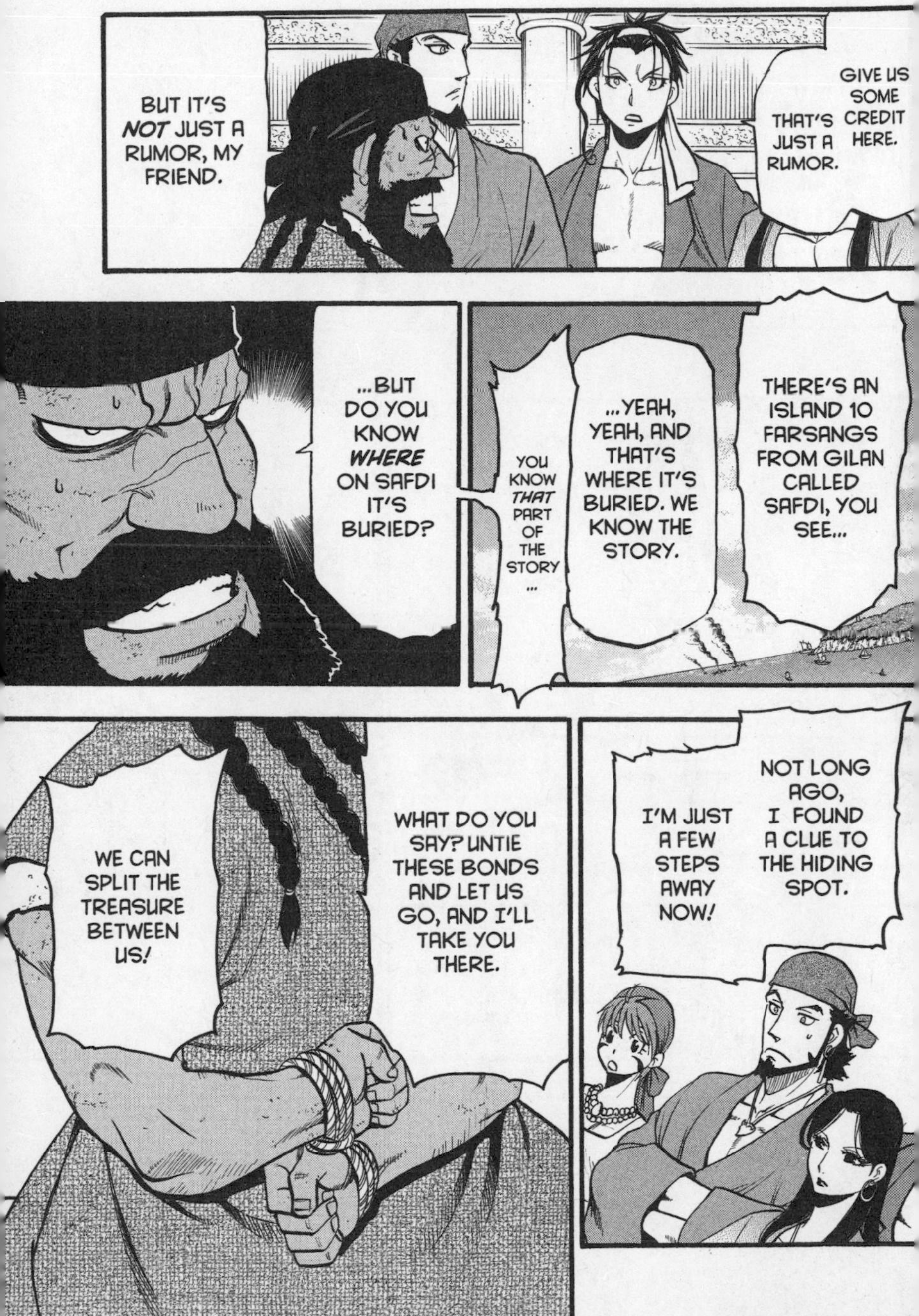
GIVE US SOME CREDIT HERE.
THAT'S JUST A RUMOR.
BUT IT'S *NOT* JUST A RUMOR, MY FRIEND.
THERE'S AN ISLAND 10 FARSANGS FROM GILAN CALLED SAFDI, YOU SEE...
...YEAH, YEAH, AND THAT'S WHERE IT'S BURIED. WE KNOW THE STORY.
YOU KNOW *THAT* PART OF THE STORY...
...BUT DO YOU KNOW *WHERE* ON SAFDI IT'S BURIED?
NOT LONG AGO, I FOUND A CLUE TO THE HIDING SPOT.
I'M JUST A FEW STEPS AWAY NOW!
WHAT DO YOU SAY? UNTIE THESE BONDS AND LET US GO, AND I'LL TAKE YOU THERE.
WE CAN SPLIT THE TREASURE BETWEEN US!

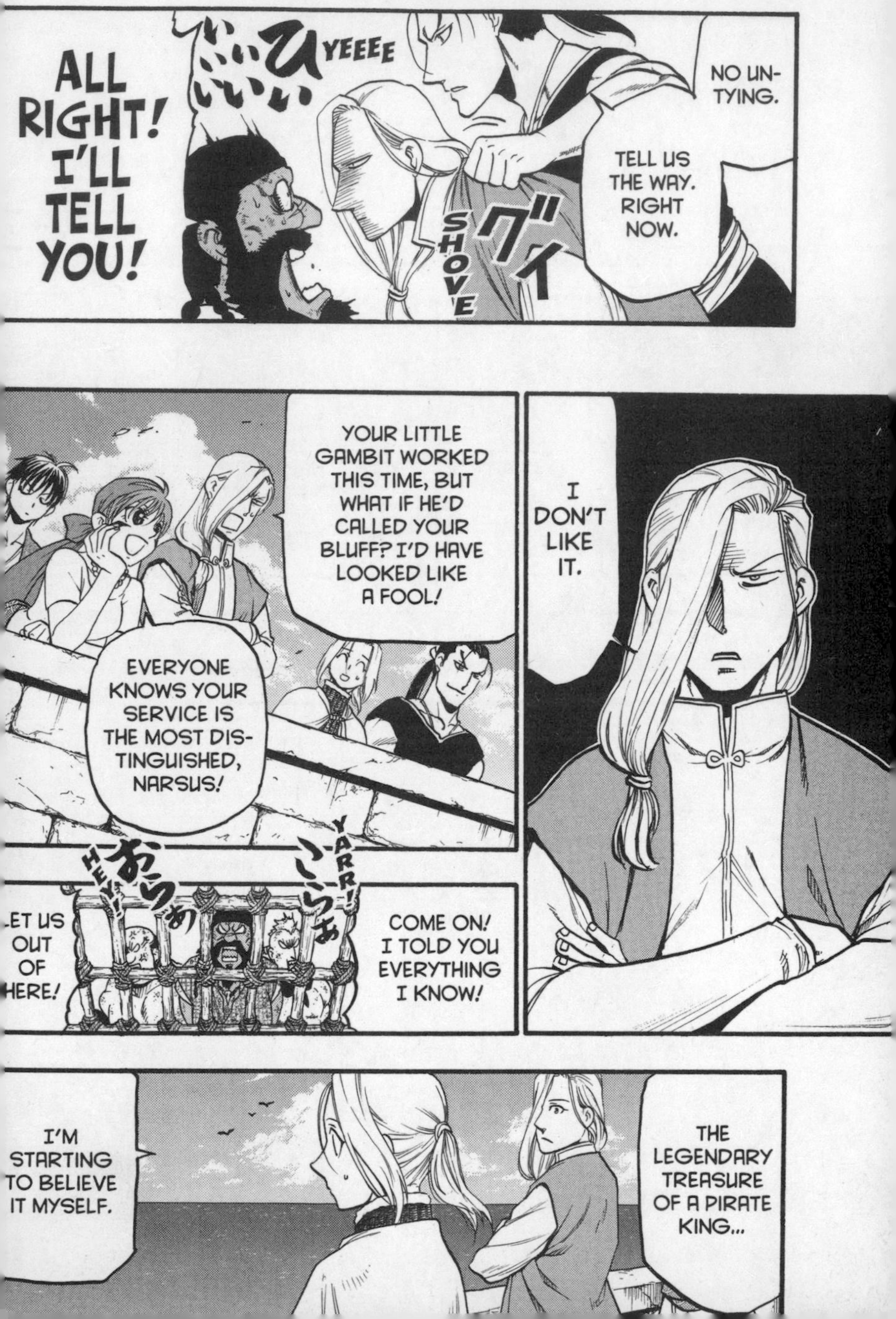
NO UN-TYING.
TELL US THE WAY. RIGHT NOW.
SHOVE
グイ
YEEEE
ALL RIGHT! I'LL TELL YOU!
I DON'T LIKE IT.
YOUR LITTLE GAMBIT WORKED THIS TIME, BUT WHAT IF HE'D CALLED YOUR BLUFF? I'D HAVE LOOKED LIKE A FOOL!
EVERYONE KNOWS YOUR SERVICE IS THE MOST DIS-TINGUISHED, NARSUS!
COME ON! I TOLD YOU EVERYTHING I KNOW!
YARR!
HEY!
ET US OUT OF HERE!
THE LEGENDARY TREASURE OF A PIRATE KING...
I'M STARTING TO BELIEVE IT MYSELF.

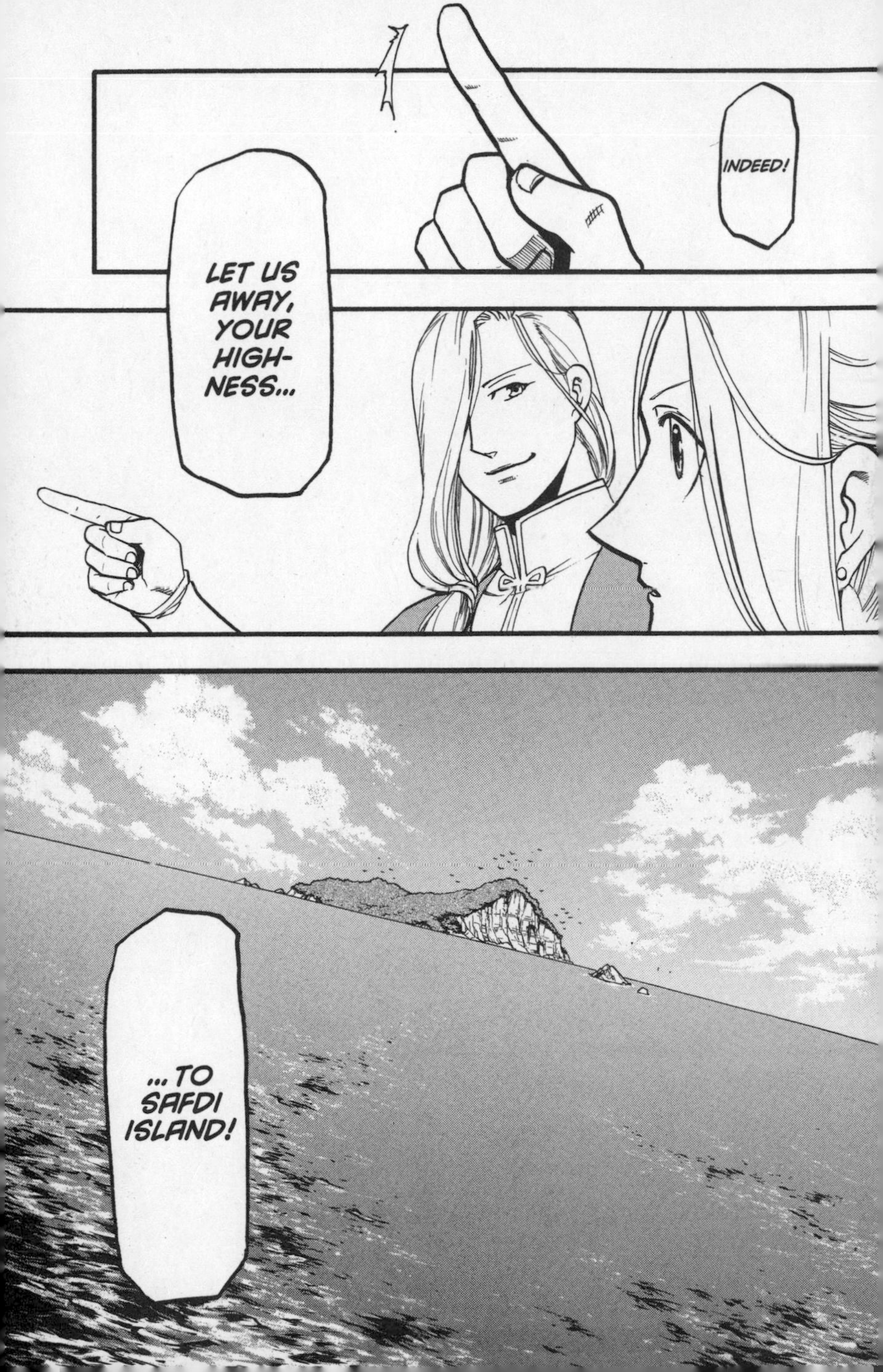
INDEED!
LET US AWAY, YOUR HIGH-NESS...
...TO SAFDI ISLAND!

THE HEROIC LEGEND OF
ARSLAN

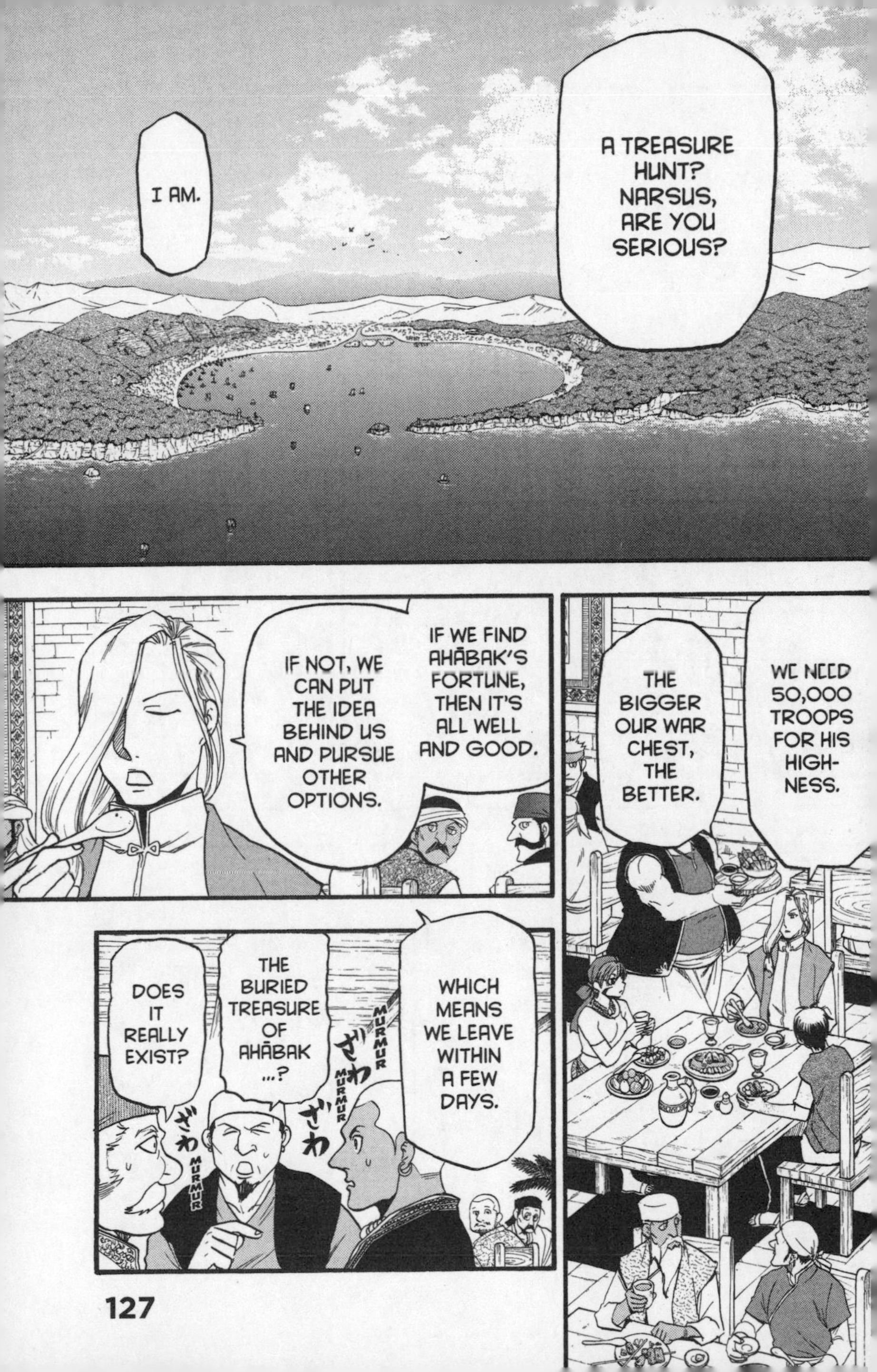
A TREASURE HUNT? NARSUS, ARE YOU SERIOUS?
I AM.
WE NEED 50,000 TROOPS FOR HIS HIGHNESS.
THE BIGGER OUR WAR CHEST, THE BETTER.
IF WE FIND AHĀBAK'S FORTUNE, THEN IT'S ALL WELL AND GOOD.
IF NOT, WE CAN PUT THE IDEA BEHIND US AND PURSUE OTHER OPTIONS.
WHICH MEANS WE LEAVE WITHIN A FEW DAYS.
ざわ MURMUR
ざわ MURMUR
THE BURIED TREASURE OF AHĀBAK ...?
ざわ MURMUR
DOES IT REALLY EXIST?

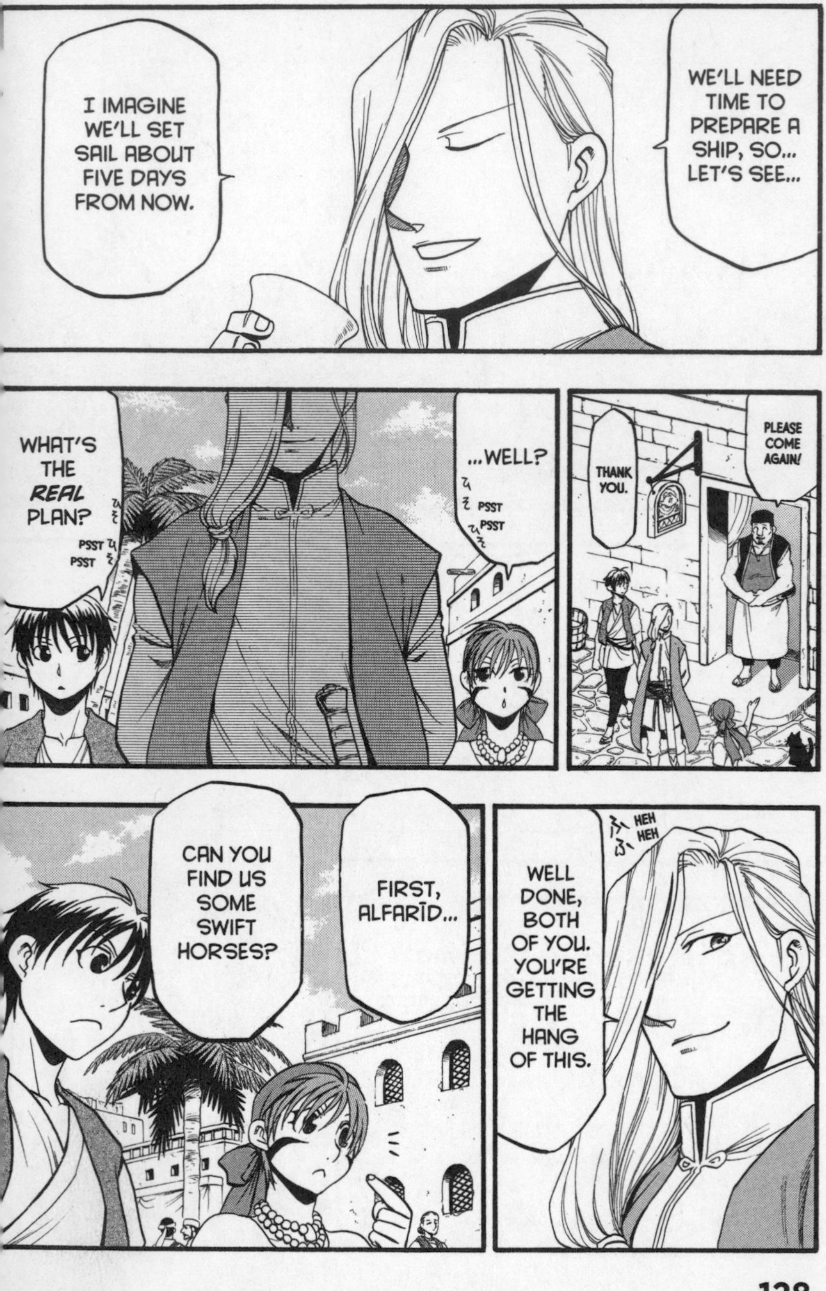
WE'LL NEED TIME TO PREPARE A SHIP, SO... LET'S SEE...
I IMAGINE WE'LL SET SAIL ABOUT FIVE DAYS FROM NOW.
PLEASE COME AGAIN!
THANK YOU.
...WELL?
PSST PSST
WHAT'S THE *REAL* PLAN?
PSST PSST
HEH HEH
WELL DONE, BOTH OF YOU. YOU'RE GETTING THE HANG OF THIS.
FIRST, ALFARĪD...
CAN YOU FIND US SOME SWIFT HORSES?

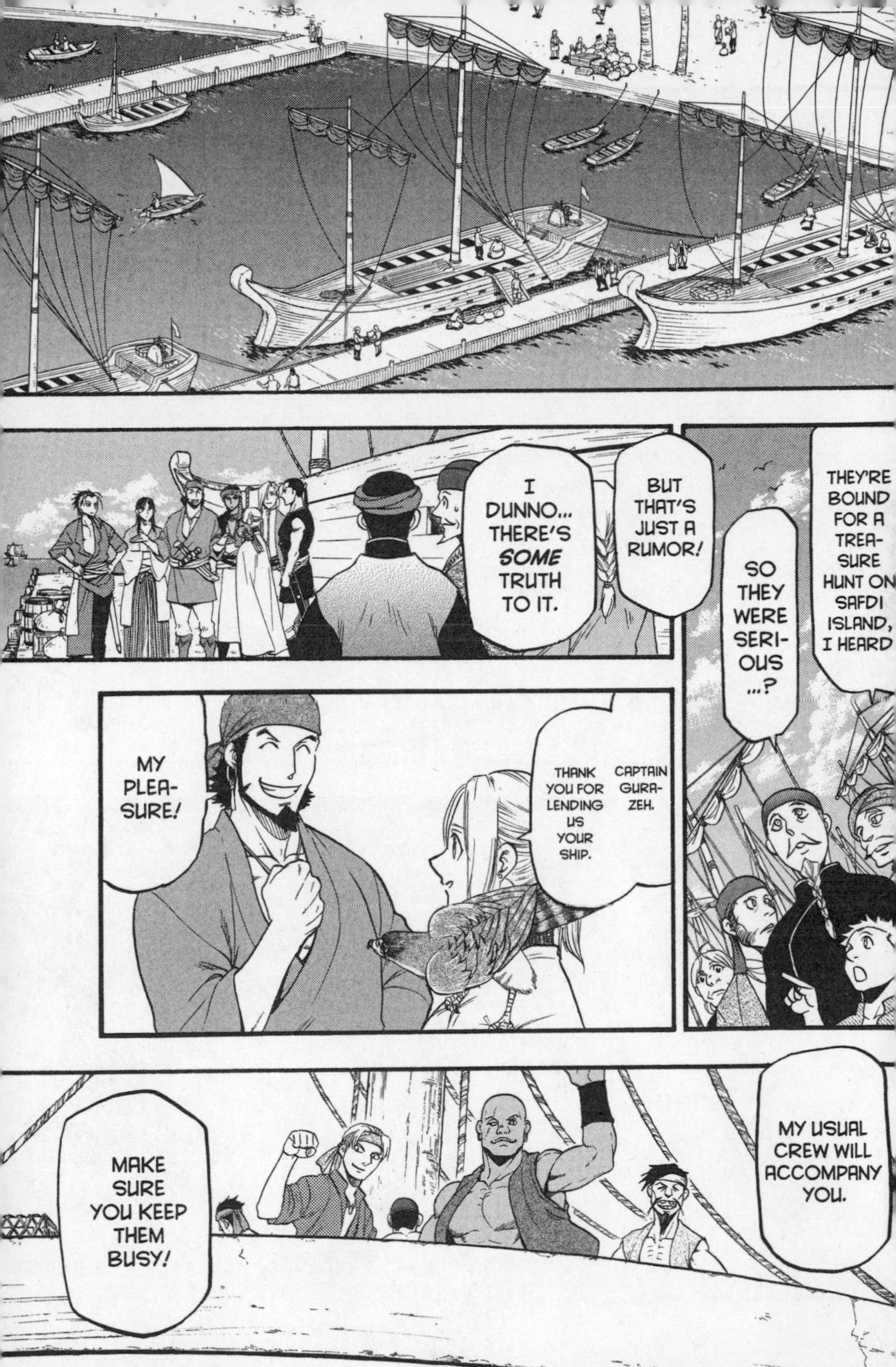
THEY'RE BOUND FOR A TREA-SURE HUNT ON SAFDI ISLAND, I HEARD
SO THEY WERE SERI-OUS ...?
BUT THAT'S JUST A RUMOR!
I DUNNO... THERE'S *SOME* TRUTH TO IT.
CAPTAIN GURA-ZEH.
THANK YOU FOR LENDING US YOUR SHIP.
MY PLEA-SURE!
MY USUAL CREW WILL ACCOMPANY YOU.
MAKE SURE YOU KEEP THEM BUSY!

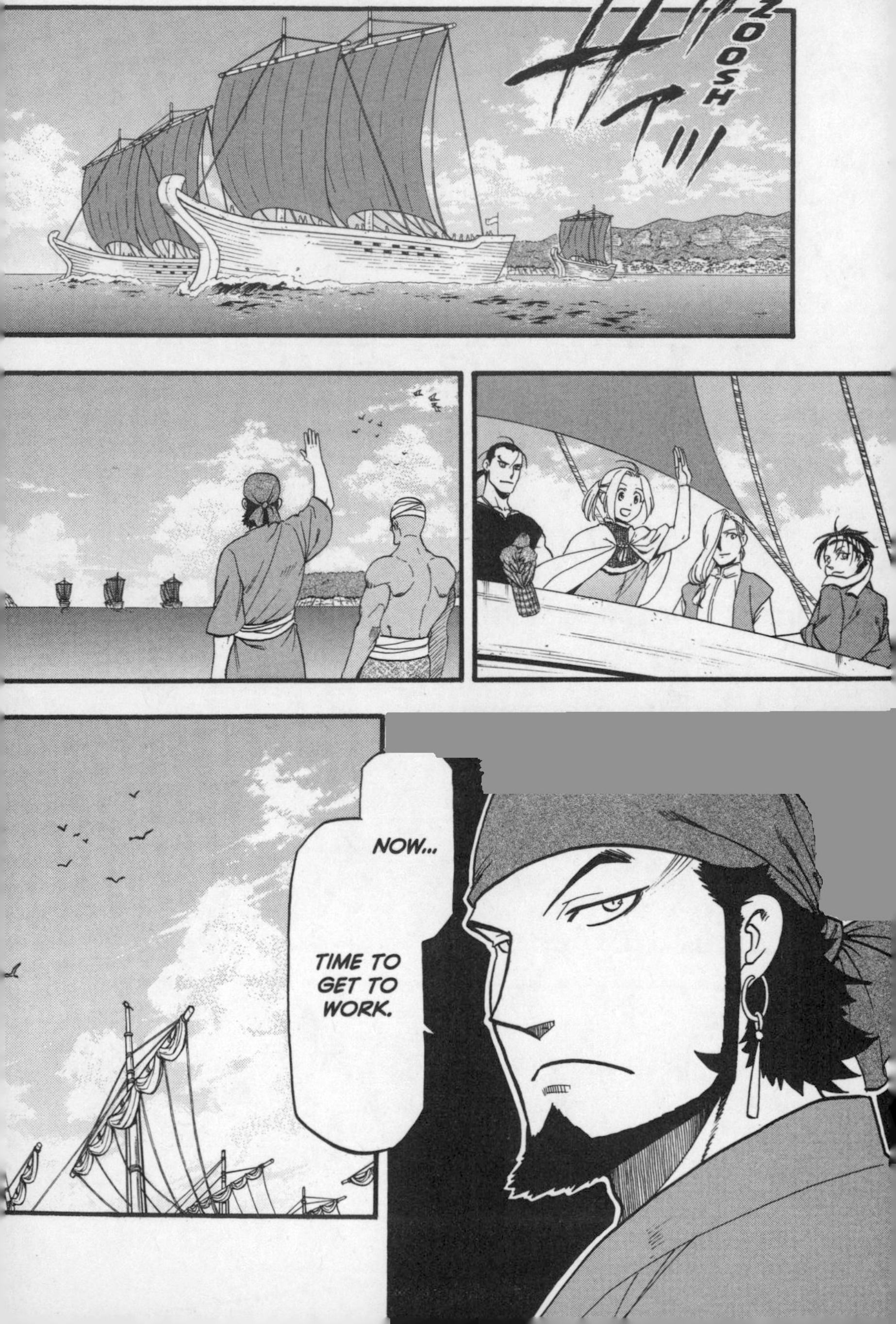
ZOOSH
NOW...
TIME TO GET TO WORK.

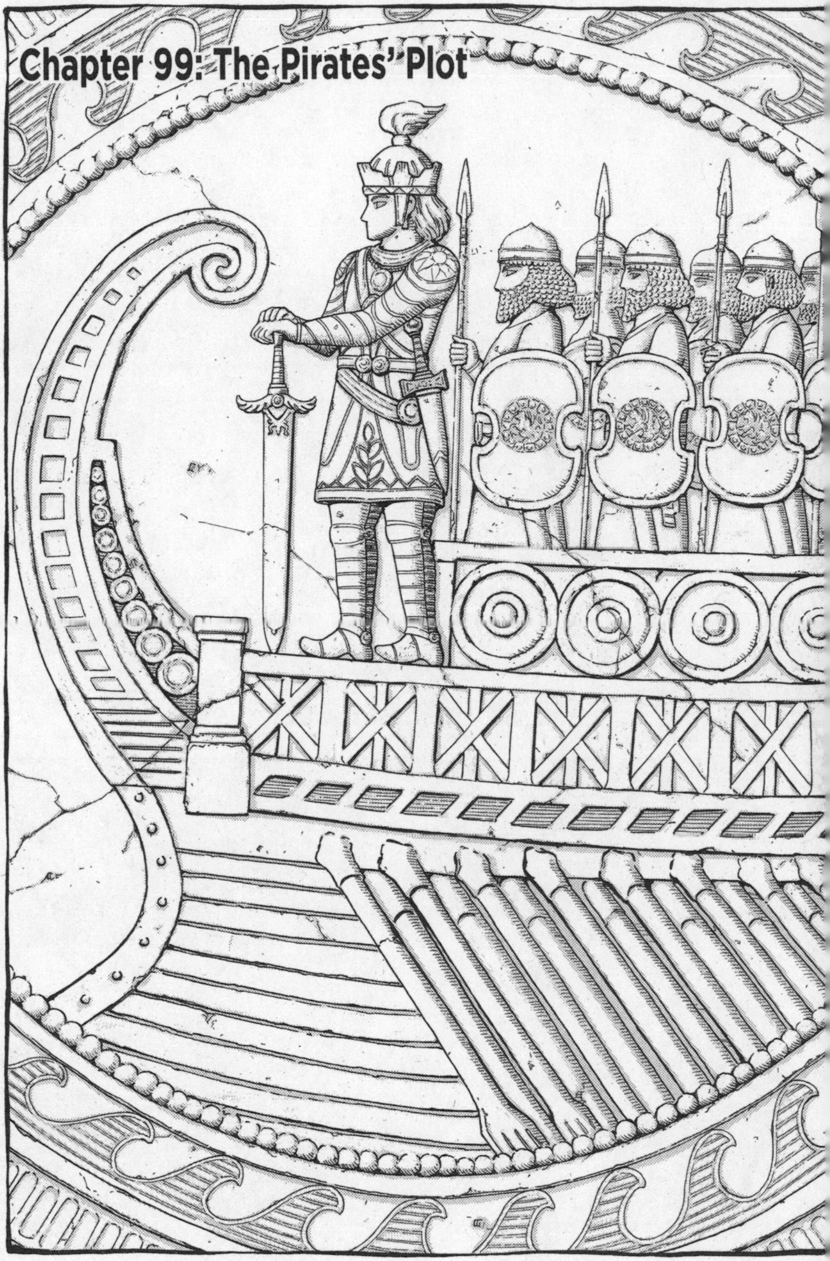
Chapter 99: The Pirates' Plot

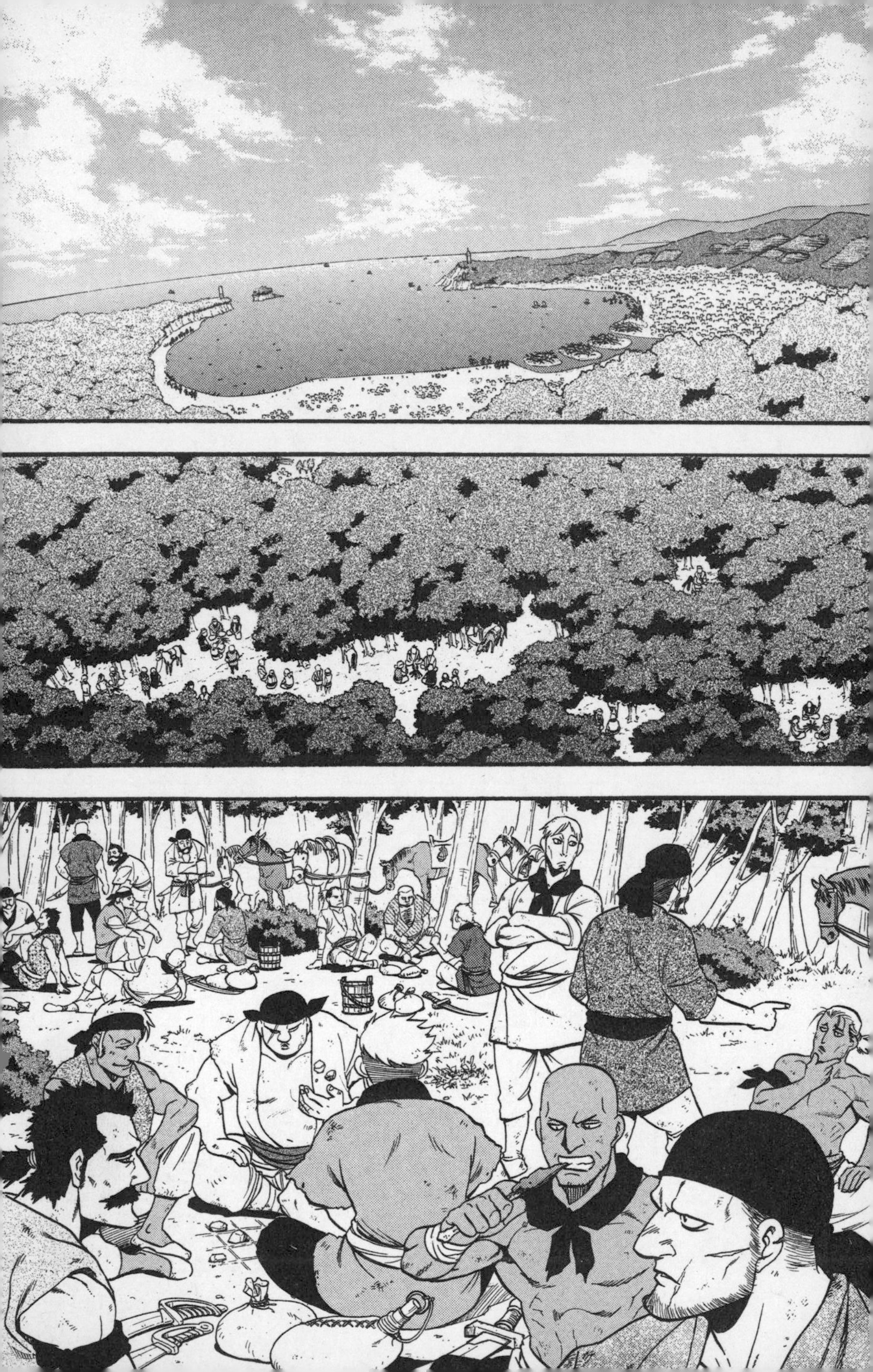

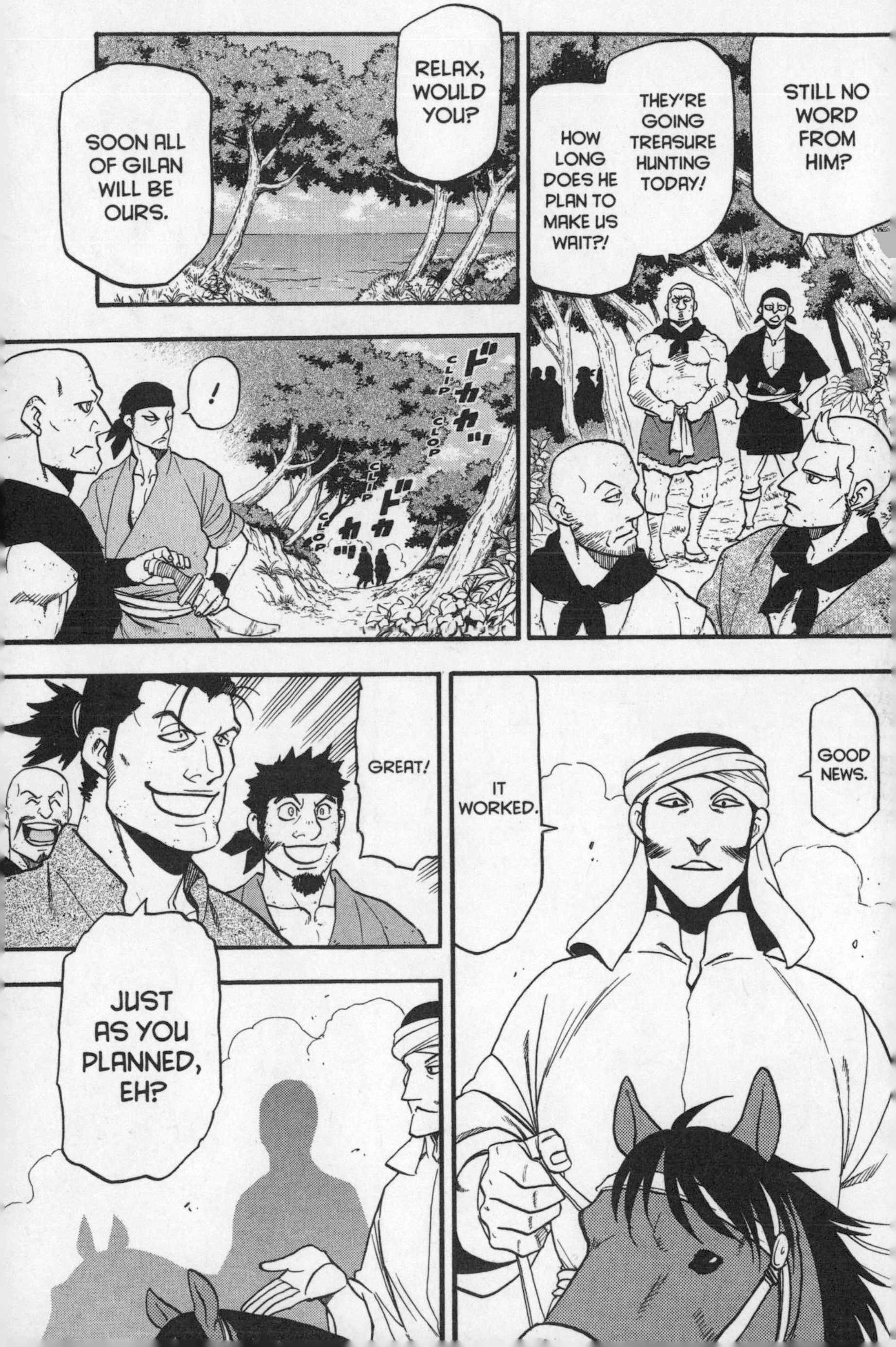
STILL NO WORD FROM HIM?
THEY'RE GOING TREASURE HUNTING TODAY!
HOW LONG DOES HE PLAN TO MAKE US WAIT?!
RELAX, WOULD YOU?
SOON ALL OF GILAN WILL BE OURS.
ドカカッ
CLIP CLOP
ドカカッ
CLIP CLOP
!
GOOD NEWS.
IT WORKED.
GREAT!
JUST AS YOU PLANNED, EH?

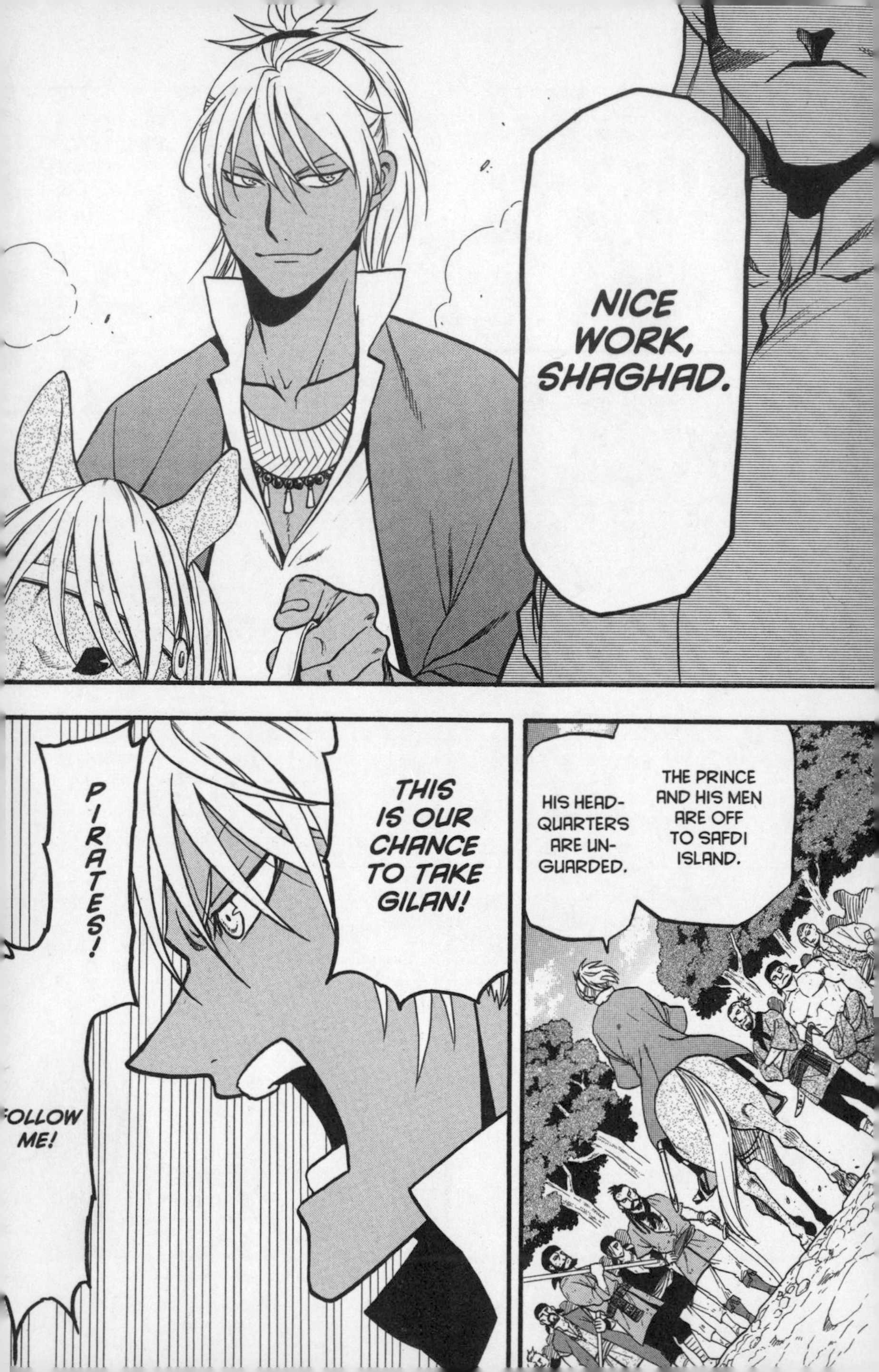
NICE WORK, SHAGHAD.
THE PRINCE AND HIS MEN ARE OFF TO SAFDI ISLAND.
HIS HEADQUARTERS ARE UNGUARDED.
THIS IS OUR CHANCE TO TAKE GILAN!
PIRATES!
FOLLOW ME!

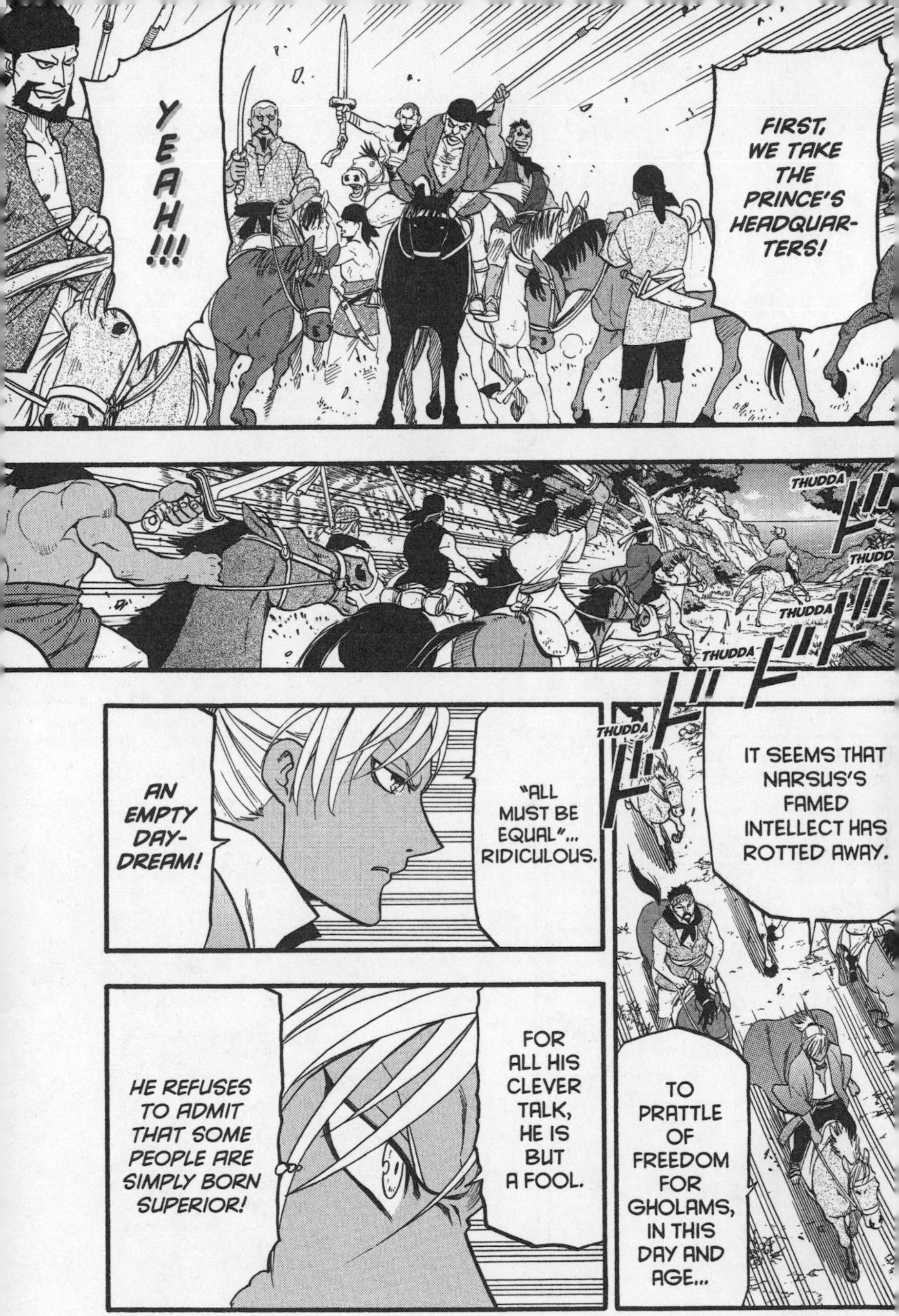
FIRST, WE TAKE THE PRINCE'S HEADQUARTERS!
YEAH!!!
THUDDA
THUDDA
THUDDA
THUDDA
THUDDA
IT SEEMS THAT NARSUS'S FAMED INTELLECT HAS ROTTED AWAY.
TO PRATTLE OF FREEDOM FOR GHOLAMS, IN THIS DAY AND AGE...
"ALL MUST BE EQUAL"... RIDICULOUS.
AN EMPTY DAY-DREAM!
FOR ALL HIS CLEVER TALK, HE IS BUT A FOOL.
HE REFUSES TO ADMIT THAT SOME PEOPLE ARE SIMPLY BORN SUPERIOR!

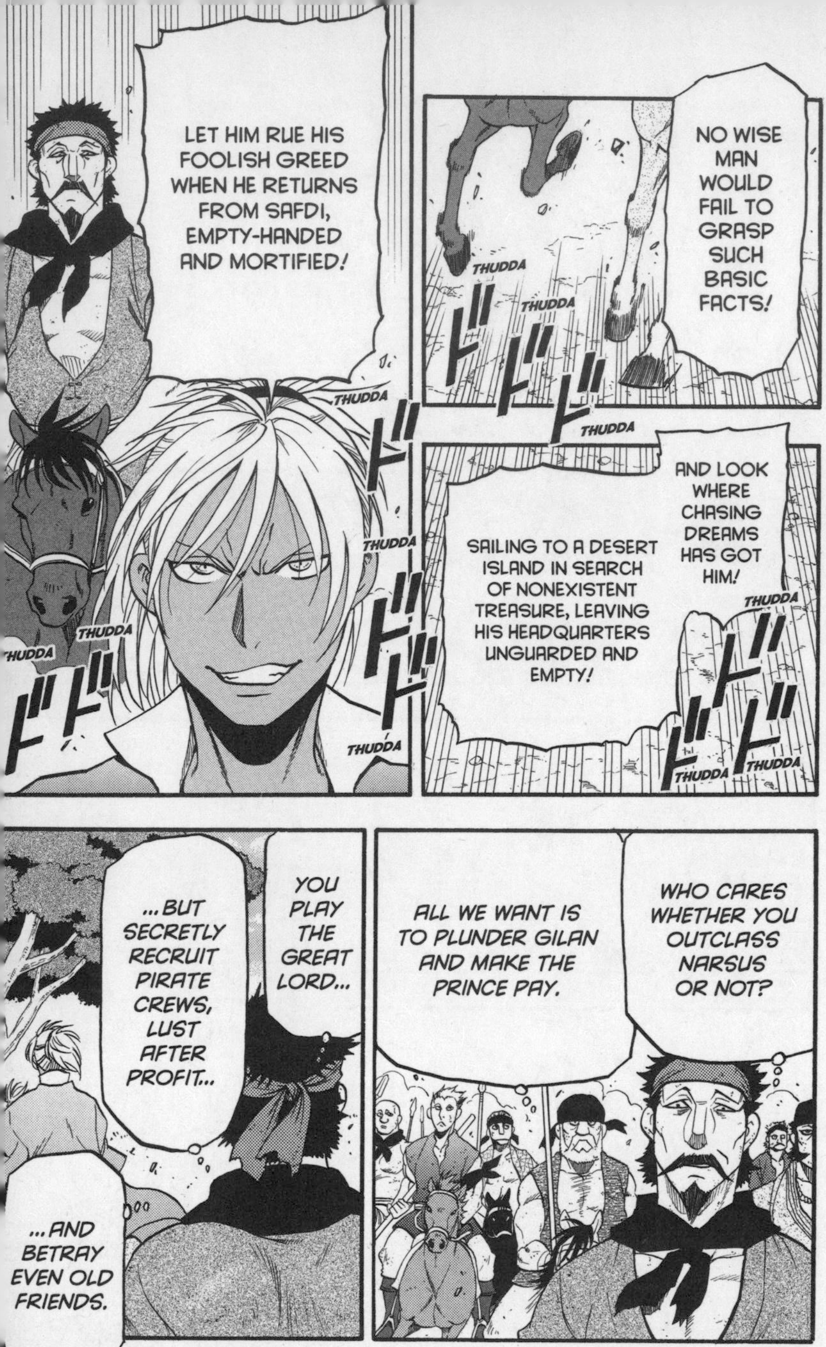
NO WISE MAN WOULD FAIL TO GRASP SUCH BASIC FACTS!
THUDDA
THUDDA
THUDDA
AND LOOK WHERE CHASING DREAMS HAS GOT HIM!
SAILING TO A DESERT ISLAND IN SEARCH OF NONEXISTENT TREASURE, LEAVING HIS HEADQUARTERS UNGUARDED AND EMPTY!
THUDDA
THUDDA
THUDDA
LET HIM RUE HIS FOOLISH GREED WHEN HE RETURNS FROM SAFDI, EMPTY-HANDED AND MORTIFIED!
THUDDA
THUDDA
THUDDA
THUDDA
THUDDA
WHO CARES WHETHER YOU OUTCLASS NARSUS OR NOT?
ALL WE WANT IS TO PLUNDER GILAN AND MAKE THE PRINCE PAY.
YOU PLAY THE GREAT LORD...
...BUT SECRETLY RECRUIT PIRATE CREWS, LUST AFTER PROFIT...
...AND BETRAY EVEN OLD FRIENDS.

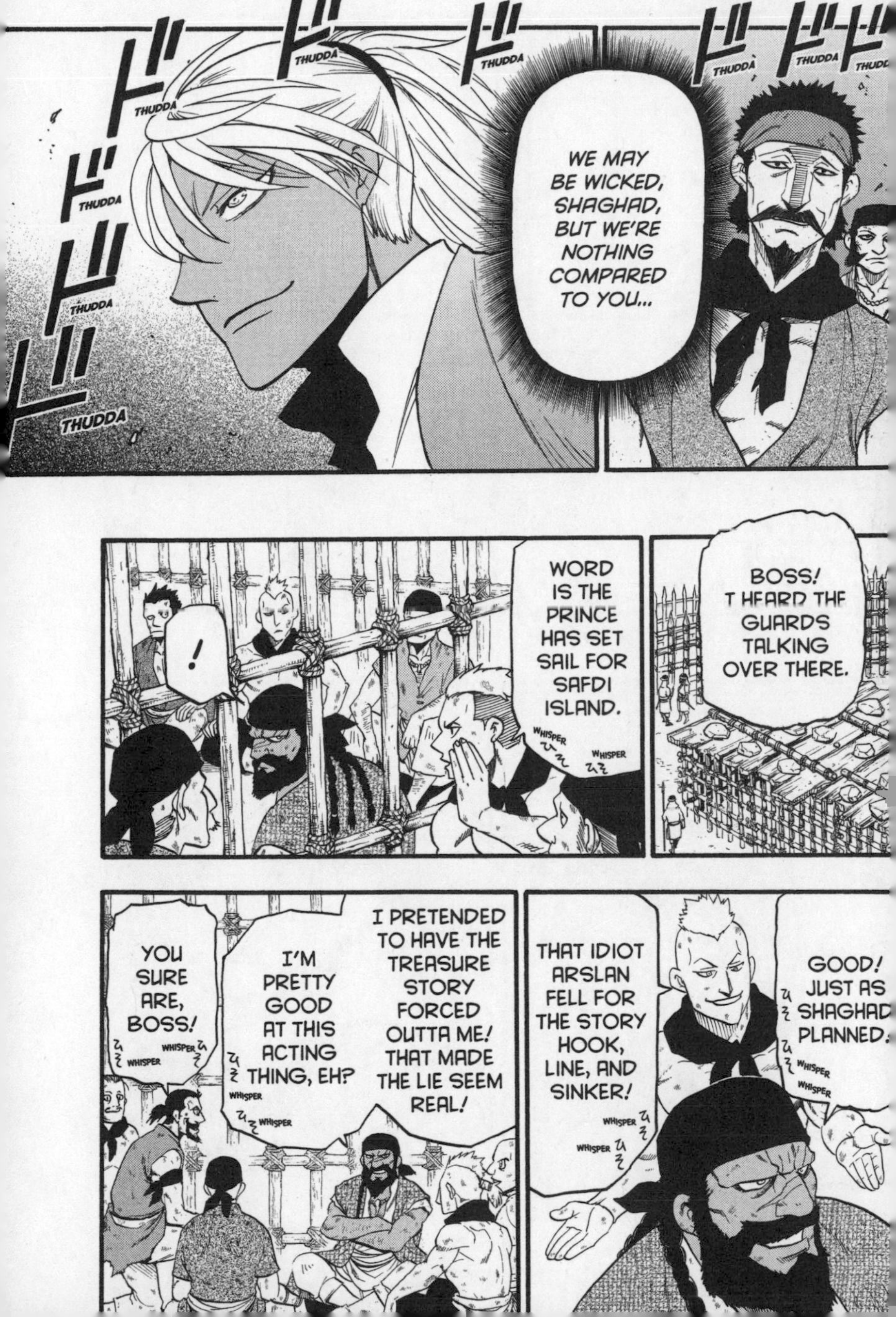

THUDDA
THUDDA
THUDDA
WE MAY BE WICKED, SHAGHAD, BUT WE'RE NOTHING COMPARED TO YOU...
THUDDA
THUDDA
THUDDA
THUDDA
THUDDA
THUDDA
BOSS! I HEARD THE GUARDS TALKING OVER THERE.
WORD IS THE PRINCE HAS SET SAIL FOR SAFDI ISLAND.
WHISPER
WHISPER
!
GOOD! JUST AS SHAGHAD PLANNED.
WHISPER
WHISPER
THAT IDIOT ARSLAN FELL FOR THE STORY HOOK, LINE, AND SINKER!
WHISPER
WHISPER
I PRETENDED TO HAVE THE TREASURE STORY FORCED OUTTA ME! THAT MADE THE LIE SEEM REAL!
I'M PRETTY GOOD AT THIS ACTING THING, EH?
WHISPER
WHISPER
YOU SURE ARE, BOSS!
WHISPER
WHISPER

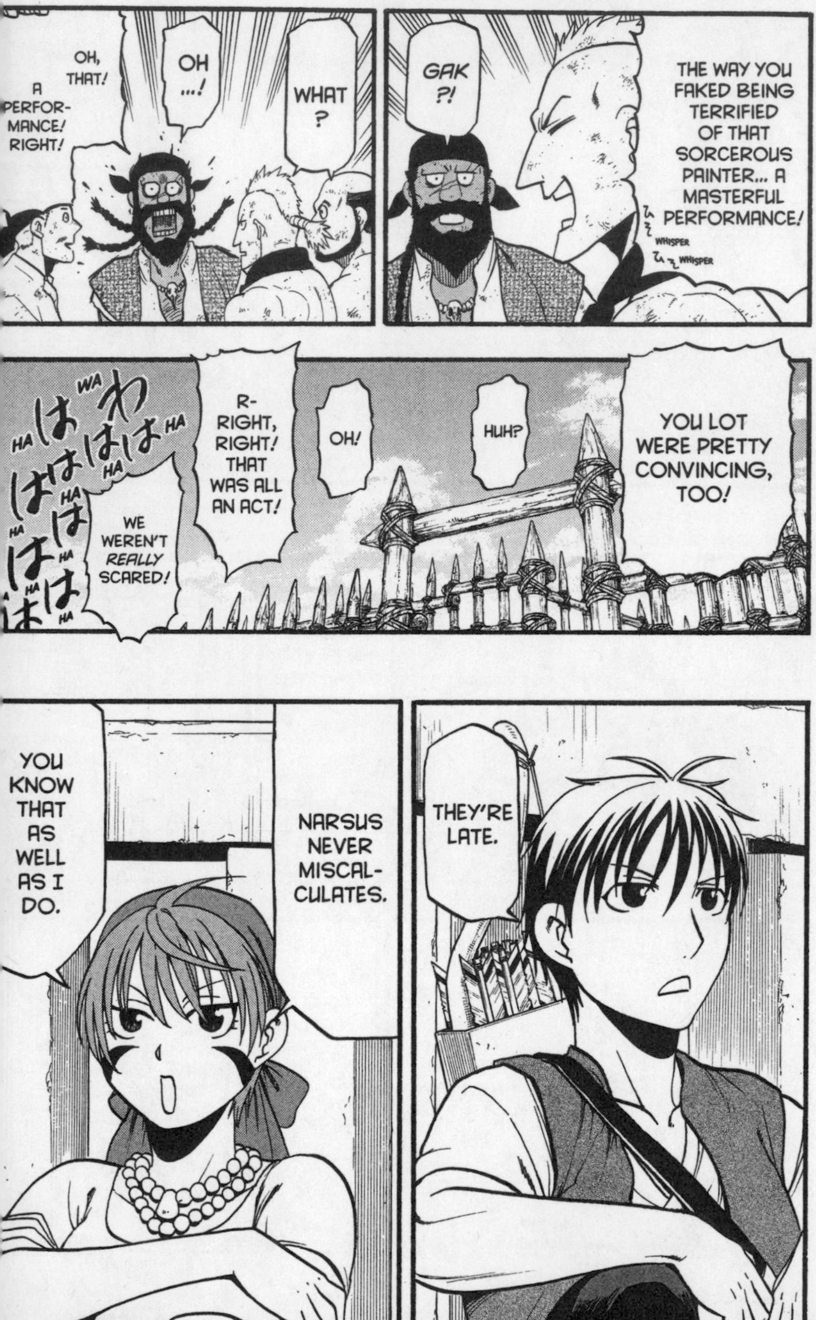
THE WAY YOU FAKED BEING TERRIFIED OF THAT SORCEROUS PAINTER... A MASTERFUL PERFORMANCE!
WHISPER
WHISPER
GAK ?!
WHAT ?
OH ...!
OH, THAT!
A PERFORMANCE! RIGHT!
YOU LOT WERE PRETTY CONVINCING, TOO!
HUH?
OH!
R-RIGHT, RIGHT! THAT WAS ALL AN ACT!
WE WEREN'T *REALLY* SCARED!
WA HA HA HA HA HA HA HA HA
THEY'RE LATE.
NARSUS NEVER MISCALCULATES.
YOU KNOW THAT AS WELL AS I DO.

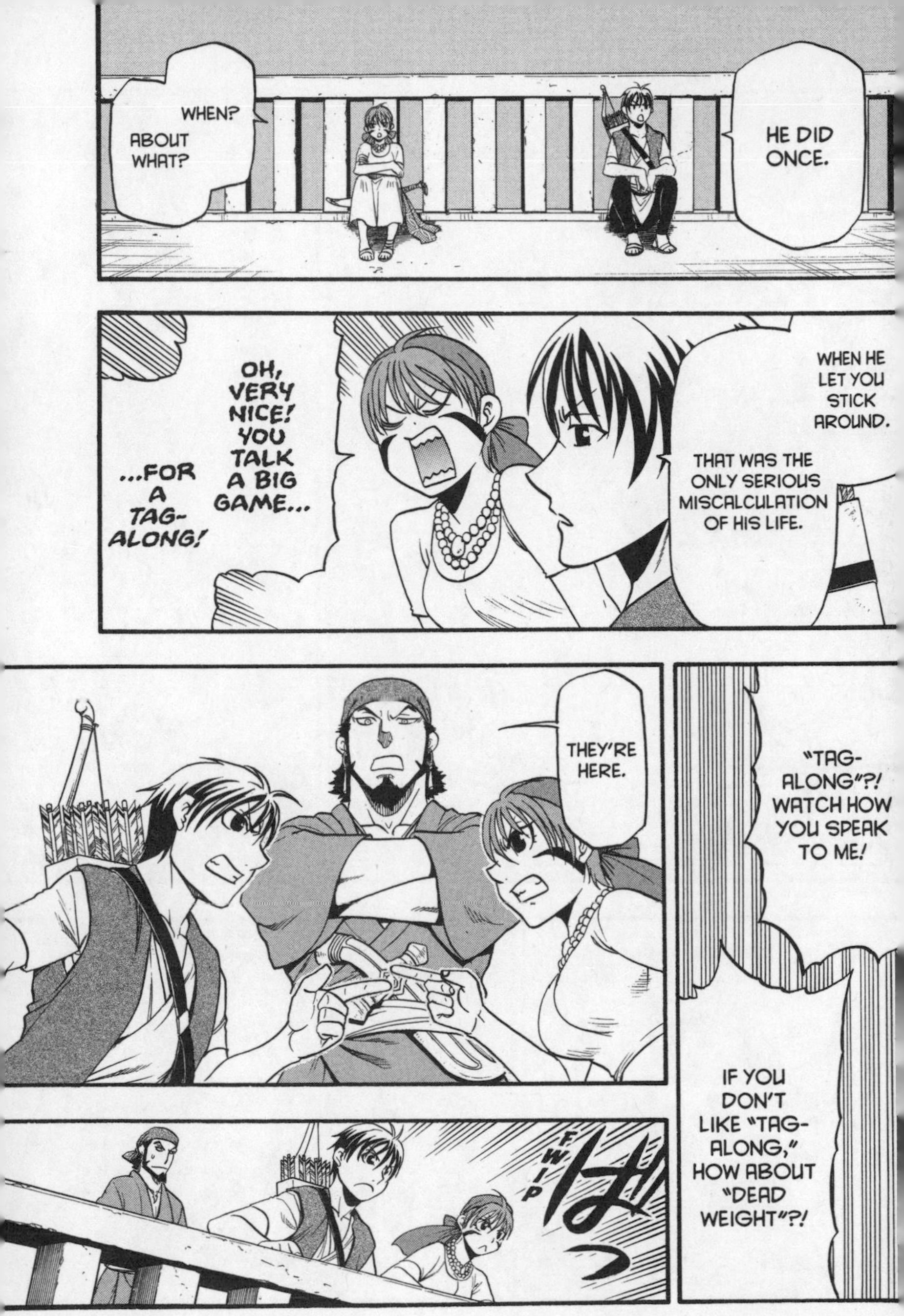
HE DID ONCE.
WHEN? ABOUT WHAT?
WHEN HE LET YOU STICK AROUND.
THAT WAS THE ONLY SERIOUS MISCALCULATION OF HIS LIFE.
OH, VERY NICE! YOU TALK A BIG GAME...
...FOR A TAG-ALONG!
"TAG-ALONG"?! WATCH HOW YOU SPEAK TO ME!
IF YOU DON'T LIKE "TAG-ALONG," HOW ABOUT "DEAD WEIGHT"?!
THEY'RE HERE.
FWIP
はっ

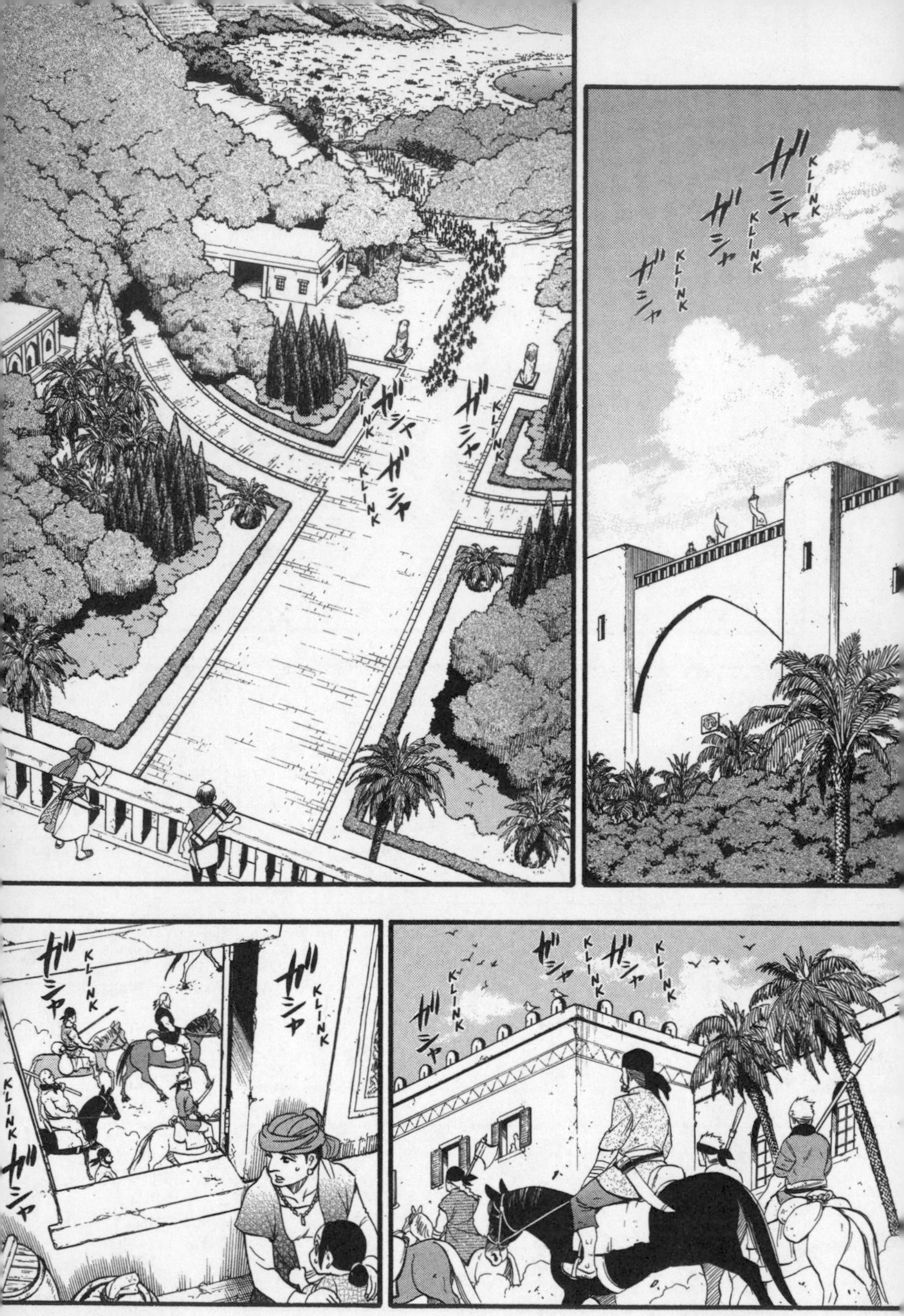
ガシャ KLINK
ガシャ KLINK
ガシャ KLINK
ガシャ KLINK
ガシャ KLINK
ガシャ KLINK
ガシャ KLINK
ガシャ KLINK
ガシャ KLINK
ガシャ KLINK
ガシャ KLINK
ガシャ KLINK

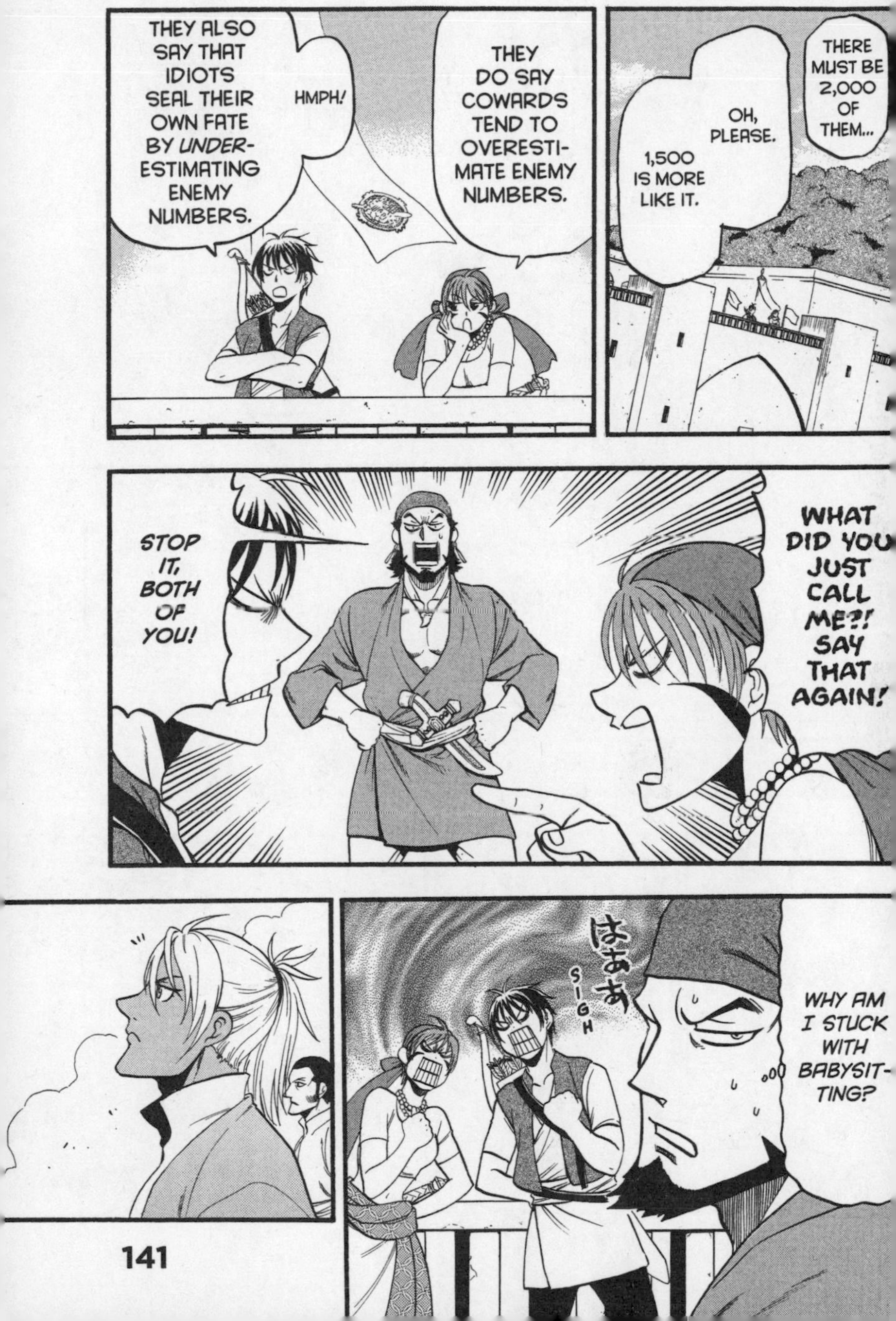
THERE MUST BE 2,000 OF THEM...
OH, PLEASE.
1,500 IS MORE LIKE IT.
THEY DO SAY COWARDS TEND TO OVERESTIMATE ENEMY NUMBERS.
HMPH!
THEY ALSO SAY THAT IDIOTS SEAL THEIR OWN FATE BY *UNDER*-ESTIMATING ENEMY NUMBERS.
WHAT DID YOU JUST CALL ME?! SAY THAT AGAIN!
STOP IT, BOTH OF YOU!
WHY AM I STUCK WITH BABYSITTING?
はあぁ
SIGH

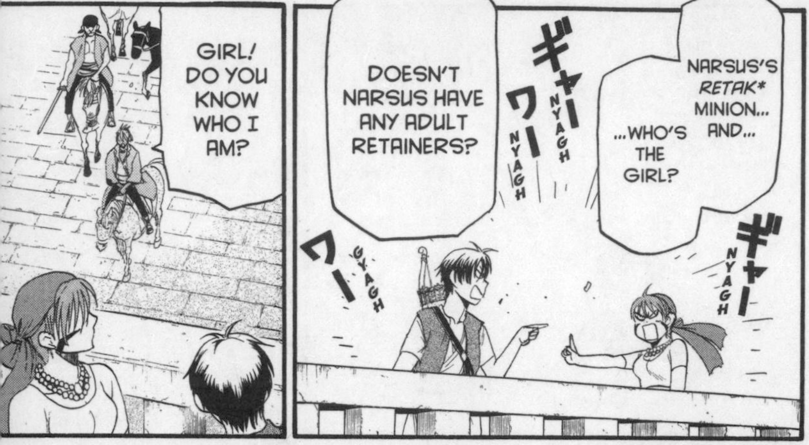
NARSUS'S *RETAK** MINION... AND...
...WHO'S THE GIRL?
ギャー NYAGH
ワー NYAGH
DOESN'T NARSUS HAVE ANY ADULT RETAINERS?
ギャー NYAGH
ワー GYAGH
GIRL! DO YOU KNOW WHO I AM?

*CHILD ATTENDANT OF SORT

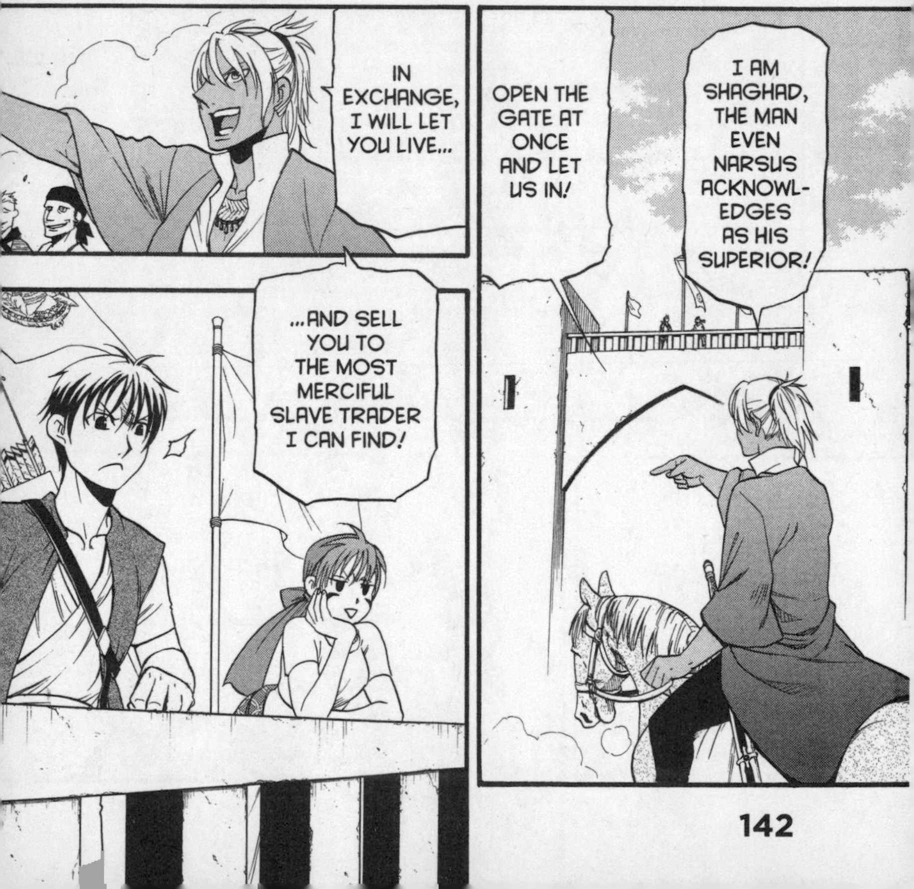
I AM SHAGHAD, THE MAN EVEN NARSUS ACKNOWLEDGES AS HIS SUPERIOR!
OPEN THE GATE AT ONCE AND LET US IN!
IN EXCHANGE, I WILL LET YOU LIVE...
...AND SELL YOU TO THE MOST MERCIFUL SLAVE TRADER I CAN FIND!

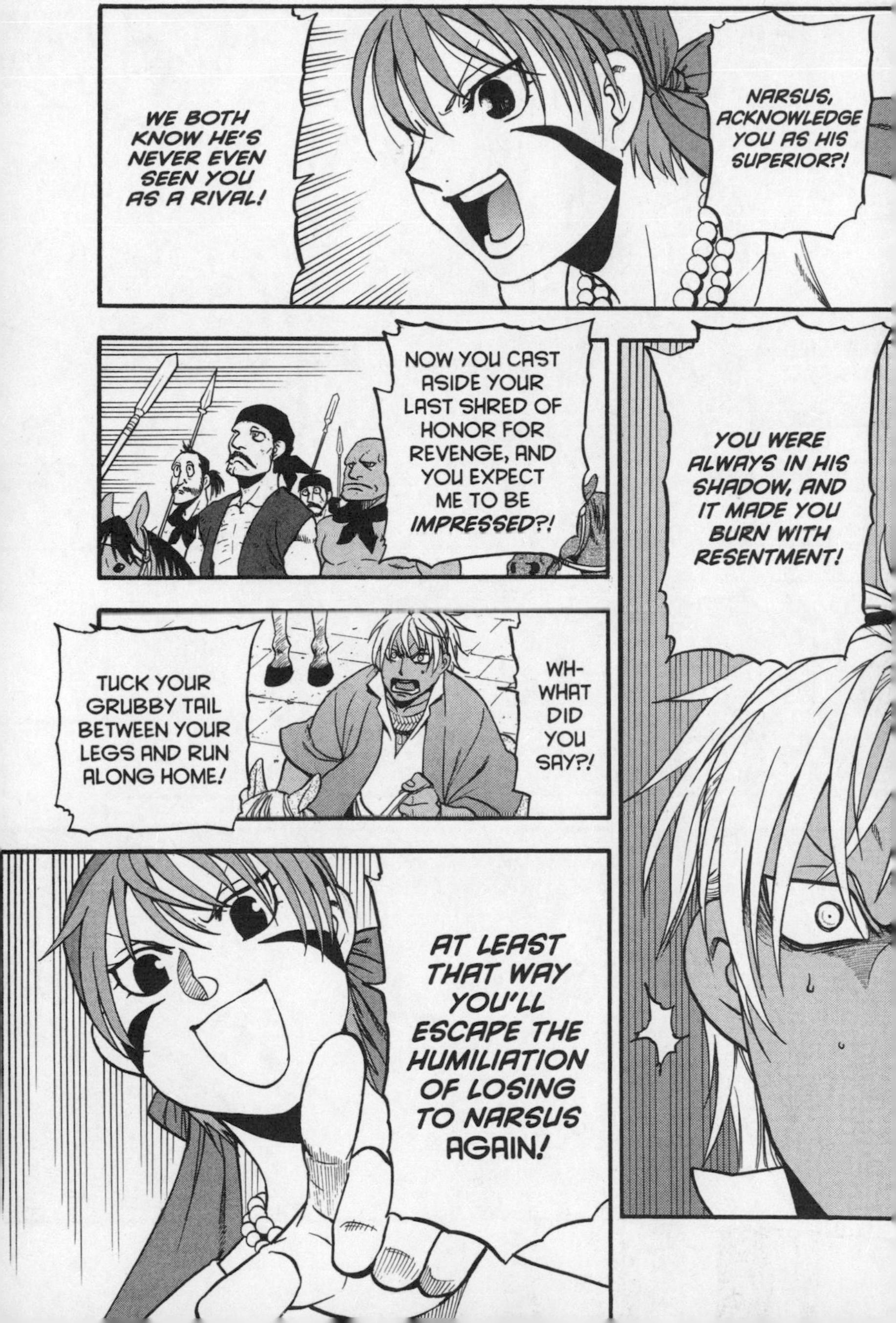
NARSUS, ACKNOWLEDGE YOU AS HIS SUPERIOR?!
WE BOTH KNOW HE'S NEVER EVEN SEEN YOU AS A RIVAL!
YOU WERE ALWAYS IN HIS SHADOW, AND IT MADE YOU BURN WITH RESENTMENT!
NOW YOU CAST ASIDE YOUR LAST SHRED OF HONOR FOR REVENGE, AND YOU EXPECT ME TO BE IMPRESSED?!
WH- WHAT DID YOU SAY?!
TUCK YOUR GRUBBY TAIL BETWEEN YOUR LEGS AND RUN ALONG HOME!
AT LEAST THAT WAY YOU'LL ESCAPE THE HUMILIATION OF LOSING TO NARSUS AGAIN!

NNGG
...

I'LL TEAR THAT IMPUDENT TONGUE OUT OF YOUR HEAD, GIRL!

GO ON! SCRAM!

AYE! AYE!

BREAK DOWN THE GATE!

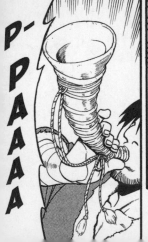

P-PAAAA

144

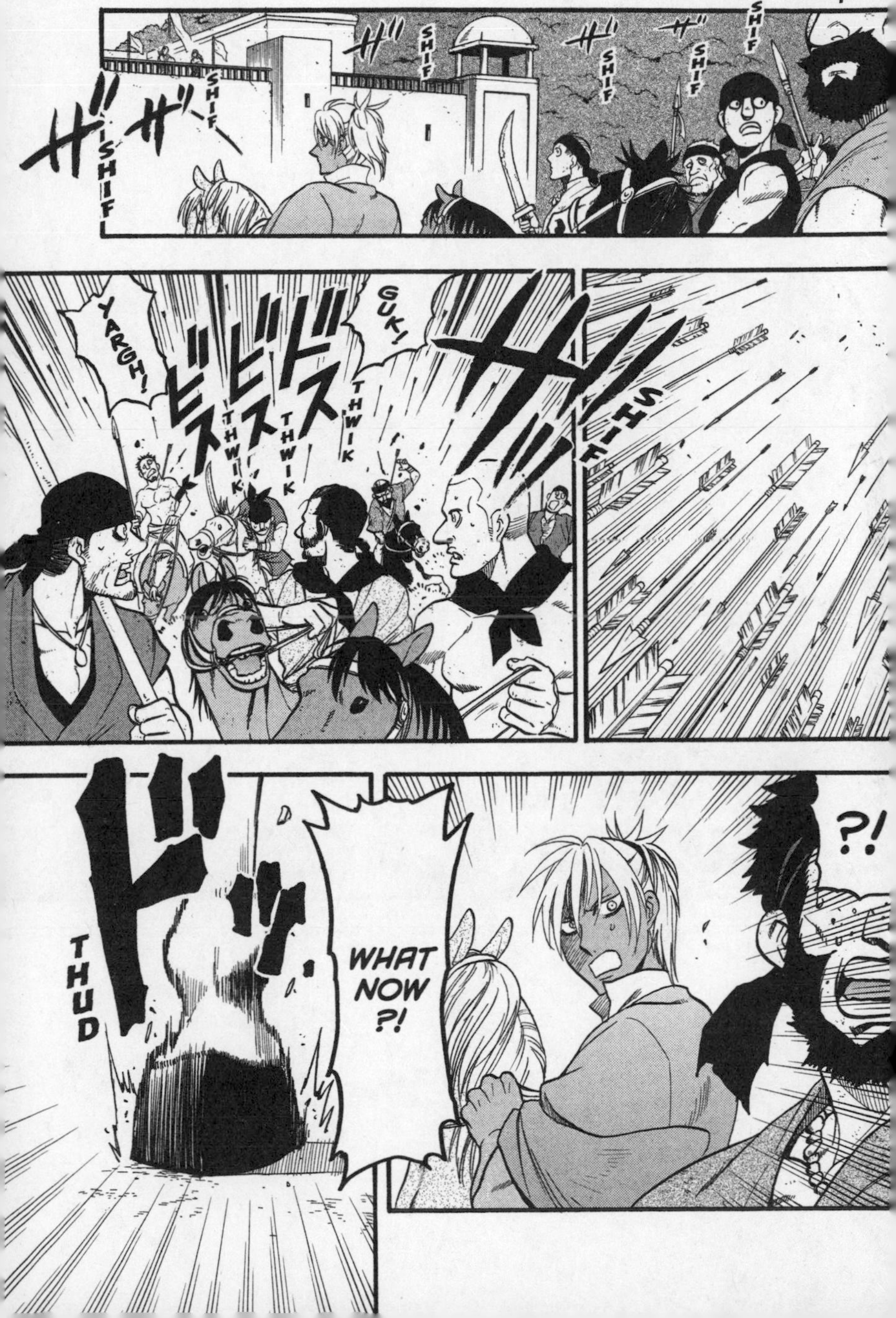

ザ
SHIF
ザ
SHIF
ザ
SHIF
ザ
SHIF
ザ
SHIF
ザ
SHIF
ザ
SHIF
ザ!!
SHIF
ザ
SHIF
GUK!
ドス
THWIK
ビス
THWIK
ビス
THWIK
YARGH!
?!
WHAT NOW ?!
ドッ
THUD

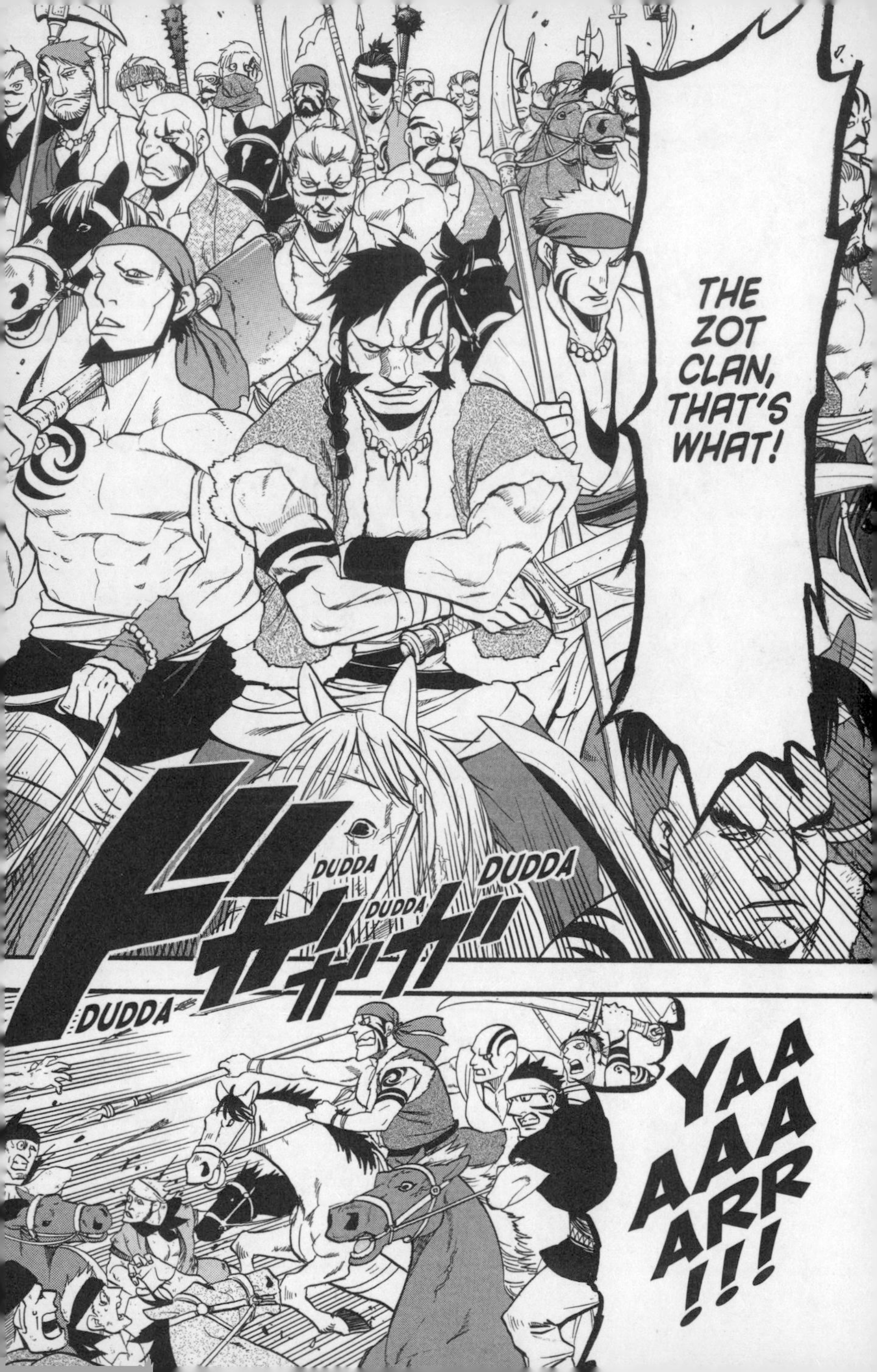
THE ZOT CLAN, THAT'S WHAT!
DUDDA
DUDDA
DUDDA
DUDDA
YAAAAAAARR!!!

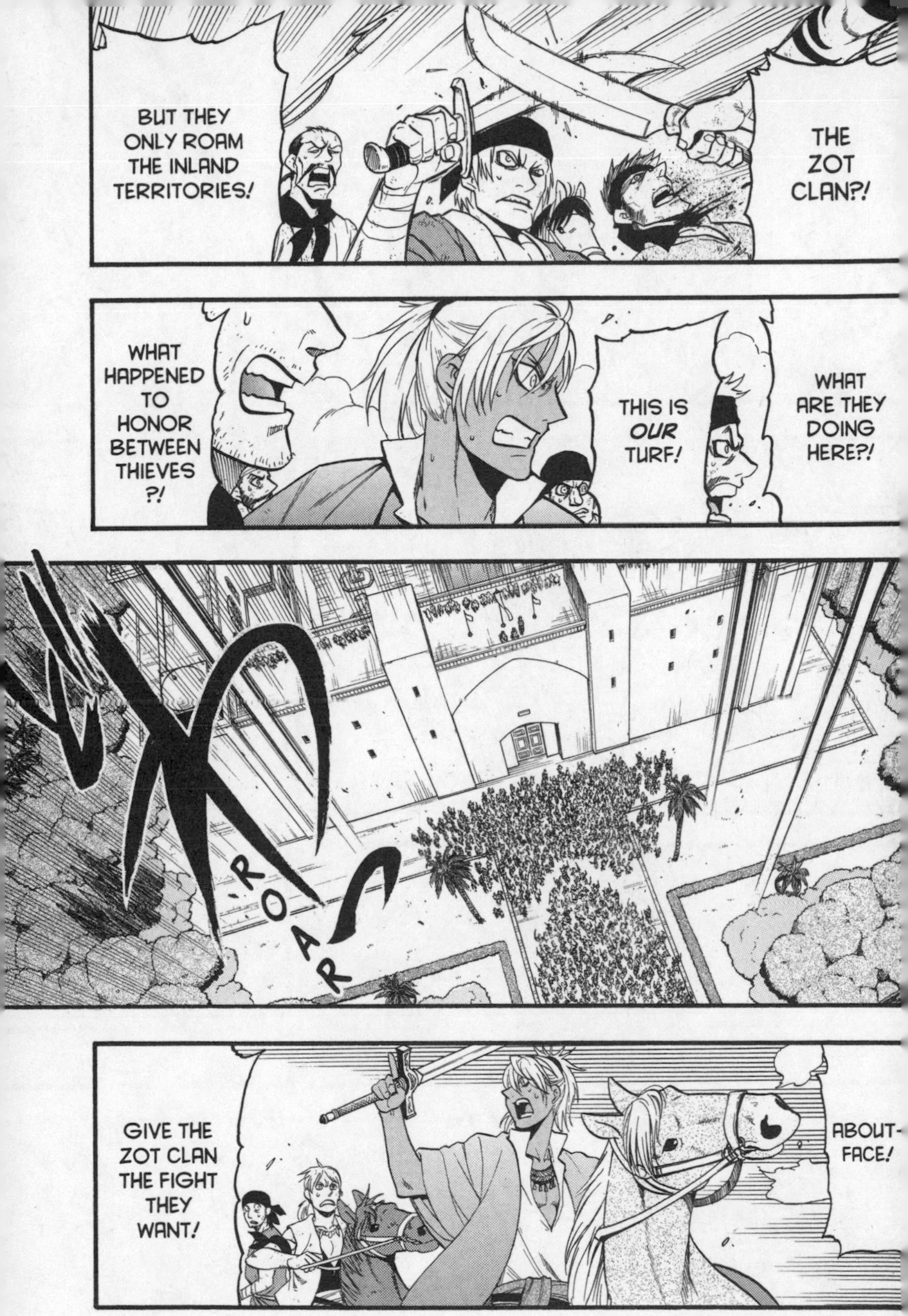
THE ZOT CLAN?!
BUT THEY ONLY ROAM THE INLAND TERRITORIES!
WHAT ARE THEY DOING HERE?!
THIS IS *OUR* TURF!
WHAT HAPPENED TO HONOR BETWEEN THIEVES?!
ROAR
ABOUT-FACE!
GIVE THE ZOT CLAN THE FIGHT THEY WANT!

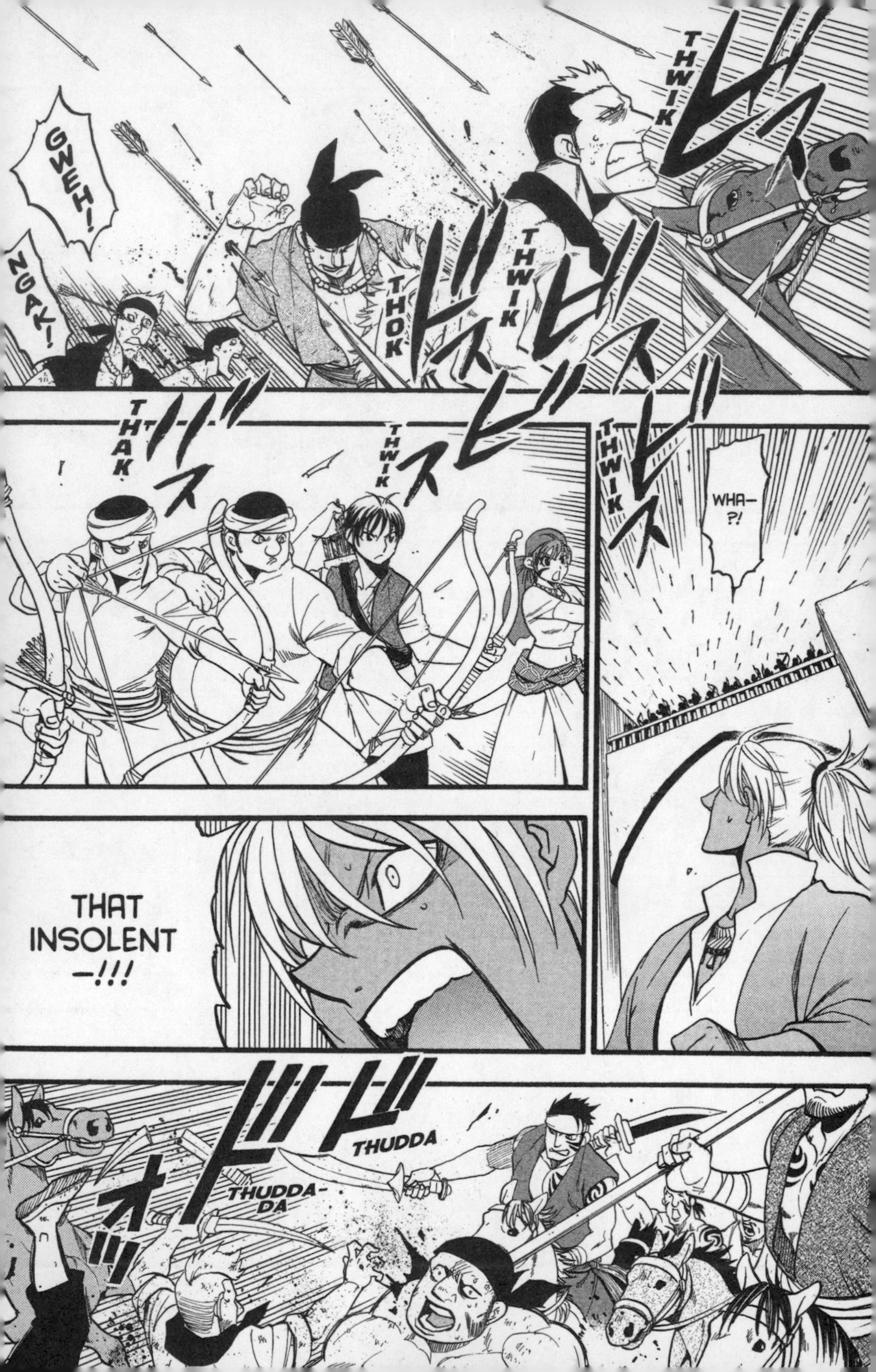
THWIK
THWIK
THOK
GWEH!
NGAK!
THWIK
WHA—?!
THWIK
THAK
THAT INSOLENT—!!!
THUDDA
THUDDA-DA

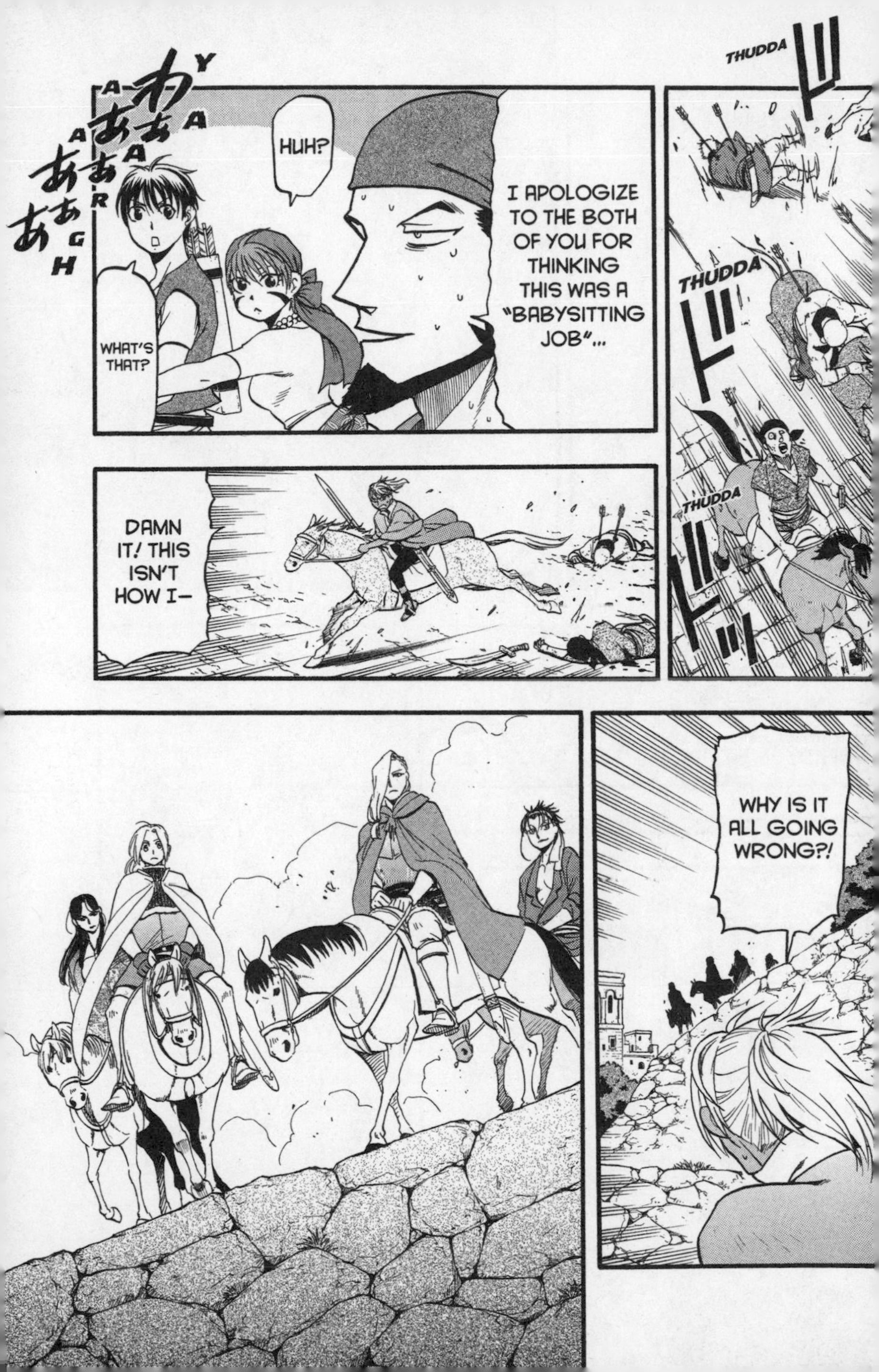
THUDDA
THUDDA
THUDDA
YAAAARGH
HUH?
I APOLOGIZE TO THE BOTH OF YOU FOR THINKING THIS WAS A "BABYSITTING JOB"...
WHAT'S THAT?
DAMN IT! THIS ISN'T HOW I—
WHY IS IT ALL GOING WRONG?!

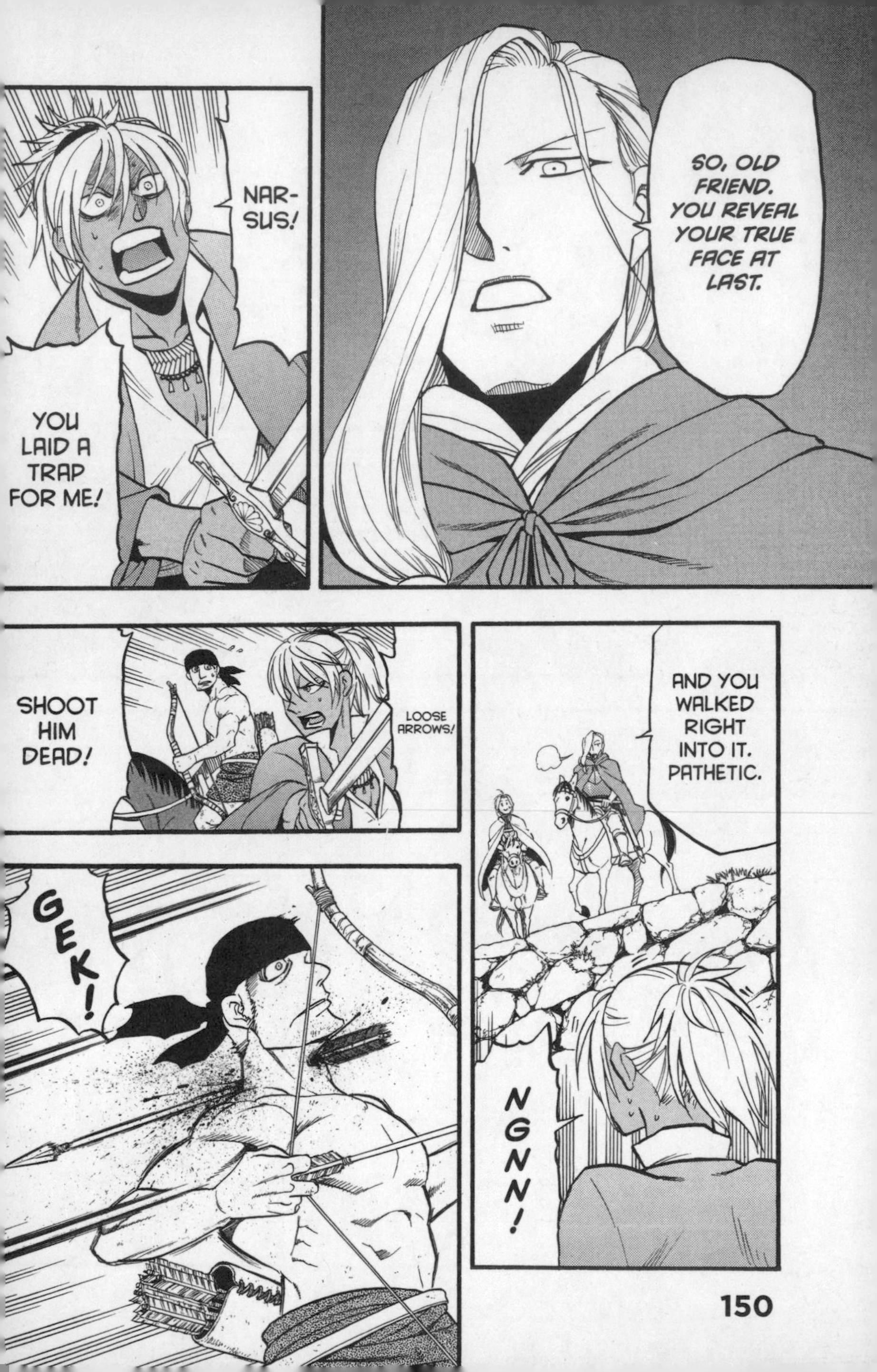
SO, OLD FRIEND. YOU REVEAL YOUR TRUE FACE AT LAST.
NAR-SUS!
YOU LAID A TRAP FOR ME!
AND YOU WALKED RIGHT INTO IT. PATHETIC.
NGNN!
LOOSE ARROWS!
SHOOT HIM DEAD!
GEK!

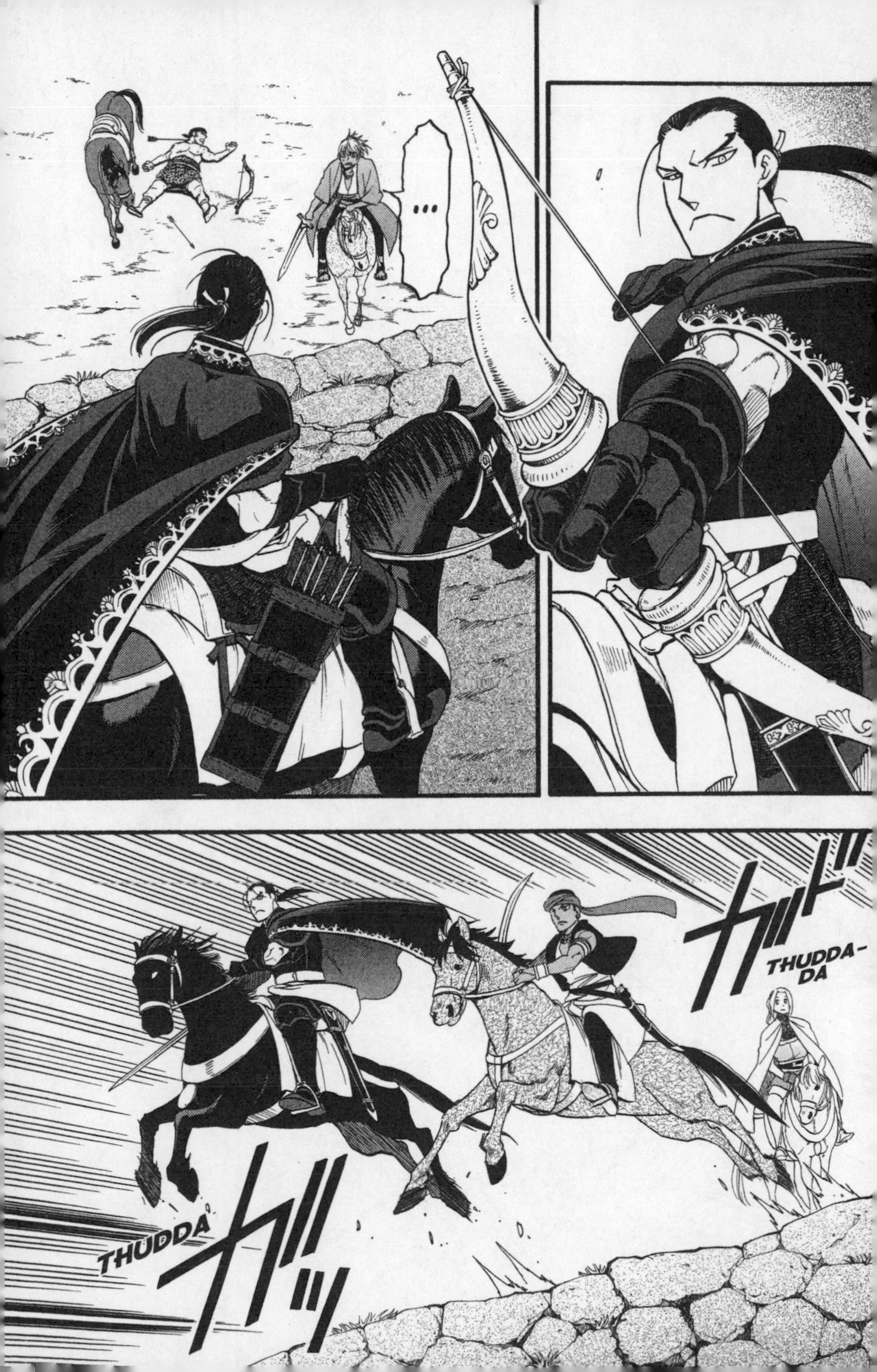
...
THUDDA-DA
THUDDA

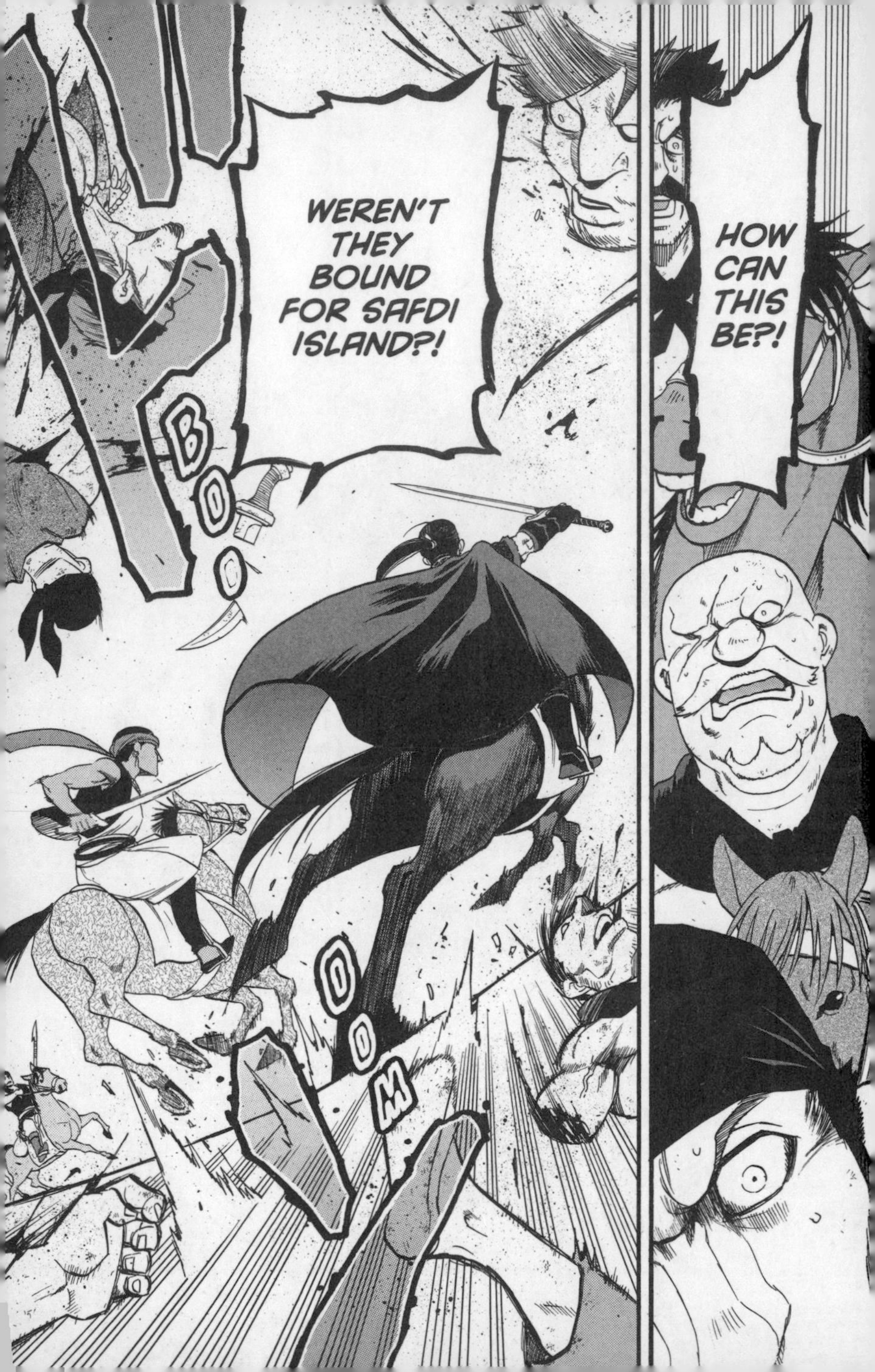
HOW CAN THIS BE?!
WEREN'T THEY BOUND FOR SAFDI ISLAND?!
BOOOOOM

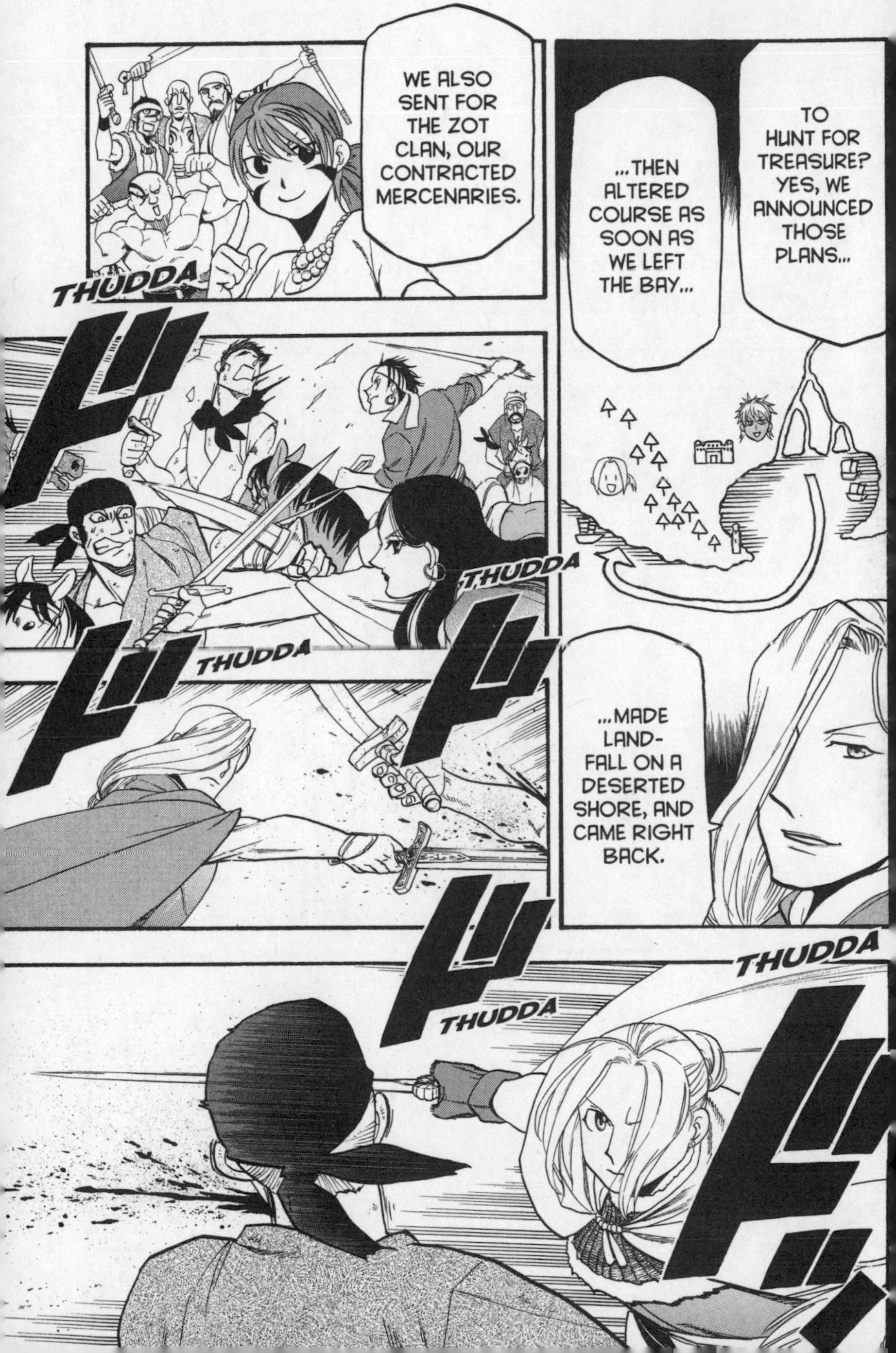
TO HUNT FOR TREASURE? YES, WE ANNOUNCED THOSE PLANS...
...THEN ALTERED COURSE AS SOON AS WE LEFT THE BAY...
...MADE LAND-FALL ON A DESERTED SHORE, AND CAME RIGHT BACK.
WE ALSO SENT FOR THE ZOT CLAN, OUR CONTRACTED MERCENARIES.
THUDDA
THUDDA
THUDDA
THUDDA
THUDDA

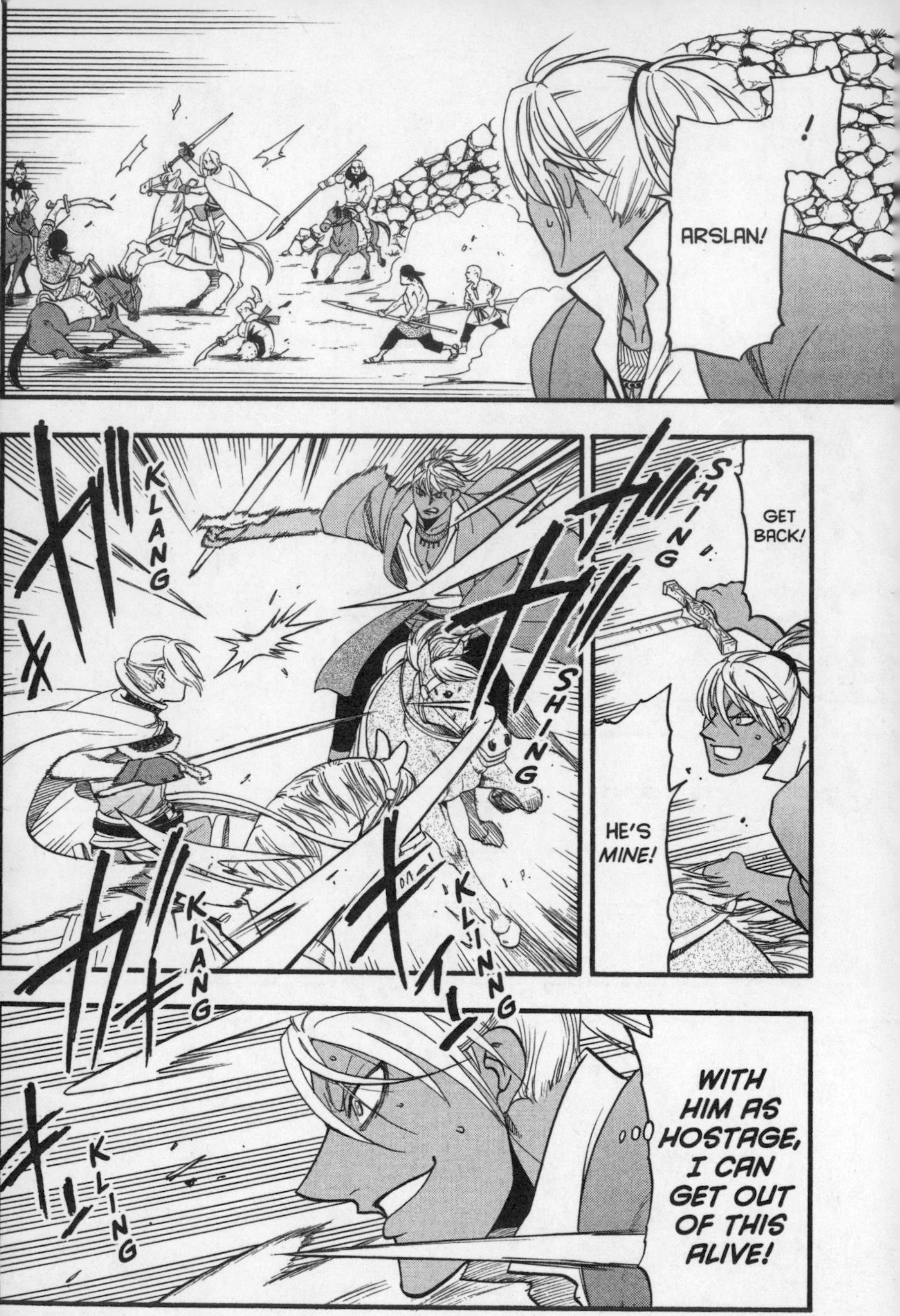
!
ARSLAN!
GET BACK!
SHING
SHING
HE'S MINE!
KLANG
KLANG
KLING
KLING
WITH HIM AS HOSTAGE, I CAN GET OUT OF THIS ALIVE!

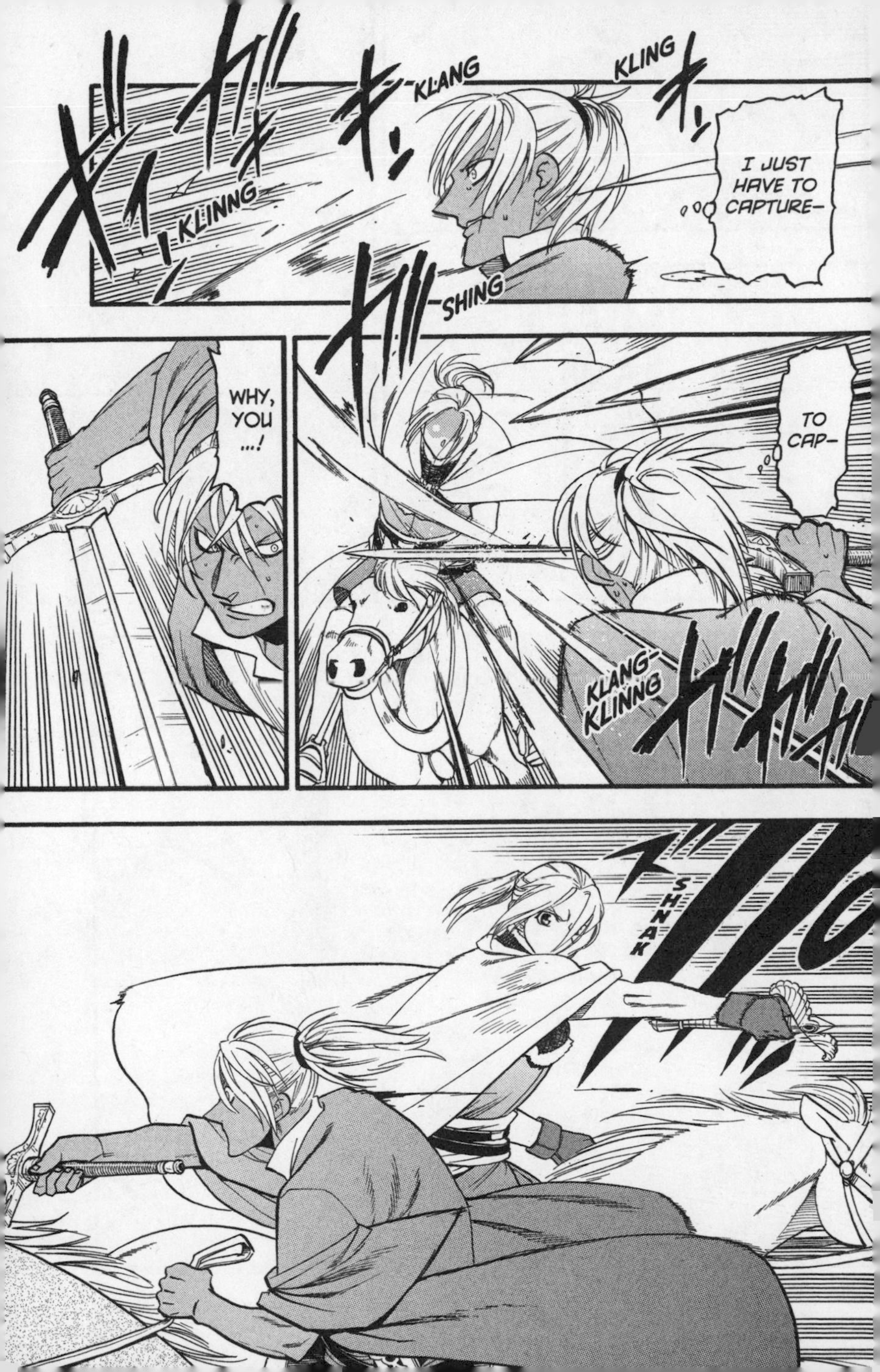
KLING
I JUST HAVE TO CAPTURE–
KLANG
KLINNG
SHING
TO CAP–
KLANG-KLINNG
WHY, YOU ...!
SHNAK

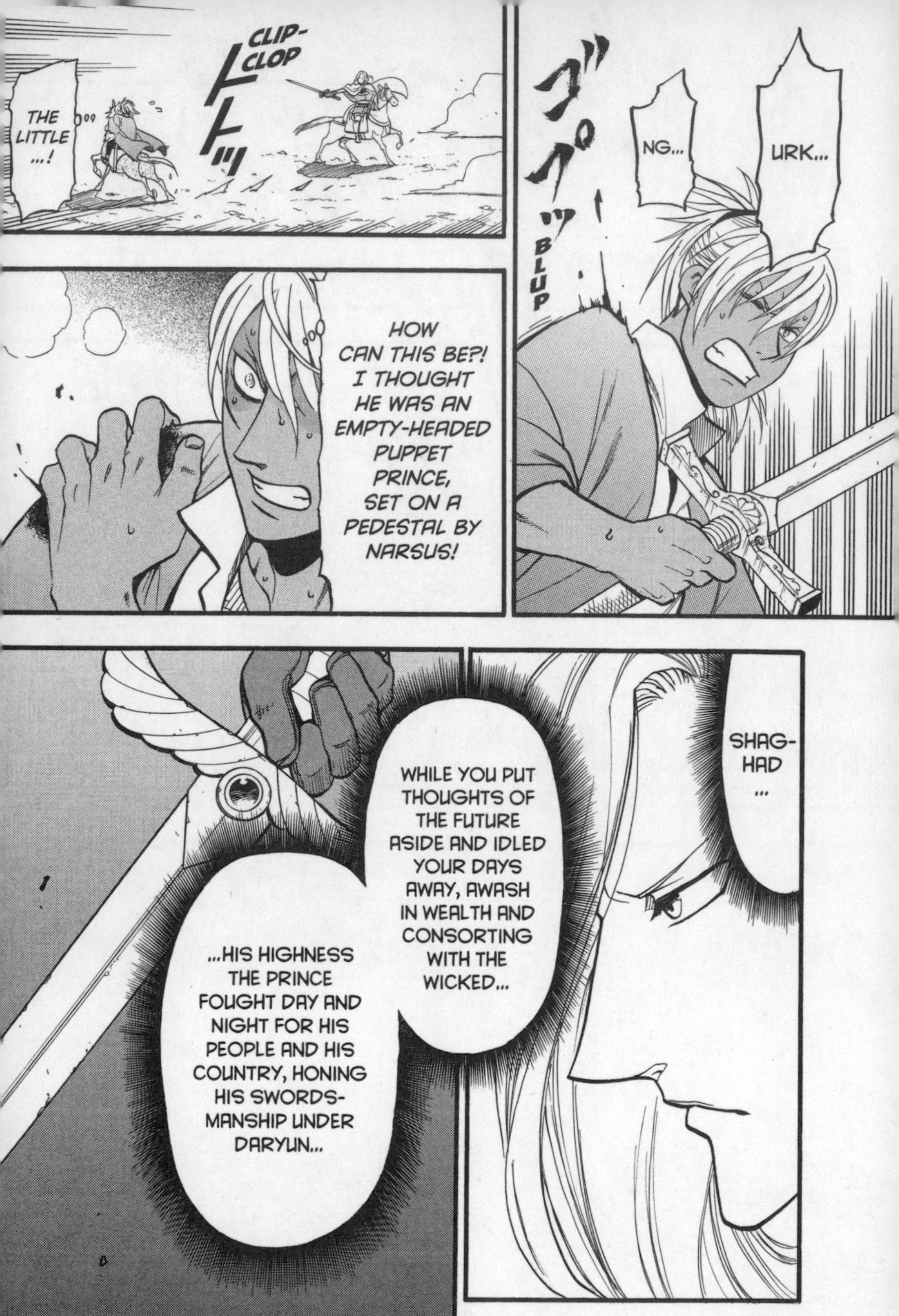
URK...
NG...
ゴプッ
BLUP
CLIP-CLOP
トトッ
THE LITTLE ...!
HOW CAN THIS BE?! I THOUGHT HE WAS AN EMPTY-HEADED PUPPET PRINCE, SET ON A PEDESTAL BY NARSUS!
SHAG-HAD ...
WHILE YOU PUT THOUGHTS OF THE FUTURE ASIDE AND IDLED YOUR DAYS AWAY, AWASH IN WEALTH AND CONSORTING WITH THE WICKED...
...HIS HIGHNESS THE PRINCE FOUGHT DAY AND NIGHT FOR HIS PEOPLE AND HIS COUNTRY, HONING HIS SWORDS-MANSHIP UNDER DARYUN...

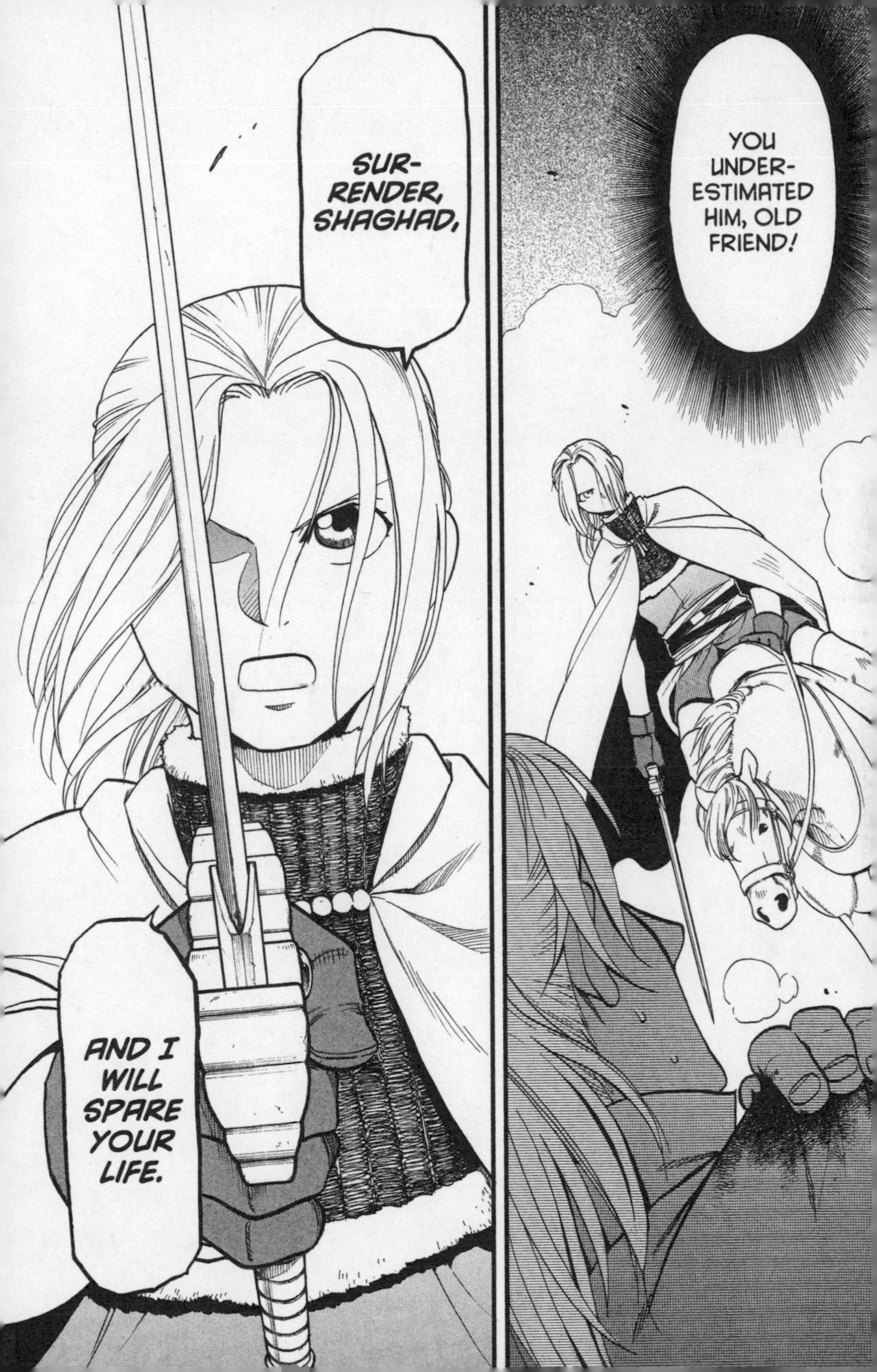
YOU UNDER-ESTIMATED HIM, OLD FRIEND!
SUR-RENDER, SHAGHAD,
AND I WILL SPARE YOUR LIFE.

THE HEROIC LEGEND OF
ARSLAN

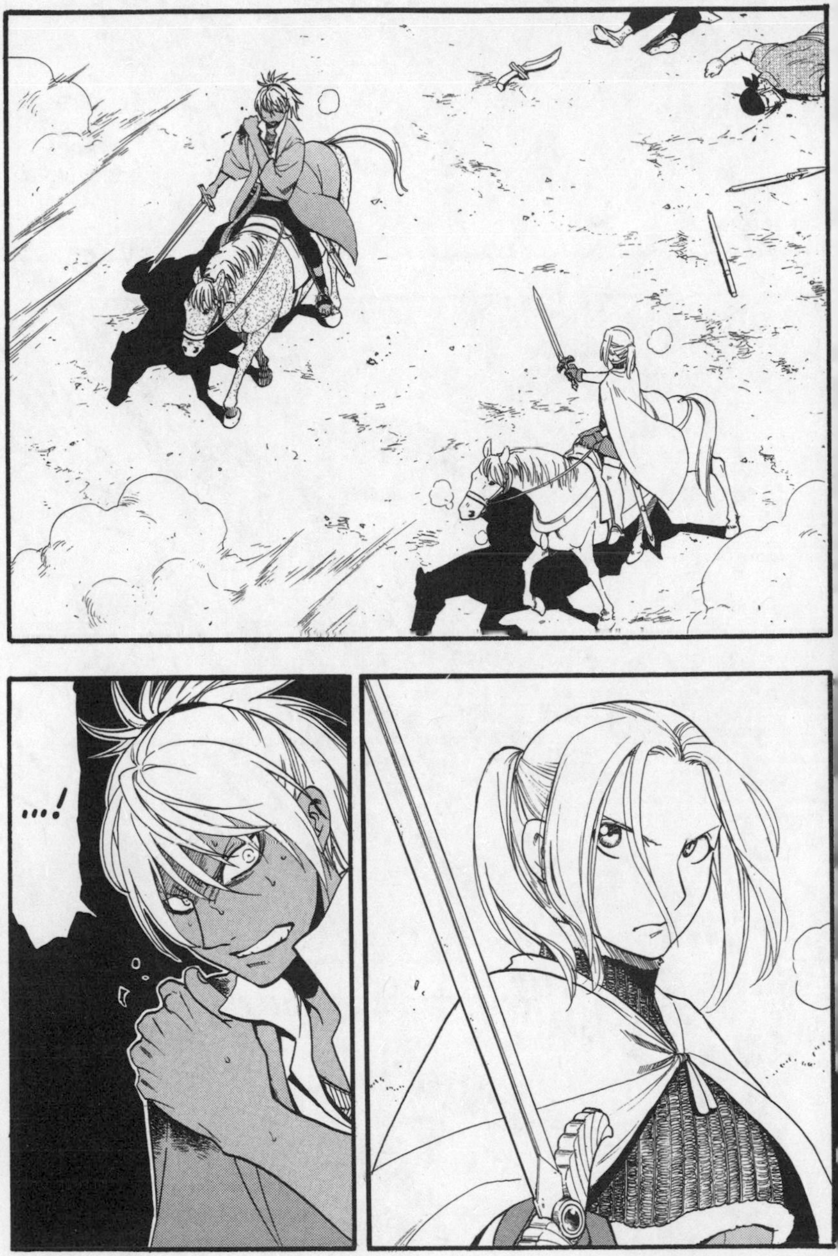
...!

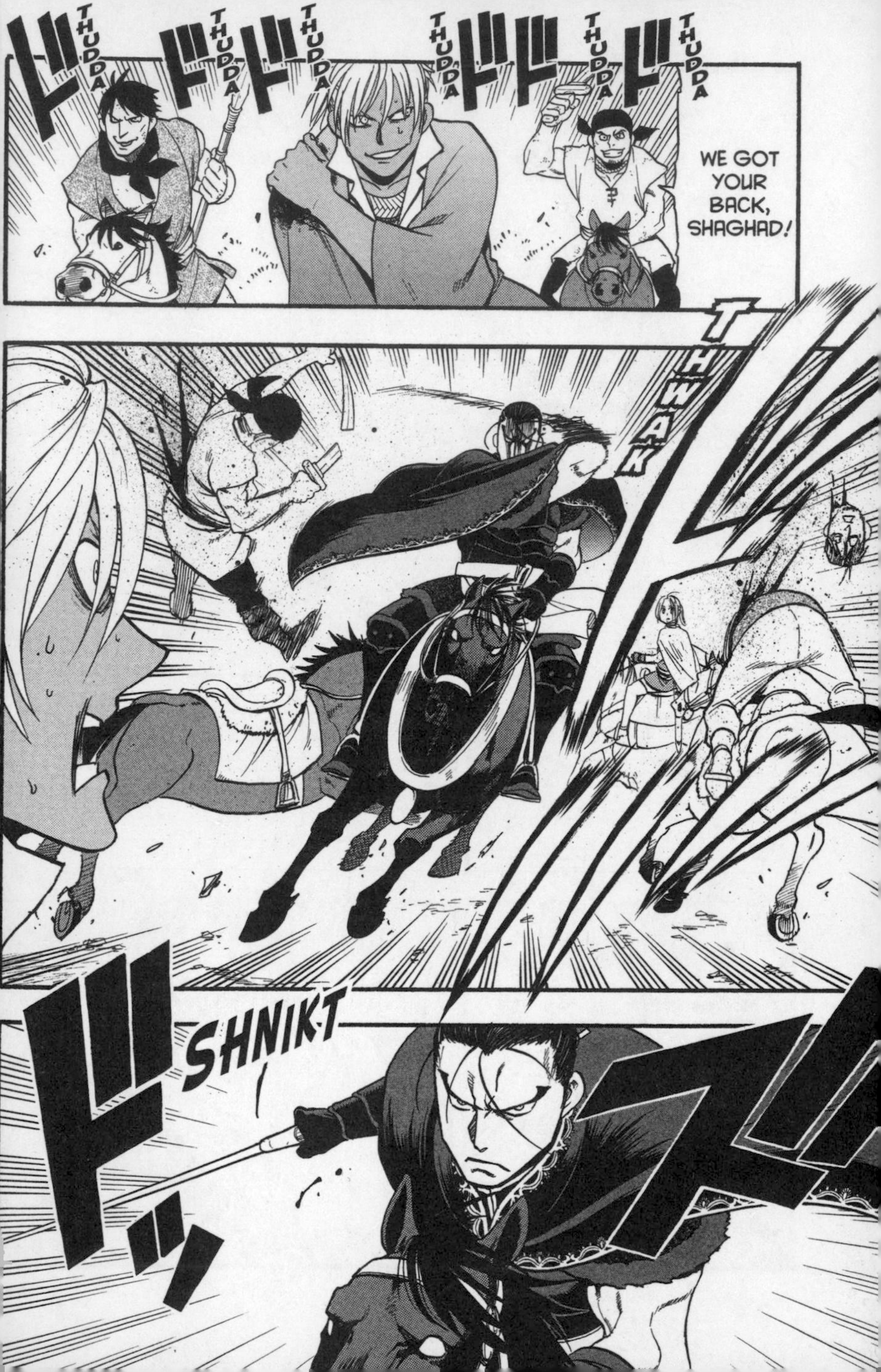
THUDDA
THUDDA
THUDDA
THUDDA
THUDDA
THUDDA
WE GOT YOUR BACK, SHAGHAD!
THWAK
SHNIKT

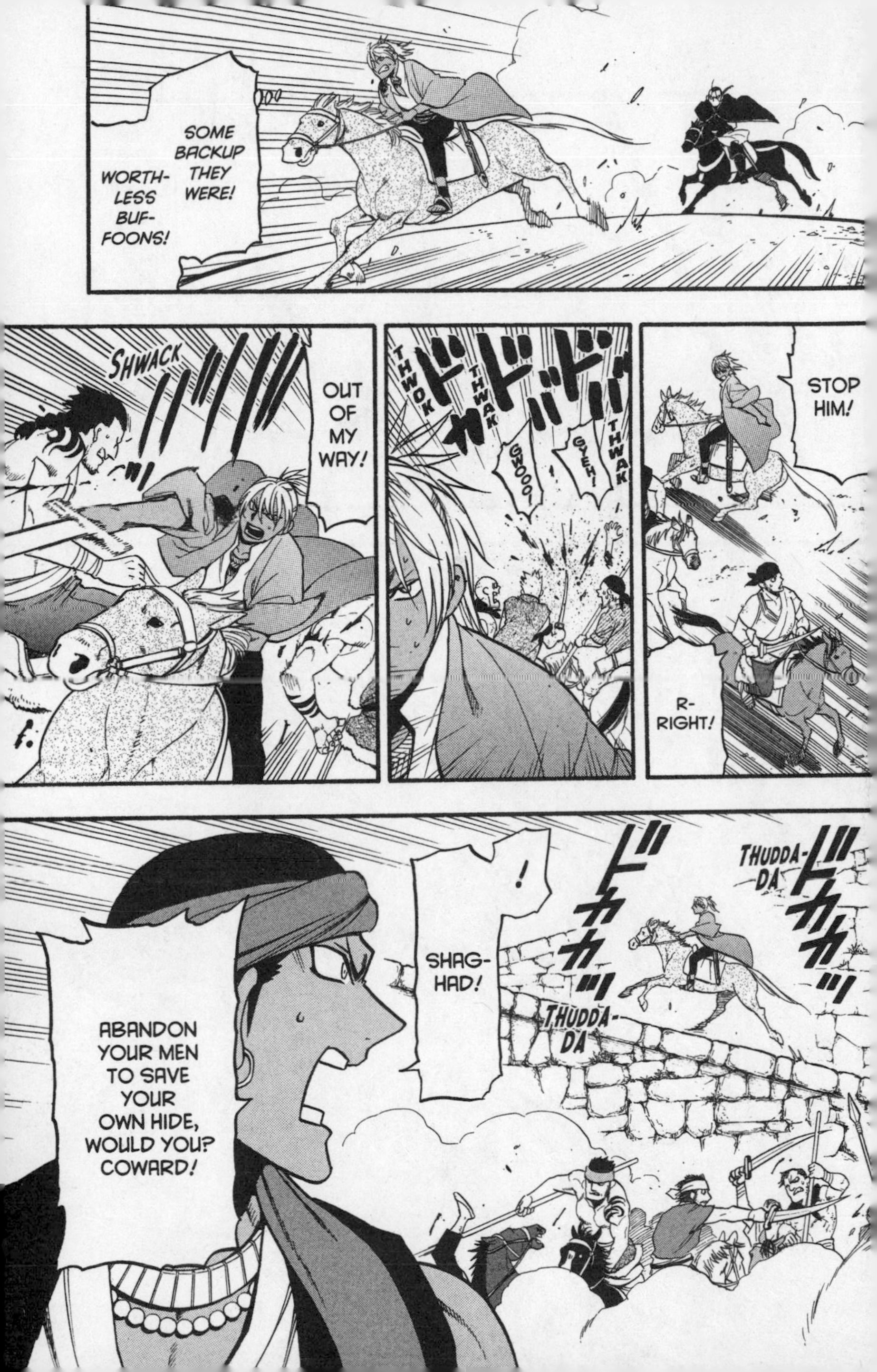
SOME BACKUP THEY WERE!
WORTH-LESS BUF-FOONS!
STOP HIM!
R-RIGHT!
THWAK
GYEH!
GWOOO!
THWAK
THWOK
OUT OF MY WAY!
SHWACK
THUDDA-DA
!
SHAG-HAD!
THUDDA-DA
ABANDON YOUR MEN TO SAVE YOUR OWN HIDE, WOULD YOU? COWARD!

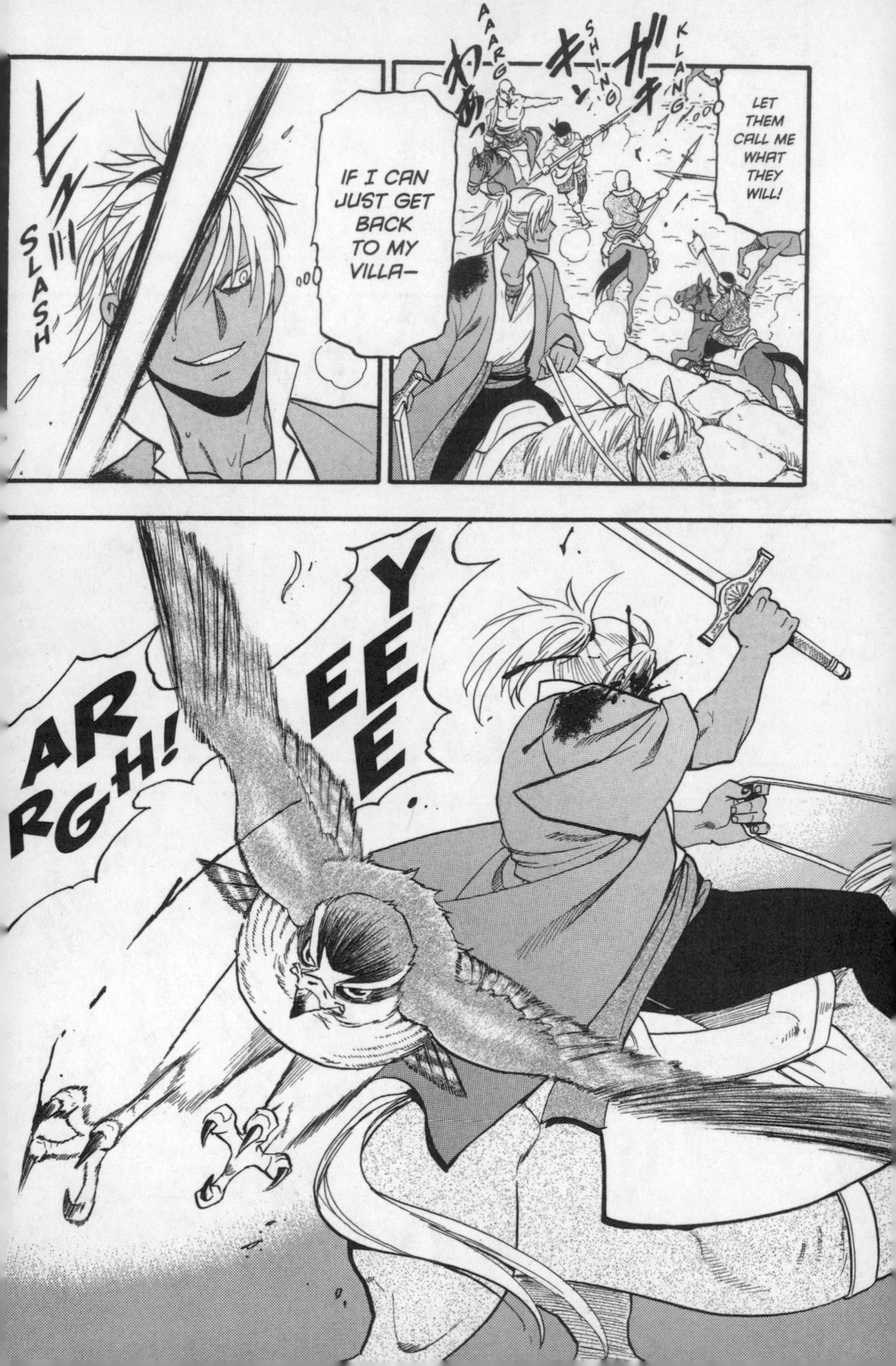
LET THEM CALL ME WHAT THEY WILL!
KLANG
SHING
AAARG
IF I CAN JUST GET BACK TO MY VILLA—
SLASH
YEEEE
ARRGH!

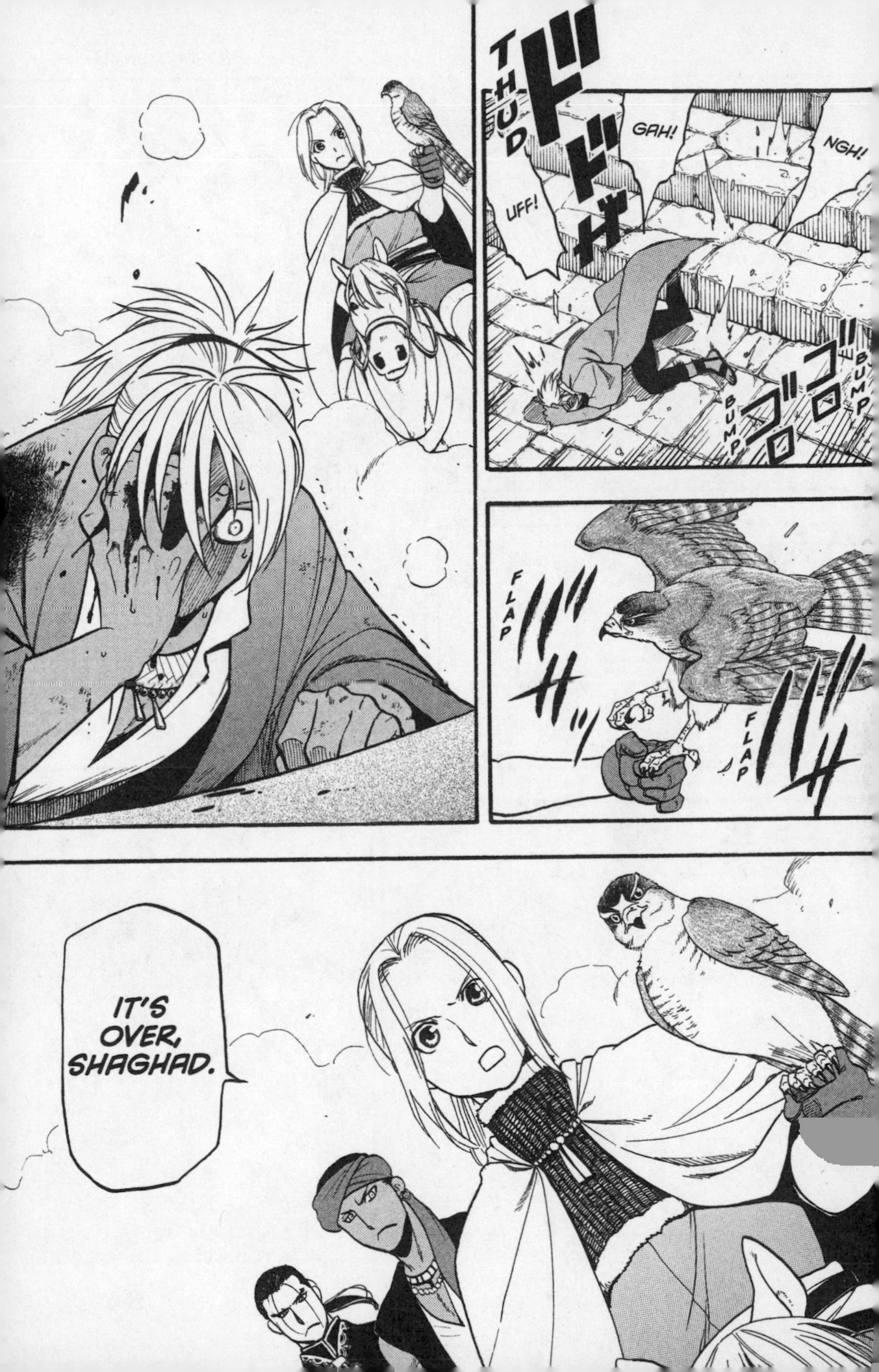
NGH!
GAH!
THUD
UFF!
BUMP
BUMP
FLAP
FLAP
IT'S OVER, SHAGHAD.

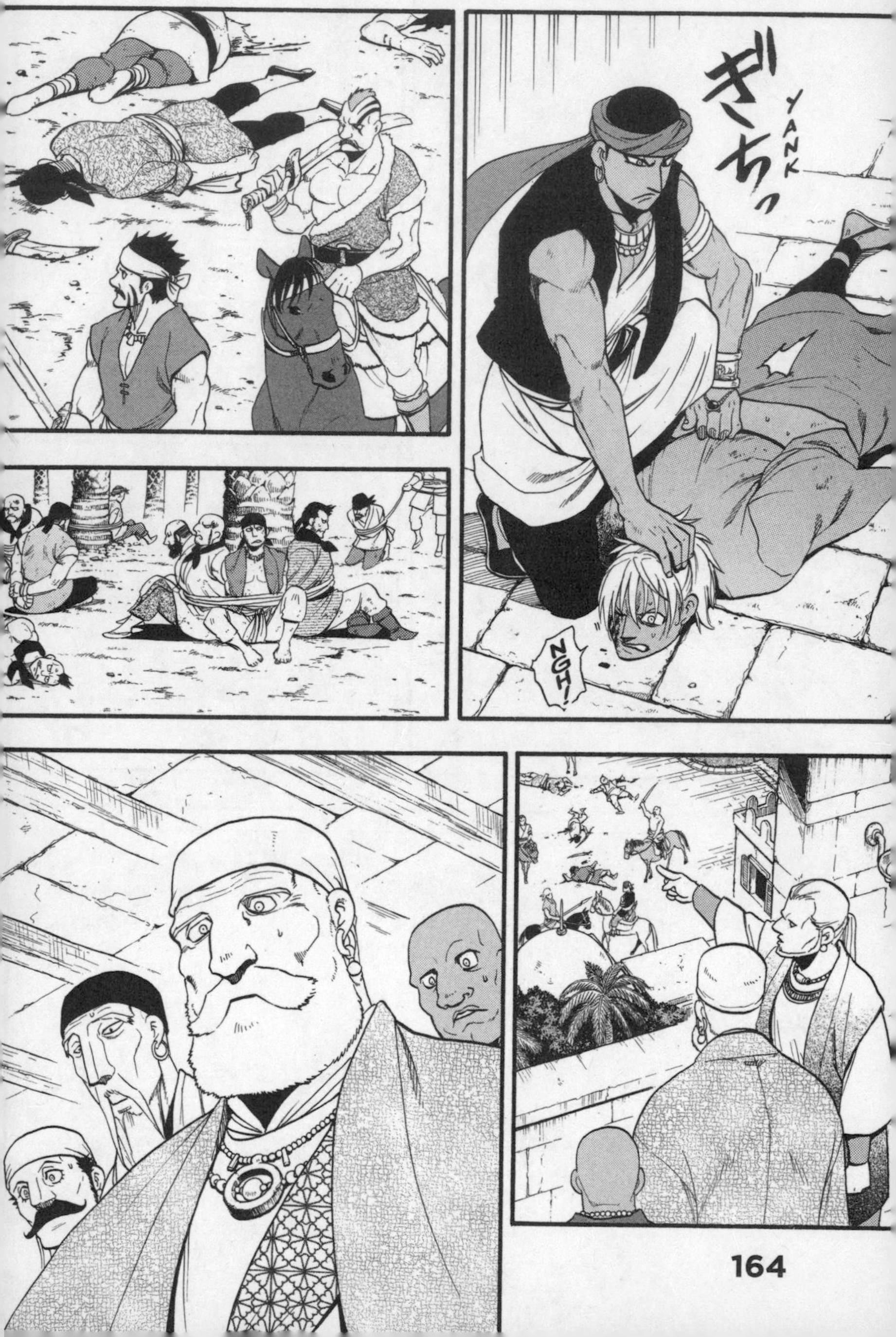
ぎちっ
YANK
NGH!

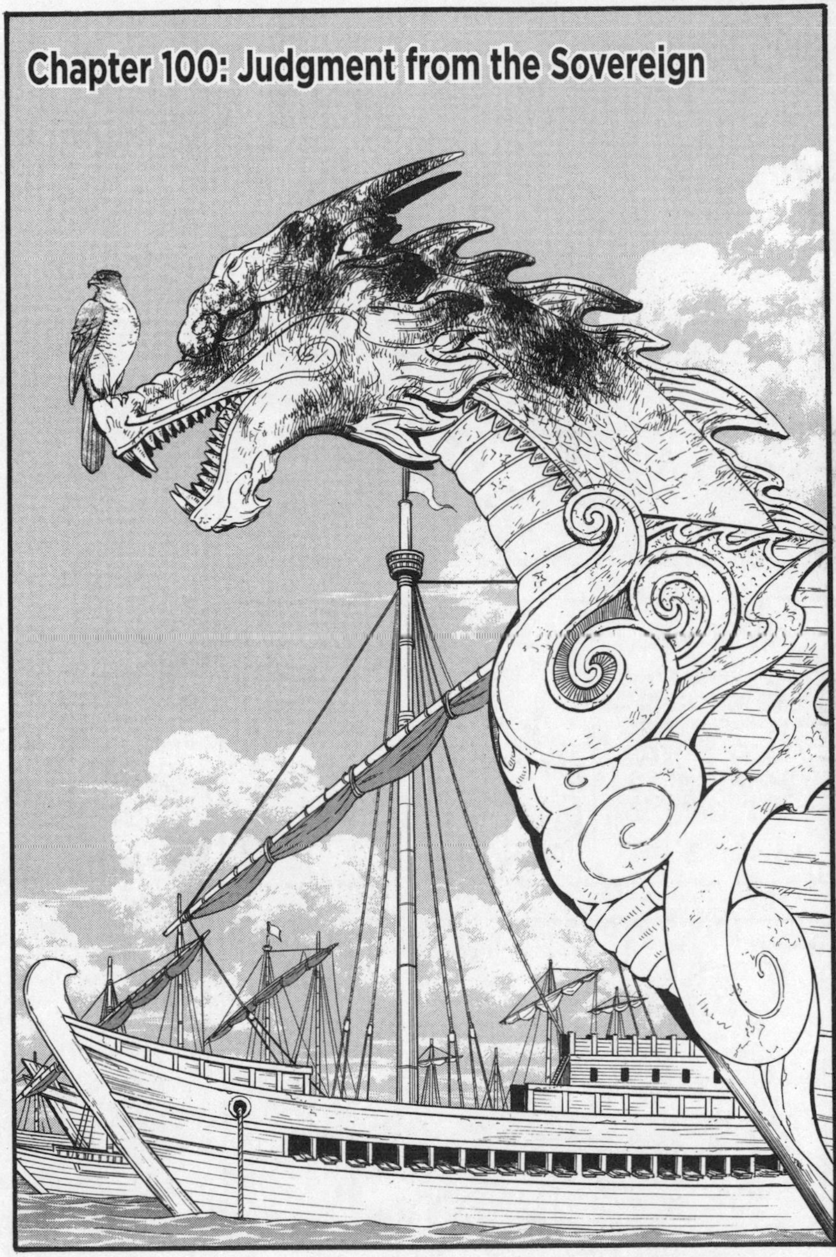
Chapter 100: Judgment from the Sovereign

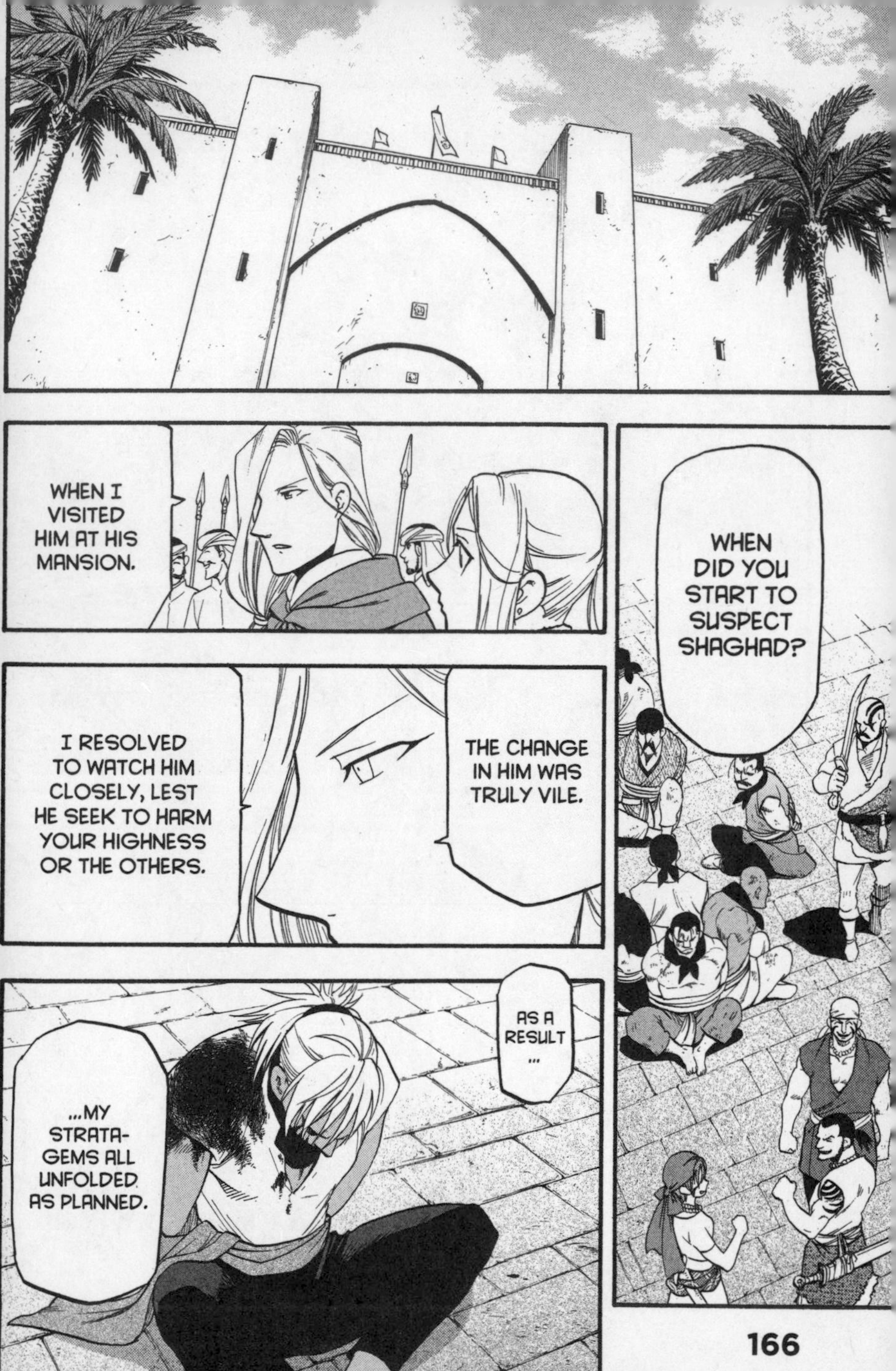
WHEN DID YOU START TO SUSPECT SHAGHAD?
WHEN I VISITED HIM AT HIS MANSION.
THE CHANGE IN HIM WAS TRULY VILE.
I RESOLVED TO WATCH HIM CLOSELY, LEST HE SEEK TO HARM YOUR HIGHNESS OR THE OTHERS.
AS A RESULT...
...MY STRATAGEMS ALL UNFOLDED AS PLANNED.

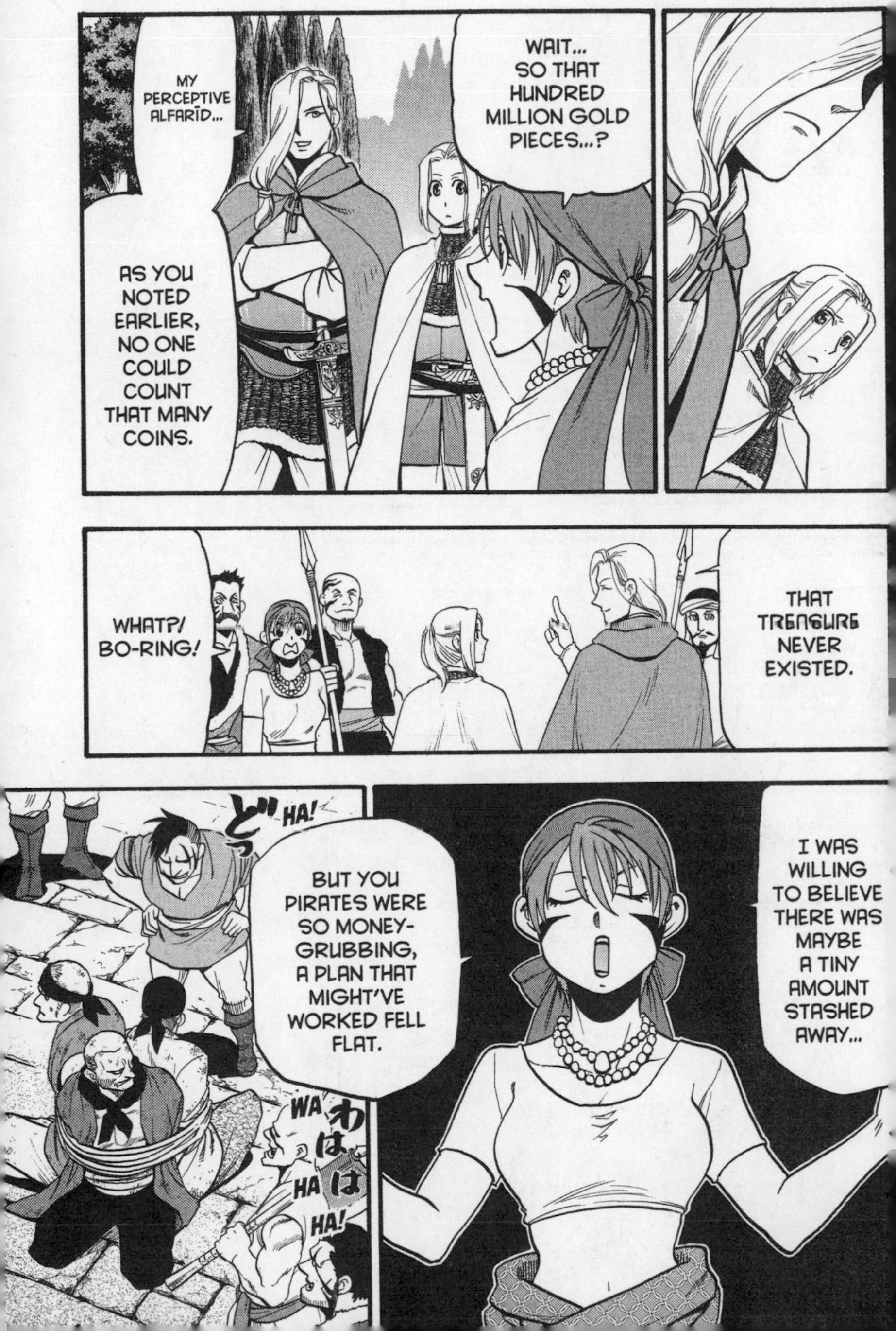
WAIT... SO THAT HUNDRED MILLION GOLD PIECES...?
MY PERCEPTIVE ALFARĪD...
AS YOU NOTED EARLIER, NO ONE COULD COUNT THAT MANY COINS.
THAT TREASURE NEVER EXISTED.
WHAT?! BO-RING!
I WAS WILLING TO BELIEVE THERE WAS MAYBE A TINY AMOUNT STASHED AWAY...
BUT YOU PIRATES WERE SO MONEY-GRUBBING, A PLAN THAT MIGHT'VE WORKED FELL FLAT.
どっ HA!
WA わ HA は HA!

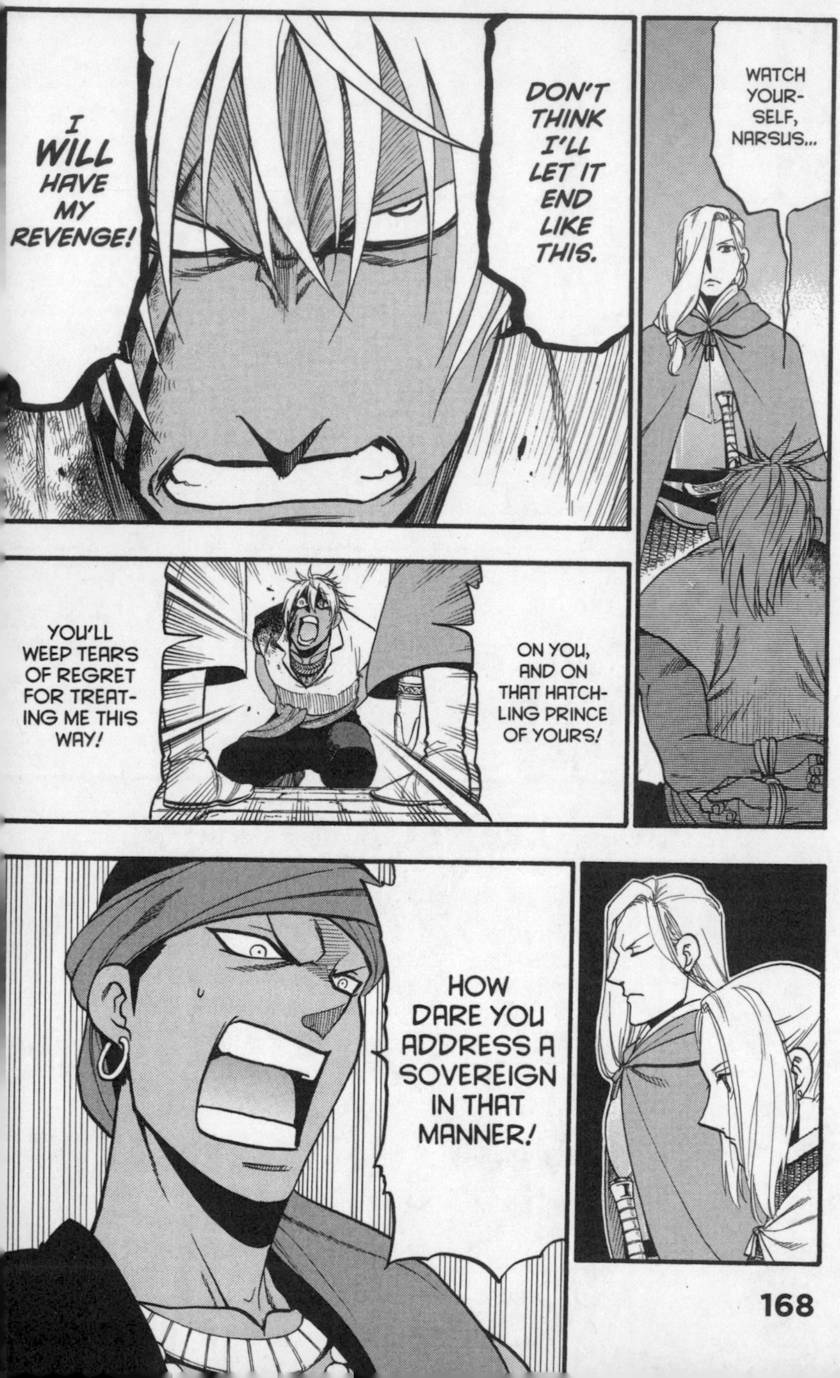
WATCH YOURSELF, NARSUS...
DON'T THINK I'LL LET IT END LIKE THIS.
I WILL HAVE MY REVENGE!
ON YOU, AND ON THAT HATCHLING PRINCE OF YOURS!
YOU'LL WEEP TEARS OF REGRET FOR TREATING ME THIS WAY!
HOW DARE YOU ADDRESS A SOVEREIGN IN THAT MANNER!

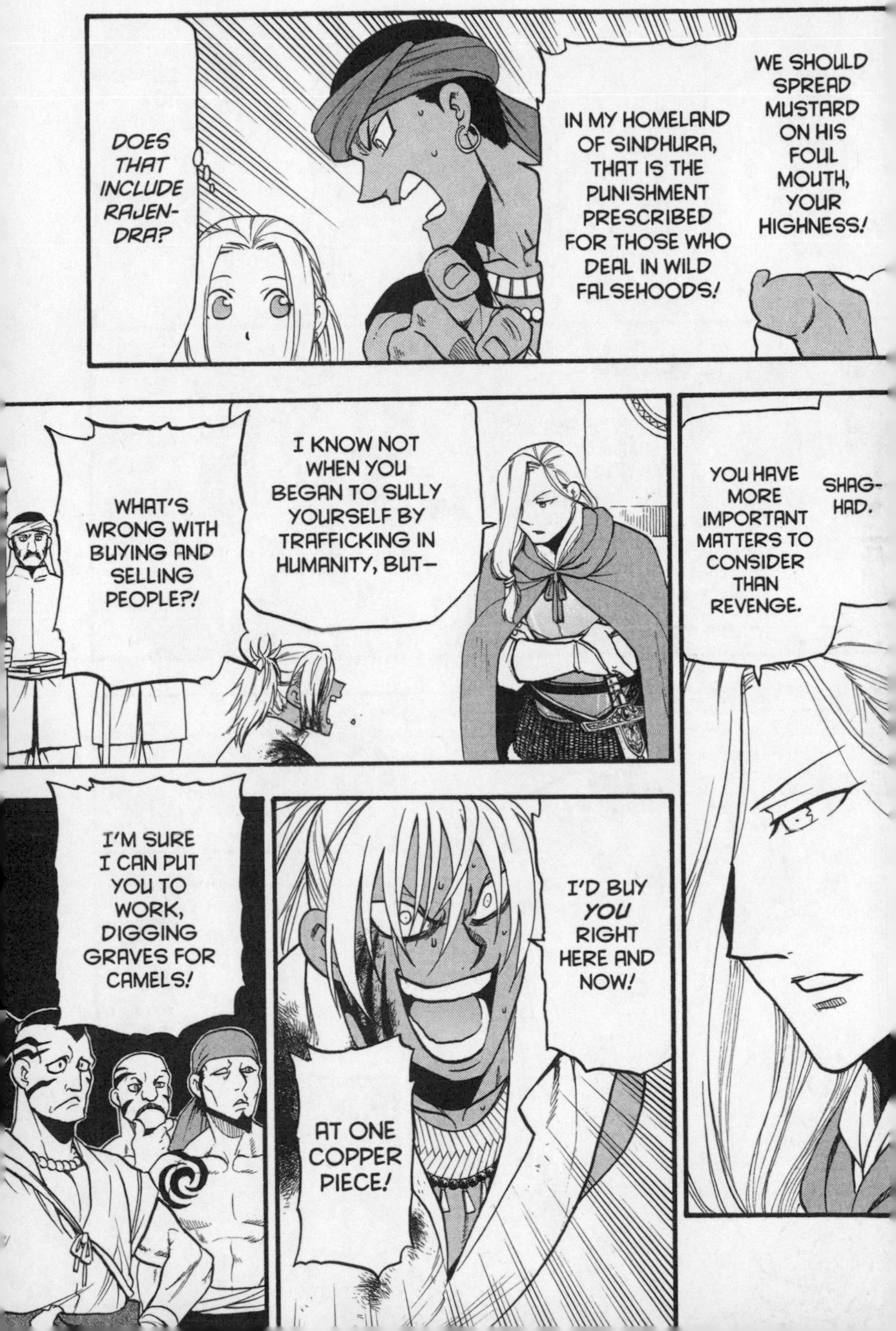
WE SHOULD SPREAD MUSTARD ON HIS FOUL MOUTH, YOUR HIGHNESS!
IN MY HOMELAND OF SINDHURA, THAT IS THE PUNISHMENT PRESCRIBED FOR THOSE WHO DEAL IN WILD FALSEHOODS!
DOES THAT INCLUDE RAJENDRA?
SHAGHAD.
YOU HAVE MORE IMPORTANT MATTERS TO CONSIDER THAN REVENGE.
I KNOW NOT WHEN YOU BEGAN TO SULLY YOURSELF BY TRAFFICKING IN HUMANITY, BUT—
WHAT'S WRONG WITH BUYING AND SELLING PEOPLE?!
I'D BUY *YOU* RIGHT HERE AND NOW!
AT ONE COPPER PIECE!
I'M SURE I CAN PUT YOU TO WORK, DIGGING GRAVES FOR CAMELS!

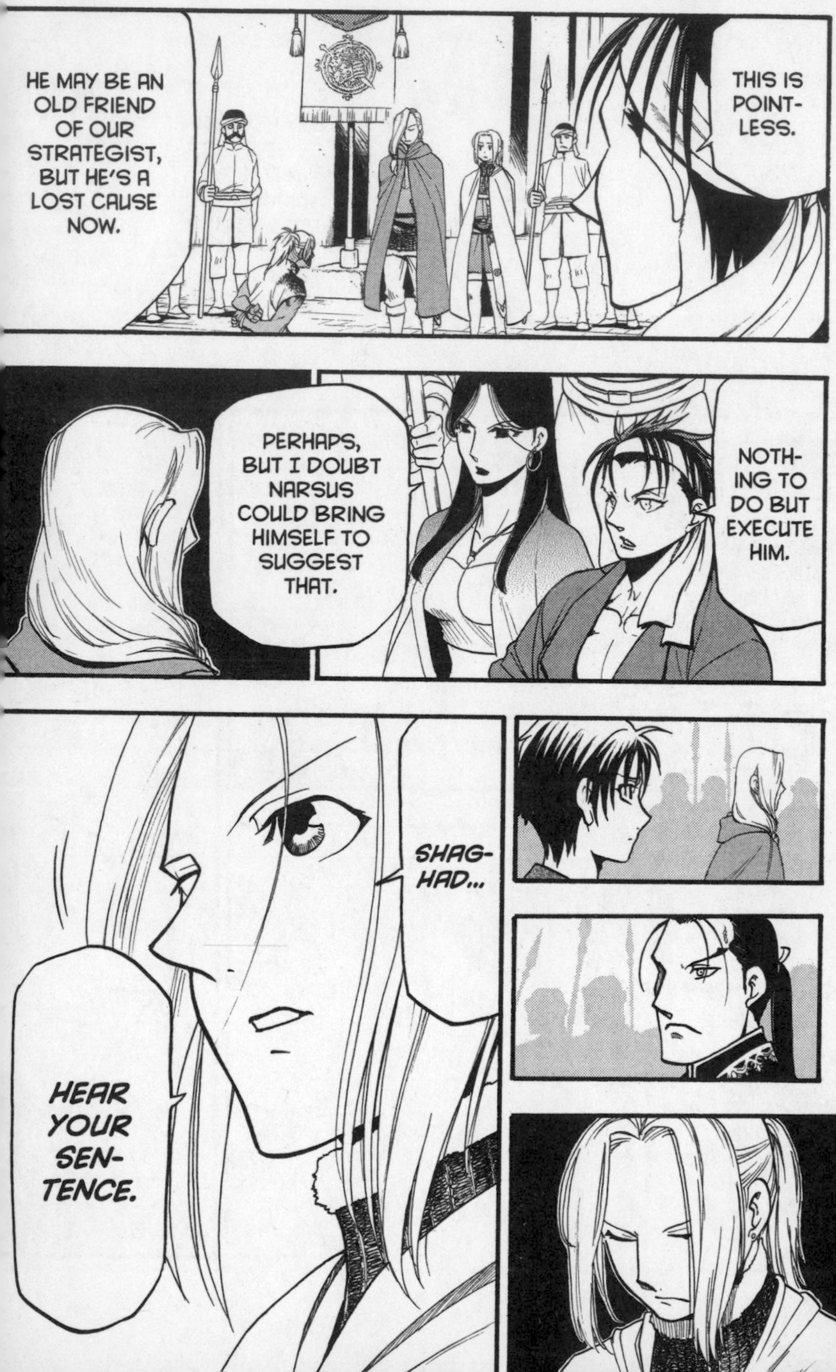
THIS IS POINT-LESS.
HE MAY BE AN OLD FRIEND OF OUR STRATEGIST, BUT HE'S A LOST CAUSE NOW.
NOTH-ING TO DO BUT EXECUTE HIM.
PERHAPS, BUT I DOUBT NARSUS COULD BRING HIMSELF TO SUGGEST THAT.
SHAG-HAD...
HEAR YOUR SEN-TENCE.

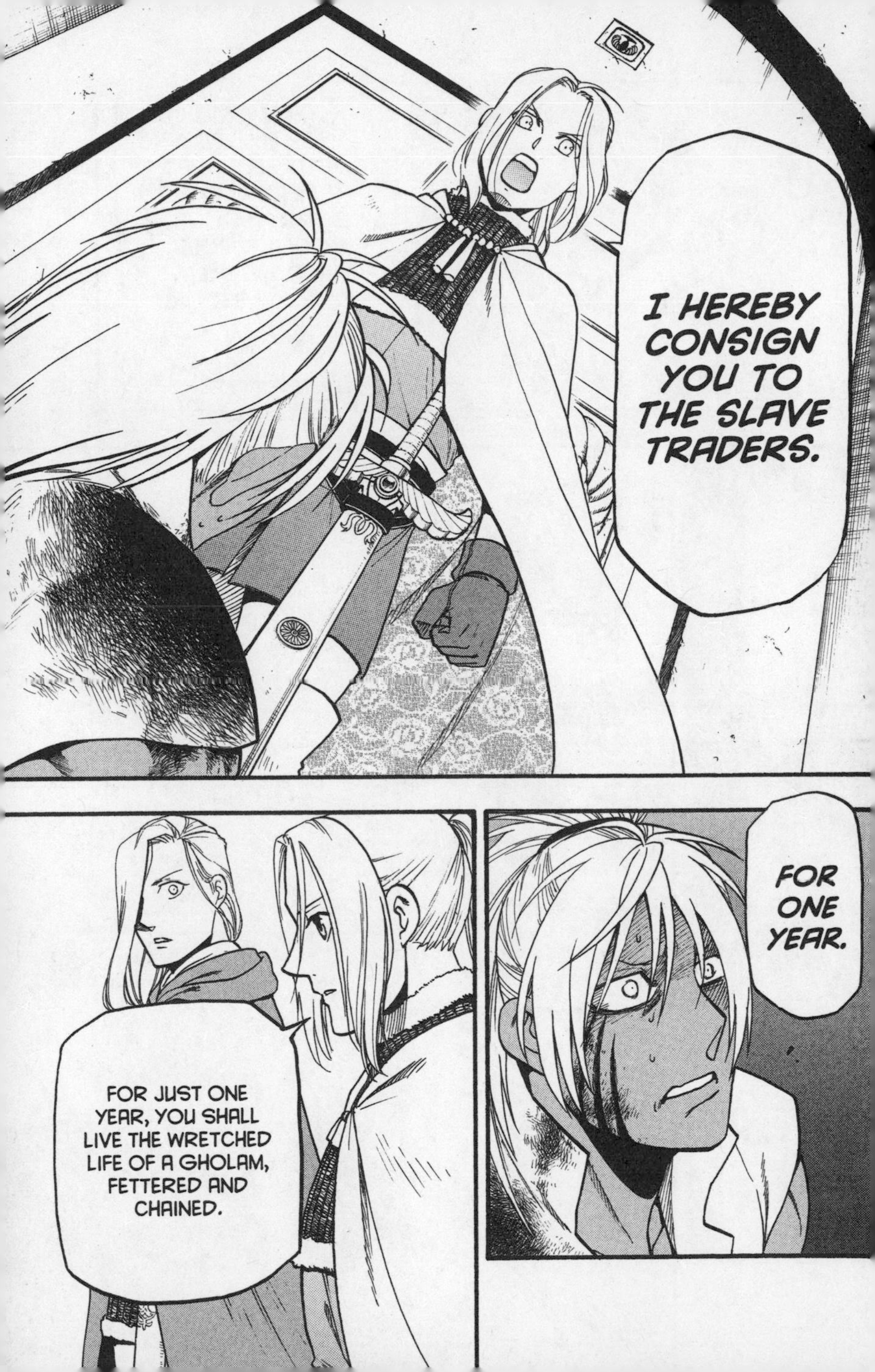
I HEREBY CONSIGN YOU TO THE SLAVE TRADERS.
FOR ONE YEAR.
FOR JUST ONE YEAR, YOU SHALL LIVE THE WRETCHED LIFE OF A GHOLAM, FETTERED AND CHAINED.

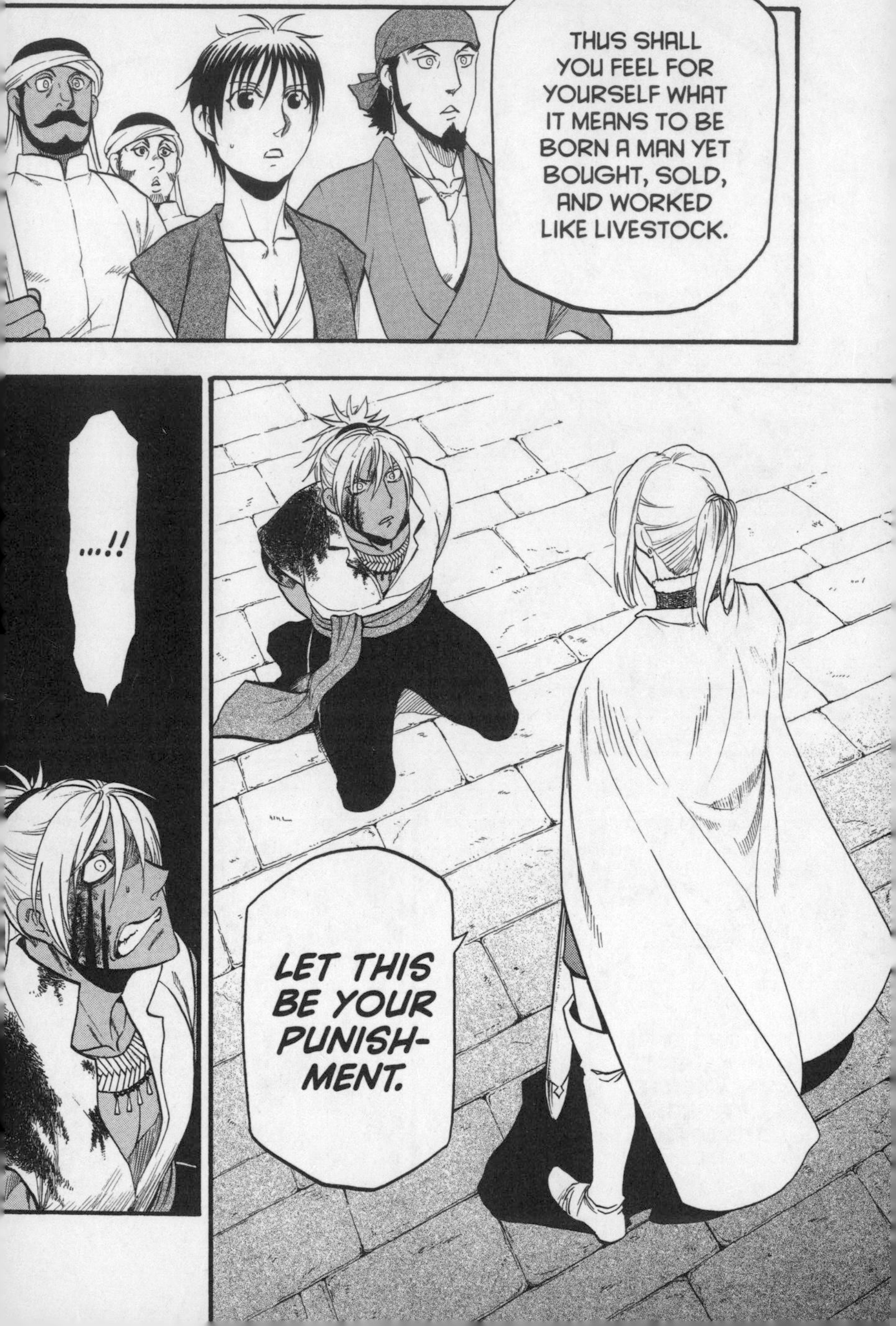
THUS SHALL YOU FEEL FOR YOURSELF WHAT IT MEANS TO BE BORN A MAN YET BOUGHT, SOLD, AND WORKED LIKE LIVESTOCK.
LET THIS BE YOUR PUNISH-MENT.
...!!

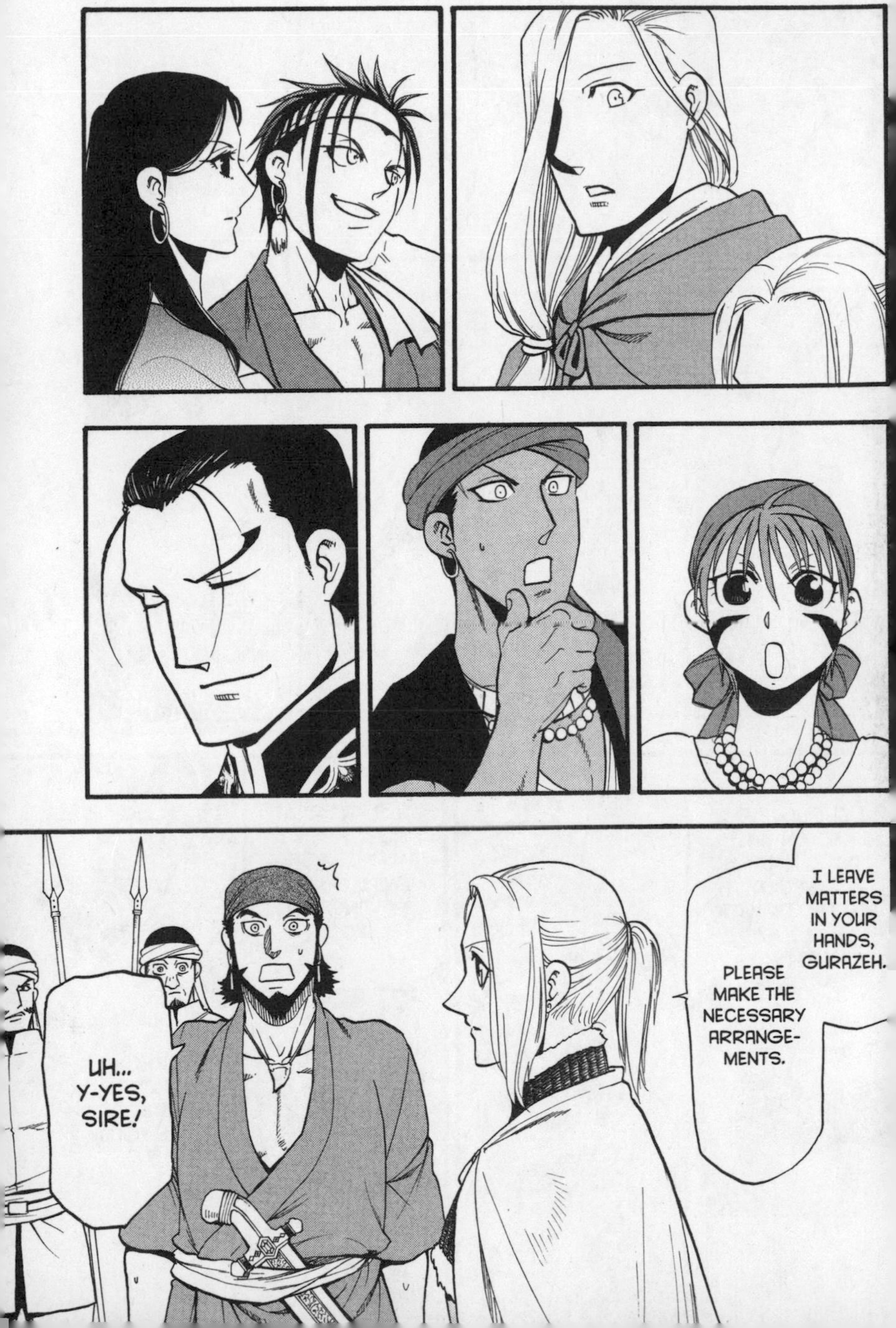
I LEAVE MATTERS IN YOUR HANDS, GURAZEH.
PLEASE MAKE THE NECESSARY ARRANGE-MENTS.
UH... Y-YES, SIRE!

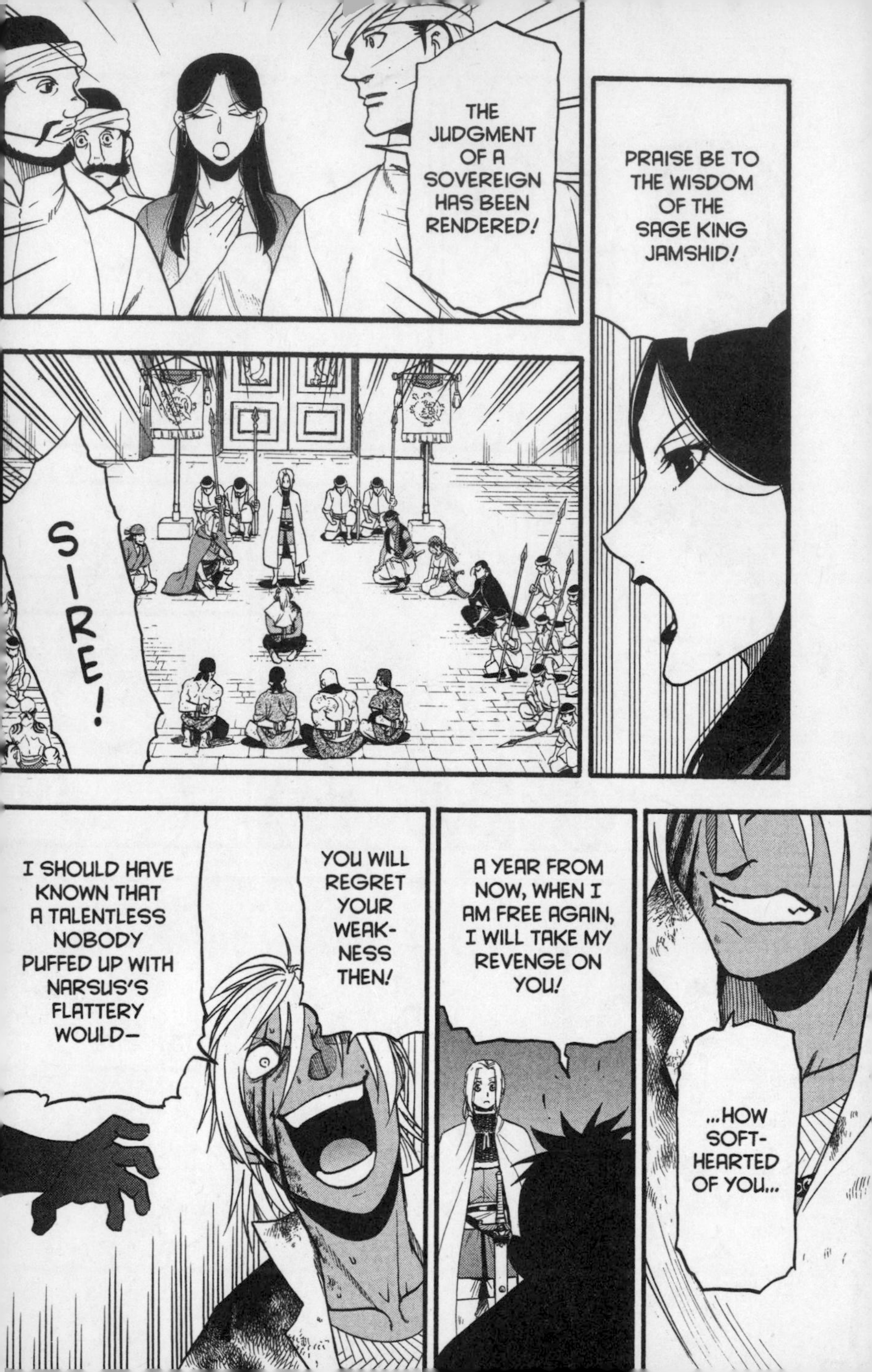
PRAISE BE TO THE WISDOM OF THE SAGE KING JAMSHID!
THE JUDGMENT OF A SOVEREIGN HAS BEEN RENDERED!
SIRE!
...HOW SOFT-HEARTED OF YOU...
A YEAR FROM NOW, WHEN I AM FREE AGAIN, I WILL TAKE MY REVENGE ON YOU!
YOU WILL REGRET YOUR WEAK-NESS THEN!
I SHOULD HAVE KNOWN THAT A TALENTLESS NOBODY PUFFED UP WITH NARSUS'S FLATTERY WOULD—

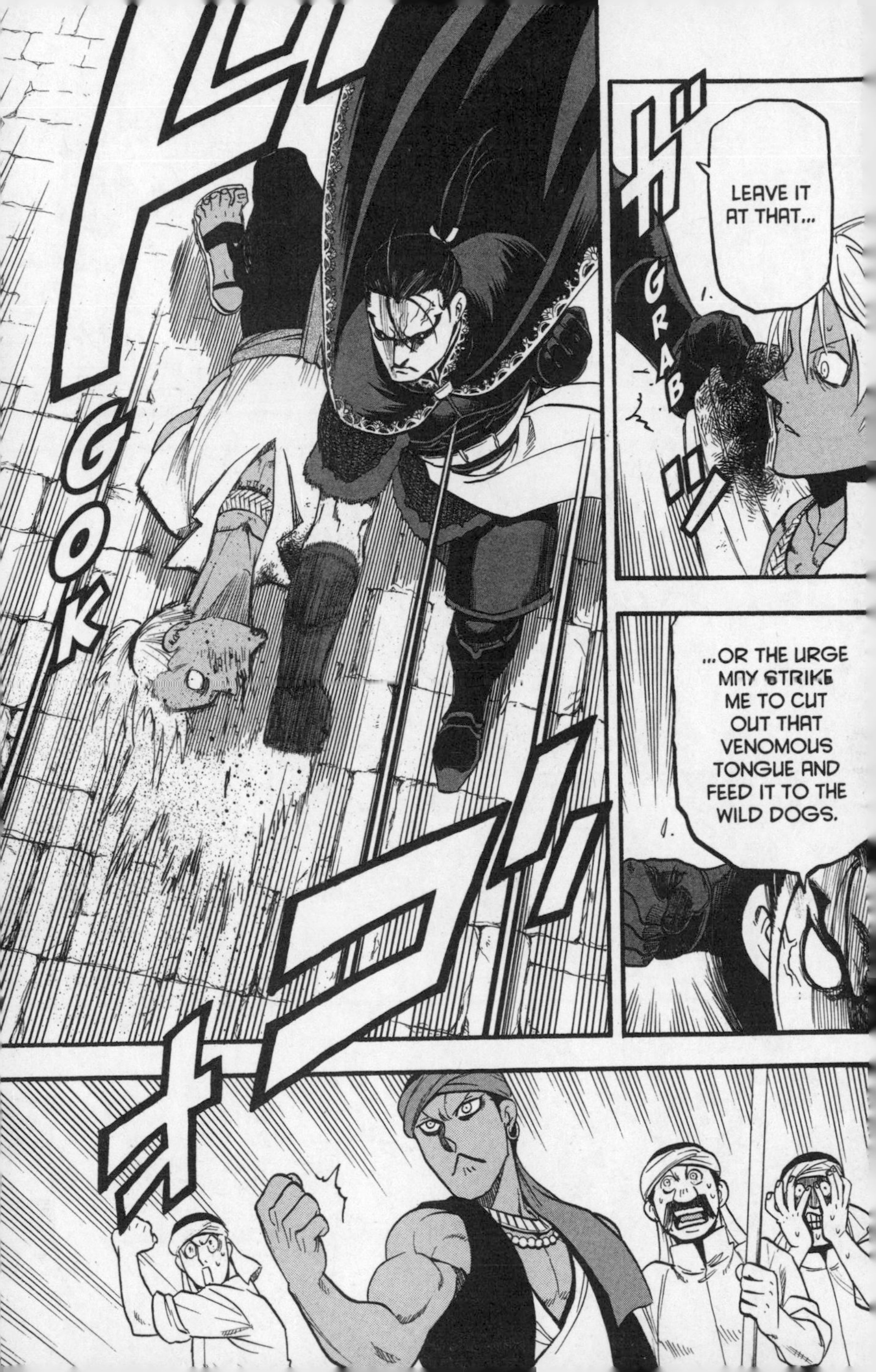
LEAVE IT AT THAT...
GRAB
...OR THE URGE MAY STRIKE ME TO CUT OUT THAT VENOMOUS TONGUE AND FEED IT TO THE WILD DOGS.
GOK

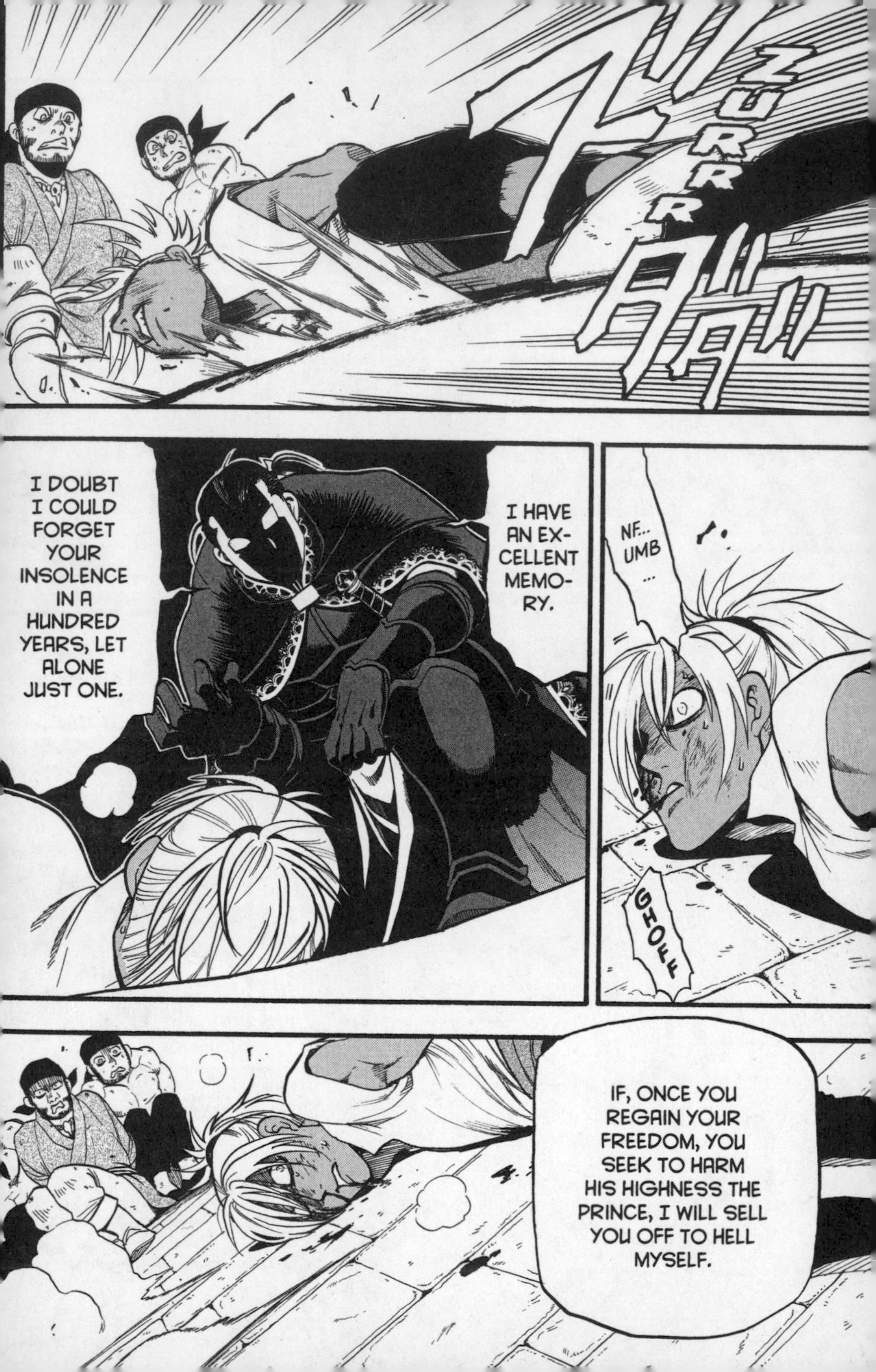
ZURRR
NF... UMB ...
GHOFF
I HAVE AN EX-CELLENT MEMORY.
I DOUBT I COULD FORGET YOUR INSOLENCE IN A HUNDRED YEARS, LET ALONE JUST ONE.
IF, ONCE YOU REGAIN YOUR FREEDOM, YOU SEEK TO HARM HIS HIGHNESS THE PRINCE, I WILL SELL YOU OFF TO HELL MYSELF.

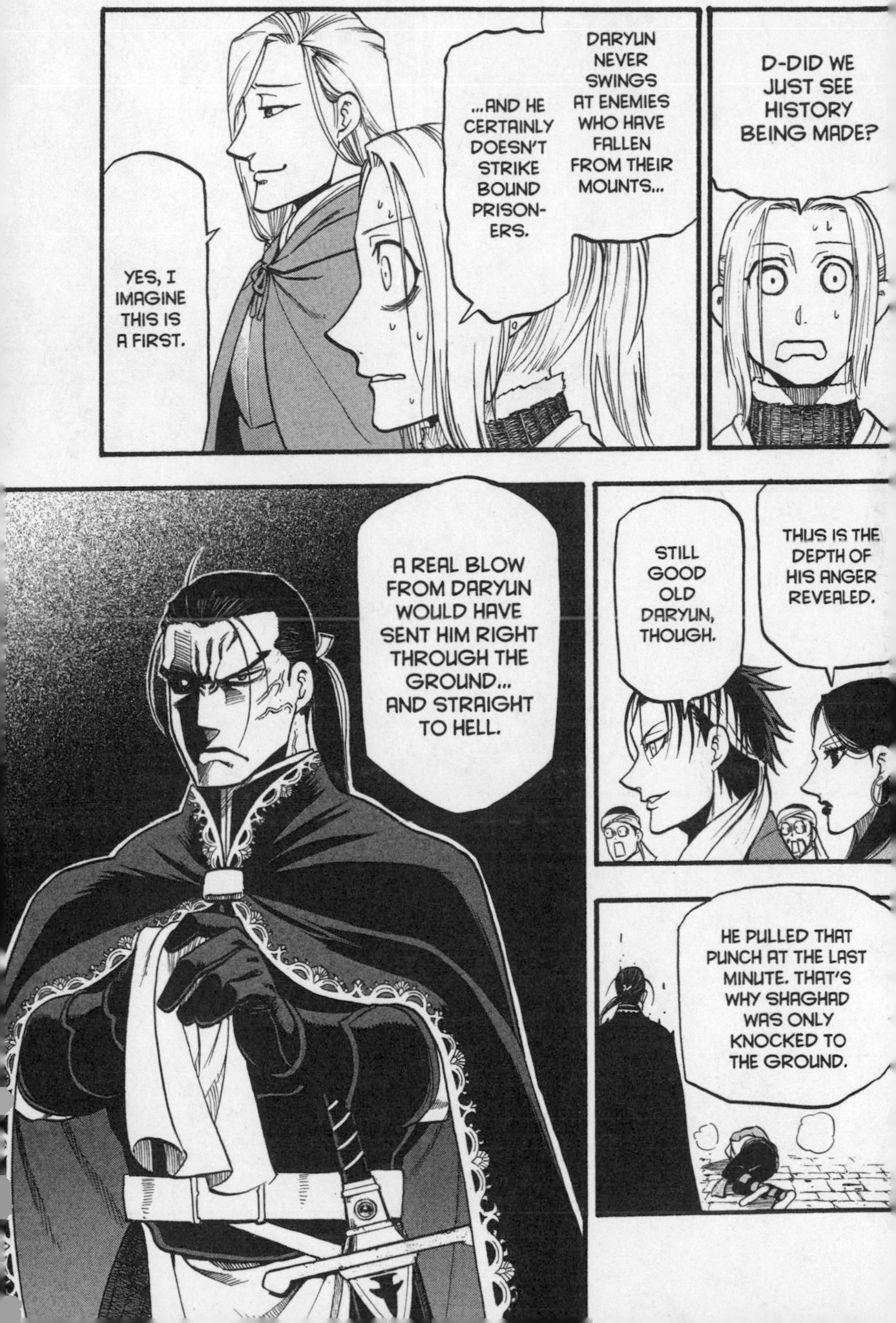
D-DID WE JUST SEE HISTORY BEING MADE?
DARYUN NEVER SWINGS AT ENEMIES WHO HAVE FALLEN FROM THEIR MOUNTS...
...AND HE CERTAINLY DOESN'T STRIKE BOUND PRISON-ERS.
YES, I IMAGINE THIS IS A FIRST.
THUS IS THE DEPTH OF HIS ANGER REVEALED.
STILL GOOD OLD DARYUN, THOUGH.
HE PULLED THAT PUNCH AT THE LAST MINUTE. THAT'S WHY SHAGHAD WAS ONLY KNOCKED TO THE GROUND.
A REAL BLOW FROM DARYUN WOULD HAVE SENT HIM RIGHT THROUGH THE GROUND... AND STRAIGHT TO HELL.

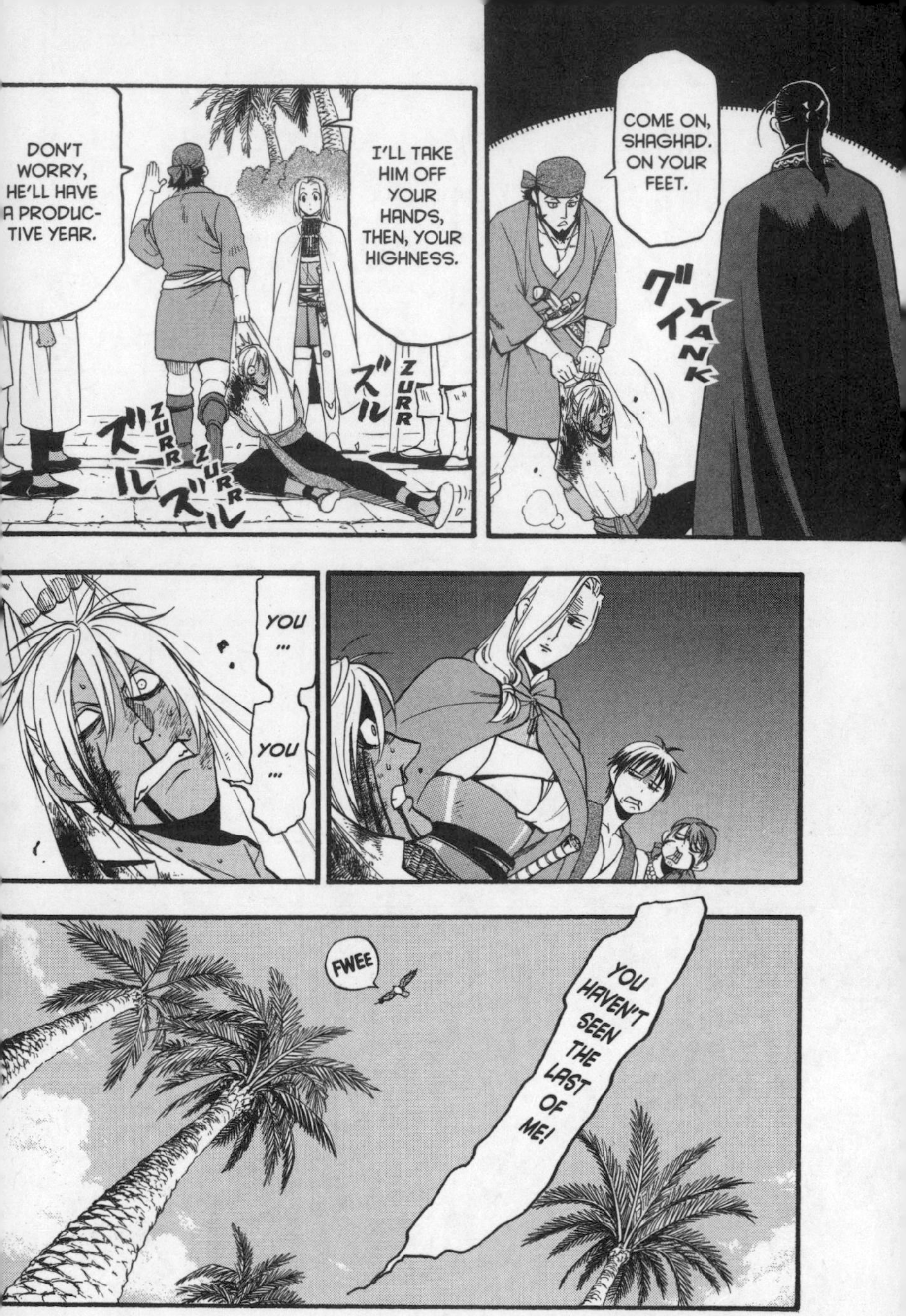
COME ON, SHAGHAD. ON YOUR FEET.
グイ YANK
I'LL TAKE HIM OFF YOUR HANDS, THEN, YOUR HIGHNESS.
DON'T WORRY, HE'LL HAVE A PRODUCTIVE YEAR.
ズル ZURR
ズル ZURR
ズル ZURR
YOU ...
YOU ...
FWEE
YOU HAVEN'T SEEN THE LAST OF ME!

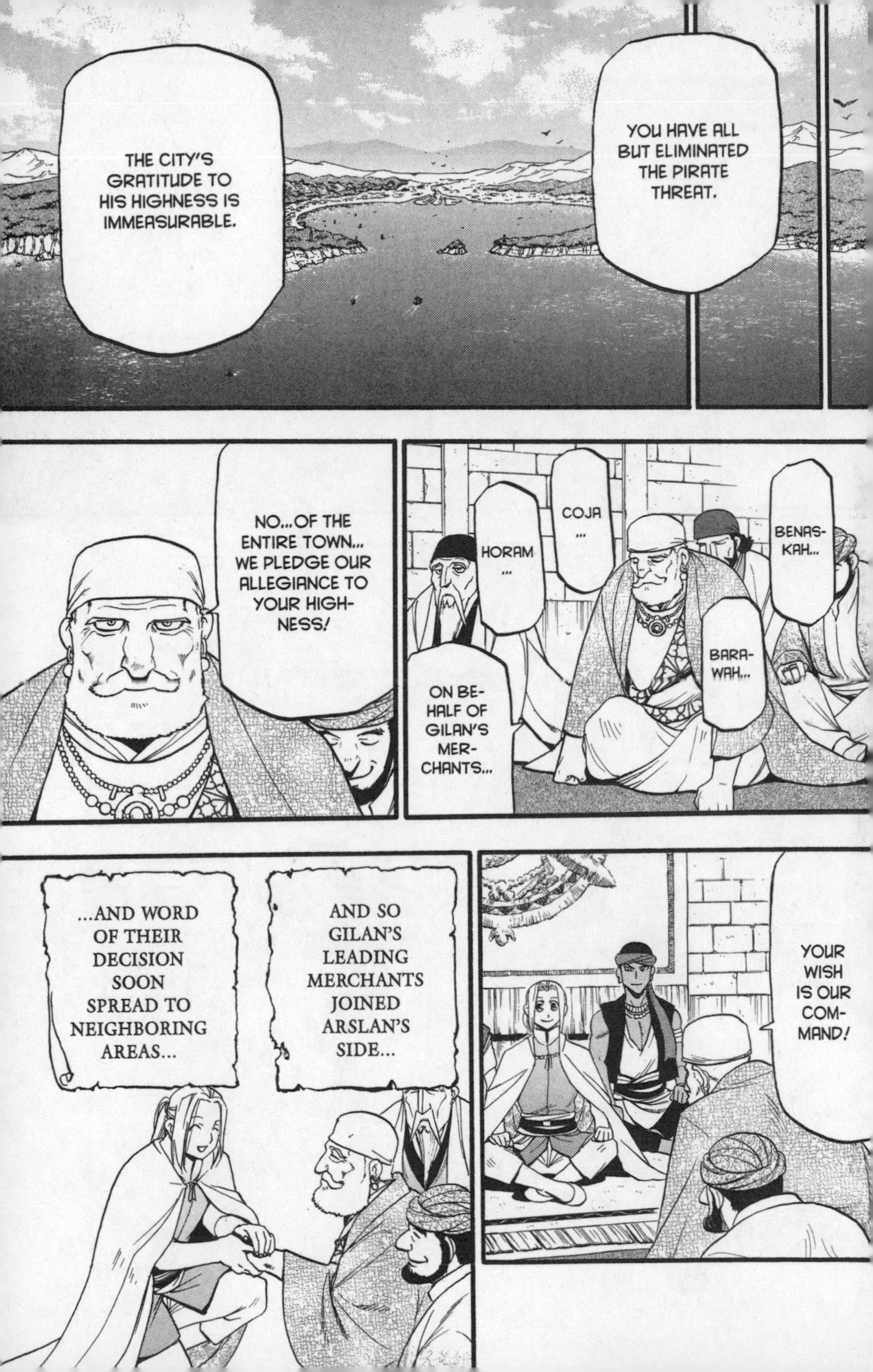
YOU HAVE ALL BUT ELIMINATED THE PIRATE THREAT.
THE CITY'S GRATITUDE TO HIS HIGHNESS IS IMMEASURABLE.
BENAS-KAH...
COJA...
HORAM...
BARA-WAH...
ON BE-HALF OF GILAN'S MER-CHANTS...
NO...OF THE ENTIRE TOWN... WE PLEDGE OUR ALLEGIANCE TO YOUR HIGH-NESS!
YOUR WISH IS OUR COM-MAND!
AND SO GILAN'S LEADING MERCHANTS JOINED ARSLAN'S SIDE...
...AND WORD OF THEIR DECISION SOON SPREAD TO NEIGHBORING AREAS...

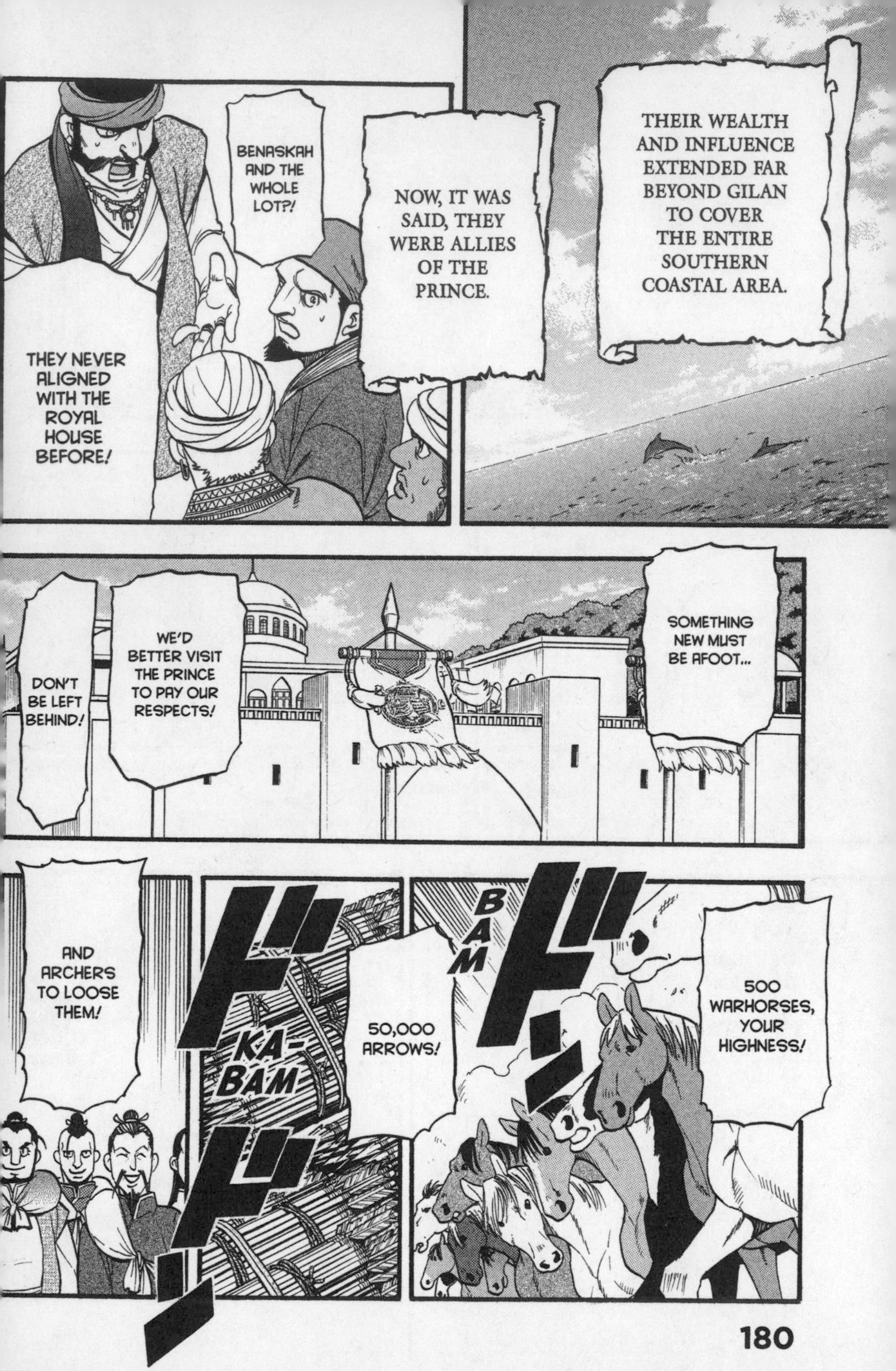
THEIR WEALTH AND INFLUENCE EXTENDED FAR BEYOND GILAN TO COVER THE ENTIRE SOUTHERN COASTAL AREA.
NOW, IT WAS SAID, THEY WERE ALLIES OF THE PRINCE.
BENASKAH AND THE WHOLE LOT?!
THEY NEVER ALIGNED WITH THE ROYAL HOUSE BEFORE!
SOMETHING NEW MUST BE AFOOT...
WE'D BETTER VISIT THE PRINCE TO PAY OUR RESPECTS!
DON'T BE LEFT BEHIND!
BAM
500 WARHORSES, YOUR HIGHNESS!
50,000 ARROWS!
KA-BAM
AND ARCHERS TO LOOSE THEM!

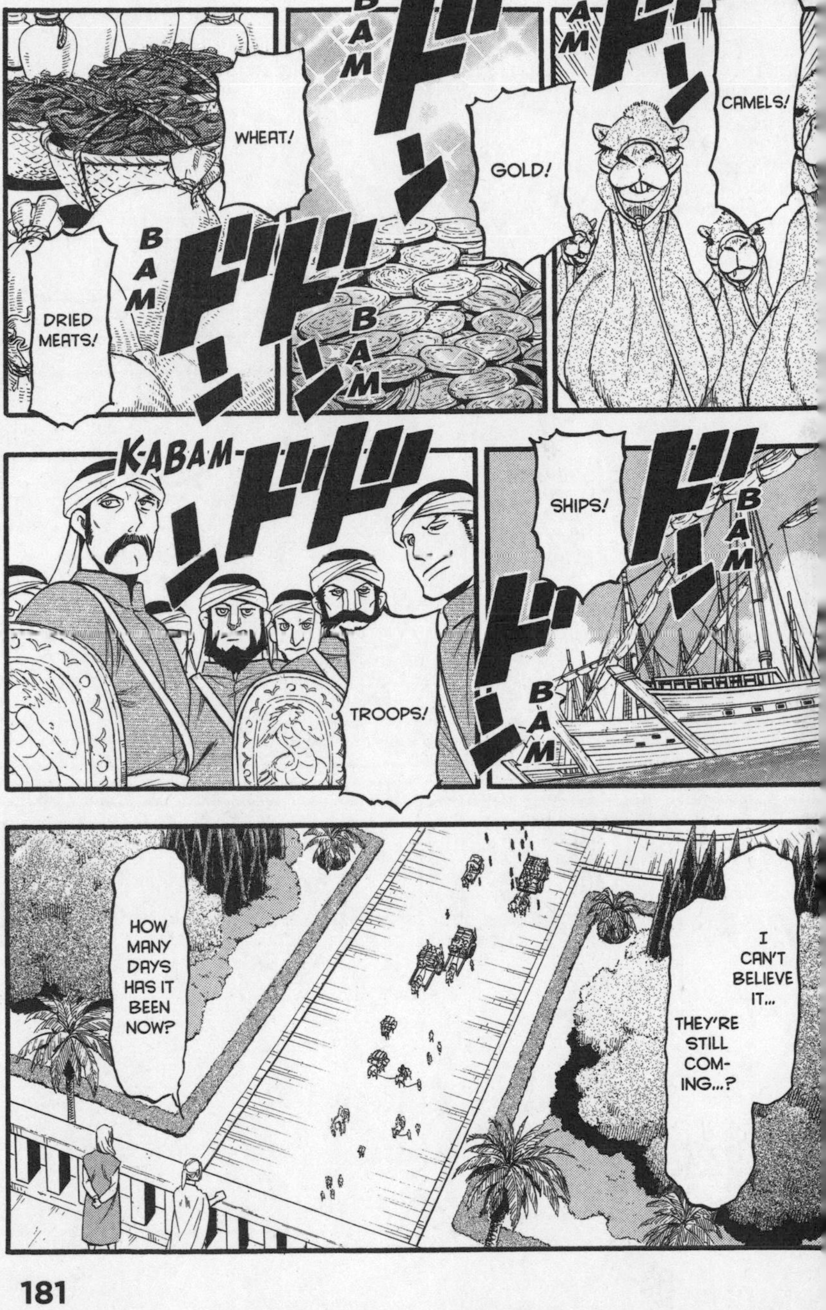
BAM
CAMELS!
BAM
GOLD!
BAM
WHEAT!
BAM
DRIED MEATS!
BAM
SHIPS!
BAM
K-ABAM-
TROOPS!
I CAN'T BELIEVE IT...
THEY'RE STILL COM-ING...?
HOW MANY DAYS HAS IT BEEN NOW?

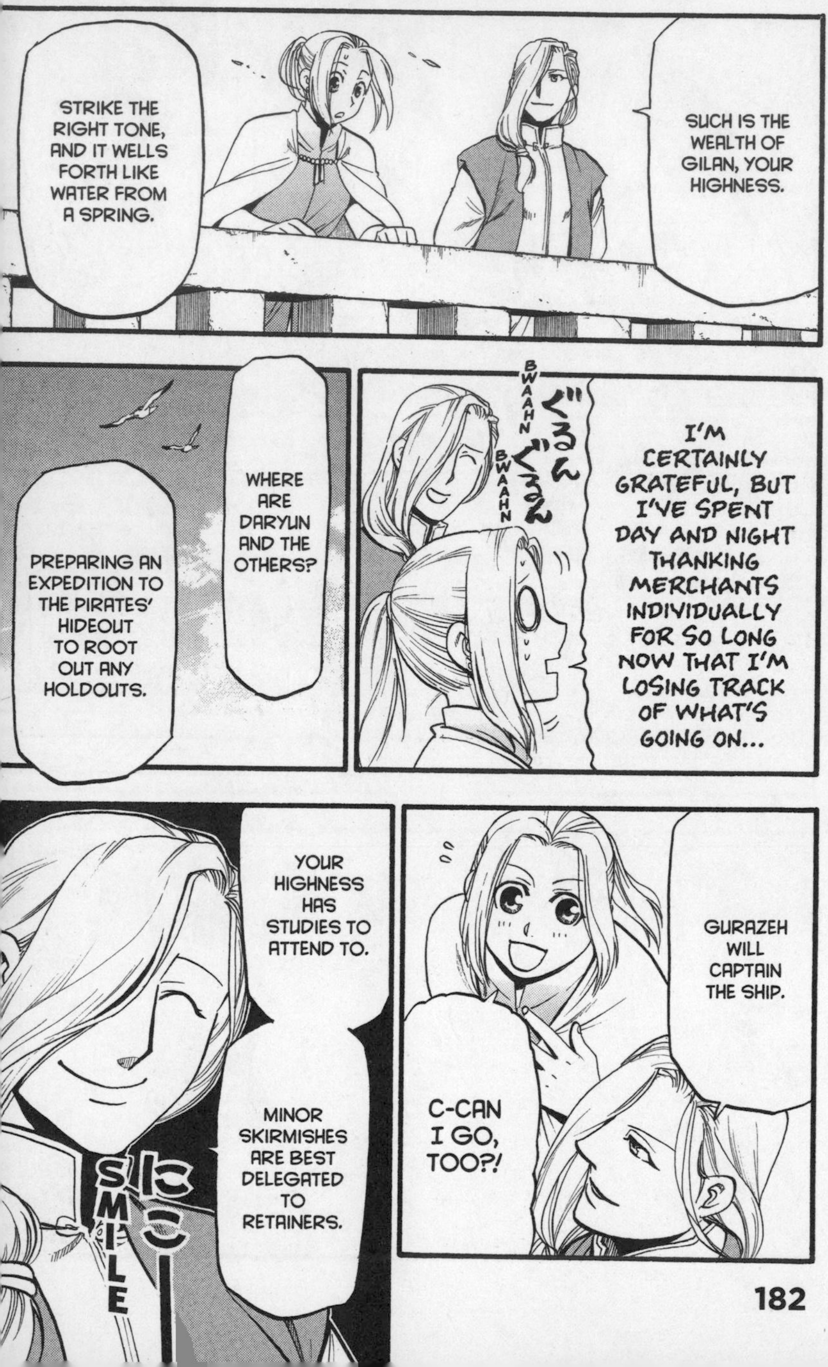
SUCH IS THE WEALTH OF GILAN, YOUR HIGHNESS.
STRIKE THE RIGHT TONE, AND IT WELLS FORTH LIKE WATER FROM A SPRING.
I'M CERTAINLY GRATEFUL, BUT I'VE SPENT DAY AND NIGHT THANKING MERCHANTS INDIVIDUALLY FOR SO LONG NOW THAT I'M LOSING TRACK OF WHAT'S GOING ON...
BWAAHN ぐるん
BWAAHN ぐるん
WHERE ARE DARYUN AND THE OTHERS?
PREPARING AN EXPEDITION TO THE PIRATES' HIDEOUT TO ROOT OUT ANY HOLDOUTS.
GURAZEH WILL CAPTAIN THE SHIP.
C-CAN I GO, TOO?!
YOUR HIGHNESS HAS STUDIES TO ATTEND TO.
MINOR SKIRMISHES ARE BEST DELEGATED TO RETAINERS.
SMILE にこ

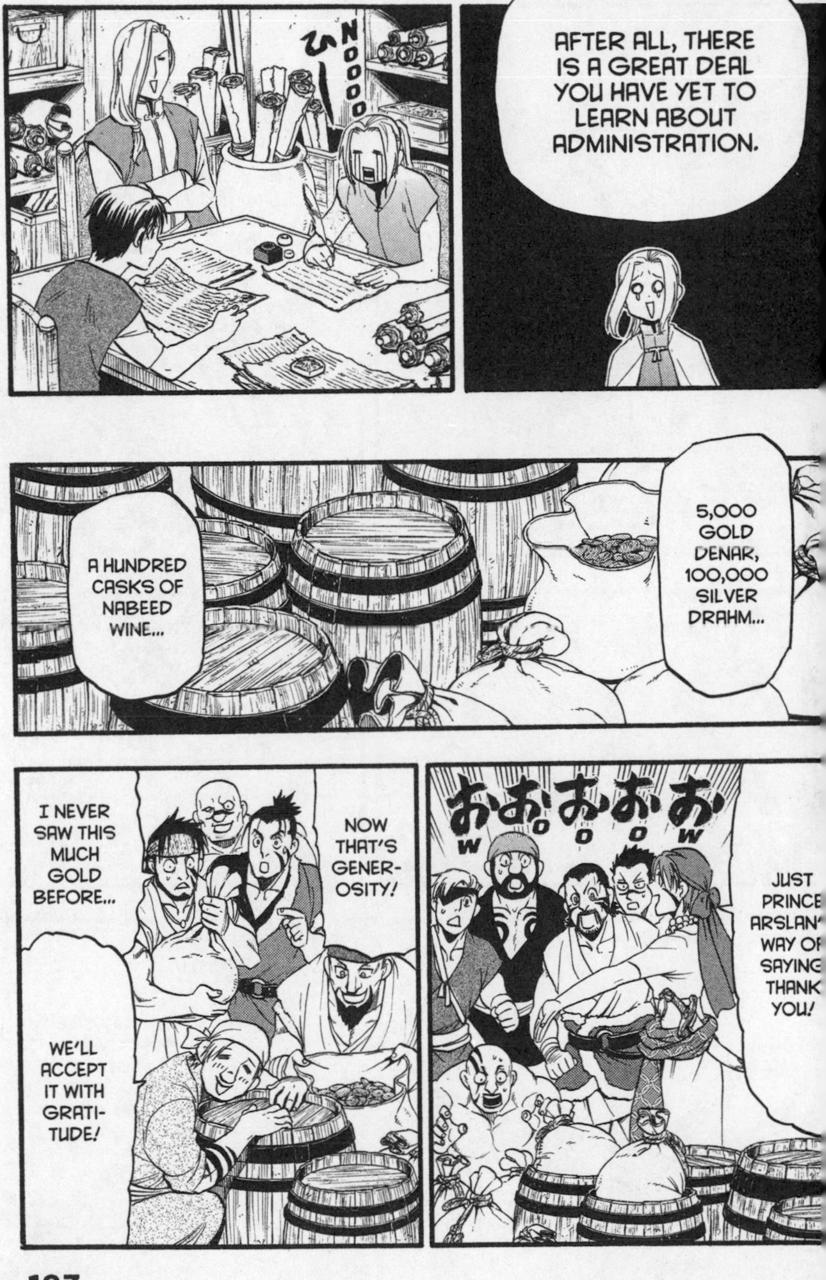
AFTER ALL, THERE IS A GREAT DEAL YOU HAVE YET TO LEARN ABOUT ADMINISTRATION.
ひー
NOOOO
5,000 GOLD DENAR, 100,000 SILVER DRAHM...
A HUNDRED CASKS OF NABEED WINE...
おおおおお
WOOOW
JUST PRINCE ARSLAN' WAY OF SAYING THANK YOU!
NOW THAT'S GENER-OSITY!
I NEVER SAW THIS MUCH GOLD BEFORE...
WE'LL ACCEPT IT WITH GRATI-TUDE!

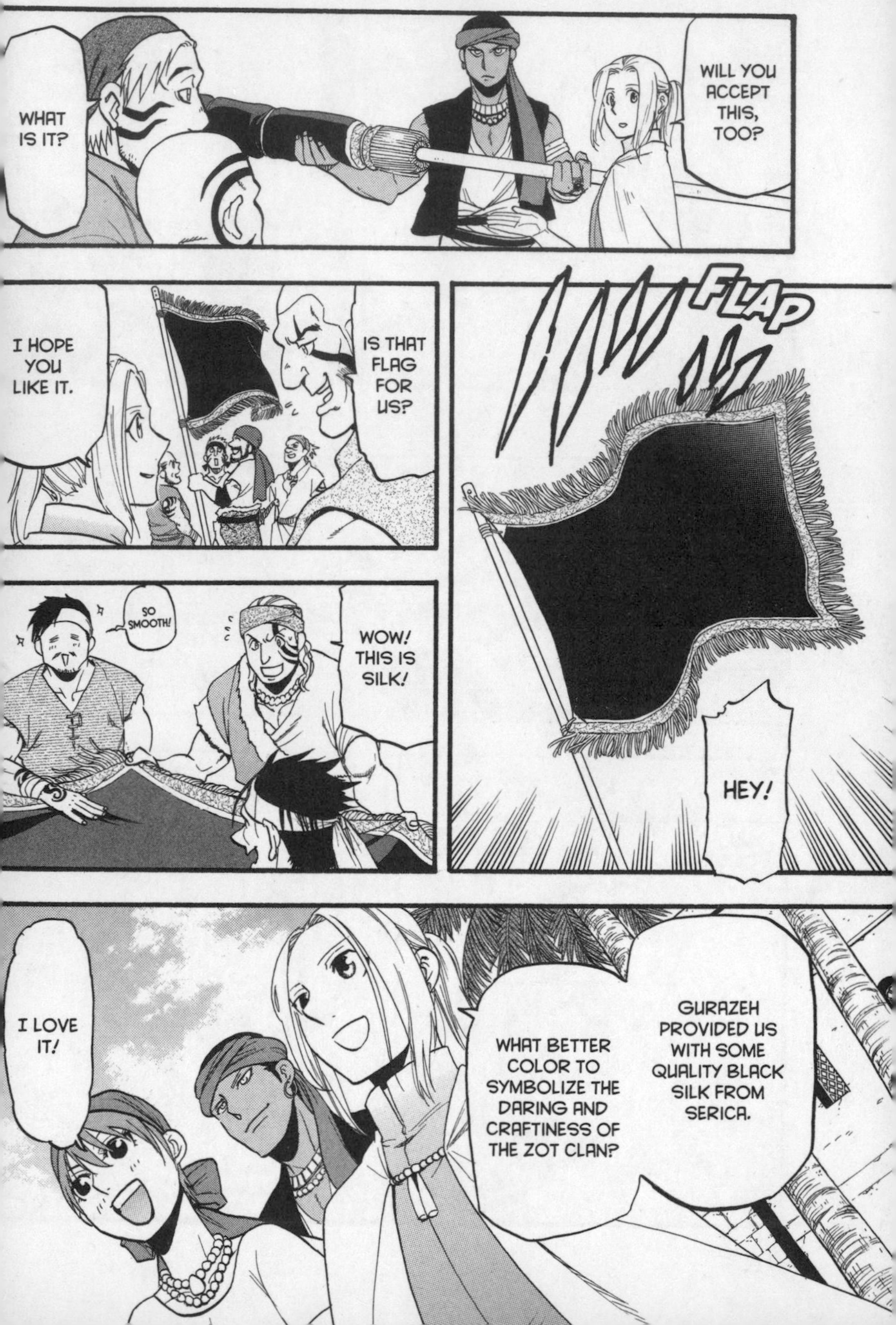
WILL YOU ACCEPT THIS, TOO?
WHAT IS IT?
FLAP
HEY!
IS THAT FLAG FOR US?
I HOPE YOU LIKE IT.
WOW! THIS IS SILK!
SO SMOOTH!
GURAZEH PROVIDED US WITH SOME QUALITY BLACK SILK FROM SERICA.
WHAT BETTER COLOR TO SYMBOLIZE THE DARING AND CRAFTINESS OF THE ZOT CLAN?
I LOVE IT!

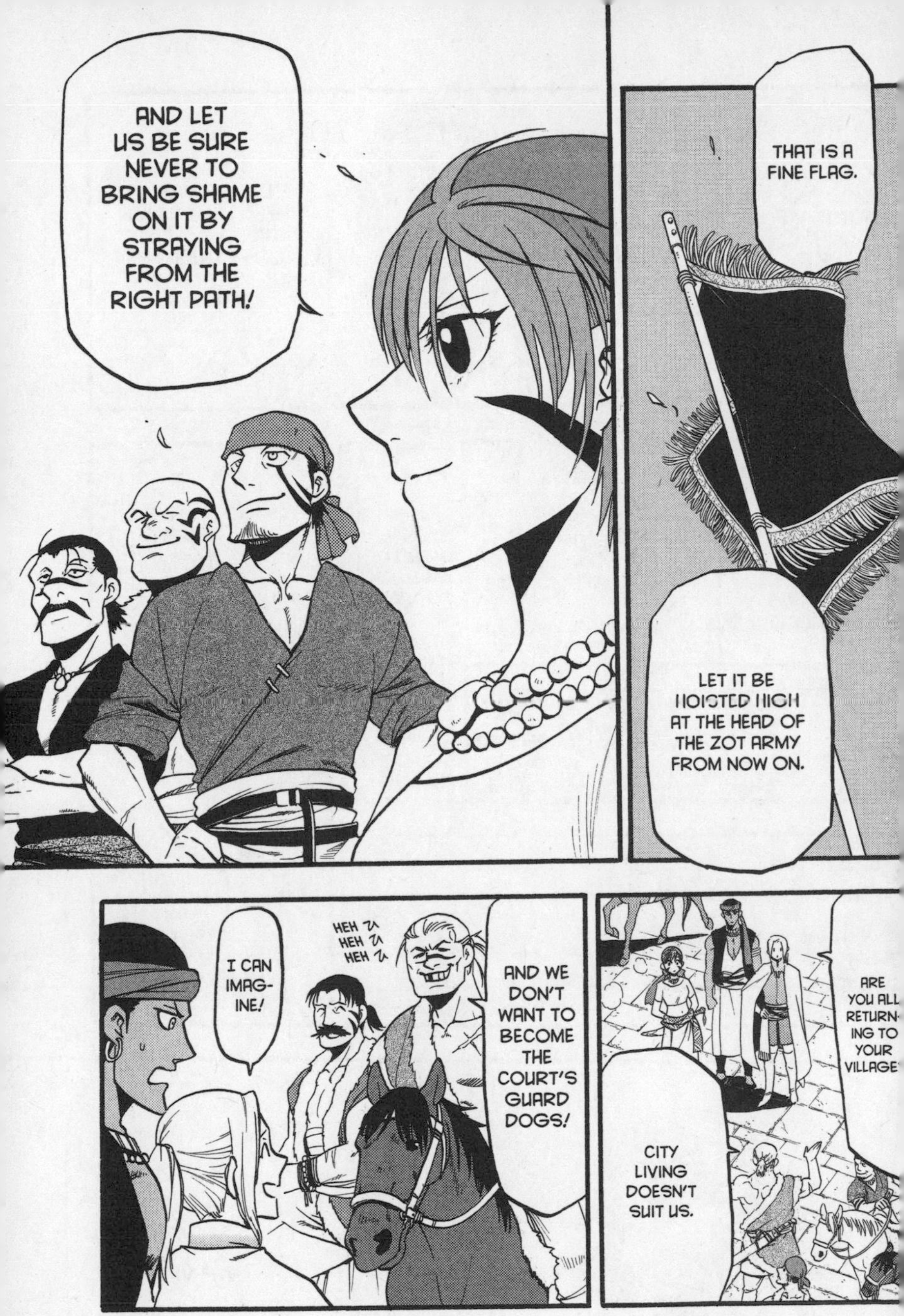
THAT IS A FINE FLAG.
LET IT BE HOISTED HIGH AT THE HEAD OF THE ZOT ARMY FROM NOW ON.
AND LET US BE SURE NEVER TO BRING SHAME ON IT BY STRAYING FROM THE RIGHT PATH!
ARE YOU ALL RETURNING TO YOUR VILLAGE
CITY LIVING DOESN'T SUIT US.
AND WE DON'T WANT TO BECOME THE COURT'S GUARD DOGS!
HEH HEH HEH
I CAN IMAGINE!

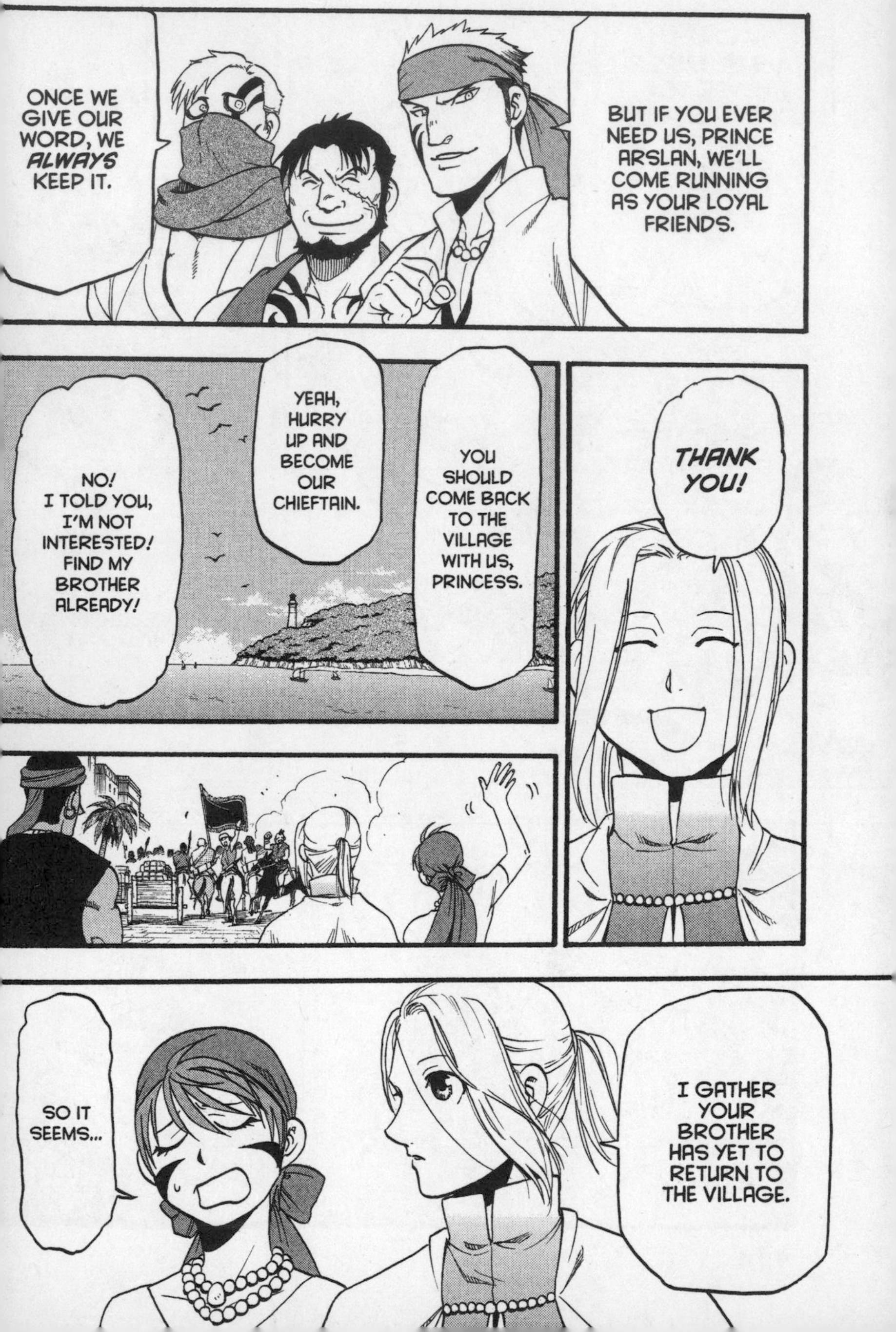
BUT IF YOU EVER NEED US, PRINCE ARSLAN, WE'LL COME RUNNING AS YOUR LOYAL FRIENDS.
ONCE WE GIVE OUR WORD, WE *ALWAYS* KEEP IT.
THANK YOU!
YOU SHOULD COME BACK TO THE VILLAGE WITH US, PRINCESS.
YEAH, HURRY UP AND BECOME OUR CHIEFTAIN.
NO! I TOLD YOU, I'M NOT INTERESTED! FIND MY BROTHER ALREADY!
I GATHER YOUR BROTHER HAS YET TO RETURN TO THE VILLAGE.
SO IT SEEMS...

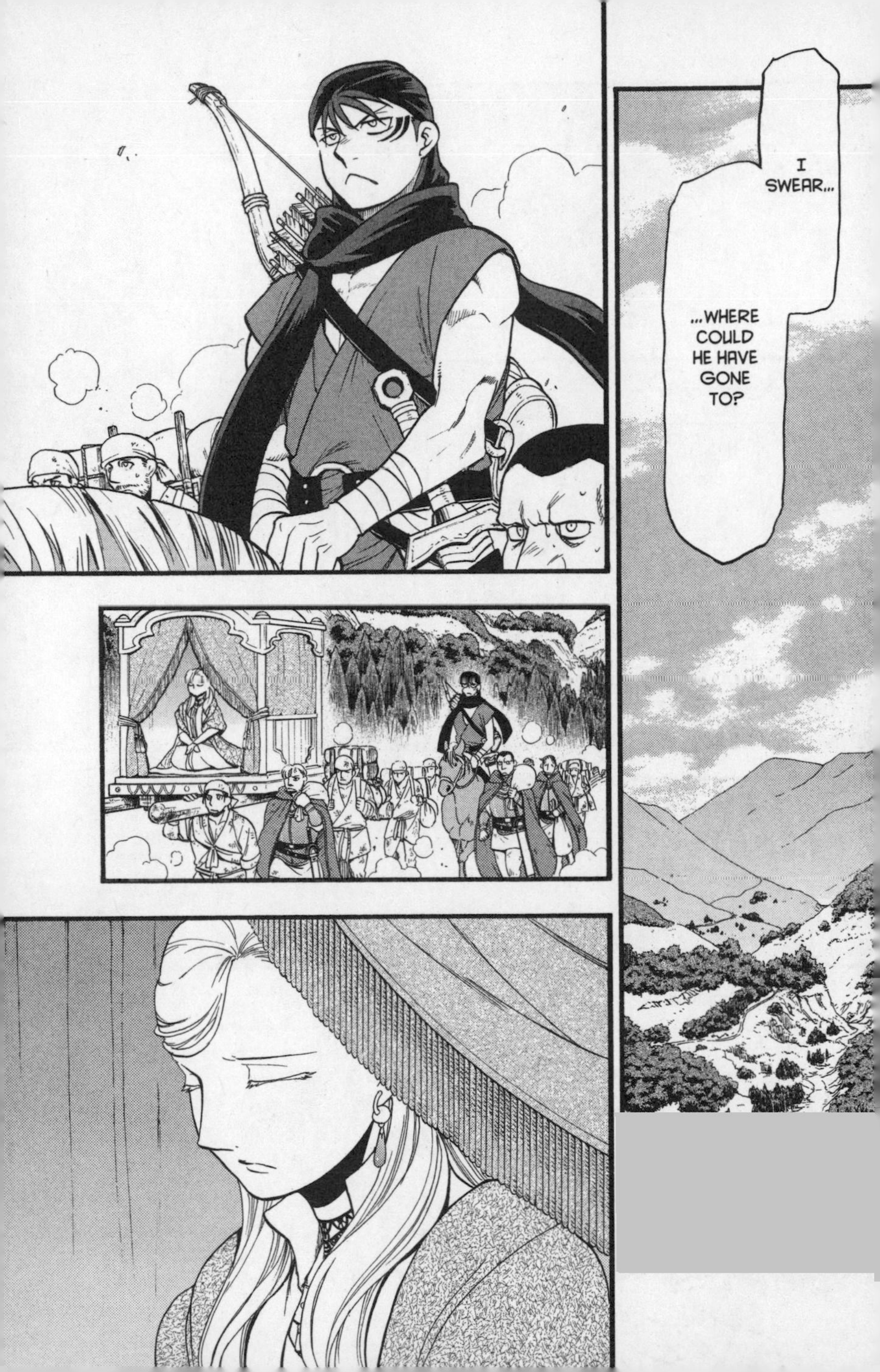
I SWEAR...
...WHERE COULD HE HAVE GONE TO?

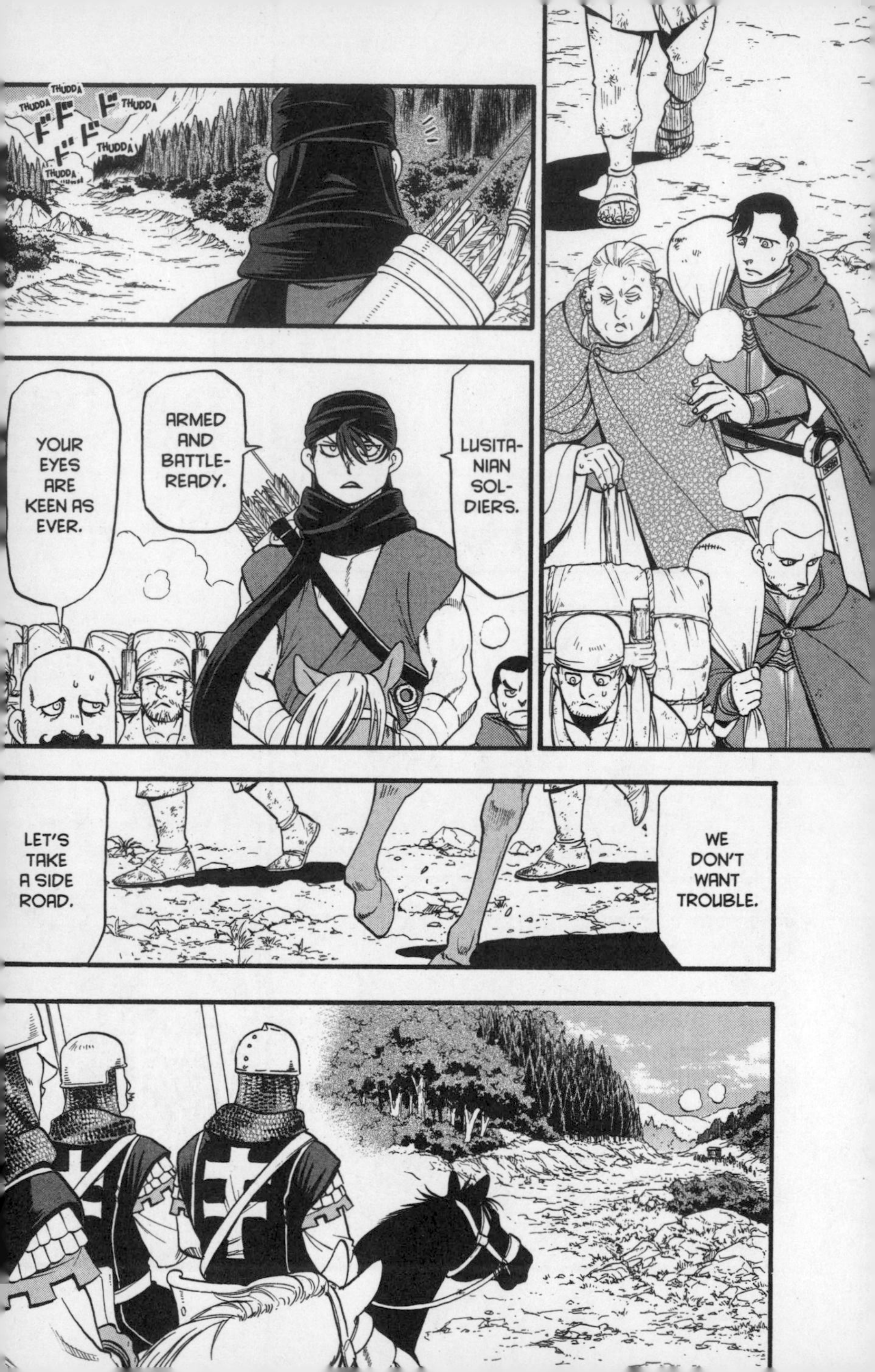
ドドドド THUDDA THUDDA THUDDA THUDDA THUDDA
LUSITANIAN SOLDIERS.
ARMED AND BATTLE-READY.
YOUR EYES ARE KEEN AS EVER.
WE DON'T WANT TROUBLE.
LET'S TAKE A SIDE ROAD.

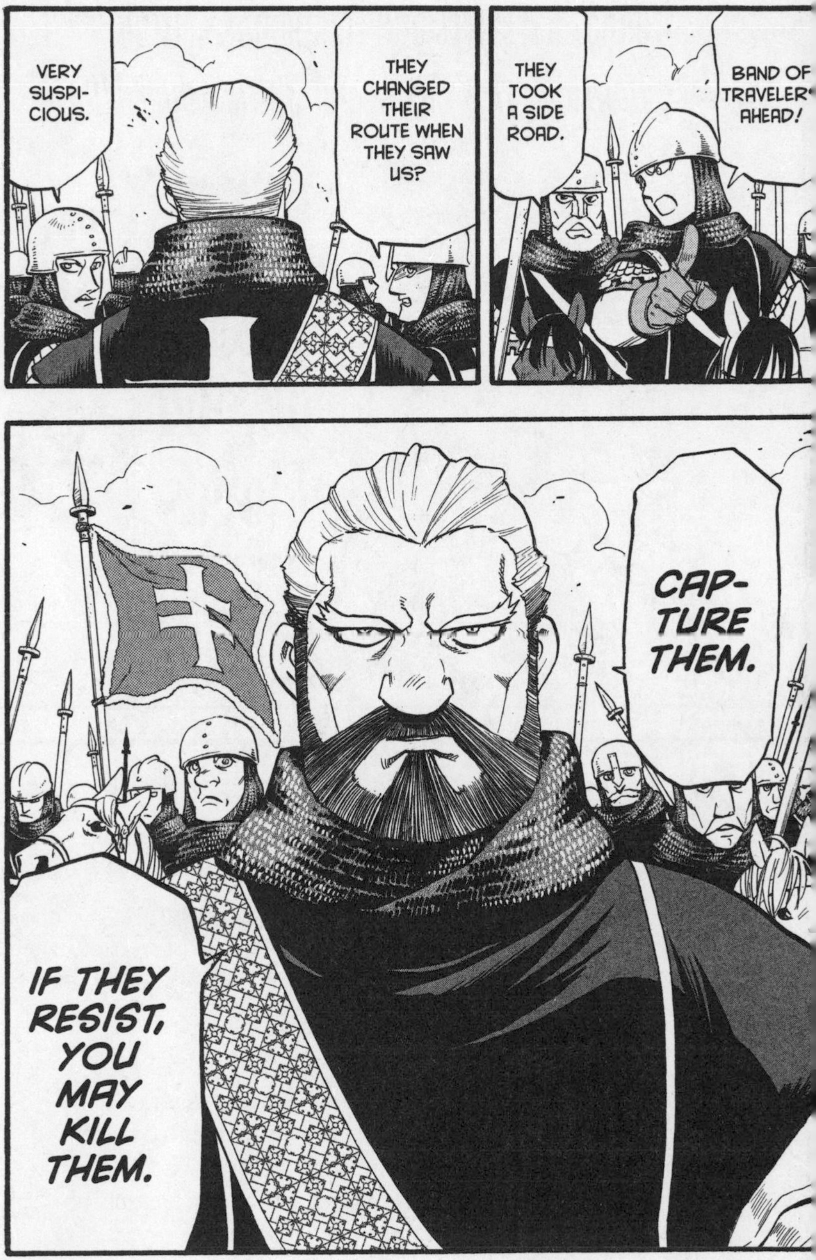
BAND OF TRAVELER AHEAD!
THEY TOOK A SIDE ROAD.
THEY CHANGED THEIR ROUTE WHEN THEY SAW US?
VERY SUSPI-CIOUS.
CAP-TURE THEM.
IF THEY RESIST, YOU MAY KILL THEM.

Young characters and steampunk setting, like *Howl's Moving Castle* and *Battle Angel Alita*

Beyond the Clouds © 2018 Nicke / Ki-oon

A boy with a talent for machines and a mysterious girl whose wings he's fixed will take you beyond the clouds! In the tradition of the high-flying, resonant adventure stories of Studio Ghibli comes a gorgeous tale about the longing of young hearts for adventure and friendship!

Knight of the Ice ©Yeyoi Ogawa/Kodansha Ltd.

SKATING THRILLS AND ICY CHILLS WITH THIS NEW TINGLY ROMANCE SERIES!

A rom-com on ice, perfect for fans of *Princess Jellyfish* and *Wotakoi*. Kokoro is the talk of the figure-skating world, winning trophies and hearts. But little do they know... he's actually a huge nerd! From the beloved creator of *You're My Pet* (*Tramps Like Us*).

Chitose is a serious young woman, working for the health magazine *SASSO*. Or at least, she would be, if she wasn't constantly getting distracted by her childhood friend, international figure skating star Kokoro Kijinami! In the public eye and on the ice, Kokoro is a gallant, flawless knight, but behind his glittery costumes and breathtaking spins lies a secret: He's actually a hopelessly romantic otaku, who can only land his quad jumps when Chitose is on hand to recite a spell from his favorite magical girl anime!

A Kodansha Comics Trade Paperback Original
The Heroic Legend of Arslan 16 copyright © 2021 Hiromu Arakawa & Yoshiki Tanaka
English translation copyright © 2022 Hiromu Arakawa & Yoshiki Tanaka

Published in the United States by Kodansha Comics, an imprint of Kodansha USA Publishing, LLC, New York.

Publication rights for this English edition arranged through Kodansha Ltd., Tokyo.

First published in Japan in 2021 by Kodansha Ltd., Tokyo as *Arslan Senki*, volume 16.

ISBN 978-1-64651-438-0

Printed in the United States of America.

www.kodansha.us

9 8 7 6 5 4 3 2 1
Translation: Matt Treyvaud
Lettering: James Dashiell
Editing: Megan Ling
Kodansha Comics edition cover design by Phil Balsman

Publisher: Kiichiro Sugawara

Director of publishing services: Ben Applegate
Director of publishing operations: Dave Barrett
Associate director, publishing operations: Stephen Pakula
Publishing services managing editors: Madison Salters, Alanna Ruse
Production managers: Emi Lotto, Angela Zurlo